User-Centered Website Development

Development

A Human–Computer Interaction Approach

Daniel D. McCracken
City College of New York

Rosalee J. Wolfe
DePaul University

PEARSON
Prentice
Hall

Pearson Education, Inc.
Upper Saddle River, New Jersey 07458

Library of Congress Cataloging-in-Publication Data

McCracken, Daniel D.
    User-centered Website development: a human-computer
    interaction approach / Daniel D. McCracken, Rosalee J. Wolfe.
    p. cm.
    Includes bibliographical references and index.
    ISBN 0-13-041161-2
    1. Website development. 2. Websites—Design. 3. Human-computer interaction.
    I. Wolfe, R.J. (Rosalee Jean) II. Title.

    TK5105.888.M376 2004
    005.2'7—dc21

                          2003048288

Vice President and Editorial Director, ECS: *Marcia Horton*
Executive Editor: *Petra Recter*
Vice President and Director of Production and Manufacturing, ESM: *David W. Riccardi*
Executive Managing Editor: *Vince O'Brien*
Managing Editor: *Camille Trentacoste*
Production Editor: *Irwin Zucker*
Manufacturing Manager: *Trudy Pisciotti*
Manufacturing Buyer: *Lisa McDowell*
Director of Creative Services: *Paul Belfanti*
Art Editor: *Greg Dulles*
Creative Director: *Carole Anson*
Art Director: *John Christiana*
Cover Designer: *Anthony Gemmellaro*
Cover art: *Todd Davidson/Getty Images Inc./Illustration Works, Inc.*
Interior/Insert Designer: *Dina Curro*
Executive Marketing Manager: *Pamela Shaffer*
Marketing Assistant: *Barrie Reinhold*

 © 2004 Pearson Education, Inc.
Pearson Prentice Hall
Upper Saddle River, New Jersey 07458

Printed in the United States of America

10 9 8 7 6 5 4 3 2 1

ISBN 0-13-041161-2

Pearson Education Ltd., *London*
Pearson Education Australia Pty. Limited, *Sydney*
Pearson Education Singapore Pte. Ltd.
Pearson Education North Asia Ltd. *Hong Kong*
Pearson Education Canada Inc., *Toronto*
Pearson Educación de Mexico, S.A. de C.V.
Pearson Education—Japan, Inc., *Tokyo*
Pearson Education—Malaysia Pte. Ltd.
Pearson Education Inc., *Upper Saddle River, New Jersey*

Contents

CHAPTER 9   Color   150

CHAPTER 10   Typography   171

Foreword

by Jared M. Spool

Founding Principal, User Interface Engineering

I like this book, but why should you care? I'm guessing that you are reading it because you're interested in what it takes to make a website that people find usable. If that's the case, then I have just one question for you: *Why bother?*

Why Bother?

It's hard enough to build a working website. A website that produces the right pages at the right time with all the links and buttons in the right positions—that's hard. Why now put in all the extra effort to make that site usable?

Let's say we wanted to build our own airline reservation service. Just creating a database to contain an up-to-date schedule of more than 2,500,000 flights for 150 different airlines over the next three years would be a huge technical achievement. The idea that you could create an interface—any interface—where every user can choose a specific flight and reserve a seat that no other user (whether using your website or buying a ticket any other way) can subsequently reserve is a monumental task.

In the book you're about to read, you'll find out that we'll have to go to tremendous effort to make our design usable. Why go to all that effort to make it usable? Haven't we done enough just to make it work? Moreover, once we start making it usable, when do we stop?

To understand my answer for these questions, you first have to understand where I'm coming from. Over the years, I've had the opportunity to watch hundreds of people interact with website designs.

I've watched these people buy shirts, order pizzas, rent movies, trade stocks, and reserve flights. I've seen them find important medical information, learn cool facts about Mt. Everest, and find a hotel at Walt Disney World. I've seen them upload pictures of their newborn baby, determine the x-ray diffusion of a protein, and isolate fluid distribution problems in an automated undersea oil rig that is 1,750 miles away. As I've watched all these users try to do all these things, I've come to an interesting conclusion: *We can't actually tell when a website is usable. We can only tell when it is unusable.*

When Is a Site Usable?

Sure, we can tell when the user you are watching has accomplished their goal. If someone comes to our airline reservation site and wants to fly from Boston to Salt Lake City in three weeks, we can tell if they successfully made the reservation.

In addition, we can tell if the folks developing the site have achieved *their* goals. Maybe our company's goal is to have every potential travel customer book and pay for their reservation. That is certainly measurable.

However, just because the user and the organization each achieve their goal, does that mean that the design of the site is usable? Let's say the users can book the reservations, but spend a lot of time hitting the wrong buttons, getting error messages, feeling confused, cursing at the screen, and needing to ask customer support for help. Was that a usable design? After all, there are many websites where, given enough patience, time, intelligence, and a thorough understanding of the workings of the design, any user would eventually figure it out—no matter how much pain the user experiences in the process.

To understand when something is truly usable, you actually have to look at what happens when it is not usable.

At some point in your life, I'm guessing that you've run into a piece of technology that just wouldn't do what you wanted. Maybe you've bought a VCR and you just wanted to record a TV show when you weren't going to be around. Perhaps you've rented a car and couldn't locate the fuel door latch to fill it with gas. Possibly, you've spent hours unsuccessfully searching a website for a piece of critical information that you know you've seen on that site before.

When you had these incidents of failure, what did you feel? Well, if you're like the hundreds of folks I've watched using websites, you've felt what they felt. You've felt *frustrated*.

Focusing on Frustration

If I asked you to tell me about a website that you thought was perfectly usable, it would probably be difficult to find one. However, it would be easy for you to tell me about one that frustrated you, with many sites from which to choose. Frustrating sites are far more common than usable sites. Why is that? Why is frustration so common a result of design?

In design terms, *frustrating* is the opposite of *usable*. They live at opposite ends of the design spectrum.

Just as cold is the absence of all heat, a usable design is a design devoid of any frustration. You can't tell when a site is usable, except by looking for frustration. It is only after we've watched every possible user attempt every possible use without any resulting frustration that we can declare a site usable.

"What Are Those Designers Thinking?"

When, in our research, users have encountered a site they consider extremely frustrating, they usually say the same thing: "How could the people who created this site think this was acceptable?" They are baffled that a designer could have let such a monster out of the lab.

When we talk with the designers of these sites, they are completely unaware that users are becoming frustrated. Until we talk with these designers, it never even occurs to them that there might be a problem. This doesn't happen because the designers are clueless or they have some hideous disdain for the user population. Instead, the developers had focused their efforts on the technical aspects of the project, and didn't pay any attention to the users.

However, why should we put all this effort into building something if everyone will become frustrated when using it? That is the motivation behind user-centered design.

Adaptation Isn't Possible on the Web

In the early days of computing, the designers of technology didn't have to think about the users. Users were a very small part of the general population, often highly trained and specialized. The work they did was typically repetitive (such as entering information about new customers) with little variance or exception. On a given day, a user, such as a data-entry clerk or call center operator, only used one, maybe two, program interfaces, performing the same, limited set of tasks, over and over. It was easy for these users to learn all the nuances of the system and adapt to the interface.

However, the Web is a very different environment from those early information systems. Most Web users only use a given site sporadically, like once or twice a month. Nobody has trained them, there are no manuals, and they've never really thought about how they will interact with the site. They can't adapt to a site's very specific interface.

Instead, they must rely on the clues given them. It is your responsibility, as a designer, to understand the clues users will respond to.

Content is Critical on the Web

Here's a little story from our research labs: One day, a gentleman, while participating in one of our studies, told us that he wanted to buy a sweater for his girlfriend. He knew which sweater he wanted to buy. He knew where he wanted to buy it. He knew what the price would be. He even knew he needed a size 6.

He sat in front of a machine and brought up the site that had his sweater. He had no trouble finding the sweater on the site—it took only a couple of clicks. They had the color he wanted in stock. The sweater was exactly what he wanted, at the price he was ready to pay.

He *didn't* buy it.

Why not? Well, he knew his girlfriend was a size 6. To buy the sweater, he had to choose between Small, Medium, Large, and Extra Large. Being a guy, he had absolutely no idea how to map his girlfriend's size 6 into the available sweater sizes.

Fortunately, there was a link labeled "Size Chart." With great anticipation, he clicked this link, only to get a chart that converted "Chest Sizes" into "Sweater Sizes", with no mention of "Dress Sizes." He could try to guess his girlfriend's chest size, but this could get expensive—the wrong guess could cost him, not only the price of the sweater, but also the cost of flowers and possibly even jewelry.

Therefore, he decided *not* to buy the sweater.

You can divide the design of a site into two categories: functionality and content. In the case of our sweater-buying gentleman, the *functionality* of the site worked perfectly for him. However, the *content* of the site failed him miserably—it had everything he needed, except for one critical piece of information.

Questions You Need to Answer

If you were the designer of this site, how would you know that this problem even existed? Once you found out, what would you do to fix it? How would you know if your fix actually worked?

If you're going to bother to make your site usable, you need to answer these questions for every source of frustration on your site. Of course, some problems are more frustrating than others are. Therefore, you'll need to do some research to find out what problems are most important to tackle first.

Why go through all of this effort to make something usable? For some designers, it's because a more usable site means that their site will capture and retain users from sites that are less usable. For others, their reason might be that they like the challenge of eliminating frustration from the user's experience. Others might be in a situation where a more usable site means more revenues to their organization. Yet others might do it just because they believe it's always worth the effort.

This book will help you know *how* to make your site more usable. You'll need to find your own reason to know *why* you need to make it more usable. Once you do, you'll have all the pieces—the desire to create a usable site and the expertise to make it happen.

Preface

This text combines an introduction to human–computer interaction (HCI) with an exposition of website development.

No one today needs convincing that the World Wide Web is a major phenomenon. Students are surely convinced, and they desire instruction in developing websites, but they usually see the subject in terms of writing HTML and of associated implementation tools. They often undervalue what the established field of HCI has to contribute to a good website.

This book is intended for such a student and for anyone else who wants to build effective interfaces between people and computers.

Goal

The goal of any course based on the book is to enable students to develop interfaces that are *usable*: they permit the user to find what he or she wants, find it quickly, and carry out any interaction effectively and efficiently. This goal has much broader applicability than the World Wide Web, of course. But with the Web being pervasive and of much interest to students, we chose to build our presentation around the Web.

Most of today's software is interactive, and most of our graduates will be called upon to write front ends or other interactive software as part of their jobs. People who have mastered the material in this book will be able to do a much better job of interaction design than they could without that knowledge. They will also be better prepared to work with HCI and website development experts in an industrial team setting.

Topics Covered

The order of presentation of the topics was given a great deal of thought, with revisions based on teaching experience. Details may be seen in the Table of Contents. Here is an overview:

- The first eight chapters build a solid foundation of HCI concepts and practice as outlined in the ACM SIGCHI's Curricula for Human–Computer Interaction. Topics include human perception, user and task analysis, content organization, visual organization, navigation, prototyping, and evaluation.

- The next six chapters are devoted to issues specific to website development: color, typography, multimedia, accessibility, globalization, and trust.

- A generous appendix presents an expository introduction to XHTML and Cascading Style Sheets. All formatting, after a first few examples, is done with Cascading Style Sheets, which has numerous advantages that are explained in the text.

Support for Instructors

The many review questions and exercises are a major feature of the book. The review questions help a student master the principles. But, as with sports, playing a musical instrument, or software engineering, a student learns to apply HCI principles to website development by *doing it*. You can't learn to swim simply by listening to lectures, and you can't learn user-centered development that way either. The way to learn is to take an assigned design task, carry it through, then compare one's work with that of other students under the guidance of the instructor. A model solution can be most helpful if presented *after* the students have tried to do it on their own.

This raises the always challenging issue of how an instructor should grade this type of project, especially if the instructor has limited experience in teaching the subject. Our response is an extensive Instructor's Manual. It contains suggestions for applications, ranging from short assignments to term-long projects, plus model solutions in the form of some of the best student work we have encountered in our teaching. The Instructor's Manual also contains tips for teaching and grading, sample syllabi, and sample exams.

The book has a companion website at `http://www.prenhall.com/mccracken_wolfe`. It contains links to illustrations in the text, URLs for simplicity in following links in the text, and other materials. A password-protected site contains the Instructors Manual and a set of PowerPoint slides for each chapter.

The bibliography for each chapter lists all literature cited in the text. These sources are both industrial and academic. Citations of relevant sources accompany design rules and guidelines as they appear in the text.

Classroom Tested

To practice what we preach, the book and supporting materials have been thoroughly use tested. Over a period of 18 months, several drafts of this book have been test-taught to approximately 1000 students at eight colleges and universities. Feedback from students and instructors has been instrumental in shaping the topic coverage and pedagogical strategy.

How to Use This Book

This organization permits great flexibility in how a course based on the text is structured. A prerequisite knowledge of Web-page authoring can be assumed or not. A prepublication version of this book has been taught successfully, using Web examples, both to students having no background in website development and to students who have extensive Web development experience.

The following outline presents two schedules, the first supporting an introductory course in Human–Computer Interaction, the second a course in User-Centered Web Development. Other possible schedules are posted on the book's companion website.

Course 1: Introduction to Human–Computer Interaction

Prerequisite: CS1
Level: Intermediate (sophomore or junior)

Students receive an overview of user-centered design principles and tools that help them develop better user interfaces in subsequent courses and in their careers as programmers.

Week	Topic	Reading
1	Why HCI; Overview of User-Centered Development Cycle	Ch. 1
2	Human Perception and Memory; Mental Models	Ch. 2
3	User and Task Analysis	Ch. 3
4–5	Content Organization	Ch. 4
6	Visual Organization	Ch. 5
7	Navigation	Ch. 6
8	Prototyping	Ch. 7
9–10	User Testing	Ch. 8
11	Color, Typography	Ch. 9, 10
12	Multimedia	Ch. 11
13	Accessibility	Ch. 12
14	Globalization	Ch. 13
	Final Exam or Final Project Presentations	

Course 2: User-Centered Web Development and XHTML

Prerequisite: CS1
Level: Intermediate (sophomore or junior)

Students learn the fundamentals of user-centered Web development, together with XHTML and a selection of Web-related topics. A project ties things together.

Week	Topic	Reading
1	Why HCI; Overview of User-Centered Development Cycle; Human Memory and Perception	Ch. 1, 2
2	User and Task Analysis	Ch. 3
3	Prototyping	Ch. 7
4	User Testing	Ch. 8
5	XHTML & Cascading Style Sheets, 1	Appendix
6	Content Organization	Ch. 4
7	XHTML & CSS, 2	Appendix
8	Visual Organization & Navigation	Ch. 5, 6
9	XHTML & CSS, 3	Appendix
10	Topics in Color and Typography	Ch. 9, 10
11	Multimedia	Ch. 11
12	Accessibility	Ch. 13
13	Globalization, Trust	Ch. 14, 15
14	Final Project Presentations	
	Optional Final Exam, or Project Evaluations	

Acknowledgments

We wish to express our appreciation for the support of the National Science Foundation, through grant DUE 0088184, which made the test-teaching and a careful evaluation effort possible. The grant is under the Educational Materials Dissemination part of the program in Course, Curriculum, and Laboratory Instrumentation. We are deeply grateful to the National Science Foundation and to the reviewers of our proposal for their backing of our approach, together with the endorsement of our conviction that more emphasis on HCI in undergraduate CS education is needed. MaryJo Davidson, Jorge Toro, and Mei Xu skillfully assisted with various aspects of the evaluation activities related to the grant.

Many people contributed time, expertise, and materials, which greatly enhance the richness of the book. Roymieco Carter and Steve Luecking lent support and expert advice regarding color and visual design. Prabhakar Srinivasan wrote the color software for the Chapter 9 exercises. Rebecca Shaftman, Susy Chan, Mei Xu, and Ehab El-Shaer generously gave of their expertise and time in developing several of the examples for Chapter 13. Rhonda Schauer gave major assistance on technical aspects of XHTML and Cascading Style Sheets. Bill Yurcik of Illinois Wesleyan University was also helpful in these matters. Michelle Scavella, Alani Colon, Mark Soriano and Abraham Mathai tested Web accessibility under various simulated disabilities and completed an end-to-end case study of a Web site for bartering. Bret Kroll worked all of the review questions and reported "bugs." Deborah Allen, Maggie Bruns, Tim Bruns, Alani Colon, Victoria Doyle, Dan Ethridge, Jim Futransky, Manav Gupta, I-Hsun Huang, Sugjoo Hwang, Katie Krakowiak, Bret Kroll, Lai Chen Lai, Abe Mathai, Ryan McCormack, Hiren Patel, Fernando Protti-Alvarez, Worawit Russameefeung, Michelle Scavella, Alice Shegelman, Mark Soriano, and Don Starkey contributed exemplary homework solutions.

We would also like to thank the many reviewers for their extensive, thoughtful and constructive comments. We are indebted to John Avitabile, Steve Cunningham, Karl Flores, Scott Grissom, Richard Hull, Don Kussee, Daniel Schwartz, Stephanie Smullen, John Tappin, Ellen Walker, and Peter Williams.

Thanks go to the people who test-taught the preprint: Stephanie Berger, MaryJo Davidson, Priscilla Lawyer, David Tain, and Jorge Toro at DePaul University; Susan Reiser at the University of North Carolina at Asheville; Rob Bryant at Gonzaga University; Erika Rogers at California State University, San Luis Obispo; Robert Beck at Villanova University; Mary Jane Willshire at the University of Portland; and Sister Jane Fritz at St. Joseph's College.

For contributions too varied and complex to explain, thanks go to: Paul Armer, Andrew Bernat, Helen Blumenthal, Dixon Cleveland, Zeev Dagan, Helmut Epp, Connie Heymann, Mohammad Karim, Stephen A. Kasten, Howard Kiernan, Karen Lilley, Barbara Loeding, Stephen Lucci, George G. Ross, Ellen Smiley, Arthur Sortland, Douglas R. Troeger, Ko-Yang Wang, Charles B. Watkins, Margaret Moers Wenig, Gregory P. Williams, and Alain Wolfe.

We both deeply appreciate the advice, encouragement, and patience of our editor at Prentice Hall, Petra Recter.

Daniel D. McCracken
New York

Rosalee J. Wolfe
Chicago

Human–Computer Interaction: An Overview

1.1 Introduction

Have you ever been annoyed by how hard it is to find something on the Web? Have you ever wondered why you had to give out your email address just to get into a site? Perhaps you have filled out an order form only to be sent to a page that says, "Sorry, you made a mistake – fill it out again." Have you waited on hold for hours to talk to someone in tech support because the instructions were lousy?

It doesn't have to be this way. Websites can be convenient and pleasant to experience when designers and developers take time to think about the users.

Goals of this Chapter

In this chapter, you will learn

- the benefits of making a website more usable
- the history and goals of human–computer interaction, the discipline that provides the tools for enhancing Web usability
- The methodology of user-centered development, which is essential for developing usable websites.

1.2 Benefits of Usable Websites

Since the 1993 introduction of NCSA Mosaic, the first point-and-click Web browser [Andreessen 1994], Internet use has exploded. However, in a period of less than 10 years, the novelty of using the Web has worn off. At first, just being innovative was enough for success; now, however, sites must meet user expectations in order to survive. Think about your experiences: if you visit a site and find it frustrating, what are the chances that you will go there again? On the other hand, websites that do meet user expectations enjoy many advantages. Four of the most important advantages are gaining a competitive edge, reducing development and maintenance costs, improving productivity, and lowering support costs [Donahue 1999].

1.2.1 Gaining a Competitive Edge

It's not the number of hits a site receives that matters; it's what people do once they get there that counts. Did they actually purchase something? Did they fill out the registration form? Essential to the success of a website is its *conversion rate*, which is the percentage of visitors who take action on the site. Taking action can mean "buy something," if it's an online shopping site; it can mean "register to receive information," if it's a travel information site. For a personal website, it might mean using the "sign my guest book" feature. The average conversion rate for shopping sites is somewhere between 3 and 5 percent.

Suppose your company spends $2,500 on advertising that generates 5,000 visits to its shopping site. This sounds like a pretty good deal on the surface – your site is receiving a lot of hits. Suppose, though, that the conversion rate is only 2 percent. With a little bit of calculation, we can find the number of purchases:

$$2\% \text{ of } 5{,}000 \text{ visits } = 100 \text{ purchases.}$$

Divide 100 purchases into $2500 and each purchase costs $25 in advertising! But if the conversion rate is just a little higher, say 4 percent, then in the same 5,000 visits your site will attract 200 purchases, and the cost per purchase drops to $12.50. The higher the conversion rate, the better the sales and the greater the profit margins [Gurley 2000]. IBM experienced this phenomenon when they rolled out their redesigned "Shop IBM" website. In the first month, hits went up 120 percent, but sales increased 400 percent [Battey 1999].

What drives conversion rates? The top factor for high conversion rates is ease of use. Usable websites consistently have the highest conversion rates. Studies have found that, if customers have an enjoyable experience, they are likely to spend more time on a site, make purchases, and return to the site for further shopping. If they have to waste time searching for an item or figuring out how to buy it, they quickly become frustrated and leave. All other things being equal, the site that offers the better user experience will win the market place. This holds true even when the more usable site charges a slightly higher price [Rhodes 2001].

1.2.2 Reduced Development and Maintenance Costs

Learning about the needs of real users before creating a website results in lower development costs by saving you from implementing features that people don't want. It can also save you from costly corrections that can crop up after site rollout. According to one study [Donahue 1999], over half of all software life-cycle costs occur during the maintenance phase. Most maintenance costs arise from "unmet or unforeseen" user requirements.

1.2.3 Improved Productivity

For people using a shopping site, improved productivity means being able to purchase items quickly. For a company's intranet, it can mean that employees are able to complete their work more efficiently. At Bay Networks, a subsidiary of Nortel, company officials estimated that their improved intranet will allow each member of the sales staff to save a minimum of two minutes per day when searching for documents. Two minutes may seem like a small amount, but over a year's time, this translated into a savings of over 10 million dollars [Fabris, 1999].

1.2.4 Lower Support Costs

When a website is understandable, users don't need to call customer support. This can add up to significant—even huge—savings, given that some experts estimate that the cost of a single service call ranges between $12 and $250 [Donahue 1999].

In 1999, Wal-Mart decided to shut down their shopping site for three weeks rather than leave it online until they could roll out the new redesign. The fact that they decided that it would be more cost effective to shut down the site, thus closing off any possibility of a sale, indicates that customer confusion was severely affecting the company's support systems [Weiss 2000].

1.3 What is HCI?

What makes a website usable? How is it possible to create a site that meets expectations? If your company decides that its current site needs improvement, how do you go about achieving it? How do you know whether the changes actually constitute an improvement? The answers to these questions are found in a discipline closely linked to computer science, called human–computer interaction—HCI, for short.

To understand HCI, it's helpful to know a little bit about the story of how it came to be. Its beginnings occurred slightly after the introduction of the computer. When electronic computers first appeared in the 1950s and 60s, they were extremely expensive. In 1966, a major midwestern university bought a computer called a Control Data CDC 6600. This particular computer had a 1-megahertz clock and less than 1 megabyte of memory. Its capacities were certainly modest when compared with today's computers, which typically have 2-gigahertz clocks and 512 megabytes of memory. Even so, the university spent $3,000,000 for this machine. Moreover, although $3,000,000 today is still a respectable sum, in 1966 it was worth a lot more. At the time, the average price of a house in the U.S. was $13,000, and the median salary was $7,436 [US 1968]. Compared to the cost of the computer, salaries were cheap. At the time, it made good economic sense to train experts to accommodate the computer. Little thought was given to the idea of making life easier for people using the programs.

Things began to change in the late 1970s and early 80s. Computers became smaller and cheaper. In 1981, IBM Corporation introduced the first IBM Personal Computer, targeted for home and small-business use. Because these machines cost less money, more people were able to purchase them. A new phenomenon occurred: nonexperts began using computers. For this new and rapidly growing group of people, computers were similar to cars and telephones: they were just tools to assist them in their work and lives. These people already had skills and knowledge in other areas, such as business and medicine. For them, knowledge of a computer's internal workings was not interesting, and they viewed learning this information as a waste of time.

Computer and software manufacturers noticed this trend and started considering the benefits of creating products that were "user-friendly." "If our product is easy to use," they reasoned, "then people will buy it." However, they didn't know any effective ways to discover what made a product user-friendly or how to design a product that *was* friendly. What was clear was that most programmers did not have good insights into these issues.

At the same time, researchers began studying these problems, drawing on previous work in human factors and ergonomics. The study of human factors had its origins in World War II efforts to design equipment that facilitates optimal human performance even under the most difficult circumstances, such as a combat situation. The field called *ergonomics* studies similar problems, but usually in a workplace setting. In 1982, the Association for Computing Machinery (ACM) approved the naming of a Special Interest Group on Computer–Human Interaction (SIGCHI), whose goals include promoting the use of human factors in the human–computer interaction process [Borman 1996].

One of this SIG's activities was to develop a definition for human–computer interaction. Here it is [ACM 1992]:

Human–computer interaction is a discipline concerned with the design, evaluation, and implementation of interactive computing systems for human use and with the study of major phenomena surrounding them.

An interactive computing system might be a single PC equipped with a monitor, mouse, and keyboard that's capable of displaying Web pages; it might be an embedded device such as certain components of today's cars; it might be a WAP (Wireless Access Protocol)-enabled device, such as a cell phone; or it might be software that allows hundreds of people from around the world to collaborate on a single project. The major phenomena surrounding interactive computing systems include accommodations for physical limitations and considerations of the environment where the system is located. A system in a noisy hotel lobby will have requirements different from these of a system located in the quiet and privacy of a user's home.

On any development team, the role of an HCI practitioner is to serve as an advocate for the users of the system. An HCI practitioner listens to users and communicates their needs to the developers responsible for implementation. Some have likened the role to that of a family therapist, attempting to provide clear avenues of communication among users and developers [Kreitzberg 2000].

1.4 Goals of HCI

What does HCI try to accomplish? HCI strives to make people's experience with computers more productive, more time-efficient, and more pleasant. Eason gives a concise answer when he states the following:

The goals of HCI are to develop or improve the

- safety
- utility
- effectiveness
- efficiency
- usability
- appeal

of systems that include computers [Eason 1988].

Safety can mean "safety of users," "safety of data," or both. Safety of users is a primary consideration in systems such as air-traffic control and the monitoring equipment in a hospital's intensive care unit. Safety of data includes protection of files from unintentional or malicious tampering and issues such as privacy and security for websites.

Utility has to do with the services that the system provides. *Effectiveness* concerns a user's ability to accomplish a desired goal or to carry out work. Utility and effectiveness are distinct aspects of an interactive system. A website might provide all the information, instruction, and server-side support required to complete a purchase, which are all examples of utility. However, if users can't figure out how to find the items they want to buy, then the site lacks effectiveness.

Efficiency is a measure of how quickly users can accomplish goals or finish their work when using the system. *Usability* includes ease of learning and ease of use, and *appeal* describes how well users like the system, including such considerations as first impressions and long-term satisfaction.

The priority among these six aspects will vary, depending on the type of system or website you are creating. As mentioned in the previous paragraph, safety would be an overriding concern for air-traffic control systems. Another example would be monitoring software for nuclear power plants. Can you think of interactive systems where safety is less of an issue?

1.5 User-Centered Development Methodology

The user-centered development methodology is essential for developing successful user interfaces. A *user interface* comprises "those aspects of the system that a user comes in contact with" [Moran 1981]. The methodology outlined here is useful for creating any sort of interface, from spreadsheet programs to video games to websites. This development methodology differs from the more traditional software engineering methodologies in three key areas:

1. User-centered development is user centric, not data centric. It involves users in the process as much as possible with the goal of creating an interface that meets user expectations. This may include such activities as observing users while they work, inviting users to participate on the design team, and asking users to try out the product and following up on their feedback.

2. User-centered development is highly interdisciplinary and draws on knowledge from a multitude of areas, including art, psychology, technical writing, and computer science, among others. Figure 1–1 demonstrates the variety of disciplines that contribute to HCI.

3. The methodology is highly iterative and involves as much testing and revision as possible. In this book, you will see techniques to test and "debug" an interface before it is implemented, thus avoiding costly revisions once the interface has been coded.

The following is an overview of the user-centered development methodology. The initial stages involve the gathering of information; the later stages involve the designing, building, and testing of a prototype of the interface.

1.5.1 Needs Analysis

Needs analysis summarizes the nature and purpose of the interactive system you plan to develop. It describes the type of system—is it a website, a video game, or a spreadsheet? It mentions the people the system will serve and the benefits it will provide. This is very brief, typically no more than a couple of sentences that explain why it is a good idea. Here is an example:

> The Woods Bay website will promote tourism for Woods Bay Cottages in Bamfield, British Columbia. It will describe the accommodations, surroundings, fishing, snorkeling, hiking, and other local attractions for potential visitors. In addition, it will provide information about traveling to Bamfield, current rates, and booking a cabin.

Here is another:

> The redesigned website for the Plains Art Council in Burkmere, South Dakota will foster greater participation in the arts in the local community by providing a comprehensive

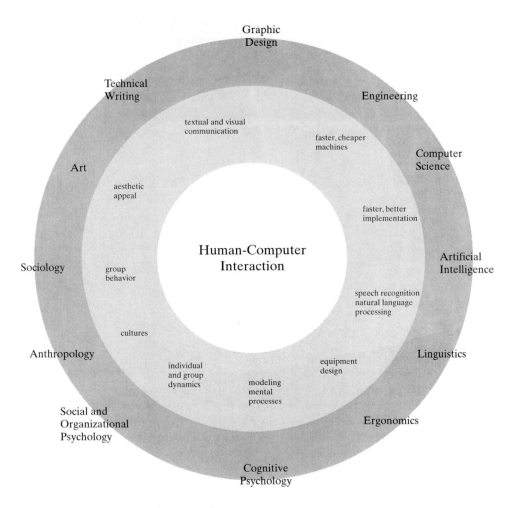

Figure 1–1 Disciplines that contribute to HCI.

listing of available art programs and services and by creating a virtual gallery or display space for local artists.

In the first example, the interactive system is a website and the audience is people who are planning a vacation to British Columbia. The site will tell them about the town and what to do there and will promote the hotel accommodations. In the second, who is the audience?

1.5.2 User and Task Analysis

User analysis characterizes the people who will use your site. This includes some general considerations, such as age, education level, and experience with computers. You will also look into users' experience and expectations with sites similar to yours. *Task analysis* looks at the type of work users will do at your website. It examines user *goals*, which are what users want to accomplish when visiting a site like yours. It also looks at *tasks*, or the activities they carry out to achieve their goals. If your site is an entertainment site, these "tasks" could actually be part of some sort of leisure activity.

Too many products fail because the development team didn't take the time to find out who their users are or what they want to do. A thorough user and task analysis will put you ahead of the game when it comes time to create your site. Chapter 3 will discuss techniques for conducting user and task analyses.

1.5.3 Functional Analysis

In a *functional analysis*, you identify the functionality—the computer services that users will need to carry out their tasks. For instance, for a travel site, tasks could include finding all of the flights to a particular location during a specified time range, ordered by price. To help users complete this task, your site will need a search function and a sorting capability. For a site selling music CDs, one of the tasks will be "Buy a CD." In this case, you will need secure on-line transaction functionality. Usually, there is a close correspondence between functions and tasks.

In this stage, you also decide what aspects of the tasks should be automated and which should be completed by humans. For example, on the Woods Bay Cottages site, the developers did not create an automated reservation system for the cottages. Instead, the site lists a toll-free phone number. In contrast, many major hotel chains allow you to book rooms directly on their sites. Access to computing resources and availability of skilled developers will influence decisions about what to automate.

1.5.4 Requirements Analysis

A *requirements analysis* describes the formal specifications required to implement any system, including websites. Depending on the application, the formal specification can include data dictionaries, entity–relationship diagrams, and object-oriented modeling. These are the same types of specifications that you would develop in a systems-analysis or software-engineering course. This particular step is well covered in other branches of the computing discipline, so this text will not cover it.

1.5.5 Setting Usability Specifications

You will need to answer the question, "How good is your website?" Setting usability specifications will help you determine this. Usability specifications include *performance measures*, such as "number of tasks completed" and "number of errors," which are directly observable user behaviors. Usability specifications also include *preference measures*, which give insights into a user's opinion about your site. Examples of preference measures include "first impression" and "overall satisfaction." Chapter 3 will discuss usability specifications and how to set them.

1.5.6 Design

In this step, you decide on the organization and appearance of your website. When designing, you identify the content for your site and organize it according to your users' expectations. In Chapter 4, you will learn techniques for organizing content, which is one of the most critical elements for success of a website. It's during the design step that you also decide on your site's look and feel. Design also includes the layout of individual pages and how to use visual organization techniques to create clarity and consistency between pages. Chapter 5 gives some straightforward, practical advice about how to lay out a Web page even if you have never had an art class. During the design phase, you will also decide how to set up the navigation, which is the topic of Chapter 6.

It's only at this stage that you begin sketching page layouts, because you now know who your users are and what they want to do. The natural temptation is to jump the gun and begin designing screens at an earlier stage, but, without knowing your users and their tasks, the results will not be satisfactory.

1.5.7 Prototyping

The word *prototype* comes from the Greek word *proto*, meaning first, and the word *type*. Thus, a prototype is an original model or a pattern. During prototyping, you create the model from which the website will (later) be implemented. You could decide to prototype the entire site, in what is called *global prototyping*, or you could prototype only selected parts of the site, using what is called *local prototyping*.

Prototypes can also be classified as *evolutionary* or *throw-away*. If the prototype becomes part of the final project, it's evolutionary. Throw-away prototyping is exactly what the term implies: the prototype serves only as a pattern for implementation, and you actually throw away the prototype once the site is complete. An additional classification of prototypes is *high fidelity* or *low fidelity*. High-fidelity prototypes closely resemble the final product in appearance and functionality. In contrast, a low-fidelity prototype would never be mistaken for a final product. Figure 1–2 shows an example of a low-fidelity and a high-fidelity prototype of a Web page.

There is a wide range of techniques and tools available for prototyping websites. Chapter 7 will discuss these in detail.

1.5.8 Evaluation

In the evaluation step, you test your prototype. In a very real sense, this is similar to testing a program. You need to know where the problems are in your prototype. There are two types of evaluation, *user-based evaluation* and *expert-based evaluation*. In a user-based evaluation,

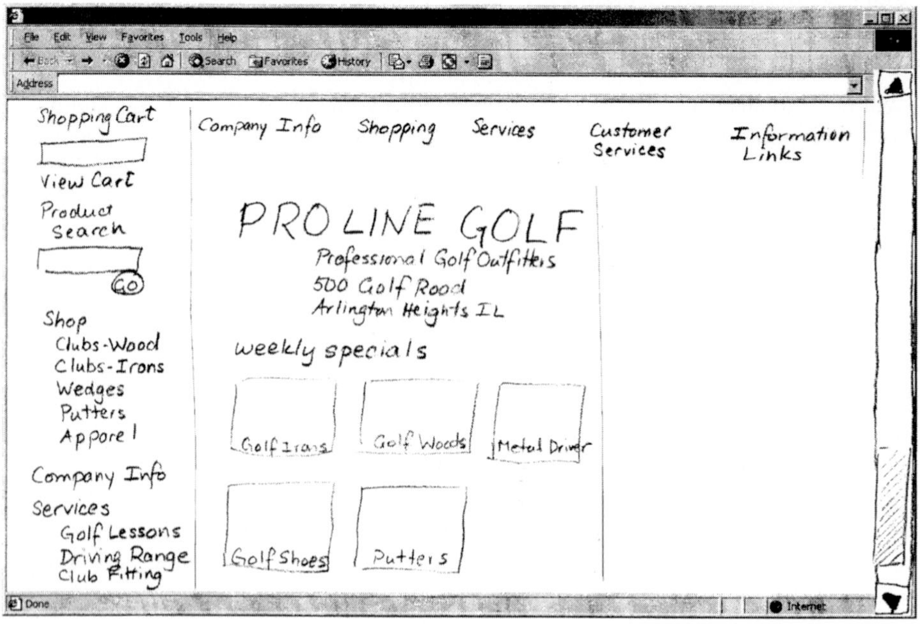

Figure 1–2 Low- vs. high-fidelity prototypes. Courtesy of Kirsten Pielstrom.

Figure 1–2   *(Continued)*

you ask actual users to perform representative tasks with your prototype. As a user carries out each task, an observer takes notes on where problems occurred. In an expert-based evaluation, a group of usability experts critique the prototype. Both approaches have their benefits, but this text will emphasize user-based testing. You will learn how to conduct user-based testing in Chapter 8. Given the results of your evaluation step, you will redesign sections of your prototype and test again.

1.6 Characteristics of User-Centered Development

User-centered development is highly iterative. There is a cycle of repetition in the design, prototype and evaluation steps of the process, as you can see in Figure 1–3. Ideally, you continue the design–prototype–evaluate cycle until you have met all of your usability specifications. The process is similar to programming, where you develop and debug programs via a cycle of design–code–test. You know that the program is working correctly when the actual outputs match the predicted outputs. Similarly, you know that your prototype is satisfactory when you meet the usability specifications.

While this book will be looking at how HCI can be used to create more effective Web sites, the principles and methodology mentioned here can be applied to any interactive system.

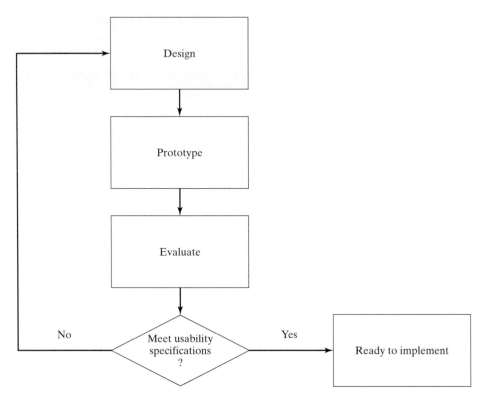

Figure 1–3 The iterative cycle of user-centered development.

1.6.1 Implementation Techniques, Accessibility, and Trust

After completing Chapters 1–8, you will be familiar with the user-centered design methodology. At this point, you will be ready to consider effective application of color (Chapter 9), typography (Chapter 10), and multimedia (Chapter 11) to enhance a user's experience.

The last chapters look at different issues in accessibility and trust. Chapter 12 examines the effect that disabilities have on a user's ability to access the Web and makes suggestions about how to design sites to accommodate users with special needs. Chapter 13 looks at how you can make a site understandable and appealing to people located around the world. Chapter 14 discusses trust building and the ethics of collecting and using personal information via the Web.

1.7 Summary

A website can offer the latest technology and include exciting interactivity and multimedia, but without consideration of the audience of users, the site is doomed to fail. On a more positive note, applying a user-centered design methodology results in websites that meet user expectations and contribute to the success of the site. This industry-proven methodology is straightforward and can facilitate cost-effective and timely implementation.

While reading this book, you will become familiar with the techniques of user-centered development and learn about effective ways of applying technology to enhance the user experience.

1.8 Other Resources

Several useful websites address issues of HCI in general and the usability of websites in particular. Here is a short list of top sites:

`www.useit.com`

> Jakob Nielsen's website contains resources for "usable information technology." In addition to guidelines for designing and developing websites, Nielsen also discusses other forms of technology, ranging from WAP devices to video games. His biweekly AlertBox feature provides current discussions about Web usability. The site also offers searching of the AlertBox archives.

`www.usableweb.com`

> Created and maintained by Keith Instone, the Usable website contains over 1400 links pertaining to Web usability. Quoting from the site, "Usable Web is a collection of links about information architecture, human factors, user interface issues, and usable design specific to the World Wide Web." In addition, the links all have descriptions and are accessible via multiple organizational schemes (by date, topic, destination, author, popularity), and search-engine queries lead to even more resources.

`www.hcibib.org`

> The HCI Bibliography site allows you to search over 20,000 books and articles in the HCI Bibliography database. Many of the articles are online and downloadable. In addition to the search capacity, you can also browse by topic. If you are looking for research results in the area of HCI, this is the definitive resource. Gary Perlman is the director of the HCI Bibliography, which is one of the resources sponsored by ACM-SIGCHI.

Several national and international organizations for HCI offer student membership at very low cost:

> Association for Computing Machinery's Special Interest Group on Computer–Human Interaction (ACM SIGCHI)
>
> Human Factors and Ergonomics Society (HFES)
>
> Usability Professionals Association (UPA)

1.8.1 Association for Computing Machinery, Special Interest Group on Computer–Human Interaction (ACM SIGCHI)

SIGCHI focuses on work in engineering the hardware and software for interactive systems, on the nature of communication between human and machine, on characterization of the use and contexts of use for interactive systems, on methodology of design, and on new designs themselves. It also serves as an international venue for specialists in human–computer interaction, education, usability, interaction design, and other related areas. The group helps to organize and disseminate information through online services, traditional publications, local SIGS, conferences, workshops, and symposia relating to HCI. Their website is `www.sigchi.org`. On it, you can find information about salaries, about jobs, and about schools that offer academic programs in HCI.

1.8.2 Human Factors and Ergonomics Society (HFES)

HFES was founded in 1957, making it one of the oldest professional organizations concerned with usability. Quoting from its website, `www.hfes.org`:

> The Society's mission is to promote the discovery and exchange of knowledge concerning the characteristics of human beings that are applicable to the design of systems and devices of all kinds.
>
> The Society furthers serious consideration of knowledge about the assignment of appropriate functions for humans and machines, whether people serve as operators, maintainers, or users in the system. And, it advocates systematic use of such knowledge to achieve compatibility in the design of interactive systems of people, machines, and environments to ensure their effectiveness, safety, and ease of performance.
>
> The Society encourages education and training for those entering the human factors and ergonomics profession and for those who conceive, design, develop, manufacture, test, manage, and participate in systems.

1.8.3 Usability Professionals Association (UPA)

As stated on its website, `www.upassoc.org`, the goals of the UPA are the following:

- Provide a network and opportunities through which usability professionals can communicate and share information about skills and skill development, methodology used and/or proposed in the profession, tools, technology, and organizational issues.
- Present the viewpoints of the profession to the public and other interested parties.
- Educate the general public and others on the usefulness of the profession.
- Represent the profession before governmental bodies and agencies.
- Provide the methods and means to increase the members' knowledge of the profession through seminars, newsletters, magazines, and other communication tools and through meetings and conventions.
- Serve the best interests of the usability profession.

Review Questions and Exercises

1. Which is easier to learn, a new car or a new program? Why? A car has over 100 settings for the driver to choose from, fewer than the number of menu items in a typical program.
2. What does the conversion rate of a website measure? Give an example of "taking action" on an e-commerce site. What would be an example of taking action on a college-admissions website? Many students who are seeking employment will post their résumés on their personal websites. What would be an example of taking action in this case?
3. How can user-centered development benefit users? List at least two positive outcomes.
4. How can user-centered development benefit developers? List at least three advantages.
5. What are the six goals of HCI? Describe each one.
6. Is it possible for an interactive system to be efficient without being effective? Why or why not?

7. Pick the most important HCI goals as they apply to each of the following types of applications:

- Air-traffic control
- Ticket-booking software for travel agents
- Reservation software for airline agents at the luggage check-in counter
- Flight simulators to train airline pilots
- An adaptation of a flight simulator as a video game for home use

Justify your answer.

8. In many ways, the history of computers has followed a path similar to that of automobiles. At first, automobiles were curiosities, accessible to only a small portion of the population. This changed with the introduction of the Ford Model T in 1908 [Gross 1996]. Since then, automobile makers have continued to make improvements on cars. Compare some of the differences between a Model T and today's cars in terms of the HCI goals of safety, usability, and appeal.

9. Give an example of how a shopping site can lead to improved productivity for a customer. For example, what can designers do to make a second purchase even faster than the first?

10. You are familiar with Amazon.com, one of the most popular websites. Explain at least two ways that the website meets each of the following goals of HCI:

- Safety
- Efficiency
- Usability
- Appeal

11. List the eight steps in the user-centered development methodology. Describe each step in a sentence or two.

12. The text gave two examples of needs analysis. In the Plains Art Council example, what is the interactive system? Who are the users? How will they benefit from the system?

13. Why is user-centered development methodology considered highly iterative?

14. Categorize each of the following usability specifications as a performance measure or a preference measure. Justify your answers.

   a. Users should be able to login in within 3 minutes, even if they forget their passwords.
   b. On a scale of 1 to 5 where 1 is "very difficult" and 5 is "very easy," ninety percent of the users should rate the login process a 4 or above.
   c. Users should hit the "back" button no more than twice when looking for merchandise items.
   d. Over 95 percent of our current users will prefer the redesigned site to the current site.
   e. Users should be able to find the "check out" page in one click, no matter where they are in the site.

    f. Users judge the page download time as "fast" or "relatively fast" when viewed via a 56K modem.

    g. If they have shopped online previously, users should be satisfied with the security of our site's on-line transaction system.

15. Forrester Research Inc. (`www.forrester.com`), a leading independent research firm that analyzes the future of technology change and its impact on businesses and consumers, estimates that Fortune 1000 companies spend an average of $1.5 million to $2.1 million per year on site redesign without knowing whether the redesign actually made the site easier to use [Kalin 1999]. How could these companies utilize usability specifications to evaluate whether spending the money actually improved their websites?

16. For each of the following activities, name the step of the user-centered development methodology where it occurs.

    a. The development team decides that a user should be able to reach any page on the site in three clicks.

    b. A team member asks users what they like about the current website and solicits suggestions for further improvement.

    c. A team member watches users as they complete tasks using a prototype of the new site.

    d. The team discusses possibilities for the appearance of subsidiary Web pages.

    e. The team comes to consensus on navigation aids.

17. This question will help you start building your set of persuasion tools for when you encounter managers or programmers who are unsure about the value of user-centered development. Using your Internet skills, find a news item of a story occurring within the past year that described a usability issue that caused problems. This should be a usability problem with the system's interface, not a problem of back-end functionality, such as a server crash, or an infrastructure problem, such as not having enough delivery personnel on hand for the holiday rush.

    a. Write a two- or three-sentence summary of the problem and its aftermath.

    b. List the URL, and include a printout of the story.

    c. The problem you cite should involve a computer in some way. Software and websites are good examples.

    d. Cite resulting problems experienced by the company or organization (examples: money lost because of slack sales; loss of market share; data compromised; angry customers).

18. You have used Internet search engines. List the URL of your favorite search engine and three reasons why you prefer it to others. Compare your reasons with three other classmates. Make note of any commonalities among the reasons, and relate your answers to the goals of HCI design.

Project Activities

19. One of the best ways to learn the user-centered development methodology is to develop a website for an organization or for a person other than yourself. There are

many places where you can find a "client" – many on-campus organizations would like to have a site that publicizes their activities. There are also many nonprofit organizations, such as service organizations, theater troupes, and religious groups that would like to set up Web pages, but don't have the skills or resources to do so. Another possibility might be a city department, such as a parks district, who might be interested.

When you find a client who is interested, ask what is envisioned for its website. If the conversation elicits a large wish list, feel free to ask which issues are most important. With this information in hand, ask your teacher to help you use this information to keep the project at a manageable size. After consulting your client and your teacher, write a needs analysis for your client. In it, give a brief description of your users and the benefits they will enjoy as a result of your new website.

References

[ACM 1992] ACM Special Interest Group on Computer–Human Interaction (SIGCHI) Curriculum Development Group. *Curricula for Human–Computer Interaction*. ACM, 1992.

[Andreessen 1994] Marc Andreessen and Eric Bina. *"NCSA Mosaic: A Global Hypermedia System,"* Internet Research: Electronic Networking Applications and Policy. **4**(1) 1994. 7–17.

[Battey 1999] Jim Battey. IBM redesign results in kinder, simpler site. *Infoworld.* April 19, 1999. `http://www.infoworld.com/cgibin/displayStat.pl?/pageone/opinions/hotsites/hotextra990419.htm`

[Borman 1996] Lorraine Borman. "SIGCHI: The early years," *SIGCHI Bulletin.* **28**(1) 1996. 4–6. `http://www.acm.org/sigchi/bulletin/1996.1/borman.html`

[Donahue 1999] George M. Donahue, Susan Weinschenk, Julie Nowicki. *Compuware Corporation.* 1999. `http://www.compuware.com/intelligence/articles/usability.htm`

[Eason 1988] K. D. Eason. *Information Technology and Organizational Change*. London: Taylor & Francis, 1988.

[Fabris 1999] Peter Fabris. "You think tomaytoes, I think tomahtoes," *CIO Magazine.* April 1, 1999. `http://www.cio.com/archive/webbusiness/040199_nort.html`

[Gross 1996] Daniel Gross. *Forbes Greatest Business Stories of All Time*. New York: Wiley, 1996.

[Gurley 2000] William Gurley. "The most powerful metric of all," *C/Net News.com.* February 21, 2000. `http://news.cnet.com/news/0-1270-210-3287257-1.html`

[Kalin 1999] Sari Kalin. "Mazed and Confused," *CIO Web Business Magazine.* April 1, 1999. `http://www.cio.com/archive/webbusiness/040199_use.html`

[Kreitzberg 2000] Charles Kreitzberg. "Usability as therapy," *The UPA Voice* **2**(2) May 2000. `http://www.upassoc.org/voice/vol2no2/editorial.htm`

[Moran 1981] J. Moran. "The command language grammar: a representation for the user interface of interactive systems," *International Journal of Man–Machine Studies.* **15**(1) 1981. 3–50.

[Rhodes 2000] John Rhodes. "Usability can save your company," *Webword.com.* December 21, 2000. `http://webword.com/moving/savecompany.html`

[US 1968] U.S. Bureau of the Census. *Statistical Abstract of the United States: 1968.* (89th edition.) Washington, D.C., 1968. pp. 324, 700.

[Weiss 2000] Todd Weiss. "Wal-Mart shuts Web site for renovations until Oct. 17," *ITWorld.com.* October 2, 2000. `http://www.computerworld.com/cwi/story/0,1199,NAV47_STO51731,00.html`

2

Capabilities of Human Beings

2.1 Introduction

Much of what you need to know to create a website will come from the information that you gather about your particular users and the specific tasks they perform. There is no substitute for collecting this information, and Chapter 3 will cover this topic in detail. However, there are some commonalities in how people think and perceive that provide a useful set of considerations for Web design. This information comes from *cognitive psychology*, which studies how people perceive, learn, and remember.

"Cognition" means "the act or process of knowing." For instance, if you are reading a Web-based article with your favorite browser and you come to a phrase written with blue underlined text, you can be reasonably certain that the blue text is a link. Research findings in cognition can help resolve such questions as the following:

"Confronted with a new website, how can a user capitalize on past experience to make sense of it? Can the user depend on the result?"

Anyone who is developing websites needs to know some basics about the limits of human perception, cognition, and memory. We don't have to delve into the latest research, but some basics are essential.

Goals of this Chapter

In this chapter, you will learn about

- human sense, perception, memory, and interruptions
- the concepts of mental models, metaphor, and perceived affordance
- some design guidelines based on these topics.

2.2 Senses

Our senses feed our perceptions. Most of us have at least five senses, primary among which are sight, hearing, touch, taste, and smell. As a whole, we are primarily visual beings. When a number of students were asked which sense they would most hate to lose, 75% replied sight [Synnott 1993]. Visual metaphors permeate our language:

- I see your point.
- Out of sight, out of mind.
- What does she see in him?

Designing good Web materials requires knowledge about how people see. The next section shows that seeing involves not only the eyes, but also involves the mind in crucial ways.

2.3 Perception

In a subject as vast and as important as this, it should not be surprising that there are differing schools of thought. Without surveying the others, we will borrow from the school of *constructivism* [Agnew 1987].

Central to constructivism is the idea that our brains do not create a pixel-by-pixel recording of a scene like a digital camera. Instead, our minds create or construct intervening models that abstract and summarize what comes out of the optic nerve, and these models influence what we perceive.

Consider Figure 2–1. This is a picture of a calf. The head takes up the left side of the image. Once you have recognized it, your mind recreates a summary of the picture, and you will see the calf easily when you encounter the image again.

Constructivist theory contends that when we see something, we don't remember all the information in the scene. We retain only the pieces that have meaning for us. Do you remember how many links are in the top menu of amazon.com? What are the colors on the box containing your favorite breakfast cereal? How many lines make up the IBM logo? An honest reaction to any of these questions might well be "Who knows and who cares?" Exactly so. People filter out the irrelevant parts and save the important ones.

Secondly, constructivist theory states that *context* plays a major role in what people see in an image. Figure 2–2 shows what looks like two identical shapes; in context, however, the two shapes are interpreted as two different letters, as seen in Figure 2–3.

The combination of factors revolving around what we know and what we bring to a situation is called *perceptual set* or *mind set*. Mind set can have a profound effect on the usability

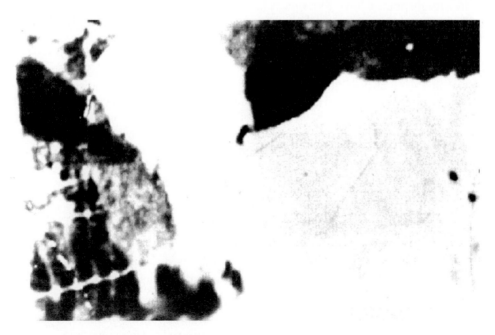

Figure 2–1   What do you see?

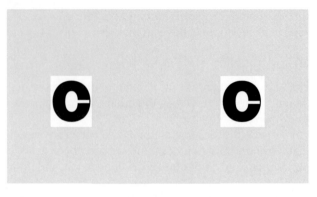

Figure 2–2   Two identical shapes [after Selfridge 1955].

Figure 2–3   Interpreting a shape on the basis of its context.

of a website. Pearrow [Pearrow 2000] gives a charming example. One of his clients had a website on which patrons could not find important links on the site, even though they were right there in plain sight. The problem came from the fact that the client had used animated graphics for the critical links. Many users have come to assume that any animation is an advertisement, and these users really never saw what the designer intended. Replacing the animations with text-only links completely solved the problem.

A third important aspect of constructivism involves the decomposition or partitioning of images into entities recognized as *figure* (foreground) and *ground* (background). This might at first seem obvious; it gets more interesting when you realize that what constitutes the figure and what the ground can be highly ambiguous. Danish psychologist Edgar Rubin devised images that exhibit a high degree of figure/ground ambiguity [Rubin 1915]. In Figure 2–4, do you see a black vase (or goblet, or bird-bath) on a white background, or silhouetted faces on a black background? Perceptual set operates in such cases too: What we see depends in part on what we are used to seeing. A glassblower might be more likely to see a vase; a person who has a habit of observing people's faces closely might be more likely to see two profiles.

We are now into the branch of psychology known as *Gestalt psychology*, which adheres to the constructivist school of thought [Schultz 1996]. "Gestalt" is the German word for "shape," but it means more than that in this context. A main idea of Gestalt psychology is that we see things not in isolation, but as parts of some larger whole. We organize what we see into meaningful wholes by using five principles—proximity, similarity, symmetry, continuity, and closure.

Proximity.   Proximity describes the process of using distance or location to create groups. Consider Figure 2–5. On the left are three groups of vertical lines. On the right are three groups of dots. People tend to perceive any closely clustered objects as a group.

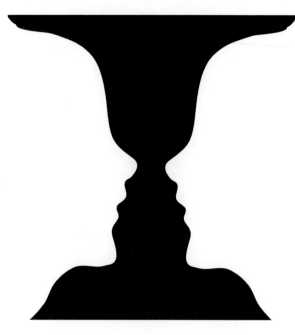

Figure 2–4   Figure-and-ground ambiguity.

Figure 2–5   Examples of proximity.

Similarity.   Similarity is a grouping by like kind or like type. The collection in Figure 2–6 has an example of grouping by similarity. There are dark dots and light dots – in other words, two groups of dots, determined by shade of gray. It is possible to use similarity in any combination of size, shape, texture, boldness, or orientation to create groups.

Symmetry.   In symmetry, the whole of a figure is perceived rather than the parts that make up the figure. On the left side of Figure 2–7 we see two overlapping triangles, not a little triangle and two complex objects [Mullet 1995]. The example on the right shows three sets of brackets. Notice that your eyes group the left two brackets together, even though the second bracket is physically closer to the third bracket than to the first [Chandler, 2001].

Continuity.   Continuity is the term for groupings created by the flow of lines or by alignment. In Figure 2–8, we see on the left two smooth curves, a–b and c–d, not two broken

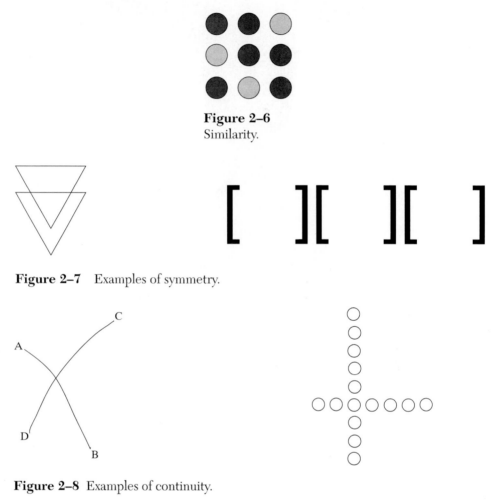

Figure 2–6
Similarity.

Figure 2–7   Examples of symmetry.

Figure 2–8 Examples of continuity.

curves, a–c and d–b. On the right are two lines created from circles. Although there are no actual lines, our eyes follow the flow formed by the circles. *Alignment* is a type of continuity. An example of alignment is the use of indentation to show hierarchy, as in an outline. In an outline, items of equal importance are aligned.

Closure.   Closure is the process by which we perceive shapes that, in a certain sense, aren't really there. We mentally complete the shape in our heads. It is a way for our minds to impose order and meaning on an incomplete set of data. Figure 2–9 displays three circles. The first has a ring of triangles surrounding it. The second has a chunk missing on the right side. The third has a dashed border. In all three cases, there is no actual circle, but your mind perceives it as such.

Three of the five visual principles of Gestalt are useful in structuring Web pages. When links are grouped together by proximity, people tend to think of those links as being related. Look at the list of links in Figure 2–10a. Considering their names, it appears that there are links to merchandise (camcorders, digital cameras, DVD players, VCRs), links to timely information (breaking news, press releases, reviews), and links to additional services (contacts,

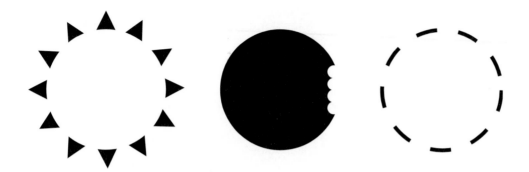

Figure 2–9 Examples of closure.

subscribe, webmaster). So there are three groups of related items: merchandise, time-sensitive information, and services. Instead of throwing them all together, which forces a user to look through the entire list, it's better to present them as three short lists. By adding a little space, the three groups are more visible, as you can see in Figure 2–10b.

The Gestalt principle of similarity says that related objects look alike. Figure 2–11 demonstrates how using this principle can improve a Web page. In all three Web pages, there are four buttons at the top of the page, but, in the first example, the buttons have different sizes and spacing that make

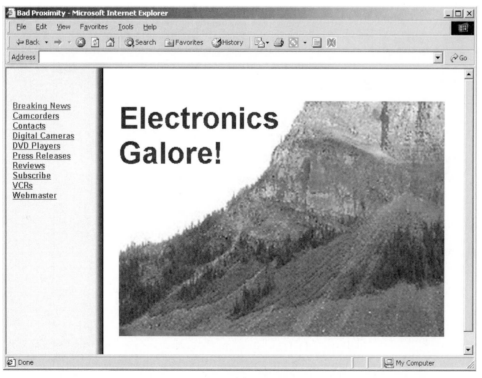

(a)

Figure 2–10 Using Proximity.

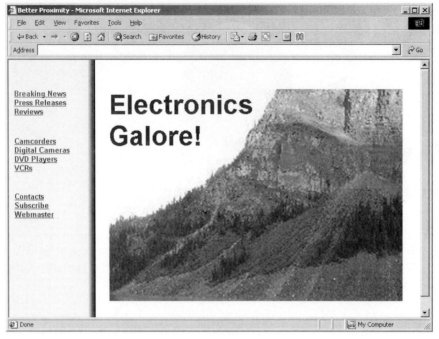

(b)

Figure 2–10   (*Continued*)

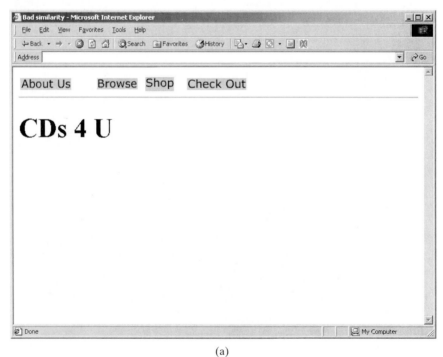

(a)

Figure 2–11   Leveraging Similarity.

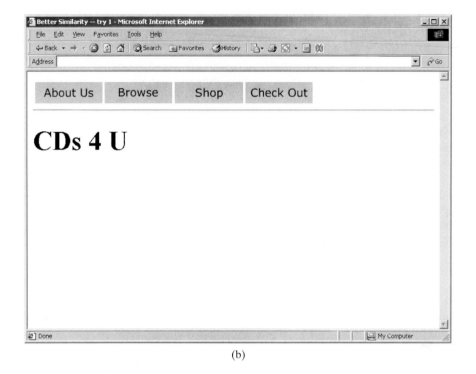

(b)

(c)

Figure 2–11 (*Continued*)

for a raggedy appearance. In the second example, the buttons are all the same size and have the same spacing. Similarity is at work. There is a third example page in the figure. Compare it to the second page. What additional feature of similarity is present in the third example but absent from the second?

Using alignment, a form of continuity, improves the Web page in Figure 2–12a. Dark lines have been added to this example to show the poor alignment at the top and bottom of the page's content area. The second example has much stronger horizontal alignment across the blocks of text. Compare the second and third pages. What has changed? Is it horizontal or vertical? Compare the first and third pages. Which one appears more professional and inspires more confidence?

These five visual principles of Gestalt psychology make up a fascinating area where psychology and graphic design come together. Chapter 5 discusses how to take advantage of this idea of visual grouping when exploring techniques to promote effective visual communication on websites.

2.4 Memory

Knowing a few facts about the types and limits of human memory will help you design better websites. For example, consider what happens if a website requires a user to type in a 10-digit part number as part of the ordering process. Very often the reaction will be, "Forget it. This isn't worth it."

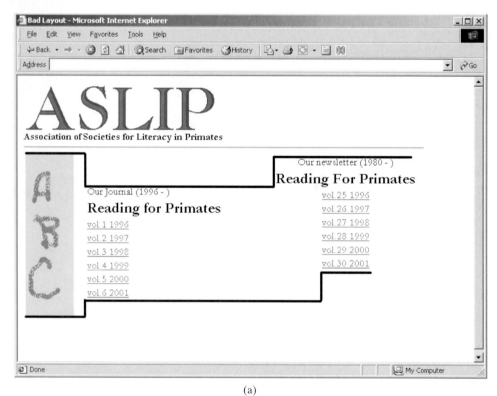

(a)

Figure 2–12 Using alignment, a type of continuity (part 1).

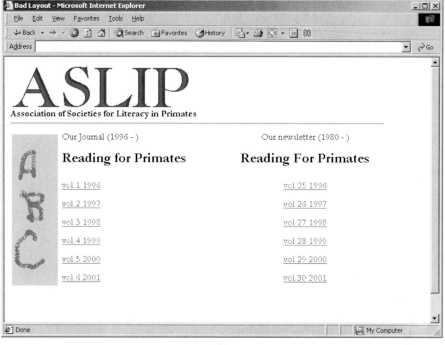

(b)

Figure 2–12 (*Continued*)

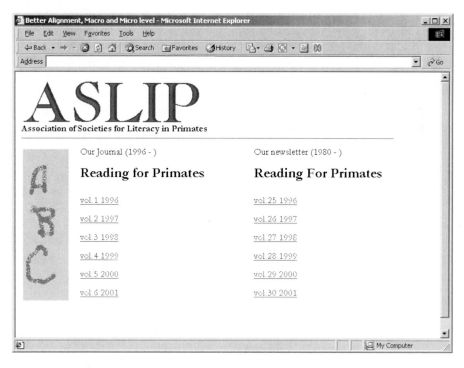

Figure 2–13 Using alignment, a type of continuity (part 2).

Memory is an astonishing capacity and variable in the extreme. One of the authors of this book can lay down his reading glasses and five minutes later have absolutely no idea where they are. In contrast, many people can remember all of the lyrics to a song that was popular in their youth, even if that youth occurred some time ago.

Knowing a few basic facts about memory will help in designing good websites. A few key concepts are the following:

- The hierarchical model of memory: sensory store, short-term memory, and long-term memory.
- The value of "chunking."
- The advantages of relying on recognition instead of on recall.
- Memory aids.

2.4.1 The Hierarchical Model of Memory

The hierarchical model of memory is just that: a model. We don't yet know how memory works at the neuron level, but the model helps explain why people can remember some things while forgetting others [Anderson 2000]. As depicted in Figure 2–14, the model consists of three stages: *sensory memory*, *short-term memory*, and *long-term memory*.

Sensory memory refers to a buffer that stores sensory input. People automatically throw most of it away without being aware of doing so. An example of this is the act of tuning out all of the voices at a cocktail party except for that of the person next to you. Consistent with this concept is the fact that people don't remember most of what they see. As an example, try remembering the commercials that played on last night's newscast.

The second level in the hierarchy is *short-term memory*. Short-term memory holds a limited amount of data for a period of time ranging from 30 seconds to two minutes. As new information arrives in short-term memory, old information is forgotten.

How much data can short-term memory hold? The answer is given in the title of a landmark 1956 paper by the psychologist George Miller: "The Magic Number Seven, Plus or Minus Two" [Miller 1956]. Many people can remember a new seven-digit telephone number long enough to dial it, but most people would not remember the number the next day. It's difficult to remember the page number where you saw an item in a catalog without the additional help of turning down the page corner. One metaphor for short- vs. long-term memory is that short-term memory is like dynamic RAM: Continuously focusing attention

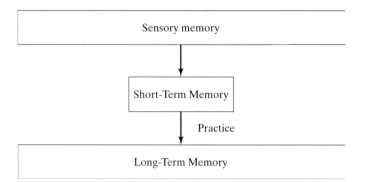

Figure 2–14 Memory Hierarchy (courtesy Maryjo Davidson).

on a set of numbers will constantly refresh the memory. If a person switches attention to something else, the information in the volatile storage medium is lost.

A person needs to expend a great deal of effort to transfer information to *long-term memory*, which is the third and final stage in the memory hierarchy. How it actually works is not known, but it is as if a connection is established between the RAM and a hard disk and the contents of the RAM are stored to disk. If you turn off your computer for a week, anything in RAM is long gone, but contents of the disk are expected to be intact. You already know that it requires a great deal of effort to move information from short-term to long-term memory: You know how much time and concentration it takes to study for an exam.

Long-term memory is quite useful and virtually unlimited, but it isn't infallible. Research has shown that long-term memory is frequently quite unreliable and is easily manipulated simply by how questions are asked. For example, a group of test participants was shown slides of an automobile collision. Later, the subjects were asked either of two questions: "How fast were the cars going when they hit each other?" or "How fast were the cars going when they smashed into each other?" A week later, all participants were asked whether they had seen broken glass in any of the slides they had been shown. Those who had been asked about the cars that "smashed into each other" were much more likely to report having seen glass than subjects who were asked about the cars that "hit each other." In fact, there was no broken glass in the scene [Loftus 1974].

Building long-term memory takes time and effort. When browsing the Web, users are not interested in expending energy to memorize a site or how to use it.

2.4.2 Chunking

In his article, Miller discussed his number seven in terms of *chunks*. A chunk might be a digit, such as the digits in a seven-digit phone number, but what constitutes a chunk will vary with the individual and the context. Consider the URL `www.bestbookbuys.com`. This URL has 20 characters in it, so at first it might seem that Miller is stating that this URL is too big to fit in short-term memory. In actuality, however, people group the characters into the following chunks:

1. www.
2. best
3. book
4. buys
5. .com

As five chunks, the URL fits nicely into short-term memory.

2.4.3 Recognition vs. Recall

Why is it easier to take a multiple-choice test than an essay test? In a multiple-choice test, it's possible to *recognize* the correct answer among the choices; with an essay exam, one is forced to *recall* the correct answer. When listening to a "golden oldies" radio station, you may *recognize* a tune but fail to *recall* the title. It is easier to read a newspaper in a second language than it is to speak in it, because speaking requires recalling the words you want to say. When using computers, it is far easier to recognize commands in a menu on a graphical user interface than to remember abbreviations in a command-line system.

An effective way of reducing a user's memory burden is to design systems that rely on people's ability to recognize information rather than forcing them to recall it. One way to do this is through *memory aids*. Memory aids are familiar from everyday life. Many of us do things like sticking Post-It® notes on the fridge to remind ourselves to buy milk. Some people might put their wristwatch on the wrong arm, so that when they get to work and try to look at the time, they will say, "What on earth is my watch doing *there*?" and then they will remember, "Oh, yes. I have to send Joe a fax."

Closer to home, the Microsoft Windows keyboard alternative to clicking on File is alt + F. The fact that F is the first letter of File is a memory aid, and the fact that on the File menu the F is underlined is another. Once the File menu drops down, we are reminded that ctrl + N means New, ctrl + O means Open, ctrl + C means Close, and ctrl + S means Save. These choices seem "natural" to us by now.

Many people use the Favorites list or Bookmarks to store URLs for later use. Hypertext links themselves can be memory aids if they give an indication of the contents of the target page.

2.5 Interruptions

Two phenomena, focusing of attention and handling of interruptions, are closely linked with memory. We have all had the experience of being in a crowded room, at a cocktail party perhaps, where many conversations are going on simultaneously. It is quite easy to focus on just one speaker, blocking out all the competing sounds.

Knowing how and when to focus a user's attention is important in such time-critical applications as the control of nuclear power plant operations, the directing of air traffic, or the monitoring of patients in an intensive-care unit. It is also important for such applications as websites, because people often encounter interruptions.

We are all capable of juggling several things at one time. Many people can cook while carrying on an animated conversation. Sometimes, though, people are interrupted in a way that does not permit doing two things at once. You are typing email when you hear a scream in the hallway; it turns out to be a scream of laughter, but when you get back to the email you have to recover your train of thought. There are definite limitations on the ability to resume an interrupted task because it relies on short-term memory. Have you ever tried to count coins while carrying on a conversation? If the talk gets too interesting, it is easy to lose count.

Consider a situation where you are writing an email message when a visitor knocks on the door. You begin a conversation with the visitor when the phone rings. After finishing the phone call, you need to remember where you were in the conversation with your visitor. If you don't recall, you can ask, "Where were we?" Similarly, when your visitor leaves and you return to your email message, you can read the last sentence or two to recognize your train of thought in the email message. In both cases, you were able to pick up the train of thought, but you relied on external cues, or *knowledge in the world* [Norman 1988] to do it.

For Web designers, it's important to give people cues or memory aids for resuming interrupted tasks. With a fill-out form, users can see where they left off, because some of the text boxes are still blank. Today's browsers return to the exact position within a Web page in response to the "back" button. Followed links have a different color, to tell a user which pages have already been visited. A more sophisticated example is the persistent shopping cart available in e-commerce sites: A user can place items in a cart and return to it even days later. These are all examples of using memory aids to ease the burden on a user's memory while resuming an interrupted task.

Web designers also need to know the answer to the question, "What constitutes an interruption?" Another way to ask this is as follows:

How fast does a system have to respond before the user's attention becomes diverted from the task at hand?

A widely quoted paper by Robert Miller [Miller 1968] gives the answer:

Response time	User reaction
Less than 0.1 second	User perceives this as instantaneous.
Less than 1.0 second	User notices the delay, but has no break in thought stream.
More than 10.0 seconds	User switches to another task.

For a response taking between 1 and 10 seconds, the user will usually wait, but there are some newer studies [Bouch 2000] that indicate that users will wait only 8 seconds for a page to download. For any response taking more than 10 seconds, a user will switch to doing something else, and an interruption has occurred. You will need to think about what type of feedback will help a user remember where the interruption occurred.

When a delay is unavoidable, it is important to give the user some kind of feedback to indicate that the computer isn't brain-dead. Users need an acknowledgment that a mouse click or other input has been received.

2.6 Mental Models

Closely related to how people store knowledge in memory is how people use that knowledge to understand new experiences or to make predictions about new situations. People build *mental models* to make predictions about an external event before actually carrying out actions. Examples are easy to find, both in everyday life and on the Web. A possible mental model of a car might be: If I put gas in here and put the key in there and turn it, the car starts.

Note that this is not the same mental model of a car that a mechanic has, but it doesn't stop the person from making predictions about the car's behavior. A possible prediction might be that if the tank doesn't get filled, eventually the car won't start. Mental models are essential for survival in the world, but, as the previous example suggests, they often do not correctly describe the functionality underlying the interface.

We can't ignore a user's mental models just because they aren't neat and clearly defined. Whether we like it or not, people use mental models to form expectations, and we ignore them at our peril.

2.7 Metaphors

Metaphors can help guide a user to choose the most relevant mental model. The term metaphor has the same meaning here that it does it literature. It's a way to relate a difficult or abstract topic to a more familiar one. For example, everyday language tends to use the metaphor of money to refer to the more abstract concept of time. People talk about "spending time," "saving time," and "wasting time."

When creating interfaces, we can use metaphors to help people become familiar with a new system by comparing it to a more familiar one that they already know. For example, in the 1980s, new computer users found many similarities between typewriters and word processors. When they saw the keyboard on a computer, they assumed that it behaved similarly to a keyboard on a typewriter. Today, many types of user interactions are based on concepts that existed before the computer age. The actions of copying, cutting, and pasting were well known before computers were invented.

The advantage of using a metaphor is that it speeds the learning process. When surveying a new interface, people will draw on their mental models of the presented metaphor to find similarities to things they already know. Using this comparison, they can make predictions about the interface's behavior.

The big disadvantage of metaphors is that they are brittle and do not expand to accommodate new functionality. One of the reasons voice mail was difficult for people to learn was that the telephone metaphor did not accommodate the new functionality of sending or accessing recorded messages. Another example is the trashcan icon on the Mac interface. At one time, the only way to eject a floppy disk was to drag its icon to the trashcan. Many users were paralyzed by this requirement: the trashcan also stood for erasing a file from hard disk, and users wondered whether the floppy would be erased. Apple changed the interface.

2.8 Perceived Affordance

If it is clear to users how to find and pay for items on a website, then it is much more likely that the users will buy. *Perceived affordance* is the quality that makes it easy for a user to spot and identify the services or functionalities of an interface. *Affordance* refers to the functions or services that an interface provides. A door *affords* an exit from a room; a radio button *affords* a one-of-many choice. Perceived affordance is affordance that is visible and comprehensible to the user. If users can spot and predict the functionality of a control, then they will easily understand how the control works. Perceived affordance is a happy result of leveraging memory aids and users' mental models.

An example of perceived affordance is shown in Figure 2–15. Given that these are attached to doors, we know that a handle affords pulling and crash bar affords pushing [Preece 1994]. Figure 2–16 also illustrates perceived affordance: the top switch controls the top lights.

Figure 2–15   Perceived affordance in door handles. Courtesy of Bret Kroll.

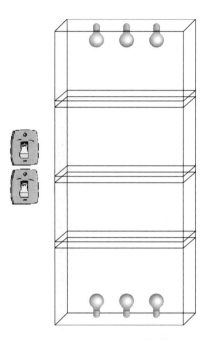

Figure 2–16   Perceived affordance: the top switch controls the top lights.

For more examples of affordance, see Don Norman's insightful and entertaining book, *The Design of Everyday Things* [Norman 1988].

2.9 Some Design Implications

The previous sections examined some key concepts of perception and memory. It covered interruptions and how memory and memory aids are important for successfully resuming an interrupted task. The careful use of metaphors and the development of perceived affordances can help a user comprehend the functionality of an interface more quickly. Here are some design guidelines for the Web that draw on this knowledge:

- Do your best to lessen the burden on a user's memory by
    - relying on recognition instead of recall
    - helping users chunk information
    - requiring as little of short-term memory as possible.
- Consider your user's mental models.
- Provide visual cues or memory aids so a user can easily resume an interrupted task.
- Provide feedback. Let the users know that their input has been received and give them an indication of how long it will take for the system to respond to it.

Review Questions and Exercises

1. According to constructivist theory, how do humans organize the data they receive from their senses?

2. Constructive theory states that context plays a major part in what we perceive. From your experience, give an example of an icon or a word that means different things, depending on the context.

3. For each of the four examples shown below, give the Gestalt principle it demonstrates.

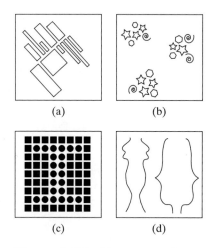

(a)   (b)

(c)   (d)

Figure 2–17   For exercise 3.

4. For each of the four examples shown in Figure 2–18, give the Gestalt principle it demonstrates.

5. What Gestalt principles are contributing to the organization of the window depicted in Figure 2–19? Explain.

6. Figure 2–20 shows a proposed home page for a website about pets.

   a. Which of the link names are most closely related? Organize them into two groups according to the meaning of the link names, and list the groups. Explain your rationale for the groups.

   b. What ways do you know to organize information visually? List all five of them. For each one, decide whether it would be useful when reorganizing the link names on the website. Explain your answer.

   c. Make a photocopy of the home page, cut it apart using scissors, and make a new version of the page where the related links appear to be part of a group.

7. What are the three levels in the memory hierarchy? How are they different?

8. For an e-commerce site, why are short domain names more desirable than long ones?

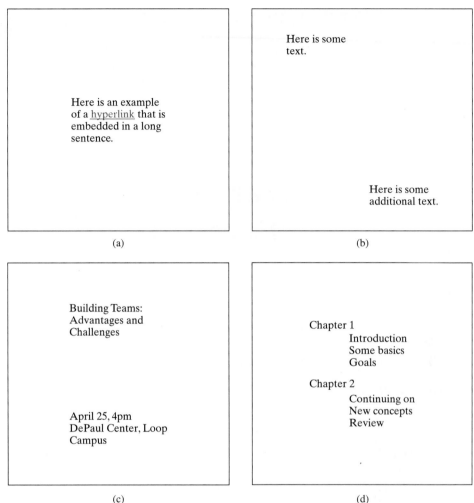

Here is an example
of a hyperlink that is
embedded in a long
sentence.

(a)

Here is some
text.

Here is some
additional text.

(b)

Building Teams:
Advantages and
Challenges

April 25, 4pm
DePaul Center, Loop
Campus

(c)

Chapter 1
    Introduction
    Some basics
    Goals

Chapter 2
    Continuing on
    New concepts
    Review

(d)

Figure 2–18   For exercise 4.

Figure 2–19   Courtesy of Apple Computer, Inc. Used by permission.

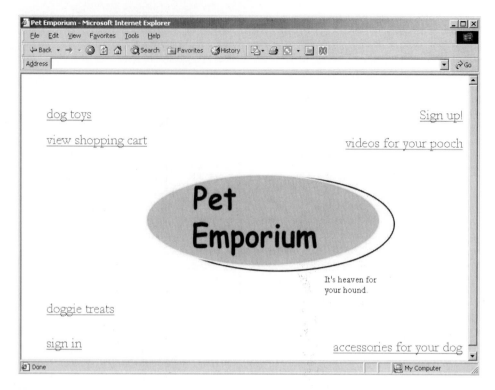

Figure 2–20 For exercise 6.

9. Why do many television ads list a phone number like 1-800 CALL ATT instead of 1-800 225 5288? After all it's easier to use the numbers on the touch pad instead of hunting up the letters. Relate this to short-term memory.

10. Both Netscape and Internet Explorer have a good number of memory aids built into them. Name at least four of them.

11. Why do most people find menu-based systems easier to use than command-line systems?

12. Suppose you are adding a new paragraph to the middle of a term paper when your computer emits a sound letting you know that email has arrived. You switch to your email client to read the new message. After you reply, you switch back to your paper. Why is it easy to know where you left off? How does it focus your attention?

13. You have selected some files that you plan to delete, but you don't get a chance to hit the "delete" key before the phone rings. When you return to your machine, how do you know which files you had chosen for deletion? Relate this to what you know about interruptions.

14. The section about metaphors mentioned that the copy and paste actions existed before the age of computers. What other metaphors do you find in today's Macintosh or Windows interfaces?

15. The following are pictures of two doors. How would you operate door A? How would you operate door B? Compare your responses to these two scenarios. Are they the same or different? How does this relate to concepts discussed in this chapter?

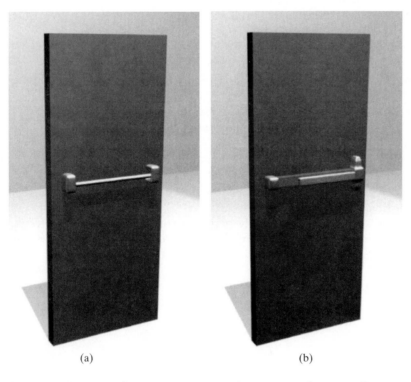

(a)   (b)

Figure 2–21   Two doors. For exercise 15. Courtesy of Bret Kroll.

References

[Anderson 2000] John R. Anderson. *Cognitive Psychology and its Implications*. New York: Worth, 2000.

[Agnew 1987] N. M. Agnew and S. W. Pike. *The Science Game*. 4th ed. Englewood Cliffs, NJ: Prentice Hall, 1987.

[Bouch 2000] Anna Bouch, Allan Kuchinsky, and Nina Bhatti. "Quality is in the Eye of the Beholder: Meeting Users' Requirements for Internet Quality of Service," Proceedings of ACM CHI 2000 Conference on Human Factors in Computing Systems 2000 vol.1. pp. 297–304.

[Chandler 2001] Daniel Chandler, Visual Perception 6: Gestalt principles of visual organization. http://www.aber.ac.uk/media/Modules/ED10510/visper06.html 2001

[Loftus 1974] E. F. Lofus and J. C. Palmer. "Reconstruction of automobile destruction: An example of the interaction between language and memory," *Journal of Verbal Learning and Verbal Behavior*, 1974. vol.13. pp. 585–589.

[Marr 1982] D. Marr. *Vision: A Computational Investigation into the Human Representation and Processing of Visual Information*. New York, W. H. Freeman, 1982. pp. 100–101.

[Miller 1956] George A. Miller. "The Magic Number Seven, Plus or Minus Two," *The Psychological Review,* 1956 vol. 63. pp. 81–97.

[Miller 1968] Robert B. Miller. "Response time in man–computer conversational transactions," *Proceedings of the Spring Joint Computer Conference 1968* vol. 33. Montvale, New Jersey: AFIPS Press, 267–277.

[Mullet 1995] Kevin Mullet and Darrell Sano. *Designing Visual Interfaces.* Englewood Cliffs, New Jersey: Prentice Hall, 1995. p. 92.

[Norman 1988] Donald Norman. *The Design of Everyday Things.* New York: Doubleday, 1988.

[Pearrow 2000] Mark Pearrow. *Web Site Usability Handbook.* Rockland, Massachusetts: Charles River Media, 2000. p. 105.

[Preece, 1994] Jenny Preece, Yvonne Rogers, Helen Sharp, David Benyon, Simon Holland, and Tom Cary. *Human–Computer Interaction.* Reading, Massachusetts: Addison-Wesley, 1994.

[Rubin 1915] Edgar Rubin. Figure and ground. In *Readings in Perception,* D. C. Beardslee and Michael Wertheimer, eds. New York: Van Nostrand, 1958. pp. 194–203.

[Schultz 1996] Duane Schultz and Sydney Schultz. *A History of Modern Psychology.* Fort Worth: Harcourt, Brace, 1996.

[Selfridge 1955] Oliver Selfridge. "Pattern recognition in modern computers," *Proceedings of the Western Joint Computer Conference.* New York: Institute of Electrical and Electronic Engineers, 1955.

[Synnott 1993] Anthony Synnott. *The Body Social: Symbolism Self and Society.* London: Routledge, 1993. p. 203.

3

Know Thy User

3.1 Introduction

A group of software developers once created a banking system that had great functionality: it provided 36 different commands for querying data. In actual practice, however, only four commands accounted for 75% of all usage, and many commands were never used [Eason 1984]. The software developers could have saved themselves a lot of work if they had interviewed the bank staff to see what they wanted.

Websites are similar to software. Simply providing a lot of cool features is not enough. Effective websites provide convenience. People can do what they want and do it quickly. Critical to the success of any website is to find out everything possible about the intended users and what they want to do.

Goals of this Chapter

In this chapter, which focuses on users, their work, and their environment, you will learn about:

- user analysis: what do you need to know about your users?
- task analysis: what are your users' goals? What tasks do they perform to achieve those goals?
- environment analysis: when a user carries out a task, what are his or her surroundings? What effect do they have?
- usability specifications: how do you plan to measure the quality of your website?
- recruiting users: how does one look for them?

3.2 User Analysis

A useful exercise at this point would be to make a big sign that reads "You Are Not Your User" and tape it to the wall above your computer. The failings of many websites can be attributed to creators who assumed that their users had the same background and expectations that they did. The more you can learn about your users and their work, the more likely it is that you will develop a usable and successful website.

3.2.1 Why User Analysis?

There are many good reasons to start a project with analysis of the users. Failure to do so results in

- Higher development and maintenance costs. One of the most commonly named reasons for website redesign at large companies such as Microsoft, 3M, and Dell is the need to better serve their customers [Kearns 2000, 3Mmeeting 2000, Mainelli 1999].
- Lost sales. Before its site rollout, boo.com mounted a massive advertising campaign that was highly successful. When the site went live, boo.com had a name recognition rate of 13% among Web users, which is phenomenal considering that typical name recognition rates at rollout are less than 1%. However, boo.com could not capitalize on the advertising. The site was so difficult for users that within two years the company went bankrupt [Rowland 2000, Warner 2000, Sprenger 2000, Nielsen 2000].

On the other hand, there is a substantial return on any investment in user and task analysis, including increased sales and lower support costs. Here are a few cases:

- When IBM redesigned its "Shop IBM" site to better serve users, it experienced a 400% increase in sales *during the first month after rollout*. This increase is all the more notable because IBM did not advertise the new site redesign in advance [Tedeschi 1999].
- In addition to enjoying increased sales, IBM found that the use of their Website's Help button dropped 84%. Previously, people had clicked on this button more often than anywhere else.
- When Frugal Fun redesigned its website with the users in mind, sales increased fourteen-fold (1400%) [Poynter 1999].
- After its Web redesign, Dell noticed a drop in service calls to their help desk: More users were finding answers to their questions on-line.

Even if your goal is to make your own personal website, it is worth going through the process of thinking about who will visit your site and why. For example many students put their résumés on their websites when they are looking for jobs. What will it take to keep a potential employer at your site long enough to read the résumé?

3.2.2 Generic User Characterizations

Most of what you need to know about users is dependent on what they're trying to accomplish, but there is some general background information you need to know for any Web project. This includes learning style, tool preference, physical differences, and cultural differences.

Learning Style

Are your users "read then do" people or "do then read" people? That is, do users want careful instructions before starting, or do they immediately start working with a new interface?

Carroll coined the term "active users" to describe "do-then-read" people [Carroll 1987]. They are impatient with the idea of instruction and just want to plunge right in. Most users today do not want to waste time on reading a manual before trying new software, let alone using a website.

Whether a user wants a step-by-step demo or wants to experiment independently will depend somewhat on the type of product. If making a mistake will incur great cost, users will be only slightly more willing to read.

Tool Preferences

Is your user population familiar with the use of drop-down menus and other Web interaction techniques? Are they in the tiny minority of the population who are familiar with Boolean algebra for forming compact, efficient search queries [Nielsen 1997] or are they in the vast majority who need a different method of specifying search criteria? Are your users keyboard people or mouse people? Other questions you might want to ask include the following:

- What computers, interfaces, and browsers are users currently using? Do they always use the same ones or are they familiar with a range of versions?
- Where did they learn these tools? School? On-the-job training? On their own?
- How familiar are they with the tools? How often do they use them? When did they learn?
- Are they familiar with technology that is similar to your intended design? Do they understand frames? Pop-up windows? Search commands?

If you are new to the subject of user-oriented design, you might have trouble accepting that there are users who don't know something as simple as what a pop-up menu is. Try to remember that, with your extensive background, you are ahead even of the curve for most computer users and far ahead of that for the general population. Scott Weiss [WeissS 2000] described user testing in which the only qualification was knowledge of what the Back button on a browser does. That eliminated about a third of the candidates.

You probably won't really believe that such users are part of your professional life and educational community until you have direct contact with them. Seek out people who are just starting to use the Internet, sit quietly, and watch them work with it. Notice what causes them confusion and frustration. Taking the time to gain this experience will give you a better understanding of the issues this chapter describes.

Physical Differences

In addition to gathering information on learning style and tool preferences, you should look for information about your users' physical characteristics, such as age, gender, colorblindness, and physical disabilities. Although Georgia Tech surveys of Web users currently indicate that the majority of Web users are under 50 and male, the surveys also show that an increasing number of women and older people are using the Web [GeorgiaTech 1998]. The main considerations are as follows:

- Physical disabilities can restrict movement. See Chapter 12.
- Some people experience color differently from most. See Chapters 9 and 12.
- Some people have difficulty seeing small objects or reading small type. Vision generally deteriorates with age, and many older people need larger font sizes. The AARP (American Association for Retired Persons) website at `www.aarp.com` displays fonts that are one size larger than what are used at most sites.
- Small children may be able to see just fine, but not have fine motor control. For this reason, they need large buttons. Further, young children do not read well. The designers of `www.funschool.com` took both of these characteristics into account when creating a site that features educational games for children from preschool through sixth grade. See Figure 3–1. When positioning the mouse over the link for "preschool," a user hears

Figure 3–1   The home page for `www.funschool.com`. Courtesy of Kaboose, Inc.

the word "preschool." The same thing occurs for the links "kindergarten," "1st grade," and "2nd grade," but for the older grades the user hears only a short "boop" sound.

Cultural Differences

Users differ in a multitude of ways that depend on where they live and work and the language they use. Many cultural differences are based on geographic location; Chapter 13 is devoted to globalization, which looks more closely into making a site work in a wide range of locales. Looking at a user's education, profession, and workplace can identify types of cultures other than geographical. Here are some characteristics that you will want to establish even for a site intended for just one geographically based culture:

- **Education.** If you are a college student or college graduate, you have a vocabulary and reading level significantly above the average. The vocabulary that would be fine for an intranet in a research lab would cause problems on an e-commerce site aimed at teens. Unless you know that your user is better educated than average, the text in your site should be at the eighth-grade reading level. (The United States Social Security Administration currently maintains a sixth- to eighth-grade reading level on most of its notices [SSA 97].)

- **Profession.** If your site is catering to a particular profession, you need to interview users to identify their terminology or vocabulary. Dentists and architects don't share much in the way of specialized vocabulary. What the term "default" means to a banker is different from what it means to a programmer. Using the proper vocabulary will

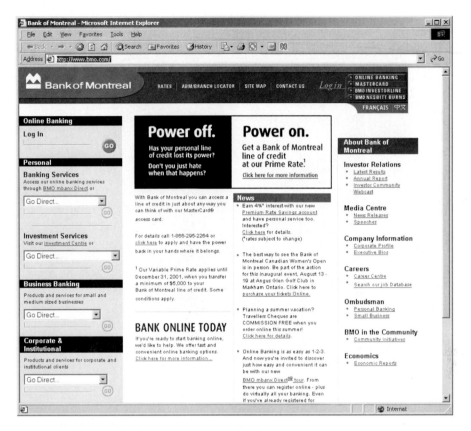

Figure 3–2   A banking website: `www.bmo.com`. Courtesy of the Bank of Montreal.

save the user from being forced to ask, "Is this the link I want?" and will empower the user with the conviction, "I want this link!"

- **Corporate style.** Organizations want to communicate their value systems to their audience. This applies not only to corporations but also to all organizations, such as universities and branches of government. Figure 3–2 shows an example of a banking website (`http://www.bmo.com/`) and Figure 3–3 gives an example of a website selling fashion cosmetics (`www.urbandecay.com`). On the banking site, the use of a restrained logo, moderate writing style, and conservative fonts creates an air of rationality and stability. To communicate excitement and a sense of the immediate, the fashion site uses bold fonts, extreme graphics and a writing style that includes a large number of exclamation points. Banks want to present a different sort of image to customers from that fashion sites want. Users want their banks to have a sense of stability, but in fashion they look for novelty.

3.2.3 Specific User Characterization

So far, the discussion has considered user characteristics in rather general terms. In addition to general user information, you need to look at users in the context of why they will use your website, what they will do there, and how they will do it. Further, you want to ask them about what familiarity they have with your website or with websites like it.

Figure 3–3   Home page for Urban Decay at `www.urbandecay.com`.
Courtesy of Urban Decay Cosmetics.

Knowledge of Jobs

If the website will support on-the-job responsibilities, then learning how users perform their jobs is crucial. When the site serves leisure activities such as entertainment or travel, learning what the user wants to do at the site is equally important. Here are some pertinent questions:

Is Web access part of a job? Are the users trained professionals who learned aspects of their jobs in school? What specialized vocabulary is part of the job?

If this website supports an office activity, do users know how their activities fit into the workflow of their business? Do they understand what has been done before the work gets to them, and do they know what happens afterwards?

Do they perform the same task all day, or do they have a variety of responsibilities?

If this website is not connected with job-related activities, what purpose does it serve? Does it provide products or services for purchase? Is it a resource for information or a center of entertainment?

Application Familiarity

In addition to analyzing the type of work they do and the degree of familiarity they have with the basic tools of technology, it is important to study users by looking at their familiarity with relevant application software or websites. Knowing users' familiarity levels will help determine the structure and services of a website. This categorization comes from Hackos and Redish's excellent book, *User and Task Analysis for Interface Design* [Hackos 1998].

Novice.   The true beginner is faced with a great and frightening unknown. Think back to the very first time you ever used a computer. Novices fear looking foolish. They fear the unknown and are impatient with learning the tool. They don't want to learn about navigating a website or using its search function. All they want to do is to complete their work. A novice who is comfortable with the subject matter and is competent with the technology will move quickly from novice to advanced beginner.

Advanced Beginner.   Like novices, advanced beginners are impatient with needing to learn concepts when they have a job to do. However, the fear of failure is no longer present, and advanced beginners are willing to experiment with accessing new functions or pages while attempting to complete their work. Advanced beginners start to develop a mental model of the application or website by learning new and progressively more complicated tasks, but they will become confused if there are too many alternatives to choose from. Further, if they encounter difficulties, they have trouble diagnosing or correcting the problem. Intermittent users fall into this category.

Competent Performer.   The two characteristics that distinguish a competent performer from an advanced beginner are an ability to diagnose simple problems and an ability to perform a series of complex tasks to achieve a goal. Competent performers are willing to learn how tasks fit into a consistent mental model of the application as a whole and are more likely to use documentation than novices or advanced beginners. If you've used a package every day for the past six months or so, most likely you are a competent performer with that package.

Expert.   Experts constitute the smallest portion of a user population. Compared to a competent performer, an expert can perform a wider range of complex tasks and can diagnose complex problems. An expert is interested in the product for its own sake and wants to develop a comprehensive mental model of the product's functionality and interface. Experts may staff support lines, teach workshops, and serve as consultants. Because these users share much in common with you, there is a danger in interviewing and listening to them: Talking with them is fun! That's not bad in itself, but you could lose perspective on what you are trying to learn about the entire range of users.

3.2.4 Gathering Information About Users

The previous section talked about what kinds of information you need to know about your users. Now you need to find people who are or might be users of your website so you can gather this information. The question is where to find them.

Managers of users are not users, and they are not a good source of information about users. They know how it's *supposed* to be done, or how it was done when they were users, but they are not currently involved in the day-to-day work.

Developers are not users. Developers have spent countless hours learning the product, but it is unreasonable to expect that users will do the same. Users don't have the time. Especially for websites, it is important that you talk to users who are *not* experts, because most users are not in the expert category. Your best bet is to focus on the novices and advanced beginners.

Primary Users and Secondary Users

All websites have primary users, but some websites will also have secondary users. *Primary users* actually use the website. *Secondary users* are people who are being assisted or served by primary users. For example, if a technical support person uses an intranet to help answer a question from a customer, the customer is a secondary user. Similarly, if a travel agent uses an airline website to search for and book plane tickets, the traveler is a secondary user. The ability to complete work in an efficient manner will be an important factor in how well a primary user can serve a secondary user.

Places to Find Information about Users

The best place to find information about users is from users themselves. Listen to users, preferably in the context of the place where they will use your website. This is the Gold Standard, the best possible source. You might want to talk to people who use your website as part of the work they do on the job and to users who access your website without assistance or interaction with others, at home or work.

Other places where you might glean information about users include Customer Service and Technical Support. You might also talk to Marketing, although this is less useful, because marketing people focus on those who purchase a system instead of on those who actually use the system.

Often a variety of people will use the website you create. Will they all be using the site for the same purposes, or will they be visiting the site for various reasons? These groups could have different needs, different frequencies of use, and different levels of experience with the system.

3.3 Task Analysis

As important as it is to know your users, it is also crucial to know what they do. Task analysis is the process of building a complete description of their duties. This includes what tasks they perform, why they perform them, and how they perform them. This information gives you a proper basis for making successful design decisions.

3.3.1 Goals, Tasks, and Actions

Always start a task analysis by learning the *goals* of a user. Goals are what people want to accomplish and form the motivation for visiting a website.

The purpose of a website is to help people do things. Sometimes this includes such work-related activities as finding a customer order, registering a hotel guest, sending a message, or buying office supplies. Sometimes the "things" aren't work related, such as playing a game with friends, throwing a party, or making travel plans. All of these are goals. Goals are technology independent, and they remain the same even when the technology changes.

Tasks are the mechanisms people use to accomplish goals. Unlike goals, tasks could change, being technology dependent. For example, suppose the goal is to send a report to a branch office. The tasks might be to find a FedEx envelope, to fill out an air bill, to put the report into the envelope, and to call for a pickup. Another set of tasks could accomplish the same goal: Type the email address, attach the document, and press "send." Figure 3–4 gives another example.

Actions are subcomponents of tasks. You can think of tasks as high-level descriptions, actions as the individual steps that compose a task. Actions are also referred to as *steps*. Deciding

Goal: Send a birthday present to your sister's three-year-old.

Task 1: Choose between a stuff toy and a set of building blocks. (Your sister said that either of these would be good.)

> Subtask 1: Check several websites for purple stuffed dinosaurs.
>
> Subtask 2: Check on the availability of the new TalkingBlox building blocks set.
>
> Subtask 3: Decide on one of these, based on price, availability, delivery and option of gift wrap.

Task 2: Buy chosen toy.

> Subtask 1: Put toy into website's shopping cart.
>
> Subtask 2: Fill out billing and shipping information. Make sure to check "gift wrap."

Task 3: Call sister; tell her that a present is on its way.

Each of these subtasks consists of multiple components. Check for the availability of the dinosaur would involve going to search site, finding the search box, typing the relevant information, and clicking "go" or "search." It could also consist of going to each site, clicking on the appropriate category, and browsing the possibilities. Each of these activities in turn could be further analyzed for subcomponents.

Figure 3–4   A set of tasks to achieve a goal.

what composes a task, what constitutes a subtask, and what counts as an action depends on the *granularity* you choose for your task analysis. This is the subject of the next section.

3.3.2 *Methodologies for Identifying Types and Granularity of Tasks*

This section discusses six techniques for gathering information about tasks. You might find that you use one or more of these techniques when collecting information for your task analysis. We begin with the ones that capture the "big picture" or broad sweep and proceed to those that operate at successively finer levels of *granularity*.

Granularity refers to the level of detail in a description. A *granule* is defined as "one of numerous particles forming a larger unit." Further, a "larger unit" with respect to one level might itself be a granule with respect to a higher level. For example, when you look at a mountain from a distance, the granules might be huge boulders. If you travel to the foot of the mountain, you might discover that the boulders are made up of many different kinds of rocks, bound together in the wake of some kind of volcanic action. Get even closer and the granularity is at the level of pebbles. In task analysis, the granularity you choose will depend on the nature and scope of your website development effort.

Workflow Analysis

Workflow analysis describes how work gets done when several people are involved. This technique gathers information at the coarsest level of granularity and provides the big picture or overview. As an example, consider how grades go from a professor's desk to a student's home. For a certain East Coast university, the workflow follows this path:

- Professor computes grades, records them on grade sheet, and gives them to departmental secretary.
- Secretary assembles grade sheets from all professors in the department, places them in a sealed envelope, and gives it to a department student aide.
- Student aide takes grades to registrar's office.
- Receptionist in registrar's office records the submission of the department's grades and gives them to Information Services.
- Clerk transfers the grades into the database.
- Computer operator prints out grade reports for each student in college.
- Postage-machine operator stuffs envelopes and runs them through postage meter.
- Transportation person takes all letters to Post Office.

A workflow could involve only two people, or it could involve many. In comparison with activities that are done in routine business work, such as hiring a new employee or filling orders for an e-commerce business, this example involves a moderate number of people.

Job Analysis

Job analysis gives a different view of a user's work by focusing on what a single person does in a day, a week, or a month. Workflow analysis focuses on work as it passes from person to person; job analysis concentrates on the activities that a single person carries out. To illustrate, the following is a list of the things that a receptionist for a small business performed in a single day:

- Call Security to get a parking permit for a visitor.
- Schedule a meeting with a prospective corporate client.
- Refer an incoming call to Customer Service (occurred 5 times).
- Type president's correspondence.
- Refer an incoming call to a sales representative (occurred 10 times).
- Call for copier service.
- Show an intern how to fill out the forms for getting paid.
- Check inventory of office supplies.
- Assemble sales data for monthly report.

How do you find out what the receptionist does? Interview the receptionist, or sit and watch.

Task List

A task list takes the granularity of job analysis to a more detailed level. Think of a task as one of the components of a job. For example, the receptionist in the previous example might engage in some or all of the following tasks when assembling the data for the monthly sales report:

- Locate sales figures from all sales reps who have submitted them.
- Compare with the list of all sales reps in the company, to find those who have not submitted yet. This results in a laggards list.

- Send a reminder e-mail to those laggards who have a history of responding to e-mail more promptly than to phone messages.
- Call those laggards who have a history of ignoring e-mail. If the person picks up the phone, cheerfully remind the person to submit figure by specified time. Otherwise, leave voicemail.
- On the day of the deadline, make more urgent requests of those who have still not responded.
- One day after deadline, send figures to president and send list of laggards to the head of the sales department.

The precise level of detail you choose is up to you, so long as you are consistent. To start, pick a target range for the number of tasks you will put in the list. If you have three, you are not recording enough detail and the list will not be helpful to you in later stages of development. If you have 500 tasks, the list will be too long and cumbersome to work with. Think in terms of 10 to 30 major tasks. You can always break them down into smaller units later, which you will do anyway when steps become the right size for menu choices.

Task Sequences

Task sequences establish the order in which the tasks take place. This may be as simple as referring to the items in your task list and arranging them. As an example, consider how a person might write a letter. One possible sequence follows:

- Write the letter.
- Address the envelope.
- Put the letter in the envelope.
- Put a stamp on the envelope.

At least that's the sequence the authors use. But there are 23 other orderings of those four tasks. Some of them are not possible: you can't put the letter in the envelope before you write it, but it is possible to do the tasks in this order:

- Address the envelope.
- Write the letter.
- Put a stamp on the envelope.
- Put the letter in the envelope.

Or this:

- Put a stamp on the envelope.
- Address the envelope.
- Write the letter.
- Put the letter in the envelope.

You learn the appropriate sequence or sequences by watching users carry out their work. Always strive to give a user the flexibility to complete the job in whatever task sequence is most comfortable. If you discover that a majority of users do things in a certain sequence, it makes sense to set up the interface to simplify things for the majority.

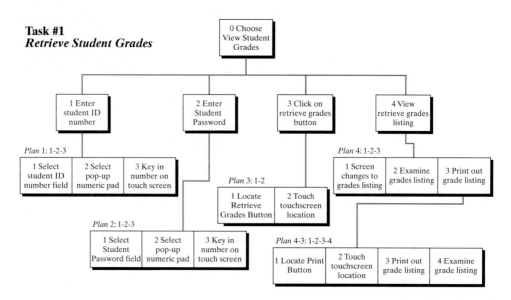

Figure 3–5   A task hierarchy. Courtesy of Wendy Fischer, Tom Drzich, and Karen Lovejoy.

This example illustrates two different reasons for picking a particular task sequence. One is based on physical realities: you can't put a letter in an envelope before you write the letter. Other times the sequence comes from the fact that the users said, "Because we've always done it that way." Unless there is an overwhelmingly compelling reason, there is no excuse not to do whatever people are used to. In fact, there is every reason to continue doing it exactly that way. A new system should disrupt users as little as possible.

Task Hierarchies

The purpose of a task hierarchy is to document the components of a task, which are called subtasks. Depending on the needs of your project, you could need to show how subtasks are comprised of actions. Figure 3–5 shows an example of a task hierarchy for a public-access kiosk equipped with a touch screen. The level of detail in such a hierarchy will depend on the type of website you are designing. In this example, the finest granularity is at the level of screen touches.

Procedural Analysis

The last approach, procedural analysis, contains the most detail of any of the techniques. A procedural analysis shows individual steps and decisions that a user goes through in carrying out a task. Figure 3–6 is an example of a procedural analysis for the task of supplying a payment method for a purchase on an e-commerce website. Notice that the procedural level is different from the other types of task analysis because it considers the constraints of the user interface. It shows *how* users carry out their tasks with the interface.

3.3.3 Techniques for Observing and Listening to Users

You now know what information you need to gather about users and their tasks. This section introduces several techniques that will help you acquire this information. Users are in

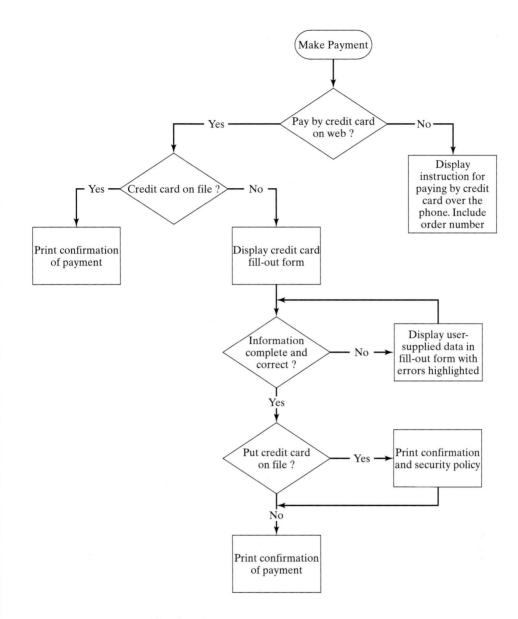

Figure 3–6 A procedural analysis.

the business of *doing* their jobs, not *explaining how* they do their jobs, so simply asking "How do you do your job?" will not give you the insights you need. There are several interviewing techniques available to you that can help you learn what you need to know. They are *think aloud*, *talk right after*, *role playing*, and *cueing recall*.

Think Aloud

In this technique, you ask users to give a running commentary on their work as they perform it. The idea is to encourage users to explain everything they are doing while they are doing it. If you are there with the users at their workplace, you can listen to users telling you about the work, you can experience the environment in which they work, and you can ask questions. This is the best way to understand how users work.

Your challenge is to keep the user talking, because they will tend to stop speaking when the work becomes difficult. Difficult tasks are things you especially want to understand, so you have to keep asking questions. For example, if a user becomes silent and hesitates while looking at a particular data entry form, you might ask, "You paused while you were filling in the form. Why was that?" If they do something that they don't explain, then you can ask such questions as "Can you always leave that field blank?"

At all times, you are seeking to learn what they are doing and why they are doing it. Thinking aloud is the best way to discover the information you need to design a good interface.

Talk Right After

In some jobs, it is impossible or inappropriate for a user to talk while carrying out a task. For example, the user might be a customer-service representative or a travel agent who is helping someone with a question. The agent can't talk to the customer and you at the same time. Other situations where thinking aloud would be inappropriate would include activities involving critical safety issues and ones where the user is under time pressures.

In cases like these, where it's too disruptive for the user to chat with you while working, take notes, and ask the user about the task once they have time to talk.

Role Playing

Sometimes, you will want to know about tasks that occur so infrequently that there is no way to observe them firsthand. For example, you could be observing a customer-service representative at a software firm on a day when no one called wanting to return the software. In this case, there is no way to observe the work except to stage it. Either you or one of the user's colleagues can play the role of the customer.

If this is the best that can be done, that's what you do. But it's not as credible as watching the real thing, and considerably less useful than having the user talk to you while performing the task.

Cueing Recall with Videotape

This technique is useful when the user does not want an interviewer present in the work situation. In this case, you set up a video camera to record the user's activities. After the taping session, review the tape and take notes. In a later interview, you can replay selected segments of the tape to help the user recall the task being performed, so that you can ask questions about what the user was doing and why.

A word of caution: anyone who is taped, including other employees and customers, must be informed that taping is occurring and asked to sign releases. This is a limitation of the technique.

3.3.4 Other Techniques

Marketing people have used a variety of surveying and interviewing techniques for many years. However, as tools for understanding users and their work, these techniques have serious limitations and should be avoided.

Focus Groups

In this technique, a moderator or group organizer invites a number of people to meet in a conference room to discuss a number of prepared questions. The goal of the questions is to elicit useful information about the users. The participants should be actual users or people who resemble actual users. Sessions typically last from an hour to an hour and a half, and the participants are usually paid something in the range of $25 to $150 each.

There are several disadvantages with this technique. The meeting takes place outside the context of an actual work situation and so potentially involves conversing with other people, serious distractions, and other influencing factors that the members of the focus group might not think to mention. An equally serious problem is that one or two people can easily dominate the entire discussion. Most of us have been in conversations where one person feels obligated to respond to everything anyone else says. In a social setting, that might be merely annoying. In a focus group, it means you paid for six people but got the opinions of two. An effective moderator will attempt to draw everyone into the discussion, but will not always be successful. People are often reluctant to offer opinions that run counter to those expressed by the loudest member of the group.

Mailed Surveys

These have the advantage of being cheap to distribute. Unfortunately, they have several disadvantages: First, it takes a lot of skill to write a questionnaire that will elicit the information you want. There is a danger of writing questions whose wording suggests the answer that you want to hear. Responses to leading questions aren't fully useful.

Second, there are other problems that can bias the results. Perhaps you had a particular user group in mind as you wrote the questions, not realizing that another group would interpret the questions differently. It could be that the distribution list is inherently biased. The famous example of this is the survey taken in the 1936 presidential election, in which, after collecting two million surveys, the pollsters from the *Literary Digest* predicted that Alf Landon would win, whereas in fact Franklin Roosevelt won in a huge landslide.

What was the cause of this mistake? The magazine had mailed postcard ballots to individuals whose names appeared in automobile registration lists and telephone books. In 1936, the United States was in the grip of the Great Depression, and most people could not afford a car or even a telephone. Americans who did not have these luxuries were missing from *The Literary Digest's* sample, and it was these Americans who overwhelmingly supported Roosevelt in the 1936 election [CNN 2000].

A third disadvantage of questionnaires is that very few people respond to them. A return of 10% of the surveys is considered very good. A rate of one to two percent would be more common [Walker 2001].

3.4 Environment Analysis

Thinking about a person browsing the Web usually conjures up images of a person using a computer at home or at the office. However, people are using computers and the Web in an ever-widening variety of locales.

One is information kiosks. These are used now at colleges, stores, and airports. Perhaps they are limited to providing directions, maps, and telephone numbers, but the possibilities are much wider.

The interface could be outdoors. In this case, environmental considerations would likely preclude a conventional keyboard, so you will be working with a touch screen or touch pad. Are there any special considerations? For example, is the winter weather so cold that the touch button areas on the screen would need to be huge, to accommodate people wearing gloves? It's done that way on ATMs in Sweden [Norman 1988].

Users might access your site via a handheld device. Experts foresee a steady rise of wireless usage in the next five years, and some predict that there will be 91 million mobile-commerce users by 2007 [Hobbs 2001].

3.5 Recruiting Users

Your primary access to users is through the people who hired you to create the website. Ask to have access to their users, clients, employees, and/or customers, as appropriate. Explain the benefits of your having access to their users. You might encounter such objections as "We don't have the time" or "We don't want to bother our users." Point out that most users are thrilled to have the attention. Invite the gatekeepers to observe what you're doing. Offer to share the information you collect.

If you don't have access to users this way, you are on your own. You can try agencies that provide temporary help. Explain the user profile to them and let them recruit for you. This costs serious money, because you have to pay for the services of the temp agency as well as compensating the users.

If you are in college, you might be able to post a notice on a bulletin board to attract users. Contact the psychology department; they do experiments all the time, either for education or research, and they might allow you to recruit users through their test pool. Depending on the type of user you need, you can set up in the middle of a heavily trafficked area, such as a cafeteria or lounge, and solicit users from passersby. Computer labs are not quite as good, because people here are trying to complete their own work and often view the solicitation as an interruption.

It is tempting to turn to family and friends. This is generally not a good idea. These people might be hesitant to give an honest reaction, if it is negative, yet that is what you need most.

You need to offer incentives of some kind, financial or otherwise. Money talks. In a college setting, a nominal amount, like $5, might attract some people who are either curious or willing to help anyway. The spending money sweetens the deal. Interestingly, if the people are actual users of the interface and they know that your aim is to improve it, they often are willing to participate for minimal compensation, because the outcome will result in a better tool that will make their lives easier.

There are alternatives to money that can serve as compensation. If you are working for a client, you might be able to arrange gift certificates of their merchandise. Dining certificates are in the same category. If your client distributes T-shirts or coffee mugs anyway, you should be able to get a supply of those. In a college setting, we have been able to attract people with an offer of free cookies. More substantively, you can offer to share technical information after the interview.

3.5.1 How Much Data Is Enough?

The answer is, as so often is the case, "It depends." What do you want to learn? Before you begin interviewing, define the issues you want to clarify. Together with the nature of the website, this will let you specify the profile of the users you need. Strive for breadth of representation, within the constraints of the project. If the target audience is 18–24-year-old females, you don't have to strive for gender equality or for representation of preteens or retired people. Other times, you will want to do exactly those things.

It might not be necessary to make a firm decision on the number of subjects until you are into the process. If, after a number of interviews, you see strong commonalities among the stated goals and the observed tasks, it is time to move on to determining the usability specifications.

3.6 Usability Specifications

Once you have gathered and analyzed information about your users and their tasks, the next step is to decide how to answer the question, "How good should the interface be?" [Hix 1993]. Usability specifications define the measure of success for a website and can also serve as an indicator of whether development efforts to create the interface are on the right track.

As mentioned in Chapter 1, usability specifications fall into two categories, commonly called *performance measures* and *preference measures*. Performance measures are directly observable by watching a user complete a task and encompass such considerations as "time to complete a task" and "number of errors." Figure 3–7 lists some sample performance measures. All of these are *quantifiable measures*. This means that they are expressible as numbers. For example, you can count the number of minutes it takes a user to complete a task or the number of negative comments that occur.

In contrast, preference measures give an indication of a user's opinion about the interface and are not directly observable. The way to gather preference measures is through an interview or questionnaire. Examples of measures of this type include "first impression," "long-term satisfaction," and "perceived ease of use." Figure 3–8 lists sample preference measures.

A typical way to solicit user response for a preference measure is by asking them to rate the interface or to give their reactions to statements about the interface. A preference measure can be expressed quantitatively by using a *Likert scale*. A Likert scale measures the extent to which a person agrees or disagrees with a statement. The most common scale is from 1 to 5. Often the scale will be 1 = strongly disagree, 2 = disagree, 3 = not sure, 4 = agree, and 5 = strongly agree. Figure 3–9 shows how a Likert scale might be used in a questionnaire to gather information about preference measures.

Time to complete a task. Examples:

> Time to fill out billing and shipping information.
>
> Time to find a new textbook on video games programming.

Number of clicks to locate the time of tonight's television episode of "Buffy."

Number of tasks completed correctly.

Number of errors. Examples:

> Number of times user hit the "back" button while looking for new textbook.
>
> Number of times user had to fill in additional information on the shipping form.

Number of negative comments or facial expressions.

Figure 3–7   Sample Performance Measures.

Usefulness of some aspect of a website	Appearance
Ease of use overall	Convenience
Accessibility	First impression / long-term satisfaction
Did website meet user expectations?	

Figure 3–8   Sample Preference Measures.

	Strongly Disagree	Disagree	Neutral	Agree	Strongly Agree
Overall, the ShopIt! site is easy to use.	1	2	3	4	5
When I searched for an item, the results were useful to me.	1	2	3	4	5
I could find everything I needed to know about billing and shipping options.	1	2	3	4	5
I could pay for my purchase quickly.	1	2	3	4	5

Figure 3–9   Sample questions that use a Likert scale.

Setting usability specifications involves choosing a set of performance and preference measures and specifying a numeric target for each measure. As an example, one usability specification for a shopping site might be, "Users make no more than one mistake on average when filling out the credit-card information."

Setting usability specifications requires research. A common mistake among inexperienced developers is to set specifications arbitrarily without looking for information about user preferences or user performance on the current site. A valuable resource can be found in the evaluations of the present site, if they exist. If this is a new site, gather information about the quality of comparable sites. Review the observations you made during the user interviews you conducted. As a starting point, any redesign should be at least as good as the old one.

After you have completed the activities described in this chapter, you know your users and what they will do with your site. Your next job is to organize the content of your site in such a way that the intended users can find what they need and work with it effectively and efficiently. That is the subject of the next chapter.

Review Questions and Exercises

1. To experience what new users encounter, ask the instructor who teaches the Introduction to Computers class if you can sit with students during a lab session. It is optimal to watch them while they learn to surf the Web, but watching any laboratory activity is useful for this exercise.

   From an unobtrusive distance, watch one of the class members for 20 minutes. Maintain a neutral demeanor at all times during your observation. List the top three problems that the user encountered and how they reacted to them.

2. What is an active user? Why is it important to accommodate active users when you develop a website?

3. Take a survey of ten people who are computer users, five of whom are outside your major. Ask them to rate their skill at using the following applications on a scale from 1 to 4, where 1 is "never use it" and 4 is "expert."

   a. A favorite word processor, such as Microsoft Word.

b. Surfing the Web.

c. A favorite drawing program, such as Adobe Illustrator or Corel Draw.

d. E-mail.

e. A favorite video game.

f. Amazon.com.

g. A favorite paint package, such as Adobe Photoshop or MS Paint.

Analyze the results. Is there any consistency in answers across all 10 people? If so, what was it? Is there any consistency in answers from the majors? If so, what was it? What area of user analysis is this? Why should you always ask this type of question when conducting a user analysis?

4. Suppose that Computing Services at your college or place of work is currently supporting two packages—Software XYZ and Software ABC. The company wants to drop Software ABC and offer only Software XYZ. For each user reaction, estimate the user's application familiarity with XYZ.

   a. "Software XYZ is so much better than Software ABC because it uses better memory management."

   b. "Don't get rid of ABC. I know enough about XYZ to know that I don't want to use it. For my purposes all I need is software ABC."

   c. "Why should I learn it? I don't want to be bothered with learning some stupid system."

   d. "I can pretty much do what I need to with XYZ, but it would be nice if more of the tech support people could help with my questions about XYZ."

5. What is the difference between primary and secondary users? The text gives an example of a ticket agent being a primary user of a reservation system and the ticket buyer being the secondary user. Name four examples of systems that have primary and secondary users.

6. When trying to find out about users, the Gold Standard is to watch a user in the context of the workplace. However, this isn't always possible. Who else in a company knows about the users? Suppose you are consulting for a company that sells computers and you need to find out about the people who use this equipment. However, you cannot interview the users (customers) directly. Where would you turn? What departments or people would you consult? Name at least three.

7. What is the difference between a goal and a task? How do they relate to technology?

8. One possible technology for achieving the goal "Getting Dinner on the Table" would be a stove. What other technologies might be used to achieve this goal?

9. Often a website supports different groups of users, with each group having different goals. For each of the following websites, list the different user groups and their goals.

   a. Real-Estate Website

   b. Airline Website

10. Suppose you are developing an intranet for a hospital's patient records. What distinct user groups can you identify? List as many as you can.

11. Choose one of the following activities:

    a. Getting a book via interlibrary loan
    b. Refilling a prescription
    c. Removing a grade of Incomplete

    Conduct a workflow analysis on the activity you choose. Interview the relevant users and lay out the analysis as a series of bullets similar to the example given in the text. Document where and how you got your information.

12. What is the difference between workflow analysis and job analysis?

13. List and explain the four interviewing techniques mentioned in the text for learning about users and their jobs. Explain the advantages and disadvantages of each.

14. For each of the following scenarios, which is the most appropriate interviewing technique? Give a rationale for each answer.

    a. Office manager whose main responsibilities are ordering supplies, tracking in-house inventory, and maintaining time sheets. This person has a private office and spends most of each day in that office carrying out these responsibilities.
    b. Teenager searching the Web looking for the best joystick for a new computer.
    c. Surgeon performing an operation. The surgical team is very busy performing operations during the week and can see you only for two hours on Saturday mornings.
    d. Academic advisor who is staffing the advising hot line during daily afternoon advising hours.
    e. Student using a new Web-based registration system.
    f. Air-traffic controllers running Arrival and Departure Control at O'Hare Airport, who work in very cramped quarters.

15. What are the major disadvantages of focus groups and mailed surveys as compared to interviewing techniques such as Think Aloud?

16. Suppose you have a website that your boss wants converted to run on a kiosk at the local airport. What changes will you have to consider?

17. Consider the website for your college department. Not all of the users who visit the site have the same reasons that you do. Identify different groups of users who might come to the site. Hint: there are at least six different groups.

18. Pick two of the user groups you identified from the last question and interview representatives from the groups to gather information about their tasks. You should listen to at least four people from each group.

    For each group, list the tasks. Are there any commonalities or differences?

Project Activities

19. If you are developing a website for a client, this is the time to conduct a user analysis. Describe the general characteristics of your users, including learning style, knowledge of technology, age, and general education level. If this website supports an office function, describe workers' knowledge about their jobs. Will the site have secondary users as well as primary users? Also, specify their level of familiarity with your website. Cite the sources of your information.

20. Perform a task analysis. Describe your user's goals and the types of tasks they carry out in order to complete those goals. Interview at least five users. If appropriate, employ the Think-Aloud technique. Include copies of the interviews.

21. Describe the environment in which the users will use your website. Is it at home? In private? At work? In a public area?

22. Once your user and task analysis is complete, set some usability specifications. If you are redesigning a site, check to see whether there are any performance or preference measures available. If not, check for measures of a comparable site. Also search the Web. Cite your sources to justify your choices.

References

[3Mmeeting 2000] 3M Visual Systems Division. *3M Meeting Network Enhances Web Site; Redesign Celebrates Three Years of Promoting Better Meetings.* Press Release October 25, 2000. `http://biz.yahoo.com/prnews/001025/tx_3m_visu.html`

[Carroll 1987] J. M. Carroll and M. B. Rosson. "The paradox of the active user." In J.M. Carroll, Ed., *Interfacing Thought: Cognitive Aspects of Human–Computer Interaction.* Cambridge, Massachusetts: MIT Press, 1987. pp. 80–111.

[CNN 2000] CNNfyi.com. Understanding Public Opinion Polls. *CNN.* October 16, 2000. `http://www.cnn.com/fyi/interactive/news/10/election.special/teachers/bg.5.html`

[Eason 1984] K. D. Eason. "Towards the experimental study of usability: Ergonomics of the user interface," *Behaviour and Information Technology.* 1984. vol.3 no.2 pp.133–143.

[GeorgiaTech 1998] GVU WWW Surveying Team. GVU's 10th WWW User Survey General Demographics Summary. GVU's WWW User Surveys, 1998. `http://www.cc.gatech.edu/gvu/user_surveys/survey-1998-10/reports/1998-10-General.doc`

[Hackos 1998] JoAnn Hackos and Janice Redish. *User and Task Analysis for Interface Design.* New York: Wiley, 1998.

[Hix 1993] Deborah Hix and H. Rex Hartson. *Developing User Interfaces: Ensuring Usability Through Product and Process.* New York: Wiley, 1993.

[Hobbs 2001] Minerva Hobbs. "Migrating to a Mobile Architecture," *Web Techniques* June 6, 2001. `http://www.webtechniques.com/archives/2001/06/hobbs/`

[Kearns 2000] Dave Kearns. "Microsoft's Web site – some observations," *Network World Fusion Newsletter.* February 9, 2000. `http://www.nwfusion.com/newsletters/nt/0207nt2.html`

[Mainelli 1999] Tom Mainelli. "Dell Revamps Web Site," *PC World.com* November 15, 1999. `http://www.pcworld.com/news/article.asp?aid=13786`

[Nielsen 1997] Jakob Nielsen. "Search and You May Find," *AlertBox,* July 15, 1997. `http://www.useit.com/alertbox/9707b.html`

[Nielsen 2000] "Boo's Demise," *Alertbox5 Year Retrospective.* May 2000. `http://www.useit.com/alertbox/20000528_boo.html`

[PCWorld 2000] PCWorld.com. IDG'S PCWorld.com Launches Web Site Redesign. Press Release, October 3, 2000. `http://www8.techmall.com/techdocs/TS001003-6.html`

[Poynter 1999] How a Web Site Redesign Brought In 14 Times as Much Business by Changing the Focus. Frugalfun.com 1999. `http://www.frugalfun.com/m7.html`

[Rowland 2000] Claire Rowland. "Walking the Talk: Usability Matters," *WebReview.com.* March 10, 2000. `http://www.webreview.com/2000/03_10/strategists/03_10_00_3.shtml`

[Sprenger 2000] Polly Sprenger. "More Creaks and Groans and Boo.com," *The Standard: Intelligence for the Internet.* May 4, 2000. `http://www.thestandard.com/article/display/0,1151,14775,00.html`

[SSA 1996] Social Security Administration. *Benchmarking Private Sector Policies and Practices for Distributing Customer Notices* — A-02-96-61000 — 9/22/97 `http://www.ssa.gov/oig/96-61000.htm`

[Tedeschi 1999] Bob Tedeschi. "Good Web Site Design Can Lead to Healthy Sales: E-Commerce Report," *The New York Times on the Web.* August 30, 1999. `http://www.nytimes.com/library/tech/99/08/cyber/commerce/30commerce.html`

[Walker 2001] Leslie Walker. "E-Mail Becomes Marketing Treasure for Retailers," *Washington Post.* April 26, 2001. p. E01. Also available at `http://www.washingtonpost.com/wp-dyn/washtech/techthursday/columns/dotcom/A2852-2001Apr25.html`

[Warner 2000] B. Warner. "Boohoohoo.com," *The Standard: Intelligence for the Internet.* Jan 28, 2000. `http://www.thestandard.com/article/display/0,1151,9249,00.html`

[WeissS 2000] Scott Weiss. Wireless Usability Study. Presentation given at SIGCHI-New York. December 2000.

[WeissT 2000] Todd Weiss. "Wal-Mart shuts Web site for renovations until Oct. 17," *Computer World.* October 2, 2000. `http://www.computerworld.com/cwi/story/0,1199,NAV47_ST051731,00.html`

4

Content Organization

4.1 Purpose

In the user-centered development methodology, a major component of the design phase for a website is organizing its content. According to several surveys [Festa 1999, McGovern 2001, Rosenfeld 1998], when people are asked, "What do you hate most about the Web?" the top answer is

I can't find what I'm looking for.

Spool's studies [Spool 97] confirm this. He asked users to find simple facts on sites of some major companies and organizations. Although all of the people taking part in the study were familiar with Web browsers, they could not find what they wanted, despite the fact that the information *was* available on the sites.

A big challenge in creating any website is to organize its information in such a way that it is useful and meaningful to users [Robertson 2001]. Good content organization creates the foundation for effective navigation and is crucial to the success of the site. Sections 4.2 and 4.3 of this chapter introduce the fundamentals of *information architecture*, which concerns the structuring of a site's content in a way that meets user expectations. Section 4.4 presents a practical method of identifying content and a technique for discovering a user's preferred organization for this content.

Goals of this Chapter

In this chapter you will learn about

- organizational systems, controlled vocabularies, and thesauri, and
- research and interviewing techniques to determine an effective content organization for a website.

4.2 Organizational Systems

Central to information architecture is the concept of *organizational systems*. Organizational systems consist of *organizational schemes* and *organizational structures* [Rosenfeld 1998]. An *organizational scheme* is a classification system for content items. It's a method of placing items into categories. Think of an organizational scheme as a way to cluster items into groups. An *organizational structure* determines the relationships between the groups. Putting it another way, an organizational structure reflects the encompassing scope of the content while an organizational scheme is a method of grouping individual items.

4.2.1 Organizational Schemes

These are part of everyday life. Appointment books, phone books, and shopping-mall directories all rely on organizational schemes to help people find what they seek.

Some schemes are easy. All that's necessary to find today's appointments in an appointment book is to turn to the page for today and look. Other schemes require more decision-making. When one visits a new supermarket, it can be difficult to find a particular item such as a favorite tomato sauce. Is it with the canned goods or with the pasta? If it's not explicitly mentioned on the signs overhead, there is no alternative but to walk through the aisles to find it. This might work in a supermarket, where people have made a commitment of time and location to come to the store, but Web developers don't have this sort of luxury, because a user can leave a site in a single click.

There are two categories of organizational schemes: *exact* organizational schemes and *ambiguous* organizational schemes. An appointment book is an example of an exact organizational scheme; the supermarket is an example of an ambiguous organizational scheme.

4.2.2 Exact Organizational Schemes

Exact organizational schemes divide information into mutually exclusive groups. In other words, each content item fits in exactly one category and there is no doubt about which category it is. The commonly used exact organizational schemes are *alphabetical, chronological*, and *geographical*.

Alphabetical.   Examples using an alphabetical organization scheme include dictionaries and the index of this book. Not only do you immediately know which category you should choose ("Englebart" starts with "E"), but you also know where you'll find the information—the E's appear immediately after the D's and before the F's.

Chronological.   Chronological organizational schemes use the passage of time to determine the classification of an item. Appointment books, history books, and magazine and newspaper archives all use chronological organization. This is straightforward as long as there is agreement on when events occurred. A website that houses an archive of press releases will often show the abstracts in reverse chronological order.

Geographical.   A geographical organizational scheme classifies items by location. Weather maps use a geographical organization scheme, as do floor plans.

Exact organizational schemes are effective when you already know what you want. This type of searching is called *known-item* searching. However, many times people don't know exactly what they are looking for when they begin searching. Think about looking up information in a library. How often do you use the author index, which uses an exact organizational scheme, compared to how often you use the subject index? Extensive research shows that people use the subject index more often [Rosenfeld 1998], but a subject index is not an exact organizational scheme. It's an example of an ambiguous organizational scheme.

4.2.3 Ambiguous Organizational Schemes

Ambiguous organizational schemes do not have the clear-cut categorization rules enjoyed by the exact organizational schemes. This is partly because language has a degree of ambiguity that defies exact classification. For example, the word "hit" can mean

- to strike
- to touch (as in "hit a mark")

- to reach one's goal ("hit upon an answer")
- a success ("Today's Top-40 hits")
- in baseball, the act of reaching first base without walking, without error by the opposing side, and without forcing a base runner out.

Strange though it might seem at first glance, ambiguous schemes can be more useful than exact schemes in many situations. The example of a library's subject index is a case in point. Sometimes, you don't have the exact term for what you want; some approximation is all you have when you begin. One of the marvelous things about searching through information that has an ambiguous organizational scheme is that you can encounter new items related to or associated with your initial term. These can help you find the standard term and the information you desire. With a well-designed scheme, you might even pick up some additional knowledge along the way.

Four valuable ambiguous organizational schemes are *topical*, *task-oriented*, *audience-specific*, and *metaphor-driven* schemes.

Topical. A topical scheme organizes content items by subject; it can be very useful if well designed. The Library of Congress subject index is an example of a topical organizational scheme, as are listings of academic course offerings and the chapters of most nonfiction books. Schemes of this type can range in scope from the encompassing breadth of an encyclopedia to those specialized for the products or services provided by a particular company. Most websites should provide some sort of topical access to content. Examples of sites organized by topic include `www.yahoo.com` and `www.usatoday.com`.

Task oriented. Task-oriented schemes organize content into a collection of functions, services, or tasks. This scheme will be familiar to you, because it is the organizational scheme of choice for menus in software packages. It is appropriate for situations in which it's reasonable to expect only a limited number of frequently used actions. Figure 4–1 shows a page for various tasks connected with cars.

Audience specific. When there are two or more distinct audiences that you can identify, consider an audience-specific scheme. This is a good choice when the site has repeat visitors who want to bookmark the page that pertains to them. The Bank of Montreal site has links for individuals, for small businesses, and for corporations. (See Figure 3–2 for a screen shot of the bank's home page.)

Metaphor driven. Using a metaphor to organize content can help users understand your site by relating it to something they already know. The cautions mentioned in Chapter 2 apply here. If they do not exist in the original metaphor, new functionalities or concepts can be difficult to incorporate in a way that people will accept. Figure 4–2 shows a website that uses a metaphor-driven scheme.

Hybrid schemes. These can combine multiple organizational schemes, but, unless the schemes are physically separated, confusion will result. The Nordstrom page shown in Figure 4–3 is a good example of a hybrid scheme: The topical links relating to merchandise appear in a horizontal bar across the top, and the left column has a task-oriented organization. A clear separation helps reinforce the fact that they are different from each other.

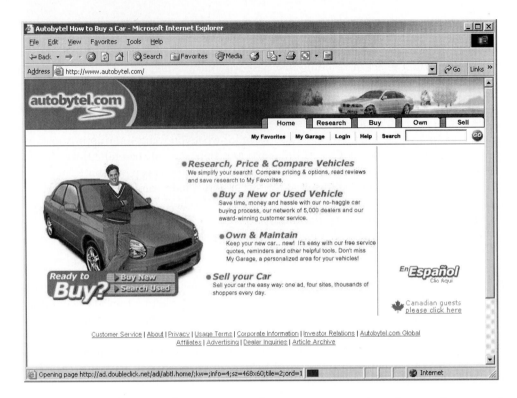

Figure 4–1 Task-oriented organization scheme at `www.autobytel.com`. Courtesy of autobytel.com.

4.3 Organizational Structures

An *organizational structure* defines the relationships among the groups created by an organizational scheme. The distinction between an organizational scheme and an organizational structure is crucial, but it can sometimes be elusive at first. Think of the difference this way:

> **Organizational schemes create groups;**
>
> **organizational structures define the relations between groups.**

Organizational structure forms the basis for how a user will ultimately navigate the site. For this reason, it is worthwhile to spend some time considering which structure to choose. The three most common ones are *hierarchy, hypertext,* and *database,* each of which has advantages and disadvantages. In some cases, it will make sense to choose one of the three; in others, it will make more sense to use a combination.

Hierarchy. A hierarchy is a structuring according to rank or level. A family tree is an example, as is a company's organization chart. In a company, at the top is a board of directors, to whom the president reports. Vice presidents report to the president. Managers report to the vice presidents. Another example is a book. A book has chapters, which have sections, which have paragraphs, which have sentences, which are made up of words.

Because people have previous experience with them, hierarchical structures have the advantage of familiarity. Hierarchies have the additional advantage of first showing users

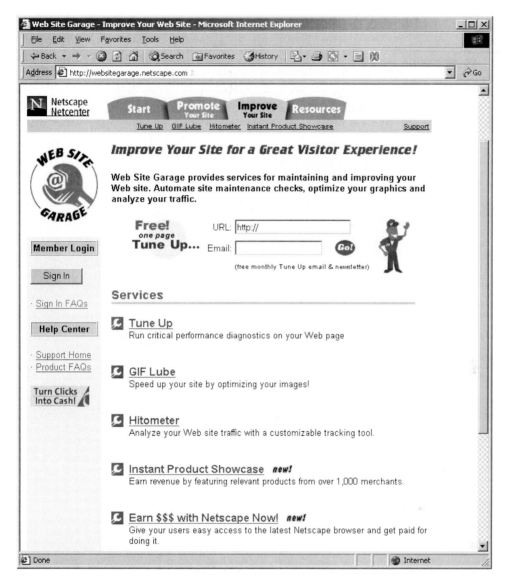

Figure 4–2   Metaphor-driven scheme: Web Site Garage website © 2002 Netscape Communications Corporation. Screenshot used with permission.

the big picture, followed by levels of successively finer detail that appear as a user drills down through the structure.

The *breadth* of a hierarchy refers to the number of links available at each level. The number of levels is the *depth* of a hierarchy. Web users prefer a hierarchy that is wide and shallow because it minimizes the number of clicks required to reach the desired information.

There is one disadvantage to a pure hierarchical structure, which occurs when a user wants to go from one lower-level page to another. Figure 4–4 illustrates the problem. A user at Page B who wishes to go to Page C will have to use the Back button and traverse three additional links.

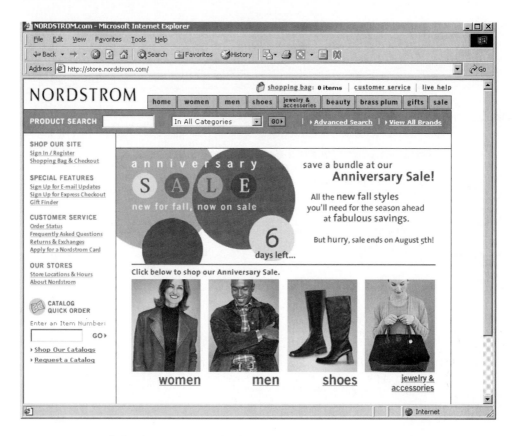

Figure 4–3 A hybrid organizational scheme, `www.nordstrom.com`. Courtesy of Nordstrom, Inc.

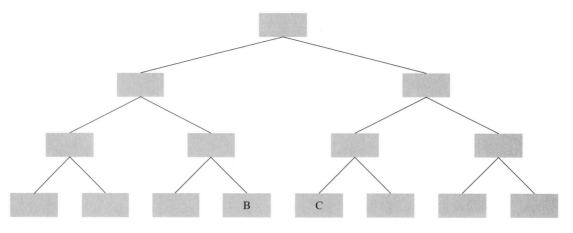

Figure 4–4 Disadvantage of pure hierarchy: getting from B to C.

Much of the time, the subject matter will not support a *completely* hierarchical structure. A book has an index as well as a chapter hierarchy. When a hierarchical structure seems to be the closest fit, feel free to accommodate the content by adding some cross-references where needed. You might identify the need for some cross-references during user and tasks analysis; the need for others might arise only in user testing during evaluation.

Hypertext.   This type of organizational structure consists type of organizational structure consists of items of information and the links connecting them. It provides the flexibility missing in a pure hierarchical system, but this same flexibility can greatly confuse users. It's easy to get lost among the links, so it's best to choose an alternative to a purely hypertext organization when planning a website. Adding links for cross-references is fine, so long as users know where they are and how they got there.

Database.   A database organizational structure provides a bottom-up view of a site, whereas the hierarchical structure provides a top-down view. A database structure permits the user to find desired information while downloading as few pages as possible. Figure 4–5 shows the **www.gmbuypower.com** site, where a customer can specify a type of car by make,

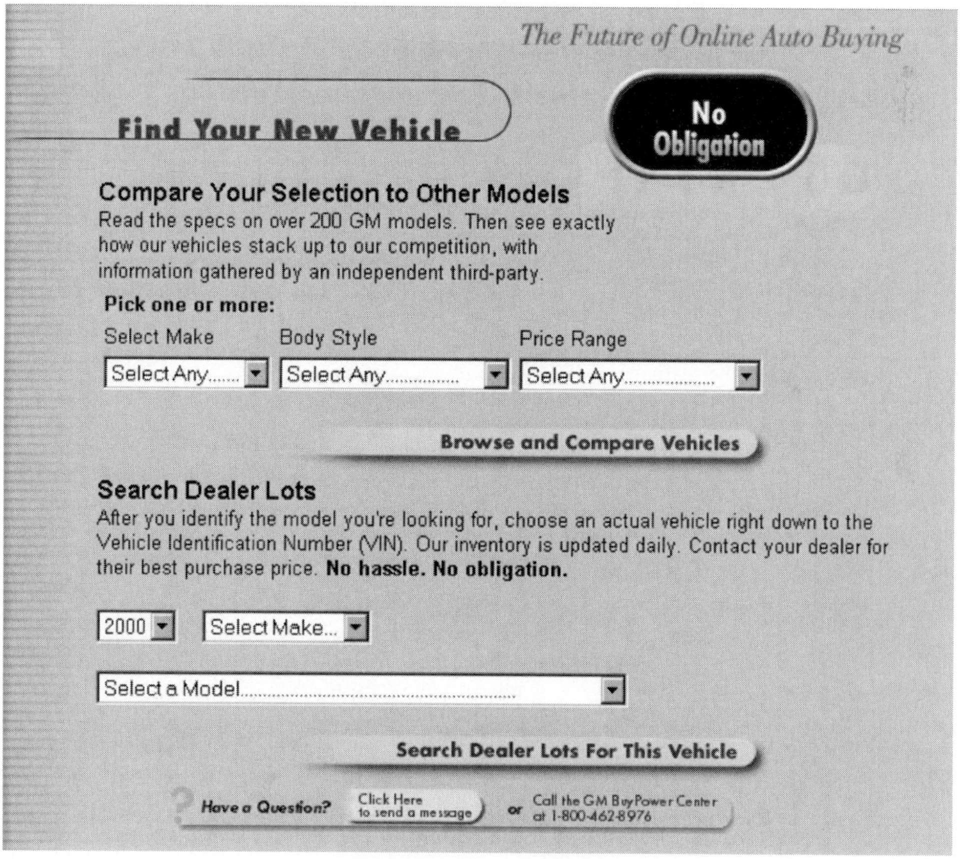

Figure 4–5   A database structure: **www.gmbuypower.com**. © 2002 General Motors Corporation. Used with the permission of GM Media Archives.

body style, and price range. This approach works well for content that's compatible with a database organization. This would include content having characteristics or attributes that can be expressed in a tabular format, as is the case in Figure 3–5.

There are many approaches to facilitating a database search. The example in Figure 4–6 lets a user specify values in multiple fields, but has no facilities for specifying a combination of search terms by using the Boolean operators AND, OR, and NOT. Not knowing how to use these operators is a source of frustration for the vast majority of people using the Web. Many successful sites, such as `www.google.com`, use a simplified search facility that returns only those entries that match *all* of the search terms typed by the user. This approach works better for most people. Even the database search facility of the Association for Computing Machinery's Digital Library `www.acm.org/dl` does not provide the option of Boolean expressions as a first choice. ACM is a technical organization for computer scientists, so this is one site where developers could safely assume that the audience would know Boolean operators. The fact that even ACM provides alternatives to Boolean expressions in their search facility is a strong indicator that it makes sense to avoid them for a general audience.

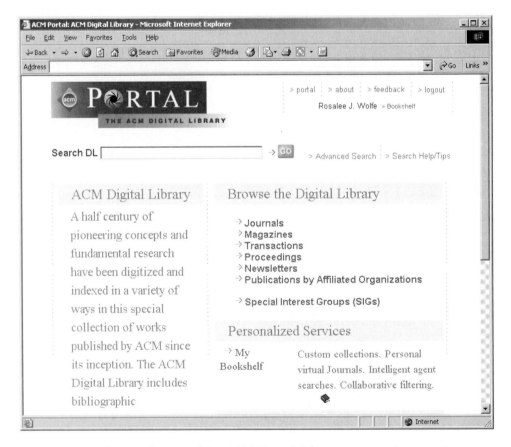

Figure 4–6   The search page of the ACM Digital Library at `portal.acm.org`. Courtesy of the Association for Computing Machinery.

When viewing the results of a database search, users like to see an indication of their relevance. Figure 4–7 shows an approach used by `portal.acm.org`, which displays a numeric percentage to indicate the degree of relevance. Another approach is to order the items by usefulness. The Google search engine does this by checking the link references to see which of them are referred to most often. This determines the order [Levin, 2000]. Try typing in the phrase "the white house" and you will see that the site *The White House* (for the residence of the President of the United States) leads the list of search results. Figure 4–8 shows the result as of February 2001, when this query returned over 1.8 million hits. The Google system had tracked what users clicked on most often in that situation, and it placed The White House site in first position.

Although it requires server-side functionality, database organization offers people the ability to search more pages than they could if they had to look at each page in turn. This structure is feasible as long as the website's content is amenable to a database organization. However, conventional database queries require precision in specifying search terms. Misspelling a word or using a variant term can severely affect the search results. This is where a *controlled vocabulary* and a *thesaurus* can help.

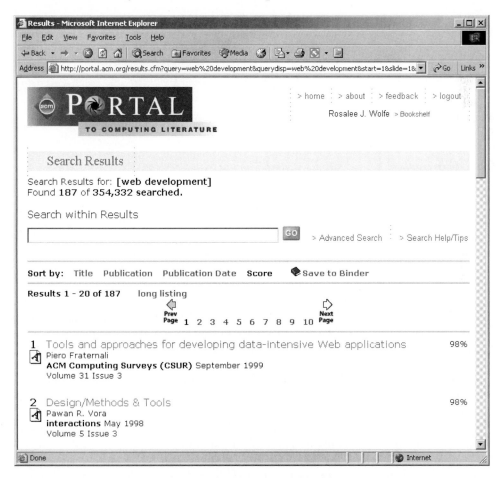

Figure 4–7   Showing relevancy in search results at `portal.acm.org`. Courtesy of the Association for Computing Machinery.

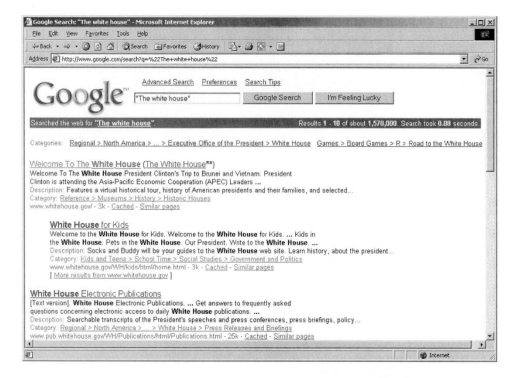

Figure 4–8   Placing the most relevant items first at `www.google.com`. Courtesy of Google Inc.

4.3.1 Controlled Vocabularies and Thesauri

A *controlled vocabulary* is a predetermined set of terms that fit together to describe a specific domain, which can be anything from medicine to kitchen appliances to rock music [Rosenfeld 1999]. The terms of a controlled vocabulary are standardized to counteract the ambiguity of English. In a controlled vocabulary, one and only one term describes a particular concept or content item in the domain. There are no synonyms. By determining the terms in a controlled vocabulary and using them consistently when describing your site's content, you can help people find what they want. All of the pertinent information will be localized in one place.

A controlled vocabulary used in conjunction with a *thesaurus* can make searching even more effective. A thesaurus contains synonyms, related terms, broader terms, narrower terms, and variant terms (including misspellings) for each word in the controlled vocabulary [Morville 1998]. For example, in the Life Sciences Thesaurus, `http://www.csa.com/edit/lscthes.html`, under the term "Cognitive ability" is the broader term "Ability," the narrower term "Problem solving," and the related terms "Neural networks" and "Self-recognition." If a person types in a variant term, the thesaurus can supply the standard term, which will produce the desired search results.

Incorporating a thesaurus to aid database searching is a major undertaking, requiring extensive software support in addition to multiple iterations of user interviews and testing.

You are now familiar with some of the basic concepts and techniques of content organization. The next section discusses practical techniques to help you identify relevant content and suggests how to interview users to discover their mental organizational systems for this content.

4.4 Research and Interview Techniques

The preceding discussion of organizational systems and of how to determine information content is all well and good, but this still doesn't answer the key question: "How can I decide to organize things so people can find what they want?" The techniques in this section will help you decide what makes sense as an organization for your website. The first is a method to gather content. The second is an interviewing strategy to determine an appropriate organization.

4.4.1 Analyze Documents for Objects and Actions

This is a technique to gather content. If you are redesigning an existing website, examine it for *objects* (nouns) and *actions* (verbs). Figure 4–9 is a sample analysis of a small part of a college intranet. If this is a new website, examine any related paper documents, such as manuals, information sheets, and brochures. If it is a commercial website, examine the business case with a fine-tooth comb. If it's a shopping site geared for selling products, look at the company's current catalog. Also, refer to your user and task analyses. What documents did they use while completing their tasks? Did they employ any specialized vocabulary? All of these leads will help you identify content.

The objects you discover will form the content items of your site. The actions that result from your analysis are the tasks your user will perform on your site. These, too, will need to be organized. Does it now make more sense that it's always useful to spend serious time on user and task analysis?

4.4.2 Card Sorting

Careful user and task analysis will give you some hints, but this alone does not provide enough insight to choose an appropriate information architecture for your site. Card sorting can help you make this decision. It can reveal how users carry around content in their heads [Nielsen 1993]. Once you have this information, you can create a website that more easily meets user expectations.

CTI Student Advising System (Student has been admitted)

Objects	Actions
Student	Finding the correct student file.
Student's file	Changing status in program
Student's transcripts	Changing majors
Student's course history	Making course substitutions
Student's courses in progress	Applying for graduation
Student's degree	Qualifying for graduation
Student's communication log	Changing faculty advisors
Faculty advisor	Making an advising appointment
Staff advisor	Registering for classes
Curriculum for CTI degrees	Drop/Add class
	Drop/Add class after first week; after second week; after eight weeks

Figure 4–9   Objects and actions from an existing website.

Card sorting has several advantages. It is cheap to use and quick. A session with a user takes less than an hour; thus, many users can be involved. It draws out how people organize topics without directly asking them questions and risking undue influence to their responses. Many websites have benefited from card sorting, including such companies as Sun, Microsoft, and IBM [Nielsen 1994, Lisle 1998, Kanerva 1998] and such governmental agencies as NIST [Scholtz 1998].

Here's how it works. Get a pack of 3×5 index cards. List each content item (topic, task, etc.) on a separate card. Avoid using terms that can be mistaken as a category heading such as "Company News." Also, avoid using phrasing that would tend to imply a group. Consider the two lists of topics in Figure 4–10. In version A, three items start with the phrase "Apply for." This will influence people to place these items together, even if it makes more sense to group "graduation check," "cap and gown," and "commencement tickets."

Number the cards on the back. The technique works best when you have somewhere between 15 and 40 cards, but some projects have used as many as 78 [Fabris 1999].

Scatter the cards on a desk in a random order. Ask a user to sit down at the desk and sort the cards into piles of related items. After the cards are sorted, ask the user to give a name to each pile. You can write these on Post-It® notes and place them on the piles of cards. After the interview, turn the piles over and use the numbers on the back of the cards to record the groupings. Record the name given by the user with the group of numbers. The interview takes about 20 to 40 minutes. Repeat this process with a number of users.

Some users will want to know "How many piles should I make?" The answer: "As many as make sense to you. You're the expert." Usually this is sufficient empowerment, but some will ask again. With a smile, reply, "More than one," and let them get started. If the user says anything like, "Am I doing this right?" say, "You're doing fine."

Once you have conducted your interviews, you will look for commonalities in how people grouped the cards. One way to do this is with a cluster analysis. This involves a measure called a similarity rating. Every time two cards are in the same pile, you assign them 1 point. Add up all of the times that two cards appear together and divide by the number of groups and you have their similarity rating. Figure 4–11 gives an example using five items. From here, you can feed the similarity ratings into a statistics package to get a cluster analysis.[1] The cluster analysis will tell you how strongly items are related. The results will help you in two ways. They will help you organize information at the page level, and they will help you structure your website so that it reflects how users view the content.

Version A	**Version B**
1. Apply for graduation check	1. Graduation check
2. Apply for tuition remission	2. Tuition remission (fee waiver)
3. Apply for Incomplete	3. Incomplete
4. Request commencement tickets	4. Commencement tickets
5. Request payment deferment	5. Payment deferment
6. Request cap and gown rental	6. Cap and gown rental

Figure 4–10 Avoid wording that implies a grouping.

---

[1]Some statistical packages will let you input the pairs of cards directly, so that you can avoid calculating the similarity ratings by hand.

Card-sorting results

	User A	User B	User C	User D
	1,5	1,4,5	1,5	1
	2,3	2,3	2,3	2,3,4,5
	4		4	

Score

cards 1 and 2	0	+	0	+	0	+	0	=	0
cards 1 and 3	0	+	0	+	0	+	0	=	0
cards 1 and 4	0	+	1	+	0	+	0	=	1
cards 1 and 5	1	+	1	+	1	+	0	=	3

Similarity rating

cards 1 and 2	$0/4 = 0$
cards 1 and 3	$0/4 = 0$
cards 1 and 4	$1/4 = .25$
cards 1 and 5	$3/4 = .75$

Figure 4–11   Calculating a similarity rating. Partial results.

Instead of preparing the data required by the statistics package, there is another method, which is not as accurate, called "data eyeballing" [Nielsen 1994]. In this approach, you examine the transcribed data, simply looking for patterns. The process involves searching for pairs of numbers that appear together often.

However, both of these approaches have a time-consuming element to them: the step in which the designer has to record the results of the card-sorting session. There are some software tools available that provide a "virtual desk" on which to sort the cards. Details about these tools can be found at `http://www.depaul.edu/~rwolfe/HCItools`. When applied to software interfaces, information architecture is also effective for organizing commands into a menu structure. In other words, it applies to interface design in general. The focus of this book is on Web development, but what you are learning has much broader applicability.

Review Questions and Exercises

1. What constitutes an organization system?
2. List three types of exact organizational schemes, and explain how they differ.
3. For each of the following examples, identify its organizational scheme.

   a. Television listing
   b. Index in a book
   c. Map of hiking trails
   d. Calendar of events
   e. The white pages in a U.S. telephone book
   f. Art gallery with rooms for the Medieval, Renaissance, Rococo, Romantic, and Impressionist artists.

4. Name the organizational scheme used in each of the following examples (Figures 4–12 through 4–15). Justify your answer.

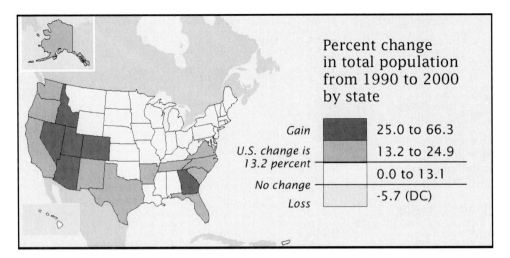

Figure 4–12   Exercise 4, part A. From `www.census.gov`.

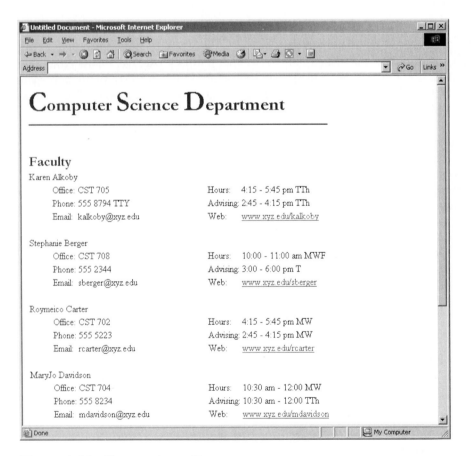

Figure 4–13   Exercise 4, part B.

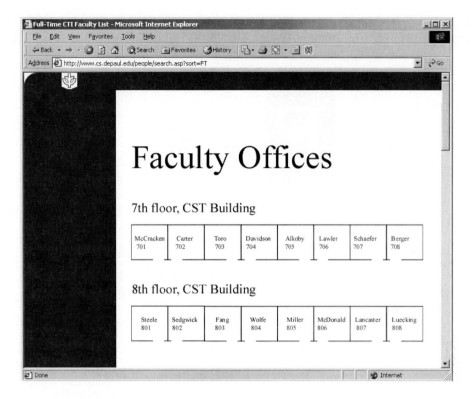

Figure 4–14   Exercise 4, part C.

5. What is the difference between an exact organizational scheme and an ambiguous organizational scheme?

6. List four types of ambiguous organizational schemes and explain them.

7. What are the advantages of ambiguous organizational schemes?

8. Name the organizational scheme in each of the following examples:

   a. The Yellow Pages in a US telephone book.

   b. A stock-brokerage home page that gives users the following options: getting a stock quote; buying, selling, or searching a stock; and reviewing their portfolios.

   c. A home page for a tile manufacturer that has links for customers, retailers, distributors, and suppliers.

   d. A music-CD retailing site offering selections in Rock, Pop, Country and Western, Jazz, and Classical.

   e. An interior designer's site set up as a well-appointed home, with different rooms displaying available services and a portfolio of previous projects.

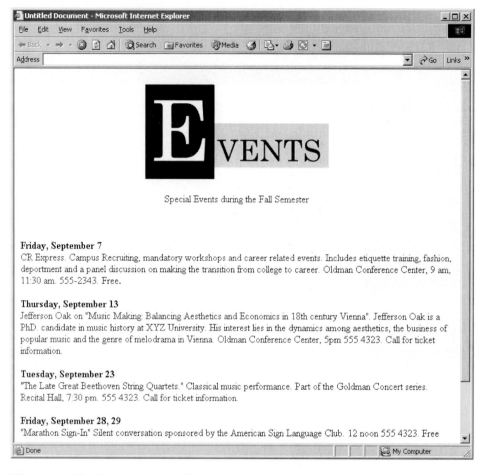

Figure 4–15   Exercise 4, part D.

9. For each of the Web pages in Figures 4–16 through 4–19, name the organizational scheme. For items c and d, consider only the regions inside the marked boxes.

10. What is the danger of a hybrid organizational scheme? What can you do to combat it?

11. What are the advantages and disadvantages of a metaphor-based organizational scheme? Use Figure 4–16 as an example.

12. Figure 4–20 is an example of a hybrid organization. What can you to do improve it? Draw a sketch.

13. What is the difference between an organizational scheme and an organizational structure?

14. Name three useful organizational structures and the advantages of each.

15. Name the organizational structure being used on each of the following Web pages in Figures 4–21 through 4–25.

16. What is a controlled vocabulary? Why is it useful?

17. How does a thesaurus enhance the usefulness of a controlled vocabulary?

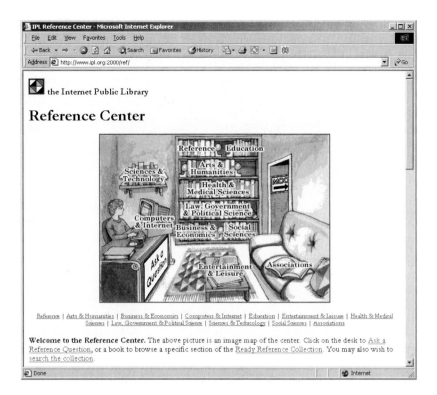

Figure 4–16   Exercise 9, part A. Courtesy of `www.ipl.org`.

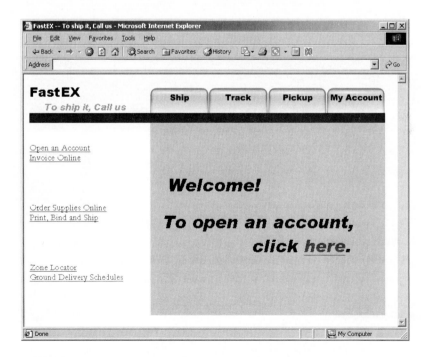

Figure 4–17   Exercise 9, part B.

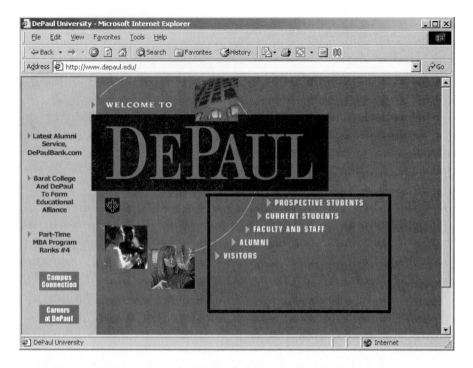

Figure 4–18 Exercise 9, part C. Courtesy of DePaul University.

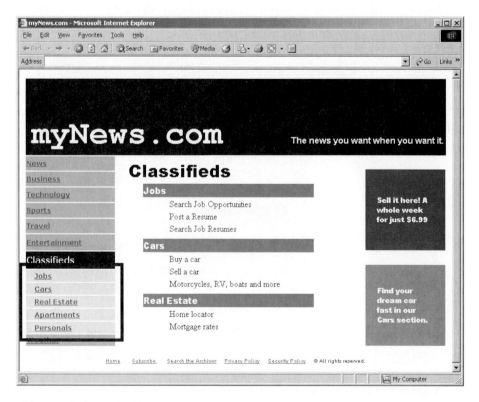

Figure 4–19 Exercise 9, part D.

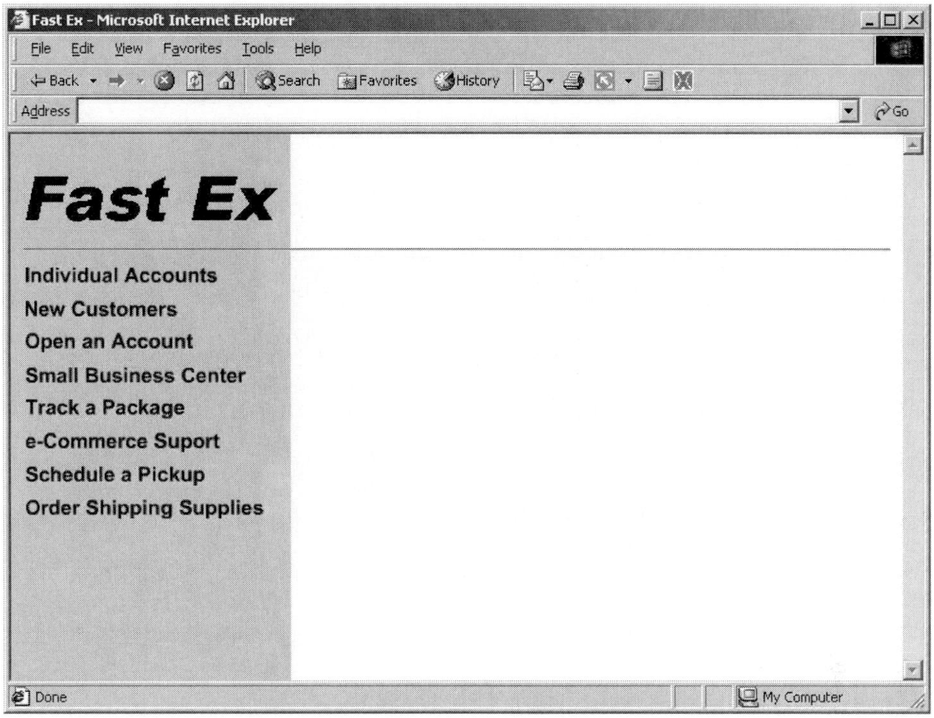

Figure 4–20   Exercise 12.

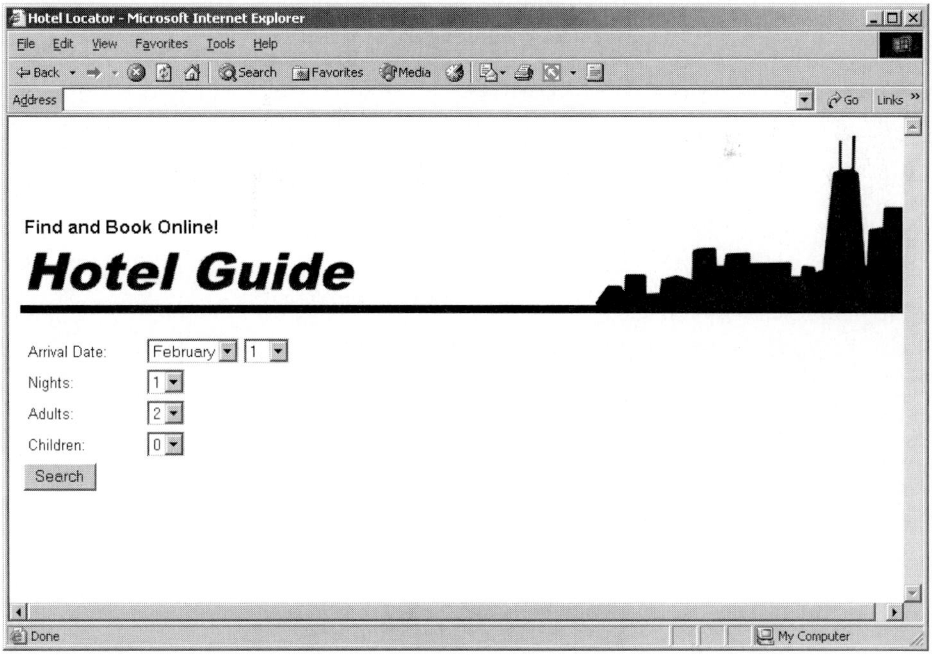

Figure 4–21   Exercise 15, part A.

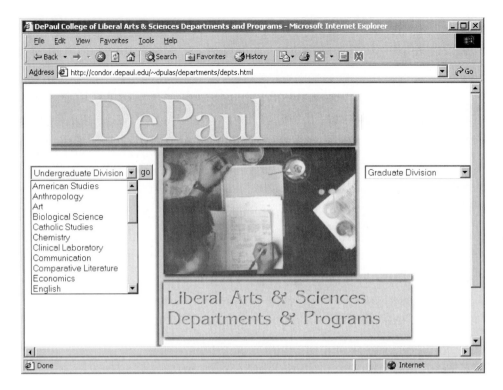

Figure 4–22   Exercise 15, part B. Courtesy of DePaul University.

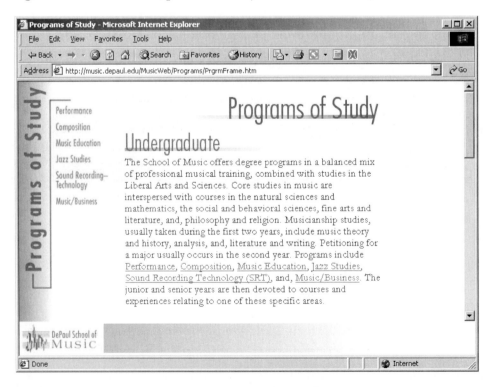

Figure 4–23   Exercise 15, part C. Courtesy of DePaul University.

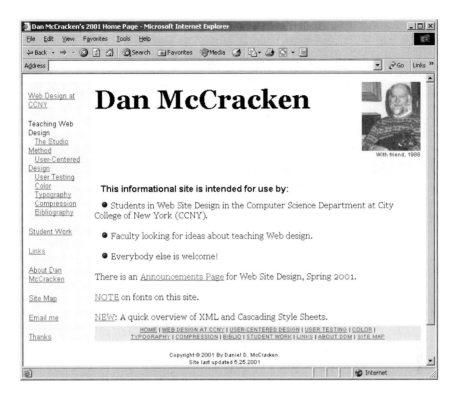

Figure 4–24   Exercise 15, part D.

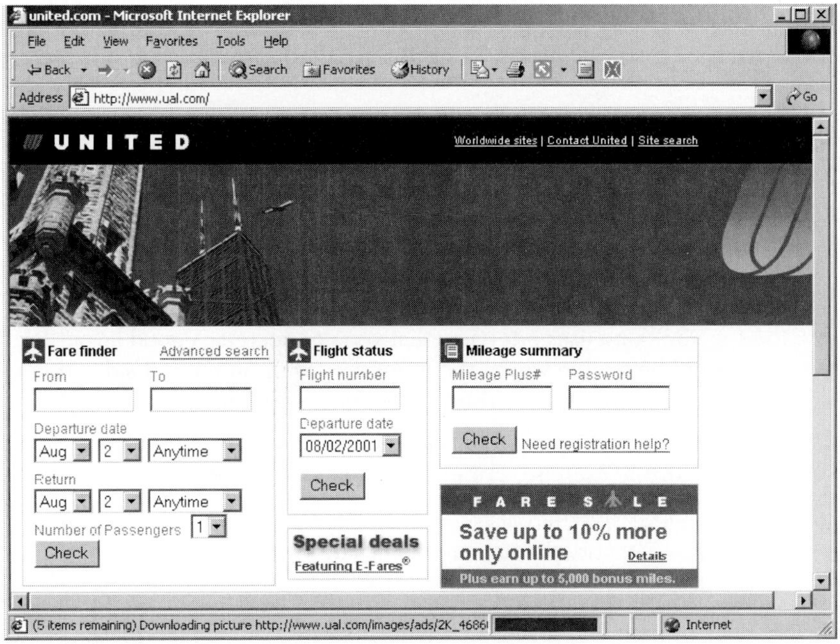

Figure 4–25   Exercise 15, part E. Home Page of www.ual.com. © 2002 United Air Lines, Inc.

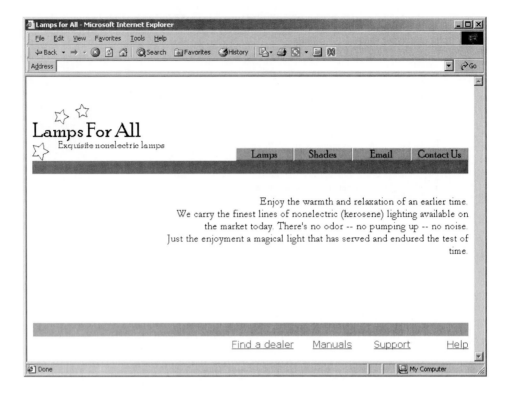

Figure 4–26 Exercise 18.

18. For the Web page in Figure 4–26, list all of the objects and actions.

19. What is card sorting? What benefits does it offer to a Web developer?

Project Activities

20. If you are working on a website for a client, this is the time to identify a list of objects and actions for the site. Begin by referring to the task list you completed and by reviewing the site, if one already exists. If it is a new site, ask your clients to show you any related paper documents. For each item, list it, and name the source where you found it. For example, the source could be the current website, a paper document (be specific), or a user interview that you conducted. A good layout for this information would be a table where the items are listed on the left side and the sources are listed as columns. To keep this process manageable, limit your topics to 30 or fewer.

21. Identify six to eight people for each of your user groups who are willing to perform the card-sorting exercise. For each person interviewed, record

- the user's first name
- the user category the person belongs to
- the date and time
- the name of the person conducting the interview
- the results of the card-sorting session, including the card numbers listed as groups and the accompanying label for each group.

Create a short report describing your findings:

a. Begin the report with your recommendations. This should be short—no more than a page.

b. Include your proposed groups of topics. Choose an easy-to-read format.

References

[Fabris 1999] Peter Fabris. "You think tomaytoes, I think tomahtoes," *CIO Magazine*. April 1, 1999. `http://www.cio.com/archive/webbusiness/040199_nort.html`

[Festa 1999] Paul Festa. "Web search results still have Human Touch," *Cnet.com*. December 27, 1999. `http://news.cnet.com/news/0-1005-200-1507039.html`

[Kanerva 1998] Amy Kanerva, Kevin Keeker, Kirsten Risden, Eric Schuh, & Mary Czerwinski. Web Usability Research at Microsoft Corporation. *Human Factors and Web Development*, eds. Chris Forsythe, Eric Grose, and Julie Ratner. NJ: Lawrence Erlbaum Associates, 1998.
`http://www.research.microsoft.com/ui/papers/webchapter.htm`

[Levin 2000] Mike Levin. Search Engine Optimization. *Mike-Levin.com* 2000.
`http://www.mike-levin.com/search-engine-optimization/`
`advice-to-get-started-topology.html`

[Lisle 1998] Linda Lisle, Jianming Dong, and Scott Isensee. Case Study of the Development of an Ease of Use Web Site. *Proceedings of the 4th Conference on Human Factors and the Web*. Basking Ridge, NJ, June 5, 1998.
`http://www.research.att.com/conf/hfweb/proceedings/lisle`

[McGovern 2001] Gerry McGovern. "The Fundamentals of Quality Search," *Clickz.com*. January 18, 2001. `http://clickz.com/article/cz.3200.html`

[Morville 1998] Peter Morville. "How do you build a thesaurus?" *WebReview.com*. October 30, 1998.
`http://www.webreview.com/1998/10_30/developers/10_30_98_2.shtml`

[Nielsen 1993] Jakob Nielsen. *Usability Engineering*. Boston: Academic Press, 1993.

[Nielsen 1994] Jakob Nielsen and Darrell Sano. SunWeb: User interface design for Sun Microsystem's internal web. *Proceedings of the 2nd World Wide Web Conference '94: Mosaic and the Web*. Chicago, IL, October 17–20, 1994. 547–557.
`http://archive.ncsa.uiuc.edu/SDG/IT94/Proceedings/HCI/nielsen/`
`sunweb.html`

[Robertson 2001] James Robertson. *Information design using card sorting*. Step Two Designs Pty. Ltd., 2001.
`http://www.steptwo.com.au/management/cardsorting/index.html`

[Rosenfeld 1998] Louis Rosenfeld and Peter Morville. *Information Architecture for the World Wide Web*. Sebastopol, CA: O'Reilly, 1998.

[Rosenfeld 1999] Louis Rosenfeld. "Cuisinarts, E-Commerce and Controlled Vocabulary," *WebReview.com*. July 9, 1999.
`http://www.webreview.com/1999/07_09/strategists/07_09_99_3.shtml`

[Scholtz 1998] Jean Scholtz, Sharon Laskowski, and Laura Downey. Developing Usability Tools and Techniques for Designing and Testing Web Sites. *Proceedings of the 4th Conference on Human Factors and the Web*. Basking Ridge, NJ, June 5, 1998.
`http://www.research.att.com/conf/hfweb/proceedings/scholtz/`

[Spool 1997] User Interface Engineering, Jared Spool, Founding Principal. Why On-Site Searching Stinks. [1997.] `http://world.std.com/~uieweb/searchar.htm`

5

Visual Organization

5.1 Introduction

Appearance matters with Web pages, just as it does in many other situations. A polished look to your résumé creates a good first impression and invites confidence. An attractively laid-out term paper gets more respect than a sloppy one. On the Web, a good visual organization lets users know what content items are related and helps them find the pages they want. Content organization and visual organization go hand-in-hand. An effective layout reinforces a site's content organization, and the result is easy navigation.

You already have experience with using instances of visual organization to your advantage. For example, when driving on an interstate highway, if you see an overhead sign for an exit over the right lane, it's a pretty fair assumption that the exit is also on the right. When you scan the table of contents of a book, the visual layout helps you understand the organization of the book's contents so you can get to the part you want.

You also have experience in creating visual organization: When you write programs, you indent to show the branches of an *if* statement or the body of a *for* loop. You perhaps enclose a block of comments in a distinctive box of suitable characters that make it a comment to the programming language, to make the internal documentation stand out visually.

Once you know how your users group content items, you can decide how the items should appear on a Web page. Simply stated,

Content organization drives visual organization.

This is a developer's point of view for designing Web page layouts. Turning it around to a user's point of view, we might say

Good visual organization makes it easy to locate content.

When looking at a Web page or the world in general, humans infer organization from the appearance and arrangement of the objects they see. The material on Gestalt principles in Chapter 2 helped you *recognize* visual organization in Web pages that already exist. In this chapter, you will learn four simple yet powerful principles that will help you *create* Web pages that have effective visual organization. Following these four principles results in Web pages that help users find things quickly. As a bonus, the pages will have a professional, finished appearance that creates a good first impression.

Goals of this Chapter

In this chapter, you will learn the following four principles of visual organization and how to apply them:

- proximity
- alignment
- consistency
- contrast.

5.2 The Four Principles

Here are the four principles, once over lightly:

Proximity. People tend to perceive items that are located close together as being related. Group related content items close together. Separate unrelated items. For example, place paragraph headings close to the paragraph they introduce.

Alignment. Place related items along an imaginary line. Align items of equal importance. Indent subordinate items. Indenting the items that belong to a main heading is an example of using alignment to clarify meaning.

Consistency. Make related items look the same. Putting a navigation bar on the left side of every page of a website is an example of consistency. Making all of the buttons the same size is another.

Contrast. Make different items look different. The large, bold lettering of a chapter title sets it apart from the smaller lettering in the body of the page.

A Web page with good visual organization draws on all four principles. Usually you will use some combination of these four principles when you are placing items on a page, but this first discussion will look at each principle in isolation.

The following discussion draws on the highly recommended work of Robin Williams. If you find this topic interesting, then read her books, *The Non-Designer's Design Book* [Williams 1994] and *The Non-Designer's Web Book* [Williams 2000].

5.3 Proximity

This is one of the Gestalt principles discussed in Chapter 2. Applying proximity can add clarity to a page by organizing related items. Figure 5–1 shows a preliminary study for the navigational plan for a department store. The application is inspired by this well-known limerick:

> A young Webmaster named Dan,
> Was building a fabulous new LAN.
>> "My site is sympathetic,
>> So I'll use alphabetic
> As my main navigational plan."

We give restrained encouragement to Dan. He had just read the previous chapter, where he learned that an alphabetic organization is sometimes an excellent choice. He didn't fully understand the limitations, and he'd forgotten about user and task analysis. Beginners make mistakes. Pretend that the lines under the title in Figure 5–1 are links.

This attempt already exhibits some use of proximity: all the top-level links are next to each other. Further they form a group that is physically separate from the phrase "Dan's Clothing Store." This makes it clear that they are not part of the title.

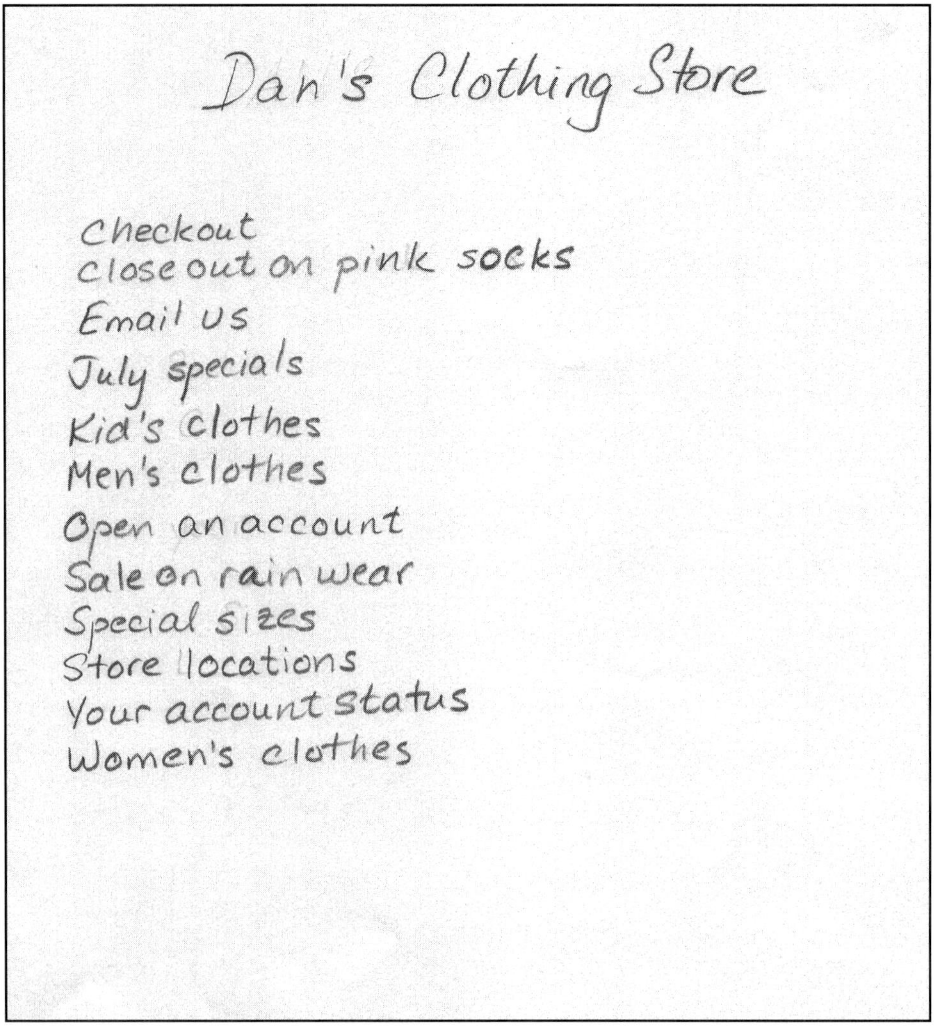

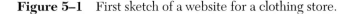

Dan's Clothing Store

Checkout
close out on pink socks
Email us
July specials
Kid's clothes
Men's clothes
Open an account
Sale on rain wear
Special sizes
Store locations
Your account status
Women's clothes

Figure 5–1   First sketch of a website for a clothing store.

What did our developer forget? Hard to say, since we can't interview him, but a reasonable guess would be that he forgot to consult his task analysis and card-sorting interviews. If he had remembered, he would have realized that people go to the website for a store with different goals. Some want to browse to find specific items; some are attracted to sales and specials; some need to interact with the store on account matters.

Suppose that the card-sorting interviews yielded the following groups:

Group 1: Women's clothes, Men's clothes, Kid's clothes, Special sizes
Group 2: July Specials, Sales on rainwear, Closeout on pink socks
Group 3: Store locations, Store hours
Group 4: Open an account, Your account status
Group 5: Check out
Group 6: Email us.

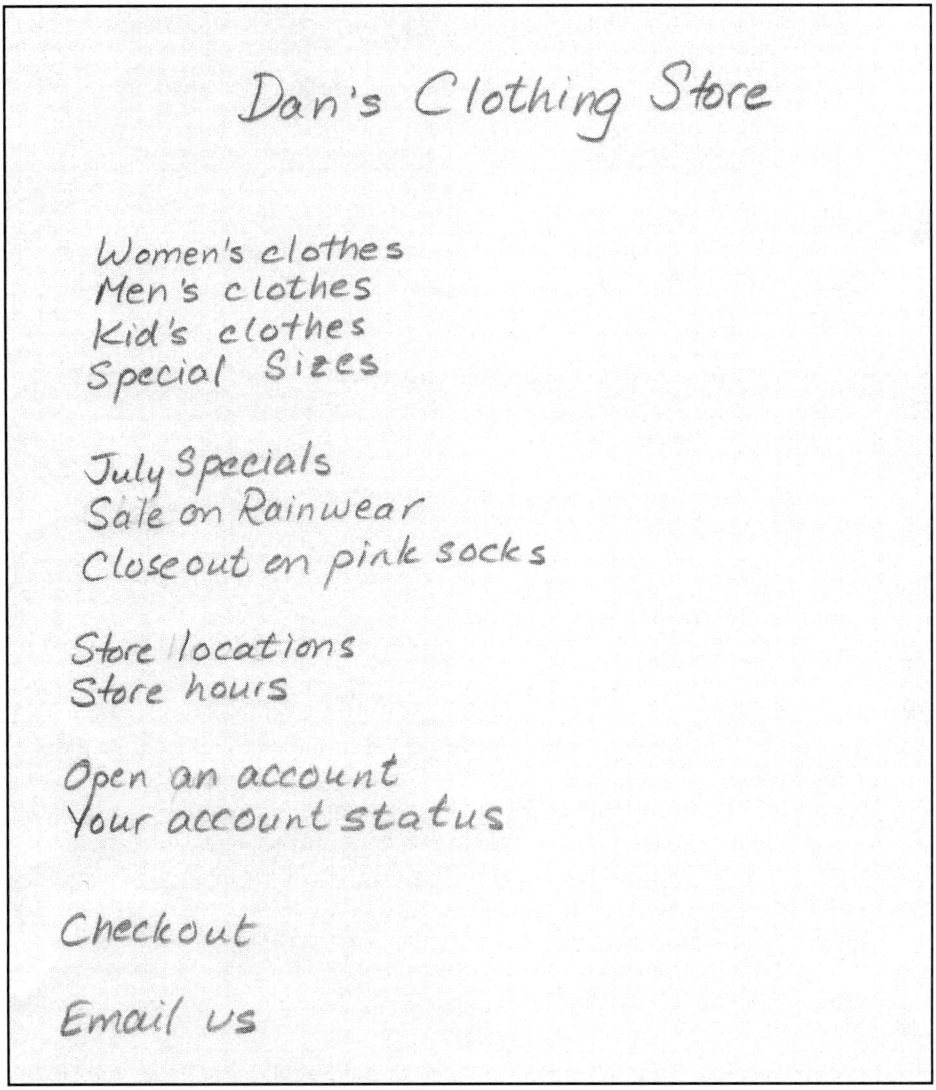

Figure 5–2   A better layout, using proximity to convey content organization.

Proximity means that things that appear close together are related. This mockup of the site shows some proximity, but it's possible to apply proximity again to organize the links into coherent groups. Figure 5–2 shows a better layout. Aside from the title, how many groups are there? Proximity created these groups. How do the groups correspond to the card-sorting results?

This tongue-in-cheek example emphasizes the basic idea of proximity, which is using visual organization to convey content organization. It isn't just that you should group similar things together; you should separate them from things that are different. As the term is used in website design, "proximity" is positive—things close together are related, but it is also negative—things that are separated are different.

Figure 5–3   Top part of the Barnes & Noble website, `www.bn.com`, in a narrow browser window. Courtesy of Barnes and Noble.

Figure 5–4   Top part of the Barnes & Noble website, `www.bn.com`, in a wider browser window. Courtesy of Barnes and Noble.

There is little hope for this developer, until he learns to read the book more carefully. However, we can see the effective use of proximity in a real website, such as Barnes & Noble. See Figure 5–3.

Several examples of proximity are at work. The items relating to accounts and customer service (top right) appear together, as do the various links for browsing and shopping. The title is set off from the site's main links, and the advertisement is physically separate from the navigational content of the page.

This screen shot was taken with the browser window set as narrow as possible without losing any content. How would you set up the page to behave as the browser window is widened? Perhaps you would put more space between the individual items? See Figure 5–4.

Not at all! The individual items are kept close together, as they were before; grouping should be reinforced by *not* spreading them apart. What is done, to keep the page from looking lopsided, is that the account-type information, with the icons and words, moves toward the right margin. Proximity is still in effect.

The concept of proximity as used to organize related items on a Web page is identical to that of proximity as elucidated by the psychologists of the Gestalt school. All four principles of visual organization are rooted in the psychology of human beings.

5.4 Alignment

The Gestalt psychology concept of continuity leads directly to the next principle of visual organization, which is *alignment*. The word "alignment" come from the Latin root for "line." In graphic design, it usually has to do with how things are positioned along a virtual or invisible line. Page layouts with strong alignment will have many unbroken virtual lines. The examples in Figure 5–5 show the normally invisible lines. In this figure, there are two versions of a table. In the first, the stretches of unbroken line are short. In the second, there is an unbroken line stretching across the entire length of the table. The second version has better alignment.

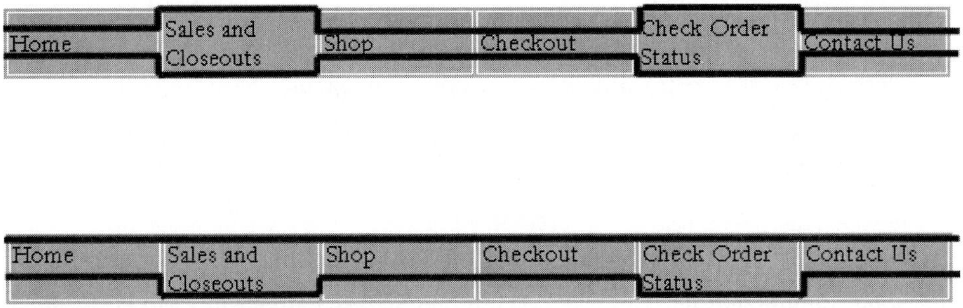

Figure 5–5   Good alignment maximizes the number of unbroken lines.

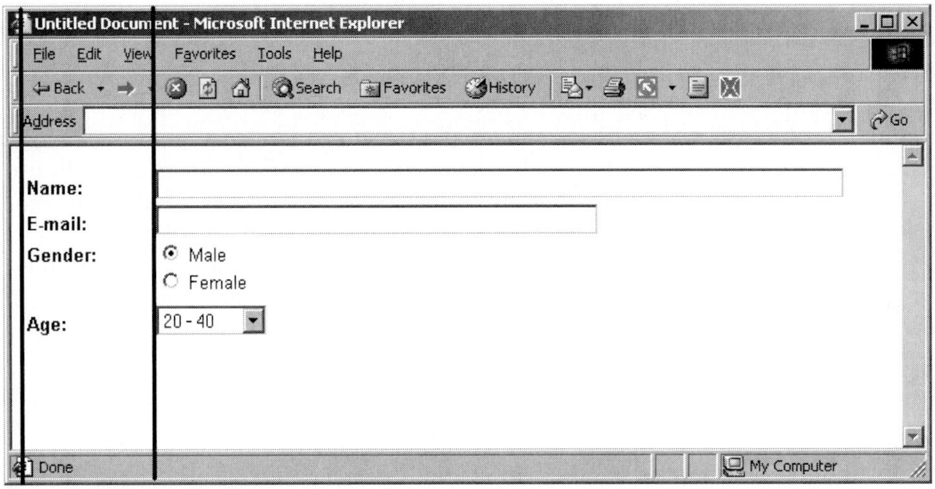

Figure 5–6   Align related items.

Align items that are related or have equal importance. In Figure 5–6, all of the labels are aligned and all of the input fields are aligned. To show that a set of items is subordinate to a header, you can indent them. Indentation is a form of alignment.

Some examples are so familiar that we don't often think about them. The lines of text in this book are aligned along an imaginary line at the left margin. This is called *left alignment*, and it is the most common form of alignment. Aligning items tells the viewer that the items are related. In printing a book, that means the lines are all part of one paragraph.

Right alignment, shown in the setting of this paragraph, aligns lines on an imaginary vertical line at the right margin. It is seldom used with bodies of text such as this, but finds use in advertising, layout of things like business cards, and occasionally on the Web. It is used with text for variety, and perhaps to attract attention by its novelty. If used for an extended body of text, with lines the length of those in this book, it is hard to read. *Centered alignment* is most commonly used for headings.

Don't use centered alignment on extended body text. You see

how bad it looks.

It can be seen very occasionally in personal Web

pages designed by people with no graphic design background.

Perhaps they think it has an "artistic" appearance. It doesn't.

What it does have is virtual illegibility.

Our eyes and brains are accustomed to flying back from the right end of

one line to the left end of the line below. This works well, so long as the lines are

spaced far

enough apart and are not too long.

That long training and habit breaks down totally in a paragraph like the next one. You will see no other examples in this book.

(It can be worse: text set in italic

and in a small font size is even harder to read.

If done on a Web page,

with white type on a dark background, the designer is inviting a lawsuit for eye damage.)

Centered alignment is the weakest type of alignment, partly because it forms fewer invisible lines than does either left or right alignment. However, if you are going to use it, make the individual lines very different in length. It always creates a bad impression if something looks *almost* aligned, like the example in Figure 5–7. Although the example has centered alignment, the beginning of each line of text is almost in left alignment, but not quite, creating a sloppy look. If you are going to use centered alignment, use very long lines of text alternating with short lines of text, as in Figure 5–8.

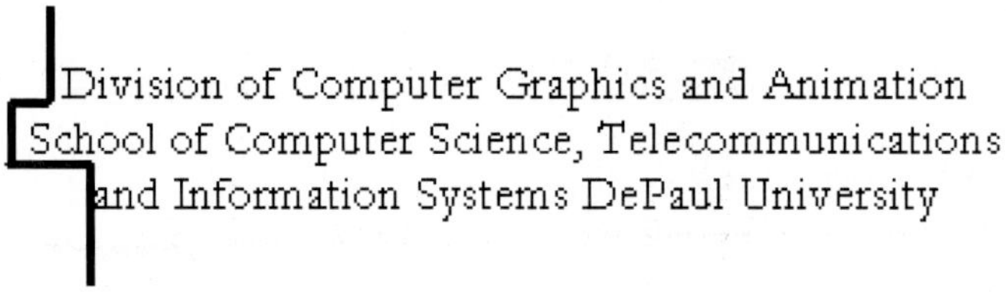

Division of Computer Graphics and Animation
School of Computer Science, Telecommunications
and Information Systems DePaul University

Figure 5–7   The danger of centering lines that are nearly equal in length.

Division
of Computer Graphics and Animation

School of Computer Science, Telecommunications
and Information Systems

DePaul University

Figure 5–8   When centering, use lines that differ greatly in length.

Text can also be *justified*, meaning that the text will align both the left and right margins; this paragraph is set justified. This is done by phototypesetting routines, which insert space between words. The amount of inserted space varies, though, as when a line is just too long and a long word has to be moved to the next line. It's best to avoid using justified text on Web pages. Strange things can happen when the user resizes the browser window.

It would be hard to find a Web page that does *not* make use of alignment. Figure 5–9 shows a page from the Eddie Bauer site.

This page has many sections to it, including a top area that contains the company logo and important links for present and past shopping as well as customer service. There is an area on the left that's reserved for seasonal or current advertising specials. Underneath this are three columns of links, taking a user to various types of merchandise. On the right of the page is a column with a darker background that offers quick shopping for users who have a paper catalog. All of these sections use left alignment.

The four graphic design principles are almost always used in combination with each other. For an outstanding example of the use of proximity and alignment, see Figure 5–10.

Proximity and alignment are seen in the grouping of the seven links at the top. Here, the "line" in alignment is not virtual: the designer has provided an actual line to reinforce the

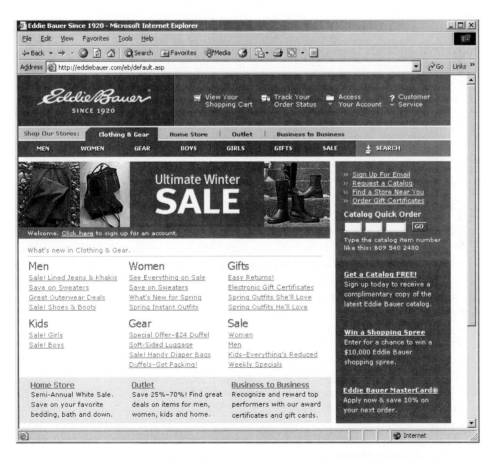

Figure 5–9   A good example of alignment. Courtesy of Eddie Bauer.

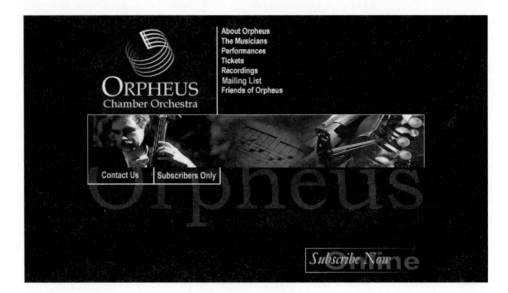

Figure 5–10   Home page for the Orpheus Chamber Orchestra at www.orpheusnyc.com. Courtesy of the Orpheus Chamber Orchestra.

imaginary vertical line created by the seven link names. Proximity is at work in the separation of the top links, which are of general interest to anyone visiting the site, from the "Contact Us" and "Subscribers Only" links, which have a narrower audience and a different purpose.

When starting out in the area of visual organization, the easiest and most effective way to use alignment is to choose a single alignment style for the whole page. It can be left aligned, right aligned or centered, but avoid mixing alignments on a page. A consistent indentation gives your pages a more polished and consistent look. Compare the two layouts in Figure 5–11. The only thing that differs between the two layouts is the choice of alignments. In the second page, there is only one alignment type. What is it?

5.5 Consistency

Consistency is one of the most powerful tools for making a website understandable and easy to navigate. Consistency here means a high degree of uniformity in layout within a page and uniformity in layout across pages. Examples abound, from putting the link to the home page in the same place on each page of a site, to consistency of alignment, to consistency of visual metaphors [Horton 1991]. Consistency can contribute to ease of navigation, as is demonstrated by a sample public-library site for children. (See Figure 5–12.)

The graphical organization consists of an illustration in the center, which is surrounded by links to other pages. The arrangement forms columns on either side of the central graphic. The links in the columns are left aligned as is the title. The link labeled "Science and Technology" leads to the page featured in Figure 5–13.

The page arrangement is consistent with Figure 5–12: a centered graphic surrounded by links to other pages. The layout and links provide the viewer with answers to the three questions that should always be immediately answerable: Where am I? (On the Science and Technology page.) How did I get here? (From Just for Kids.) Where can I go from here? (Math, Science Museums, etc.)

Figure 5–14 shows a side-by-side comparison of the Science and Technology page with another second-level page. What kinds of consistency do you see?

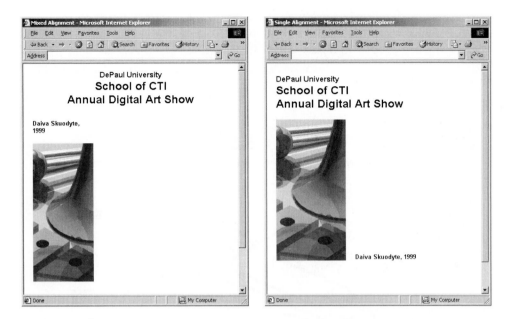

Figure 5–11 The advantages of using a single alignment style on a page.

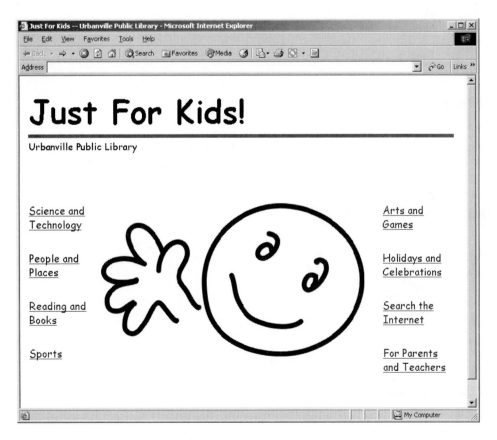

Figure 5–12 The home page from a public-library site for children.

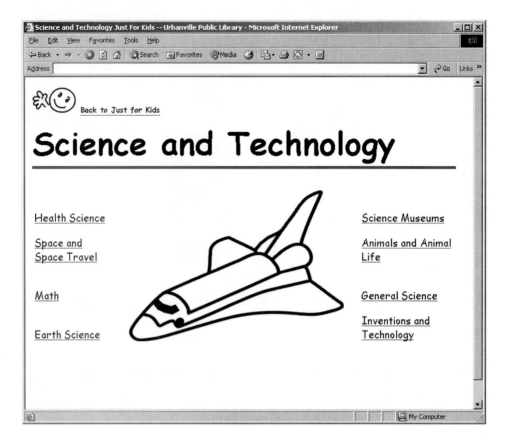

Figure 5–13   The Science and Technology page.

Figure 5–14   Two second-level pages from the site.

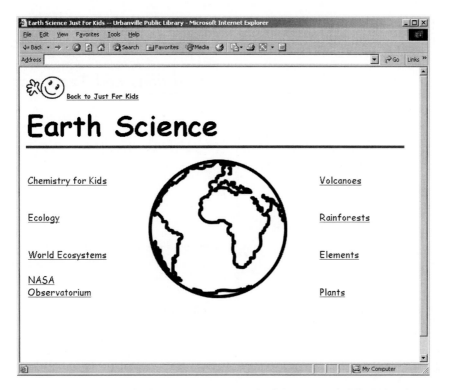

Figure 5–15   The Earth Science page, reached from Science & Technology.

Will this page layout serve all pages in the site? That is too much to expect; forcing all pages of such a large site to fit the same mold would not serve the broader purpose of using visual organization to communicate content effectively. However, even all third-level pages still retain quite a bit of consistency with the upper-level pages. Figure 5–15 shows that the viewer still knows the answers to the questions, "Where am I? How did I get here? Where can I go from here?"

Compare the four third-level pages in Figure 5–16. In addition to navigation-bar placement, what other consistencies do you see?

Creating pages with consistent placement of links and consistent alignment of text will significantly enhance the usability of your Web pages. We now turn to the fourth of the principles that you can apply, contrast.

5.6 Contrast

The final one of the four principles is contrast. Contrast can draw attention to items on your page and reinforce the content hierarchy by creating a visual hierarchy. Text that is large and bold will be perceived as being more important than smaller text.

When you decide to make two items different, make them really, *really* different. As Robin Williams says, "Don't be a wimp" [Williams 1994]. In the top example in Figure 5–17, the headings are barely different from the items that follow them. This is not a good use of contrast. If you've decided to make headings bigger, then make them *twice* the size of normal text. While you're at it, also make the headings bold, to increase the contrast further.

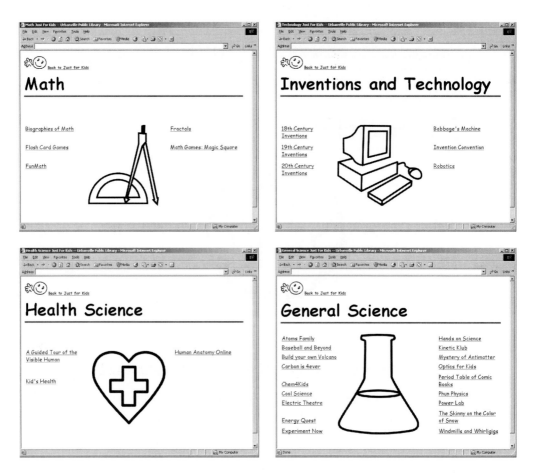

Figure 5–16 Reduced images of four pages reachable from the Science and Technology page.

5.7 Summary

If you apply the four principles—proximity, alignment, consistency, and contrast—to your Web pages, the result will be a professional-looking site that will inspire user confidence and make it easier for your users to find what they want. The next time you notice a Web page that strikes you as looking good, take a moment to analyze the page for these principles.

Although the Web is primarily a visual medium, it is increasingly used by people with limited vision. Chapter 12 presents the wide variety of technology available to help this user group. Tens of millions of people with some kind of vision limitation use the Web. Chapter 13 also covers design guidelines for making your Web pages accessible to them.

You don't have to be an artist to design visually effective Web pages. You can create some sharp-looking pages with just HTML and a text editor. You do need talent and training to create original art for Web pages, whether by paint and brushes or with Adobe Illustrator®, but you don't have to be an artist to know how to lay out text elements so that the visual organization serves to make content organization clear. Effective visual organization that reinforces content organization will result in easy navigation, which is the topic of the next chapter.

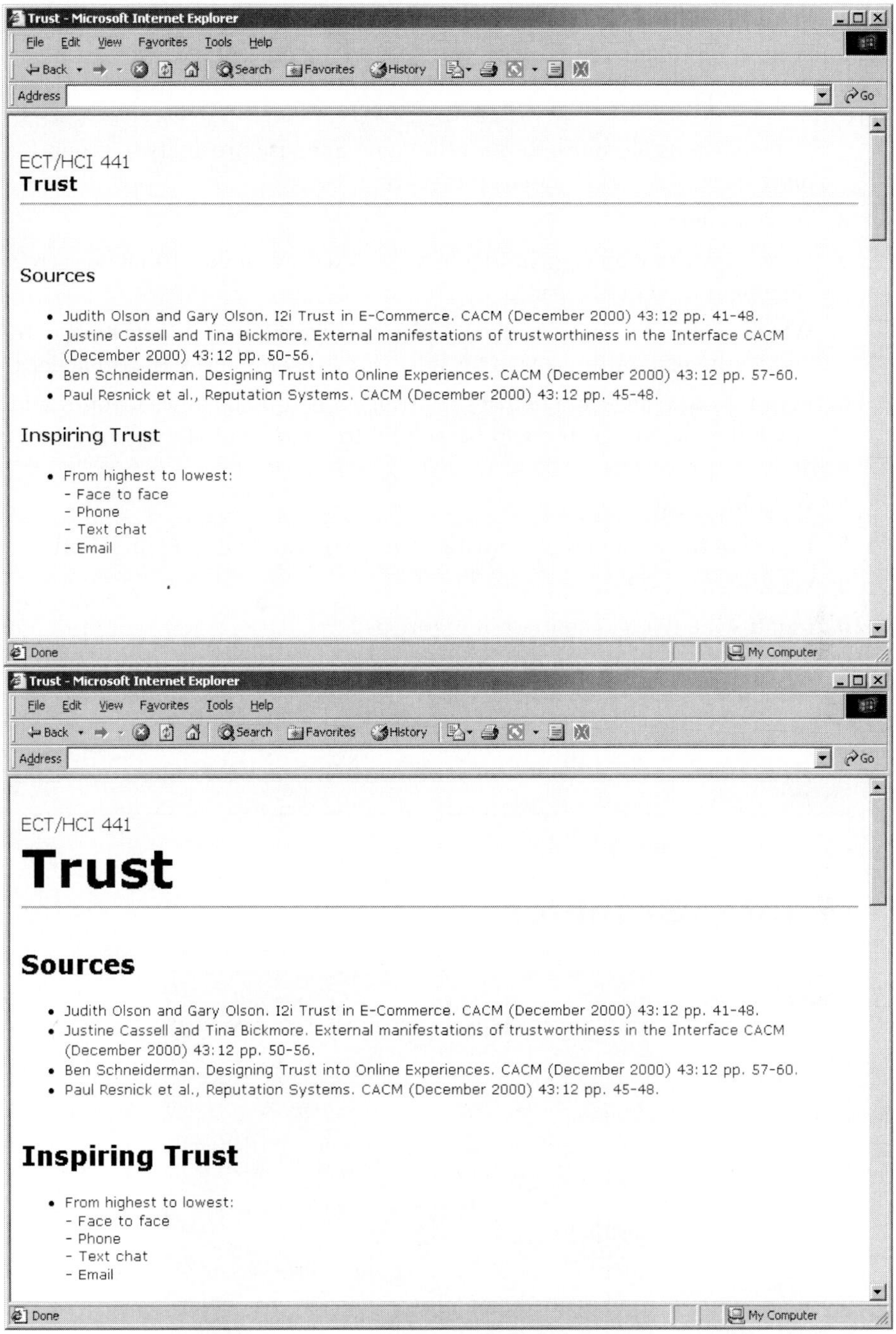

Figure 5–17   If you want the headings and text to be different, make them really different.

Review Questions and Exercises

1. What is proximity?

2. Here are four letters:

   A B C D

   While keeping all four letters on the same line, use proximity to group B and C and make each of A and D into a group of one.

3. What is alignment?

4. Photocopy the Web page in Figure 5–18 and draw in the virtual lines created by the alignment used on the page.

5. Which of the following two examples in Figure 5–19 demonstrates strong alignment—the first, or the second? Justify your answer in terms of virtual lines.

6. Figure 5–20 is an example that's not well aligned. Explain what you would do to improve the alignment. It could be helpful to create a photocopy of the example and draw on it.

7. What is consistency?

8. List all of the examples of consistency that you can find in Figure 5–21.

9. What is contrast?

10. Identify the types of contrast in Figure 5–21.

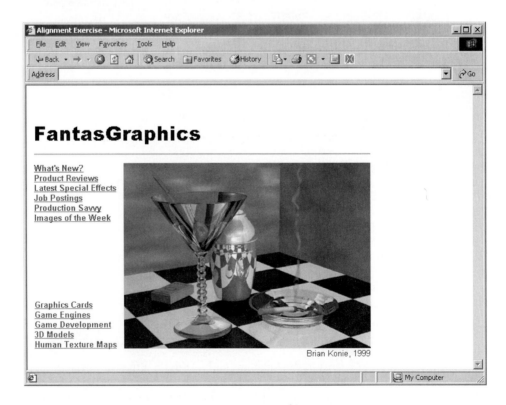

Figure 5–18   For exercise 4. Image courtesy of Brian Konie.

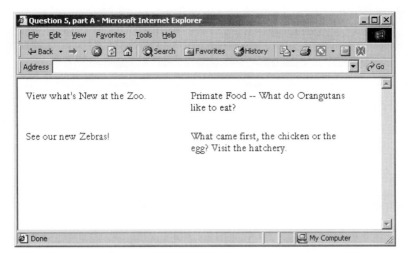

Example A

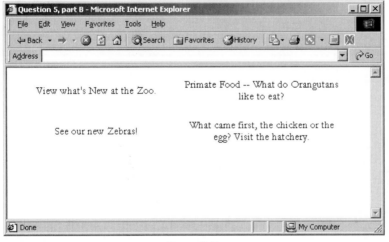

Example B

Figure 5–19   For exercise 5.

11. Figure 5–22 does not have very good contrast.

    a. What contrast is already present?

    b. How many levels of priority are there on the page? There is certainly a detail level. What other levels are there?

    c. How can you make the existing contrast more emphatic?

    d. How can you adjust the existing contrast to support the number of levels you identified in question 11-b?

    e. In addition to emphasizing the existing contrast, are there any other organizational principles you can add to show the distinction in the various levels you have identified? Describe what you would do.

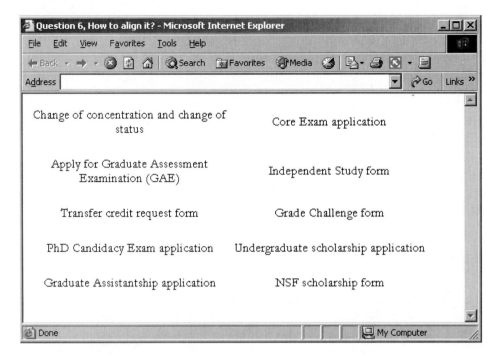

Figure 5–20   For exercise 6.

Title

Chapter 1

Section 1-1

Section 1-2

Section 1-3

Chapter 2

Section 2-1

Section 2-2

Chapter 3

Section 3-1

Section 3-2

Section 3-3

Figure 5–21   For exercises 8 and 10.

Syllabus: ECT 441 Usability Issues for E-Commerce
Description
Design, prototyping and evaluation of e-commerce web sites. Context of usability in the project development life cycle. User/task analysis with emphasis on the first time and the infrequent user. Content organization. User testing with low fidelity prototypes. Issues of perceived privacy and security.
Schedule
Click here to link to the schedule. All homeworks are available via the schedule.
Due Dates
Homeworks must be submitted in the form requested on the posted due date. No emailed homeworks. The Incomplete Policy is consistent with established school policy.
Attendance
Required. Attendance will be taken and becomes part of the individual contribution portion of the grade. Before coming to class each week, please consult this page for links to handouts and homework assignments. It is your responsibility to make a copy of web-based course material and bring it to class.

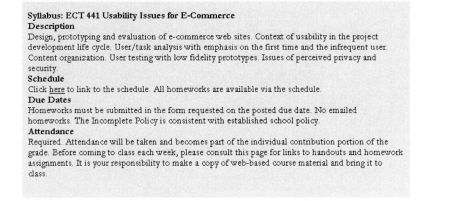

Figure 5–22 For exercise 11.

12. Name the organizational principle at work in Figures 5–23 through 5–25.
13. In the four examples in Figure 5–26 there are two or three visual organizational principles at work. For each example, name the principles.
14. This text in Figure 5–27 (shown on page 102) has a title, "A Great Time for Team Building," a subtitle, "Considering the advantages and challenges of group work," and details regarding the date and presenter.

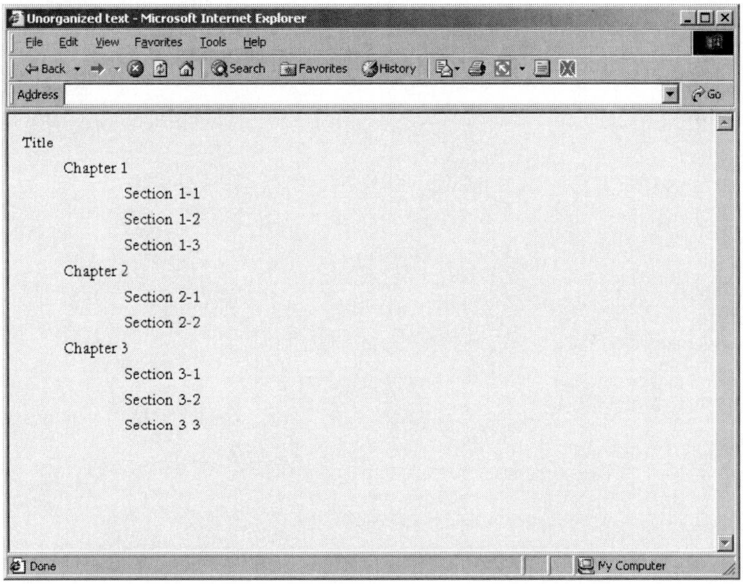

Figure 5–23 For exercise 12, Part A.

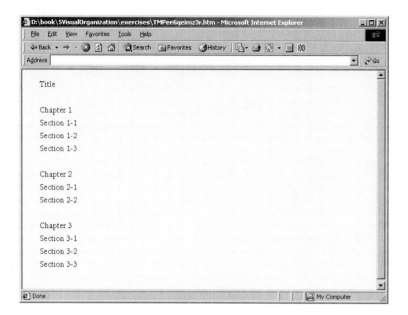

Figure 5–24   For exercise 12, Part B.

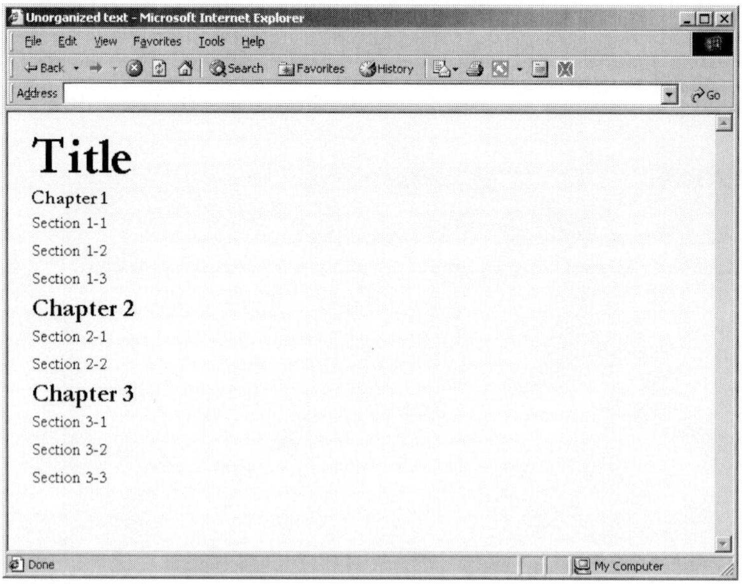

Figure 5–25   For exercise 12, Part C.

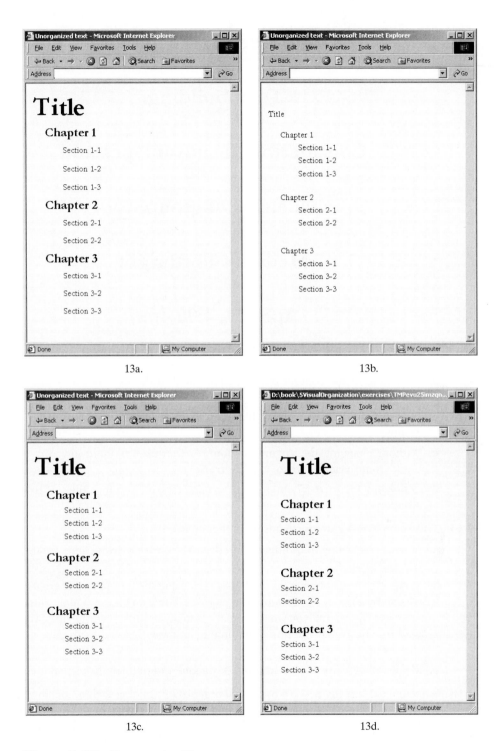

Figure 5–26   For exercise 13.

A Great Time for

Teambuilding:

Considering the advantages and

challenges of group work

Mediator Forthright

April 21, 4:00 4pm

Figure 5–27   For exercise 14.

    a. According to the content analysis mentioned in the exercise, how many groups are there?

    b. In the current version of the text layout, is there any visual indication of these groups?

    c. Without changing the alignment, font, or font size, is there any way to create these groups visually? If so, what is it?

    d. Photocopy Figure 5–27 and use scissors and tape to rearrange the text to show the groupings.

15. The example in Figure 5–28 has poor alignment.

    a. Make a photocopy of the figure and draw the current virtual lines created by the text and pictures.

    b. Make another photocopy of the figure and, using scissors and tape, create a better version by aligning the text and the pictures. You won't have to move any one element very much, but you want to create as many unbroken virtual lines as possible. Feel free to modify the horizontal line in any way that will help make a stronger alignment.

    c. Make a photocopy of your improved versions and draw in the virtual lines.

16. Someone has already tried to use visual organizing principles when making the page shown in Figure 5–29, but one principle in particular is lacking. Which one is it? Make a photocopy of the page, and, using paper and scissors, make a new version that applies the missing principle to communicate more clearly.

Great Digital Images

Mapping techniques add realism and interest to computer graphics images. Texture mapping applies a pattern of color to an object. Bump mapping alters the surface of an object so that it appears rough, dented or pitted. When creating image detail, it is cheaper to employ mapping techniques that it is to use myriads of tiny polygons. Imagine the number of polygon it would require to model the blades of grass in the lawn! Texture mapping, creates the appearance of grass without the cost of rendering thousands of polygons.

Knowing the difference between world coordinates and object coordinates is important when using mapping techniques. In object coordinates, the origin and coordinate axes remain fixed relative to an object no matter how the object's position and orientation change. Most mapping techniques uses object coordinates. Normally, if a teapot's spout is painted yellow, the spout should remain yellow as the teapot flies and tumbles through space. When using world coordinates, the pattern shifts on the object as the object moves through space.

Depending on the mapping situation, we may need to bound an object with a box, a cylinder, or a sphere. It's often useful to transform the bounding geometry so its coordinates range between zero and one. Transformed bounding boxes has coordinates that range from (0,0,0) to (1,1,1). For a

bounding cylinder, we change the cylinder's circumference to one and its height to one. For a sphere, we scale the latitude and the longitude so that both range between zero and one.

Texture mapping can be divided into two-dimensional and three-dimensional techniques. Two-dimensional techniques place a two-dimensional (flat) image onto an object using methods similar to pasting wall paper onto an object. Three-dimensional techniques are analogous to carving the object from a block of marble.

In two-dimensional texture mapping, we have to decide how to paste the image on to the object. In other words, for each pixel in the object, we encounter the question, "Where do I have to look in the texture map to find the color?"

Let's see how this works...

Figure 5–28   For question 15.

Project Activities

17. If you are creating a website for a client, ask your client whether there are any specific graphics (pre-existing images or clip art) that they want on the site. Often an organization will have an identifying logo that will need to appear, particularly on the home page.

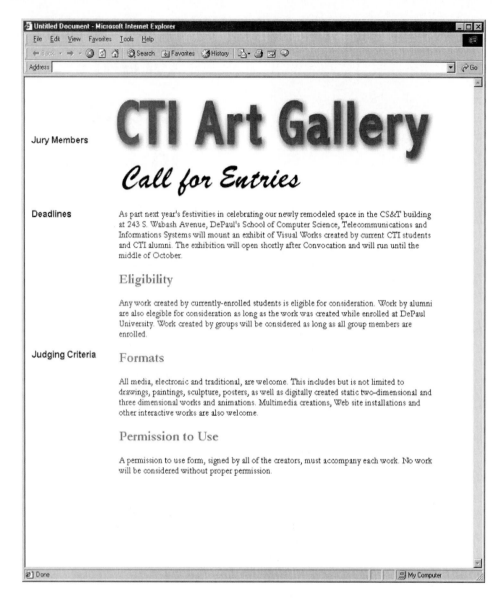

Figure 5–29 For exercise 16.

References

[Horton 1991] William Horton. *Illustrating Computer Documentation: The Art of Presenting Information Graphically on Paper and Online*. New York: Wiley, 1991.

[Williams 1994] Robin Williams. *The Non-Designer's Design Book*. Berkeley: Peachpit Press, 1994.

[Williams 2000] Robin Williams and John Tollett. *The Non-Designer's Web Book*. 2nd ed. Berkeley: Peachpit Press, 2000.

6

Navigation

6.1 Introduction

According to the *Winston Dictionary*, "to navigate" means "to steer or manage a ship or an airplane" [Winston 1954]. The idea of steering or choosing a path of travel carries over to the Web. *Navigation*, or choosing a path through a website's information space, is a key aspect of a site's usability. Its goals are to help people know where they are in a site and to give them confidence when choosing where they want to go next. Effective navigation is the product of two factors: the first is an appropriate content organization, chosen after interviewing users; the second is a visual organization that reinforces the content organization. The previous two chapters cover content organization and visual organization. This chapter shows how to use these tools to create effective navigation.

Goals of this Chapter

In this chapter, you will learn principles and techniques for

- site-level navigation
- page-level navigation.

It's important to consider navigation at two levels. *Site-level navigation* encompasses issues pertaining to understanding and moving through the information architecture of a website. The second, *page-level navigation,* includes techniques that enhance the comprehension of an individual Web page.

6.2 Strategies for Effective Site Navigation

When creating site-wide navigation, you are bringing together the knowledge you have collected about users and their tasks and about how users personally organize the content you intend to have on the site. The next step is to consider the strategies that will help you create a navigation system that's effective for your users. The main strategies are the following:

1. Choose an appropriate navigation system that reflects the content's organizational structure.
2. Choose visual navigation elements that build context for a user.
3. Be aware of the built-in services provided by Web browsers, and take advantage of them.

6.2.1 Navigation Systems

Navigation systems are closely linked with organizational structures. One way to distinguish between the two is to recognize that the navigation system is a visual implementation of an organizational structure. This section will discuss three major types of navigation systems: *hierarchical, ad-hoc,* and *database-driven.* A hierarchical navigational system implements a hierarchical organizational system and provides users with a top-down view of a site. *Ad-hoc* systems serve a hypertext organizational structure. It is rare that a site uses a purely database-driven navigational system, but the sites that come the closest are search engines.

Hierarchical

Most sites should have some sort of hierarchical navigation system. In its pure form, it is rather limiting, but, with a few additional links, it becomes flexible and powerful. As mentioned in Chapter 4, a pure hierarchy doesn't facilitate easy traversal between two pages deep in the structure. However, the additional links allow users to access pages with fewer clicks, as Figure 6–1 demonstrates. Note the lines connecting the bottom boxes; these are not part of a hierarchical system.

This type of navigation system is so useful that it comes in several different forms. For small sites, a *global navigation system* could be enough. Such a system appears consistently on every page of the site and offers navigation options for the entire site. The simplest global navigation system consists of a single navigation bar that appears on each page. The site featured in Figure 6–2 has a horizontal navigation bar located under the site name. A second example, in Figure 6–3, displays a vertical navigation bar. On a site's home page, the bar might not be necessary if the primary links are already displayed as part of the page layout. For the navigation bar appearing on secondary pages, it is almost always a good idea to provide a link back to the home page. Secondary, or second-level, pages are those reachable from the home page with one click. For a personal website, a simple global navigation system usually suffices.

A more complex site might include a second navigation bar that contains links leading to third-level pages, as demonstrated in Figure 6–4. The top-level navigation bar has four choices. The change in color indicates that the user has clicked on "Shop," and is now on the main shopping page. The secondary navigation bar, located below the first, displays shopping-page links leading to third-level pages.

When working with sites having three levels or more, it can be helpful to use *breadcrumbs*, which display a record of links that the user clicked in the process of traveling to the current page. They are a record of a user's trail through the site. In a sense, they

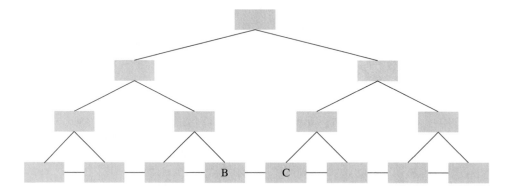

Figure 6–1   Extra links add flexibility.

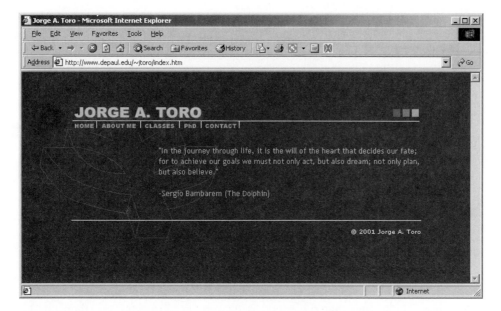

Figure 6–2 A single navigation bar in a global navigation system. Courtesy of Jorge Toro.

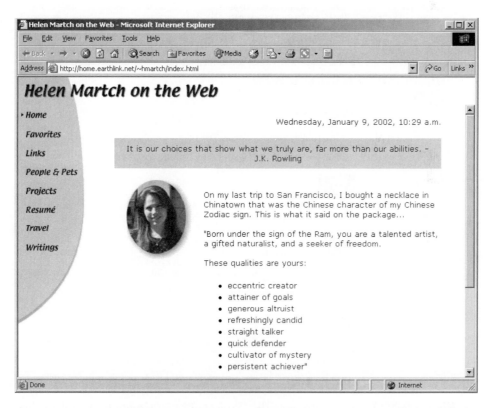

Figure 6–3 A vertical bar in a global navigation system. Courtesy of Helen L. Martch.

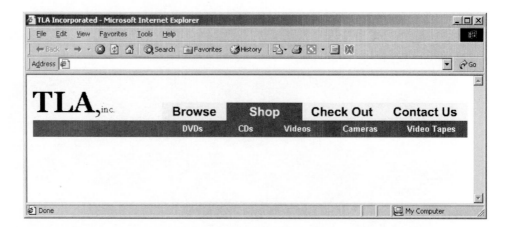

Figure 6–4   Using a secondary navigation bar.

serve as a sign that reads, "You are here." Many large sites, such as Yahoo, C|net, and Amazon, use breadcrumbs. Figure 6–5 has a breadcrumbs trail of "Projects List > Computer Graphics," indicating that the user has clicked on "Projects" and then on "Computer Graphics." In addition to the breadcrumbs, this site adds an arrow to the left of the entry in the main navigation bar to mark the current second-level page.

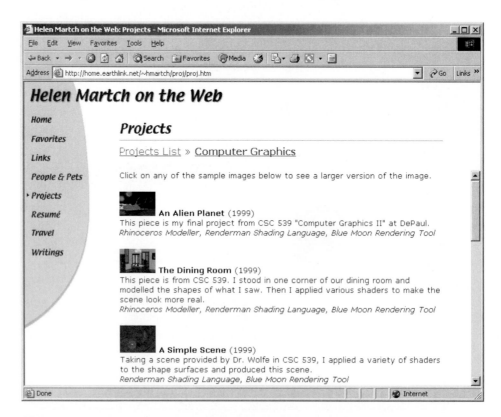

Figure 6–5   Breadcrumbs: note the "Projects List > Computer Graphics" line. Courtesy of Helen L. Martch.

For any type of navigation bar, it's important to have consistency in placement across pages on the site. When comparing Figure 6–5 with Figure 6–3, notice that the primary navigation bar is in the same place on both pages.

Sites having even greater complexity can require an additional navigational system. These sites are so large that they contain *subsites* [Nielsen 1996a]. A subsite is a collection of pages within a website that can share a common navigation system, one perhaps different in style from that of the website as a whole. A *local navigation system* helps users with accessing a subsite and complements the site's global navigation.

Both the Health and Beauty (see Figure 6–6) and the Books (Figure 6–7) subsites of amazon.com have local and global navigation. On both subsites, the top horizontal bar affords global navigation. The Health and Beauty subsite offers local navigation by way of a second horizontal bar plus a vertical column on the left. In contrast, on the Books page, a single column affords subsite navigation. Links in local navigation give access to the subsite, whereas the global navigation offers links to Welcome, Store Directory, the shopping cart, My Account, and Help.

Sometimes, a hierarchical system simply can't accommodate all of the relationships among the content items on a site. To rectify this problem, you can insert *ad hoc* links once the content is basically in place. Used as an adjective, "ad hoc" means "created for one specific purpose." Ad-hoc navigation systems are additional links that can help make the connections required by the content's relationships. As Rosenfeld notes, these are more

Figure 6–6 Screen shot of a portion of Amazon.com's Health and Beauty subsite, Drugstore.com. Copyright © 1999–2002 drugstore.com, inc. All rights reserved.

Figure 6–7 The Books subsite of Amazon.com. © 2001 Amazon.com, Inc. All Rights Reserved.

editorial than architectural [Rosenfeld 1998]. An editor or content specialist could decide to add these, perhaps after user testing. Usually, this involves converting words or phrases into embedded hyperlinks. Rosenfeld cautions that, if a link is buried in the middle of a paragraph, it could get lost. Web users often scan a page rapidly instead of reading it [Nielsen 1997], so they might miss it. If you are going to use embedded links, consider either making them into a bulleted list or placing them at the beginning or the end of a paragraph. Figure 6–8 shows an example that uses ad-hoc links effectively.

The last type of system, the *database-driven navigational system,* implements a database organizational structure. It rarely appears as the only navigational system on a website, but it's often used as a facility ancillary to the main navigational system. Even search-engine sites have additional navigation to supplement a purely database-driven system. As Figure 6–9 demonstrates, the search engine site `www.google.com` prominently features a search box, but it also offers a link to a hierarchical system that organizes content by topics and a link to a large number of discussion groups.

6.2.2 Building Context

Building context means helping users understand where they are and where they are going while visiting a website. Careful use of appropriate *navigational elements* helps build context. Navigational elements are visual organizations of text and graphics that display a user's options and current position in a site. The most common of these are navigation bars and menus.

Figure 6–8 Ad-hoc links. Home page of `www.useit.com`.

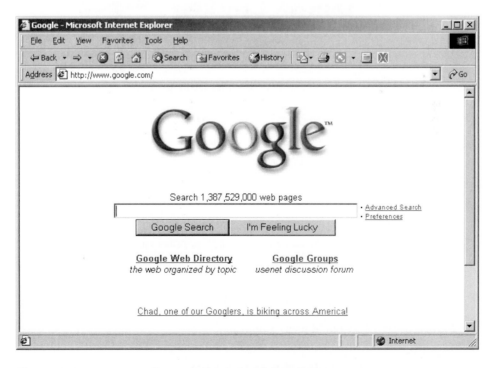

Figure 6–9 `www.google.com`. Courtesy of Google Inc.

Navigation Bars

Navigation bars are effective for implementing both global and local navigation systems. Stripped to its essence, a navigation bar is a collection of links that are grouped together on a page. In terms of implementation, there are two basic types of navigation bars: text based and graphical. Figure 6–10 shows a text-based navigation bar along the left side and another running along the bottom of the screen. Figure 6–6 and Figure 6–7 also show examples of graphical navigation bars.

Graphical navigation bars have enormous appeal, as you can see in Figure 6–11. They also have the ability to display context clearly, as is demonstrated in Figure 6–12. When looking at this image, why can you tell at a glance that you are in the Search pages of this website?

One problem, though, is that graphical navigation bars take longer to download than text. If the same global navigation bar appears throughout the site, a delay will occur only once because browsers cache the images. Also, graphical navigation bars pose a problem for people with limited-bandwidth connections who have opted to turn off image loading. For this reason, every image in the navigation bar should have an appropriately named ALT attribute.[1] One last drawback to a graphical navigation bar is the maintenance cost. It is much easier to add a link to a text-based navigation bar than it is to modify the images of a

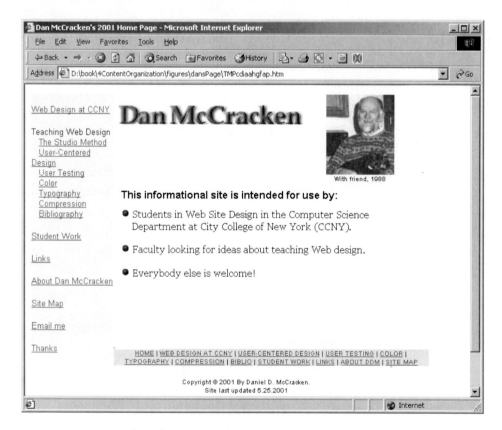

Figure 6–10 Text-based navigation bars.

---

[1] For more information about HTML markup, see the Appendix.

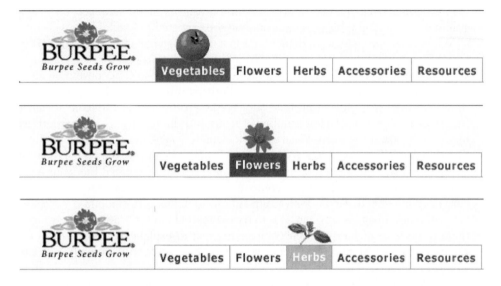

Figure 6–11   The appeal of graphical navigation bars, from www.burpee.com. Courtesy of W. Atlee Burpee & Co.

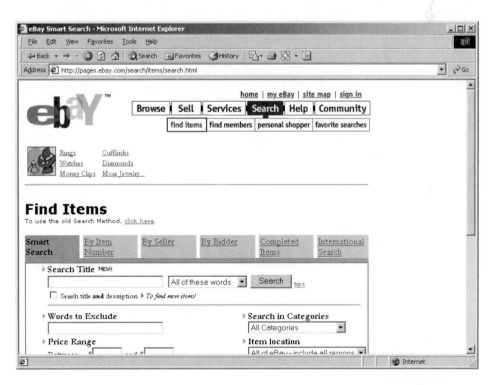

Figure 6–12   Building context with navigation bars. These materials have been reproduced by permission of eBay Inc. COPYRIGHT © EBAY INC. ALL RIGHTS RESERVED

graphical one. What you choose will depend on your intended audience, on your access to graphics tools and graphic designers, and on the expected fluidity of your website.

When considering icons to depict links in a navigation bar, always include text to explain them. Strange as it might seem, it is extremely difficult to represent concepts pictorially in a way that will be universally understood. In 1994, Jakob Nielsen reported on an icon intuitiveness test that he conducted for Sun Microsystems [Nielsen 1994]. He showed users some icons designed for an intranet site. He asked them what the icons meant to them. Figure 6–13 shows a selected number of icons and the test users' interpretations. Take a moment to look at the icons. What do they mean to you? Does your reaction match that of the test users? If you want to see the intended meanings, turn to the end of the chapter and examine Figure 6–21. Keep in mind that skilled designers created the icons and that the test users were all from the same company and had very similar user profiles. If it is this hard to create effective icons for a group as homogeneous as the employees of a single high-tech company, imagine how hard it is to try to create them for a larger user group. The best thing to do is to include some accompanying text to explain the icon. As you can see in Figure 6–14, the MetaDesign site at `www.metadesign.com` uses icons, but labels each icon with supporting text.

Deciding on the labels in a navigation bar presents challenges in communicating effectively. *Labels* are words presented as links in a navigation bar and represent paths to subsets of information held in the site. In face-to-face conversation, people use labels all the time as a faster way to exchange information, gossip, and so on. For example, people familiar with the goals of HCI might use the word *usable* as a label for anything that is "easy to learn, easy to navigate, and easy to use." People new to HCI might have trouble decoding this term completely and look at you blankly when you use it. Try going into an ice-cream shop in the Midwest and ask for a "frappe" or "cabinet," which are perfectly reasonable terms for a milk shake in New England. In conversation, you have the opportunity to notice a blank look and to explain the label that's causing problems. This is a luxury that Web developers don't have.

To create an effective set of labels, begin by looking at the results from your card-sorting interviews. They are your best resource. During the interview process, each participant gave names to each pile of cards. Any patterns or trends you find in the names will be useful in creating navigation labels.

Also, take note of current labeling systems on the Web. There are already some standard meanings for certain labels. Some examples of these conventions appear in Figure 6–15.

Figure 6–13 User interpretations for three icons. Intended meanings are shown in Figure 6–21.

Figure 6–14   Always support icons with text. Courtesy of MetaDesign.

Label	Meaning
Home	The main entry point of a website, generally containing the top-level links to the site.
Search	Find related pages by supplying a word or a phrase.
About Us	Information about the company that created the site. Includes a mailing address.
Shop	Browse for merchandise.
Check Out	Supply shipping and billing information, complete transaction.
Contact Us	Initiate an interactive dialog with a customer representative, either via email or telephone.

Figure 6–15   Conventional meanings for a selected set of labels.

Take advantage of these conventions. It does not make sense to ignore these any more than it would make sense for a single state in the United States to change the placement of Interstate road signs. Conventions help a user to navigate a site quickly.

Once you decide on a set of labels, use them consistently throughout your site. When each of two links takes you to the same page, it is not good to call the link "Continue" on one page and "Check Out" on another.

Consistency is key in choosing labels for navigation and in placing navigation bars on each page. With the possible exception of the home page, navigation bars should appear in the same place on each page. Examine clearinghouse.net, amazon.com, or ebay.com. You will see that navigation bars appear in a consistent location, have a consistent appearance, and use a consistent labeling system, no matter where you are in the site's information architecture.

There are some indications that some conventions for placing navigation elements are emerging. A recent study asked inexperienced and experienced Web users about where they expected to find various navigational elements on a Web page [Bernard 2001]. The vast majority of both types of users expected the "home" link to be in the upper left corner or at the bottom center of the page. They also expected the links that are internal to a site to be on the left side.

Menus

Menus present a list of possible links in the form of a drop-down list or a scrollable list. Users can choose the next page they visit by selecting one of the items in the menu. As navigation elements, menus help reduce the number of clicks required to reach a desired page. They can pack a large number of options onto a single page. The menus at `www.cdw.com` allow a user to link directly to a third-level page with a single click. (See Figure 6–16.) Reducing the number of clicks and subsequent page downloads is a big advantage, but some experts caution that menus carry two disadvantages. With menus, not all options are visible at any one time. Further, the user must act—by moving the cursor over an item to activate a list—before seeing the menu. Some users might not know to do that.

Menus can provide an efficient navigation alternative. When creating menus, take time to select the labels for the menu items, just as you would for a navigation bar. Also, keep in mind the organizational scheme you've chosen for the site.

Other navigational elements

Frames and site maps are also types of navigational elements. These are used less often than navigation bars and menus, but they are presented here for completeness.

Figure 6–16   Menus pack lots of options onto a single page: `www.cdw.com`.
Courtesy of CDW.

A *frame* is a scrollable pane that continuously occupies the same position in the browser window while a user navigates the site. Typically, the top-level links of a site appear in a frame on the left side of the window while the content pages appear on the right. At first glance, they seem to offer some advantages, especially from the developer's perspective. They separate navigation from content, thus freeing HTML developers from the necessity of including the code for any global navigation bars in every page of the site.

However, several drawbacks overshadow this advantage. Frames hog screen real estate. Printing them is a problem. If a user attempts to print a page, the frame normally won't appear on the paper copy. It can be difficult to bookmark the specific content page; the browser will instead save a link to the top-level page.

For these reasons, few commercial sites use frames today. See [Nielsen 1996b] for more on this topic. With the advent of sophisticated Web authoring tools, it is possible to carry out site-wide updates automatically when a global navigation bar needs to be changed. The Appendix shows how to accomplish this goal with Cascading Style Sheets.

The last type of navigational element is a *site map*. A site map is a graphical representation of a site's information architecture. See Figure 6–17. Some site maps are interactive

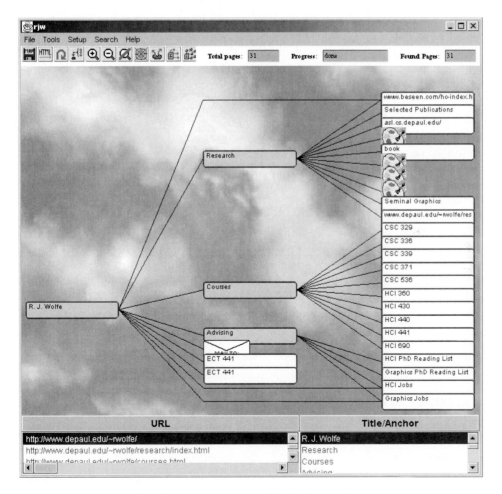

Figure 6–17   Example of a site map. Created with the Ptolomaeus site-mapping software.

image maps, allowing a user to access regions of the site by clicking on various areas on the map. There are many novel graphical representations for site maps [Kahn 2001], but the authors have noticed a trend away from graphical site maps, which can be slow to download. The trend is to a text-based table of contents that serves the same purpose.

6.2.3 Built-In Browser Services

The previous sections talked about building context by using navigation elements within a Web page. Web browsers themselves provide additional ways of building context to help users know where they are in a site. The Back and Forward buttons on a browser enable users to go backward and forward through visited pages. The History menu gives users direct access to any previously visited page; the Address textbox allows a user to jump directly to any page by typing in a URL. Browsers offer another useful context-building service in hypertext links. The links are color coded to indicate whether they have already been visited.

Current browsers are the product of a great deal of research and testing, and it doesn't make sense to override their features. In particular, using the color blue for an unvisited link and purple for a visited one has become accepted convention [Nielsen 1999]. Don't change these for aesthetic reasons.

After considering site-wide navigation issues, which include choosing navigation elements that build content and lend support to the navigation system, it is time to consider navigation issues that pertain to individual pages. The next section focuses on this area, with a special emphasis on forms.

6.3 Effective Navigation at the Page Level

The good news is that, if you have chosen an appropriate sitewide navigation system and consistently applied it to individual pages, then, for most content pages, you have already completed the page-level navigation. However, in the case of forms, there are several additional guidelines to keep in mind.

Forms can have various textfields, checkboxes, radio buttons, and menus, but they all have a "submit" button that sends a user's information to a server for processing. Be sure that the submit button appears at the bottom of the form, not higher up on the page.

Make the lengths of textfields appropriate to the foreseen size of the user information, as is demonstrated in the right side of Figure 6–18. Be careful that no textfield forces the user to scroll horizontally, because users don't like it. In the year 2004, you can safely assume that most of your audience has a screen that's at least 800×600 pixels [Bailey 2001]. Format your Web pages so that they will fit this size. If you need more space than a single-line textfield will allow, consider using a multiline textfield instead.

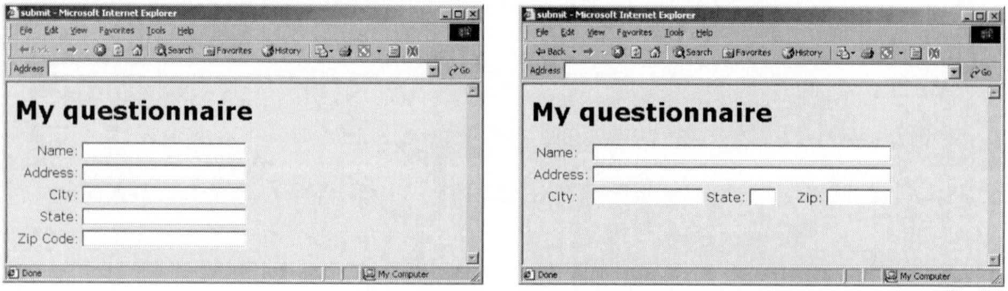

Figure 6–18   Length of textfields should conform to size of user input.

Figure 6–19 Be consistent with label placement.

Be consistent with the placement of labels. Forcing a user to decide which button is associated with a desired label does nothing except waste the user's time and increase input errors. The page on the left of Figure 6–19 shows an inconsistency in label placement. In the first set of radio buttons, the labels appear on the right; in the second set of buttons, the labels appear on the left. The page on the right of Figure 6–19 demonstrates consistency in label placement.

If your form has required fields, mark them clearly. One way to do this is to add a sentence at the top of the form that reads, "Required fields are marked with an asterisk (*)" and include an asterisk in the label of each required field. Another way to do this is to add the label "Required" to each required field.

When errors do occur, the best practice is to present the form to the user again, with all of the correct input already in place, together with a message explaining which fields still need correct input. For long forms, consider using the technique demonstrated in Figure 6–20. A user can click on the "Go to the next error" link to find the field that caused the problem. A brief explanation appears next to the field, plus a link to the next error.

If you are writing the data-validation routines for a form, check the data for the entire form, so that your response will inform users of as many errors as possible. One of the authors recently encountered an e-commerce site that did not indicate the required fields and would inform the user only of the *first* error encountered in the input. Three tries later, the author managed to complete the transaction. Your users deserve better.

6.4 Summary

Effective navigation results from a combination of good content organization and good visual organization. When planning your navigation, review the organizational scheme and organizational structure that you determined by carrying out interviews with your users. Examine the results of card-sorting sessions to find appropriate labels for the links you will create.

By using the four principles you learned in Chapter 5, you can create visual organization that reinforces the content organization and promotes communication. When planning site-wide navigation, consider what combination of navigation bars and menus will most clearly build context for users, who want to know where they are in your site's information architecture. Avoid using frames. A site map could be an appropriate supplement to your main navigational system, especially if the site is large.

Once you determine your site-wide organization and apply it to individual pages in a consistent manner, then you're pretty much set at the page level, with the exception of

Your form could not be processed. Please fix the errors indicated to the right of the field.

go to first error

Before you enter any information, please review the entire online form to get an overview of its fields and requirements.

Applications must be received by: **17 March**

Entries marked with a ▪ must be filled in.

Personal Information

(Contact information must be valid through 15 May.)

(Include all country, city, and area codes.)

First Name	▪	Rosalee
Last Name	▪	Wolfe
City	▪	Chicago
State/Province		Illinois ▾ (US/Canada only)
Country	▪	United States ▾
Postal Code	▪	60604
Daytime Telephone	▪	+1 312 362 6248
Home Telephone	▪	required Next Error
Fax		+1 312 362 6116
Email	▪	wolfe@cs.depaul.edu
		○ Male ○ Female required Next Error

School Information

Institution Name	▪	required Next Error

Figure 6–20   Error feedback in long forms. Courtesy of the Association for Computing Machinery.

forms. Design forms to minimize the number of possible errors. For example, when soliciting a mailing address, consider using a menu instead of a textbox for such items as the state. It is always better to prevent errors than to have to send an error message. If errors do occur in user input, the response should contain information about as many errors as possible. Include an explanation of the error. If the form is long, consider using links to guide the user to each field that caused problems.

Once you've decided on your navigation system, you are ready to begin prototyping. Chapter 7 covers various aspects of prototyping and focuses on the fastest, cheapest, easiest method for prototype creation.

To close, here (in Figure 6–21) are the intended meanings for the icons shown in Figure 6–13.

	*Intended Meaning:* Geographic view of the company (branch offices in different locations).
	*Intended Meaning:* Benefits.
	*Intended Meaning:* Public relations (TV with commercial).

Figure 6–21   Intended meaning for the icons shown in Figure 6–13.

Review Questions and Exercises

1. What two types of organization are essential to effective Web navigation?
2. What is the main difference between site-level and page-level navigation?
3. What is a navigation system?
4. What are the three major types of navigation systems? Explain the differences among them.
5. What is a navigation bar?
6. What is a global navigation system? In what circumstances will a global navigation system be sufficient?
7. What is meant by a second-level page? A third-level page?
8. What are breadcrumbs? What purpose do they serve? When are they useful?
9. What is a subsite? How does a local navigation system serve a subsite?
10. What are ad-hoc links? What do they add to a navigational system? Are there any special considerations you should keep in mind when using them?
11. What is the purpose of building context?
12. What is a navigational element? List three types.
13. Compare the advantages and disadvantages of graphical navigation and text bars.
14. What is the danger of using an icon without supporting text?
15. What is the usefulness of conventions for Web users?
16. What are labels? What is the best resource for developing an effective set of labels? What second resource can be helpful?
17. Refer to Figure 6–4, which is a navigation system. What links are in the top-level navigation bar? How do you know that this is the top-level navigation bar and that the links you listed are part of it? Explain in terms of proximity, alignment, consistency, and contrast.
18. What is a menu? How does it differ in appearance from a navigation bar?
19. Explain the advantages and disadvantages of menus.
20. Why should you avoid using frames?

21. Print a screen dump of your favorite Web browser. With a pencil, label the navigational aids that help build context for a user.

22. Why is it important to indicate which fields in a form are required?

23. Why is it important for the server software to scan all of the input for errors before sending a message to the user?

24. Here are the results from a series of card-sorting sessions. The first item in each group is the name that users gave to the group. The remaining items represent content pages. A hierarchical navigation system is appropriate for this information. Sketch a global navigation system that has two levels of horizontal navigation bars. You need not sketch the top-level navigation bar more than once, but your sketch should give an indication of what each secondary navigation bar will contain.

Home	Shop	Your Account	Customer Service
What's new?	VCRs	My Wish List	How to ...
Special Sales	DVD players	View Account	Return Policy
Store Locations	CD players	Order Status	Call us
About Us	DVD writers	Open an Account	Email us

25. Using the same card-sort information given in question 24, create a single vertical navigation bar with links corresponding to the individual items.

    a. All of the links are visible; do the group names nonetheless need to be links? Why or why not?

    b. Use one or more of the four visual-organization principles to set off the groups. Explain the principles you used and how you used them.

    c. How did you choose to distinguish the group name from the items within the group? Explain in terms of one or more of the four visual-organization principles.

Project Activities

26. If you are working on a website for a client, now is the time to consider navigation.

    a. What organizational scheme and organizational structure will you use? Justify your answer in terms of your card-sorting interviews. Include a copy of your card-sorting results with your answer.

    b. For the organizational structure you chose in question (a), choose a navigational system. Justify your answer.

    c. Create a sketch of the navigation bar(s) you envision for the home page. Show the relationship between the items in the navigation bars and the results of the card-sorting sessions you conducted.

    d. Create a sketch of the navigation system that you envision on the second-level pages. Explain how it is consistent with the navigation bar(s) on the home page. Also, explain how it accommodates the results of the card-sorting sessions you conducted.

References

[Bailey 2001] Bob Bailey. "Screen Resolution: When is it time to change?" *User Interface Design Update Newsletter.* March 2001.
`http://www.humanfactors.com/library/mar01.asp`

[Bernard 2000] Michael L. Bernard. "Examining User Expectations of the Location of Web Objects," *Internetworking* **3** (3). December 2000.
`http://www.internettg.org/newsletter/dec00/contents.html`

[Kahn 2001] Paul Kahn and Krzysztof Lenk. *Mapping Web sites*. Hove, East Sussex: Rotovision, 2001.

[Nielsen 1994] Jakob Nielsen and Darrell Sano. SunWeb: User interface design for Sun Microsystem's internal web. WWW2 94: Second International World Wide Web Conference. Chicago, Illinois; October 17–20, 1994. `http://useit.com/papers/sunweb/`

[Nielsen 1996a] Jakob Nielsen. "The Rise of the Sub-Site," *AlertBox.* September 1996.
`http://www.useit.com/alertbox/9609.html`

[Nielsen 1996b] Jakob Nielsen. "Why Frames Suck (Most of the Time)," *AlertBox.* December 1996. `http://www.useit.com/alertbox/9612.html`

[Nielsen 1999] Jakob Nielsen. "When Bad Design Elements Become the Standard," *AlertBox.* November 14, 1999. `http://www.useit.com/alertbox/991114.html`

[Nielsen 1997] Jakob Nielsen. "How Users Read on the Web," *AlertBox.* October 1, 1997.
`http://www.useit.com/alertbox/9710a.html`

[Rosenfeld 1998] Louis Rosenfeld and Peter Morville. *Information Architecture for the World Wide Web*. Sebastopol, California: O'Reilly, 1998.

[Winston 1954] *The Winston Dictionary: 3000 Illustrations and an Atlas of the World*. Philadelphia: The John C. Winston Company, 1954. p. 650.

7

Prototyping

7.1 Introduction

By this time, you have not only completed your user and task analysis, but also conducted additional interviews to understand how people fitting your user profile organize information mentally. You've thought about how you can use visual organization to support the content organization of your site, and you have considered what navigation strategies will be most effective. Now it's time to prototype. Prototyping creates a model, but not necessarily an implementation, of the intended website.

The goal of prototyping is to provide a way to observe aspects of the website to evaluate design ideas and to consider alternatives before committing to an implementation. The problem with implementation is that it requires a commitment to a design with no opportunity to see it, use it, or test it. Once the implementation is available, there are no resources left to make significant changes. In traditional development methodologies, developers get one shot at getting it right. According to Jared Spool [Spool 1998a], " 'Getting it right the first time' is a myth."

Prototyping solves this problem. Prototyping is a technique that supports successive refinements and is based on user feedback. Depending on the specifics of the approach, it is possible to complete a refinement cycle within a period of hours, not the weeks or months needed for an implementation.

Goals of this Chapter

In this chapter, you will learn

- the basic terminology of prototyping
- the benefits of prototyping
- the advantages of low-fidelity vs. high-fidelity prototyping
- the techniques of building a paper prototype.

7.2 Why Prototype?

In traditional software development methodology, you can't evaluate a design until it's implemented; after it's implemented, however, changes are difficult, if not impossible, to make. At the beginning, there is nothing to test, so developers begin an implementation. Implementation is expensive and time-consuming, which means that a lot of resources are committed to design choices that haven't been evaluated.

Prototyping breaks this *implementation paradox*. It fosters the opportunity to evaluate designs very early and to improve the usability of a website.

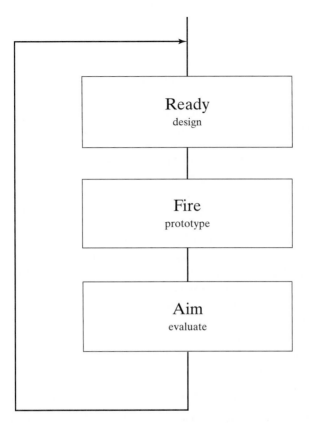

Figure 7–1   Artillery and user-centered development.

Prototyping is a technique, not a specific tool. In fact, this technique works very well without using a computer. It is helpful in fostering communication among various members of a development team, each of whom brings different skills to the table. Computer scientists often do not fully comprehend the need for user-centered design, but HCI practitioners, who do understand user-centered design, sometimes do not appreciate the technical limitations of the implementation environment. Prototyping can help the two groups work together to create a website that not only is produced on time and within budget, but also provides convenience and a pleasant user experience to people who visit the site.

Hix says that prototyping in user-centered methodology is similar to the artillery method of Ready–Fire–Aim [Hix 1993]. Gunners fire a first shot to provide a reference point. They then make adjustments so that the next shot lands closer to the target. This is similar to the design–prototype–evaluate cycle of user-centered development. (See Figure 7–1.) The firing of the shot corresponds to the prototyping step.

7.3 Basic Terminology

To get a better understanding of the types of prototypes, it's useful to review the stages of development that occur after user and task analysis, as a website progresses from design to final product:

- Design.
- One or more prototypes, each followed by testing and redesign.

- Implementation.
- Site goes live.

If a prototype becomes so nearly complete as to constitute an implementation, then it's called an *evolutionary* prototype. On the other hand, developers can start the implementation from scratch and instead use the prototype only as a specification. The actual prototype is not part of the implementation. This is a *revolutionary* or *throwaway* prototype. Developers still use the prototype to guide their implementation, but the prototype itself is discarded.

The following terms come from the completeness of functionality and range of features that a prototype offers. A *horizontal* prototype has little depth of functionality (or no functionality) but is broad in terms of the number of features it presents. Horizontal prototypes are useful for presenting an overview or the "big picture" perspective of a site's "look." (See Figure 7–2.)

A *vertical* prototype presents only a limited number of features, but the functionality of those features is fully developed. On a website, this could involve prototyping one set of links leading from the home page to a terminal page. It could instead mean prototyping the transaction page, but not completing the "search this site" function. (See Figure 7–3.)

A *global* prototype has breadth and depth. It is a prototype of the entire site, and gives users an opportunity to get a good appreciation of the look and feel of the entire site.

A *local* prototype, also called a *scenario*, models a very small part of a site. It's usually a standalone model that's not connected with the rest of the pages and typically has a very short life span. Spool recommends using a local prototype as a means to resolve "opinion wars" [Spool 1998a]. Hix calls it the "five-minute rule" [Hix 1994]. Sometimes, two parties on a project team will get involved in a heated debate about which design alternative to choose, but neither side has much to back its case other than force of opinion. If the exchange goes on longer than five minutes, Hix advises creating local prototypes to test the alternatives.

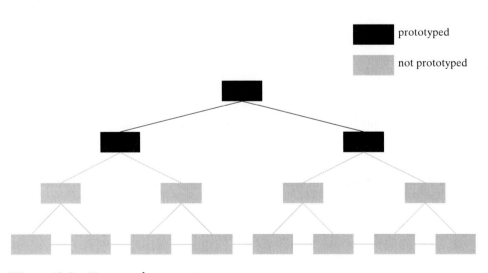

Figure 7–2   Horizontal prototyping.

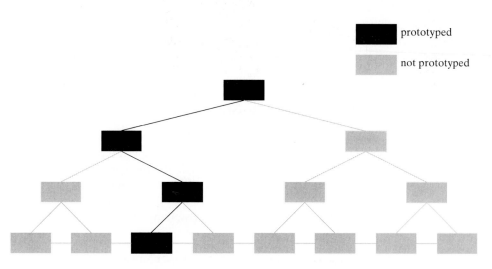

Figure 7–3   Vertical prototyping.

7.4 Benefits of Prototyping

In a traditional software-development methodology, there is only one chance to create the interface. In contrast, the user-centered approach is highly iterative and features successive refinements to a prototype before commitment to an implementation. This improves the chances of creating a usable product. Studies as far back as 1984 found that developing interactive products with the prototyping approach resulted in fewer time pressures on the development team [Boehm 1984] and higher user satisfaction and acceptance [Alavi 1984]. Part of the reason is that users can be very good at criticizing an existing system, but they are not always good in anticipating or describing future needs. After working with a first version, users sometimes change their opinion about how they want to interact with the product [Wasserman 1985].

This holds true for Web development as well. Prototyping is cost effective and works well, even for developing sites at start-up companies, where the product manager is also the user interface designer [Hansen 1997].

Similarly, development teams are not good at foreseeing every need, even after user and task analysis. As Jared Spool notes [Spool 1998a],

> The vast majority of usability problems come from a single cause: the development team was lacking a key piece of information. If team members had known it earlier, they would have designed to accommodate it and the usability problem would never have occurred.

Implementation is so expensive that in practice it's done only once. Prototyping has the advantage of resolving usability problems before implementation begins.

7.5 Disadvantages

Prototyping and user-centered development methodology are still not practiced in all work settings, so it might take some effort to persuade the stakeholders to give it a try. The good news is that HCI practitioners report that prototyping is becoming more prevalent [Baumer 1996].

Another problem can occur if the prototype is a *high fidelity* prototype, which closely resembles the final product. High-fidelity prototypes create the danger of raising false expectations in management. Management might perceive the prototype as being a fully implemented prototype that's ready to ship when, in fact, it is still entirely lacking functionality.

7.6 Low-fidelity and Other Prototyping

Low-fidelity prototyping can solve this problem. *Low-fidelity* prototypes do not resemble the final product. This section describes the fastest, cheapest, easiest tool for low-fidelity prototyping: paper. Paper prototypes don't resemble the final product, because they aren't even displayed on a computer, so management will not get any silly notions about moving up the delivery date.

You can use a paper prototype to solicit user reactions to an interface. In overview, this procedure includes the following steps:

- A test team constructs a paper prototype. "Paper" means ordinary paper, glue, colored markers, acetate, and so on. This is *not* done on a real computer.
- To test it with a user, one team member "plays computer," rearranging the interface in response to the user's actions. This will be discussed in detail in Chapter 8.
- Another member takes careful notes.
- At the end of the testing sessions, the team distills the notes to see what aspects need to be changed.

7.6.1 Paper-Prototype Advantages

It is quite natural to ask, "Why go to all that trouble with paper, glue, and scissors when I could make a prototype by using a computer?" The advantage of a paper prototype is that it can demonstrate behavior and reveal problems very early in the design cycle, when changes are cheapest. In other words, you can test just the design, as distinguished from testing a design *and an implementation*. The approach thus holds the potential for a huge increase in interface quality at very low cost. Changes are cheap when nothing has been implemented. In short, a paper prototype has the advantages that:

- It is easy to build.
- It is not necessary to wait for the developers to create a (computer-based) prototype.
- It is fast to change. Erasing one link name and writing in another is quicker than rewriting the website code.
- It maximizes the number of times the design is refined before anything is committed to implementation.
- The lack of polish does not affect user opinion of the prototype [Wiklund 1992].

The alternative to a paper prototype is a high-fidelity prototype, otherwise known as a partial implementation. This strategy seems quite attractive on the surface but causes many problems.

7.6.2 Problems with High-Fidelity Prototypes

The urge to rush ahead to a computer implementation of a prototype is enticing, but using a high-fidelity prototype risks the following pitfalls:

Correctly functioning software takes too long to build. By the time there is anything that can be used for testing the design, much of the project's development budget has already been spent.

- Changes take too long.
- One bug can destroy a user test.

As mentioned earlier, a software prototype creates unrealistic expectations in management. If the interface is appealing and makes the proper screen transitions in response to user input, some people will think that completing it will be simple and quick even though none of the functionality has yet been implemented.

When testing a high-fidelity prototype, users tend to comment on such surface issues as choice of font or color. These are referred to as "fit and finish" issues and have little effect on the overall usability of a website [Spool 1998b]. When viewing a paper prototype, which has no pretensions of resembling the final project, users comment on deeper, more important issues, such as proper use of terminology and mismatches between the content organization and the user's mental model.

Once there is an implementation, the developers have an investment in it, including time, money, lost sleep, and pride of authorship. It is only human nature in them to resist making changes that in their opinion are not worth the additional effort—at a time when they are still tired from completing the existing version.

7.6.3 Disadvantages of Low-Fidelity Prototypes

There are a few disadvantages to low-fidelity prototypes. If your low-fidelity prototype is made from paper, you might need to create some convention for indicating that an item is "clickable," because users will not be able to watch the cursor change as it passes over a link. Using a yellow marker to highlight the links works very nicely. You could also underline the hyperlink text with a pencil.

A second disadvantage of low-fidelity prototypes is that they do not "show" well to management, because they do not have a polished look to them. This is one of the reasons why it's worth spending some time promoting the benefits of prototyping to the stakeholders in the project.

A third disadvantage is that low-fidelity prototypes do not simulate response time accurately. A human computer certainly has a slower response time to a mouse click than does an electronic computer; on the other hand, a human computer can swap paper Web pages faster than Web pages can download if the user has a slow connection.

7.7 Building a Paper Prototype

Creating a paper prototype is decidedly low tech and consists of three steps. The first is to assemble a kit. A kit contains the items you will need when constructing paper prototypes. The following materials are useful:

- White, unlined heavy paper or card stock. A sheet measuring 11 × 14 inches is a good size.
- Regular 8.5 × 11 unlined paper.
- 5 × 8 index cards. Lined is slightly preferable, because they are for taking notes.
- Adhesives: rubber cement, Scotch® tape, glue sticks. Soft adhesive like that on the back of a sticky label is now available in bottles and as glue sticks.
- Markers of various colors.

- Sticky note pads, in various colors and sizes.
- Acetate sheets. No need to get more than a couple of sheets; they are slightly expensive and can be reused.
- Scissors.

The second step is to set a deadline and stick to it. Once a team starts building a prototype, there is a terrific temptation to keep improving it. Team members can argue for inordinate amounts of time over how many buttons there should be, where to put them, what text labels to use, and on and on. However, there is no way of knowing what is usable until a prototype has been presented to users. A deadline adds focus to the process and forces prioritization.

The third step is to construct the prototype. Here are some considerations to keep in mind:

- Make a generic template in the shape of a browser window. Use your heaviest stock for this.
- Make a screen dump of your favorite browser and use a paint program cut out the contents electronically. Print it. Enlarge in a copier if necessary.
- Paste the printout onto the template. (See Figure 7–4.)

Construct a model, not an illustration. The prototype will need to include representations for every element that a user will encounter. Create separate stock for anything that moves, changes appearance, or appears and disappears. This includes drop-down menus, pop-up menus, scrolling lists, highlights, and textboxes. To create a scrolling page, tape together as many sheets as it takes to create the entire page. Cut slots in the cardboard frame to accommodate the page. To simulate typing keyboard text, you can use a sheet of acetate and a felt-tip pen. Figure 7–5 shows some sample items you might need to make, including a menu bar, a scrollbar, and its indicator. You can place these items on the screen dump of the browser, as you can see in Figure 7–6.

Low-fidelity means low-tech. The first sketch should be done completely by hand; use photocopies to save time and effort. Do not spend much time on the "prettiness." You'll be doing it over. As long as it's legible, it will be fine for testing.

Figure 7–4　A generic template for paper prototyping, created from a screen dump of a browser.

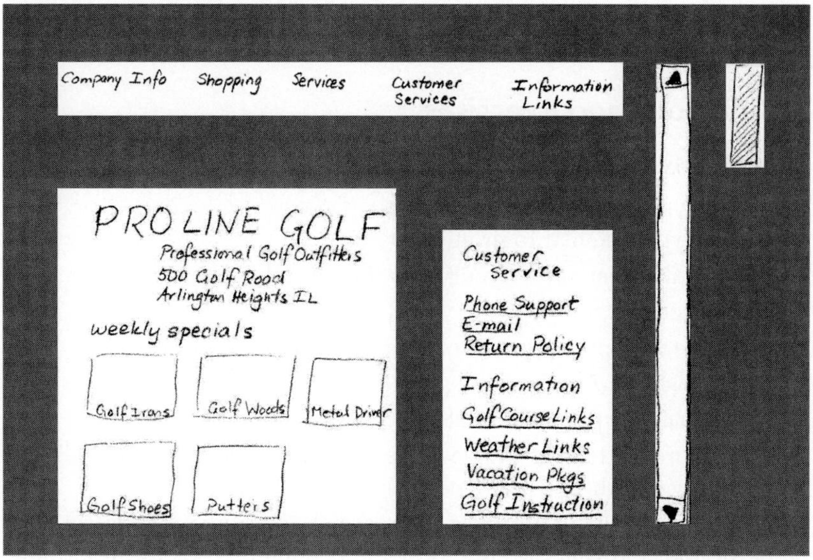

Figure 7–5 Clockwise, from top: a menu bar, a scrollbar indicator, a scrollbar, a secondary menu, and opening contents. After Kirsten Pielstrom.

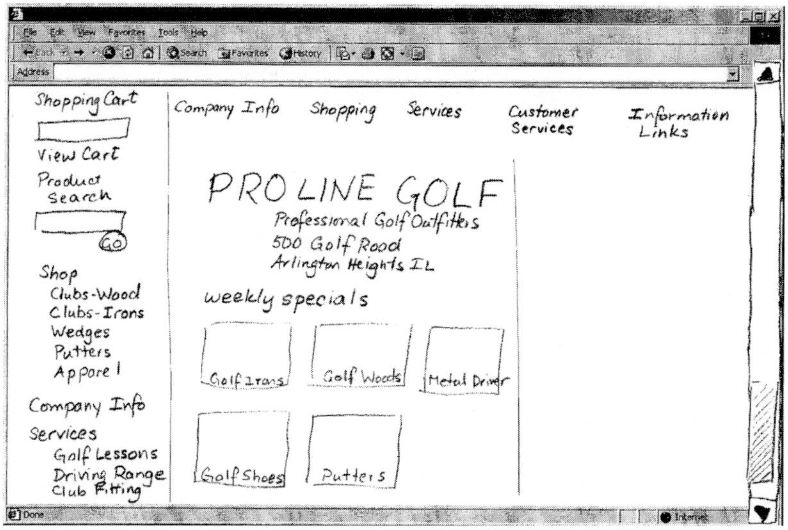

Figure 7–6 A template with pieces placed on top. After Kirsten Pielstrom.

7.8 What's next?

You don't have to prototype every single page in your intended website. Which pages you choose to make will depend on the types of testing you want to carry out. Consult your usability specifications. What measures are important? What parts of the website are related to each measure?

Once you've created a prototype, the next step is to test it with users. Turn to Chapter 8 to see how it's done.

Review Questions and Exercises

1. What is the goal of prototyping a website?
2. What is the implementation paradox?
3. How is prototyping similar to firing artillery?
4. What is an evolutionary prototype? How does it differ from a throwaway prototype?
5. What is a horizontal prototype?
6. How does a vertical prototype differ from a horizontal prototype?
7. What is a global prototype?
8. What is the main purpose of a local prototype?
9. Suppose the project team prototypes the home page and the first-level pages. What type of prototype is this?
10. Suppose the members of a project team sketch the home page and a template for each of the four levels in the site. They then create prototypes for a single page on each level, and each page is reachable from the prototyped page one level above it. What type of prototype is this?
11. The project team has created a single search page for use with a future database engine still under development. It has several fields for specifying search terms and several options for displaying the results. What type of prototype is it?
12. Is a paper prototype an evolutionary or throwaway prototype?
13. What are some of the benefits of prototyping?
14. Are there any disadvantages to prototyping? If so, what are they?
15. What is the difference between a high-fidelity and a low-fidelity prototype?
16. What advantages does low-fidelity prototyping offer?
17. What problems can occur with high-fidelity prototypes?
18. Are there any disadvantages to low-fidelity prototyping? If so, what are they?

Project Activities

19. If you are working on a website as a project, now is the time to create a paper prototype. You and your team have discussed options for visual organization and navigation. Create a prototype of the home page. You will also want to prototype at least one first-level page. The number of pages that you prototype will depend on the types of testing you will do. Consult your usability specifications. What measures are important? What parts of the website are related to each measure?

References

[Alavi 1984] Maryam Alavi. "An Assessment of the Prototyping Approach to Information Systems Development," *Communications of the ACM.* **27**(6), 556–563.

[Baumer 1996] Dirk Baumer, Walter Bischofberger, Horst Lichter, and Heinz Zullighoven. User Interface Prototyping: Concepts, Tools and Experience. Proceedings of the 18th International Conference on Software Engineering (ICSE '96). March, 1996. 532–541.

[Boehm 1984] B. Boehm, T. Gray, and T. Seewaldt. Prototyping vs. Specification: A Multi-Project Experiment. *IEEE Transactions on Software Engineering.* May 1984. 290–303.

[Hansen 1997] Allison Hansen. Reflections on I/Design: User Interface Design at a Start-up. *Proceedings of ACM CHI 97 Conference on Human Factors in Computing Systems.* 1997, v.1. pp. 487–493.

[Hix 1994] Deborah Hix and H. Rex Hartson. *Developing User Interfaces: Ensuring Usability Through Product and Process.* New York: Wiley, 1993.

[Rettig 1994] Mark Rettig. "Prototyping for Tiny Fingers," *Communications of the Association for Computing Machinery.* 37: 4 (April 1994), 21–27.

[Spool 1998a] Jared Spool, Tara Scanlon, and Carolyn Snyder. Product Usability: Survival Techniques. *Proceedings of ACM CHI 98 Conference on Human Factors in Computing Systems (Summary).* 1998, v.2. pp. 113–114.

[Spool 1998b] Jared Spool, Tara Scanlon, Will Schroeder, Carolyn Snyder, and Terri DeAngelo. *Web Site Usability: A Designer's Guide.* Morgan Kaufman, 1998.

[Wasserman 1985] A. Wasserman and D. Shewmake. The Role of Prototypes in the User Software Engineering Methodology. In *Advances in Human-Computer Interaction,* H. R. Hartson, Ed. Norwood, NJ: Ablex, pp. 191–210.

[Wiklund 1992] Michael Wiklund,Christopher Thurrott, and Joseph S. Dumas. "Does the Fidelity of Software Prototypes Affect the Perception of Usability?" *COMPUTER SYSTEMS: Usability and Rapid Prototyping: Proceedings of the Human Factors Society 36th Annual Meeting.* 1992, v.1. 399–403.

8

Evaluation

8.1 Introduction

By this stage of a project, you have already accomplished a great deal. You have gathered information to perform user and task analyses. You have applied the design techniques of content organization, visual organization, and navigation systems to create an initial prototype. Now it is time to test your prototype with actual users to determine how quickly and easily they can do their work. Involving users is key to knowing exactly how well they will accept the prototype.

Goals of this Chapter

In this chapter, you will learn

- the benefits of testing
- the differences between user-based and expert-based testing
- the proper technique for conducting a user-based test, and
- an effective method of communicating test results.

8.2 Why Test?

In today's ultracompetitive e-commerce arena, a site that is easy to use has a much better chance of surviving than one that doesn't. If your site doesn't sell products, but is an informational site for an organization, it will communicate more effectively with your intended audience if it's usable. Being usable has benefits even for a corporate intranet that employees are required to access in day-to-day operations. If it is usable, employees will need less training and will make fewer service calls to the technical support department.

It is tempting for designers and developers to think, "Why bother testing with users? I'm a user myself; I'll just make pages that make sense to me." Unfortunately, there is a fatal flaw in this reasoning. Designers and developers have spent months studying and thinking about the system, and they can forget to include small details that will cause problems for users. To paraphrase Jared Spool, most usability problems stem from the project team's lack of key information. User testing is an opportunity to check for key pieces of information that had so far gone unnoticed.

Creating a usable website has parallels with programming. Figure 8–1 demonstrates the analogy between program debugging and interface debugging. Yes, it is indeed true that developers plan carefully when designing and coding an

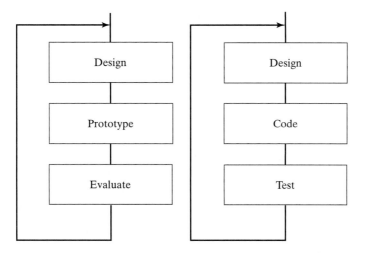

Figure 8–1   Debugging an interface compared to debugging a program.

implementation. However, is this enough guarantee that a large programming project is correct? Do developers apply techniques of program verification to prove correctness without ever actually executing it? No. They test it and debug where necessary.

It is the same with a website. Finding the problems of an interface requires testing. A project team makes successive refinements based on the results. In the user-centered methodology, the cycles of refinement continue until the usability specifications are met.

To review, the cycle of refinement contains the following steps:

- (Re)design a website to meet user needs.
- Build a prototype.
- Test the prototype with real users.

This will uncover mistakes and unforeseen requirements. It will also uncover aspects of the users and the way they do their jobs that the development team did not know. In the ideal situation, this cycle continues until the prototype fulfills the usability specifications. At this point—and only then—it is time to implement.

One characteristic of user-centered development that distinguishes it from more traditional software engineering methodologies is the role and timing of user testing. In traditional methodologies, users play a role at two stages. After an initial consultation during the needs-analysis stage, users are isolated from the process until the beta-test stage, which occurs just before product release. In beta testing, a company distributes the product to a few dozen or a few thousand potential or actual users and asks them to try it out. The company may provide it free or at greatly reduced cost, in exchange for a promise to report all problems. However, at this point, almost the entire development budget has been spent, and there is very little money left for making changes. Only the most critical problems of functionality get fixed. Problems that cause people to lose time in learning the product or in completing tasks are not considered critical and do not get fixed.

In contrast, a user-centered approach performs user testing early and often. With this approach, many usability problems can be caught and remedied before developers write any code or format any Web pages.

8.3 When to Test?

Two terms describe the role and timing of testing within a development process. *Formative evaluation* takes place during the development process; *summative evaluation* occurs after the completion of a project. As Bob Stake puts it [Scriven 1991], "When the cook tastes the soup in the kitchen, that's formative; when the guests taste the soup, that's summative."

It is a truism in software development that changes are cheaper the earlier they are made [Donahue 1999]. Correcting a mistake caught at the design stage, before programming has begun, will cost a small fraction of what it costs to correct a mistake that causes a product recall. Think of the process of building a house. Implementation, be it programming or creating HTML pages, is a lot like pouring concrete. While the house is just a design on paper, it is easy and cheap to make changes. Once the foundation is poured, changing the location of the bathroom becomes impossibly expensive and time-consuming.

The situation is the same with building websites. Changes made before writing any HTML or server-side code will cost little compared with the cost of lost business when people who are trying to buy something through your site cannot find what they want and give up in frustration.

On the other hand, summative evaluation is valuable as a method of assessing a competing product. It is also useful when management has decided that a website needs an overhaul. A first step can be to evaluate the current website to find problems that will be addressed in the new and improved version.

8.4 Expert-based Evaluation

It is reasonable to ask: "Why go to all the trouble and expense of bringing in users? Why not hire an interface-design expert to point out the problems?"

The answer is twofold. First, there is a matter of availability. Few people are qualified expert evaluators. Second, there is a heated controversy about the effectiveness of expert-based evaluation. Several studies [Bailey 1992, Kantner 1997] suggest that experts can sometimes miss the most critical usability problems or mislabel something as a problem that does not actually interfere with a user's completing a task. Further, an expert on interfaces will not necessarily know who your users are or what they are trying to accomplish with your product.

There are, to be sure, people who know a great deal about interface design in general, who might be able to do a useful review based on general principles. But even these experts go to real users to get it right. The November 2000 issue of *Eye for Design* [User 2000], published by the respected firm User Interface Engineering, was devoted to a description of how the company performed user testing to discover some fairly serious problems with one of their websites. If professionals who make a living as usability experts need to go to users to discover the problems with their website, what chance do developers have of trying to find the errors in their own websites?

"Okay," you might be thinking, "I get it—I know that I shouldn't evaluate the usability of my own website. But I'm the *only* person responsible for our company's website—I don't have any help—What am I supposed to do?" We understand. It happens. The great thing about user testing with a paper prototype is that it can help you even when you're the only one in charge. That's what the rest of this chapter is about.

8.5 User Testing with a Paper Prototype

In user-based evaluation, actual users try out the prototype. User testing with a paper prototype is a powerful tool for formative evaluation [Rettig 1994]. In overview, this procedure includes the following steps:

- A test team constructs a paper prototype. "Paper" means ordinary paper, glue, colored markers, acetate, and so on. This is *not* done on a real computer.
- To test it with a user, one team member "plays computer," rearranging the interface in response to the user's actions.
- Another member takes careful notes.
- At the end of the testing sessions, the team distills the notes to see what aspects need to be changed.

The authors sincerely hope you will use a paper prototype for initial testing, but the rest of the chapter actually applies to testing with any sort of prototype. Preparing for a test involves four steps: preparing test scenarios, creating a prototype, practicing the test, and recruiting users.

8.5.1 Preparing Test Scenarios

The tasks carried out by users during a test are called *test scenarios*. The scenarios need to be representative of the tasks that the users carry out in the normal course of work. The results from your user and tasks analyses contain valuable information that will help you create effective test scenarios.

According to Rubin [Rubin 1994], test scenarios should describe the following:

- Motives for performing the work
- The end results that the test user will try to achieve
- Actual data rather than generalities
- The state of the system when a task is initiated
- Readouts of displays and printouts that the test users will see while performing the task.

For example, in testing the usability of an e-commerce site that sells clothing, it is important to learn whether users can find the merchandise they want to order. Questions similar to "Can you find items at this site?" are too general to solicit useful feedback. Instead, a test scenario should involve actual data. For this example website, a possible test scenario might go as follows:

- Motivation and end results: "You want to buy a sweater. Find a woman's blue V-neck sweater for under $80."
- State of system: Test user is at the site's home page. The user is visiting the site for the first time, so there is no customer information on file and the user's "shopping cart" and "wish list" are empty.
- Displays include the following:
    - Home page
    - Ladies' Apparel Department
    - Sweaters page
    - Search dialog (in case test user decides to search for item rather than clicking on links)
    - List of available sweaters that meet search criteria.

8.5.2 Creating a Prototype

As discussed in the previous chapter, creating a paper prototype is the most time-effective technique for modeling a website that doesn't yet exist. In fact, even if the website already exists, it's best to create a paper prototype by printing screen dumps of the current site. In terms of depth and breadth, be sure to prototype enough of the site that you can support all of the test scenarios that you plan to use. Figure 8–2 and Figure 8–3 show the prototype of the pages necessary to support the example test scenario mentioned in the last section.

8.5.3 Practicing

As you know, programming bugs can bring software to a crashing halt. The same is true in user testing, where "bugs" in a test can compromise the value of the feedback you gather. Study the next section on conducting a test and practice administering the test until it becomes smooth and tension free.

8.5.4 Recruiting Users

Refer to your user analysis, and recruit people who fit the user profile. Recall the discussion of this topic in Chapter 2: The best source for users is the organization that requested the testing. In a college setting, a notice on a bulletin board might produce students who, for a modest inducement, are willing to serve as surrogate users. For scheduling hard-to-find users, be sure to start early, and solicit user groups and professional associations whose members match the user profile you've developed [Schroeder 1998].

Avoid using family and friends as test users. Even when they fit the user profile, they might be unwilling to offer honest criticism. The only situation where asking family or friends to act as test users is acceptable is when you are practicing the test. Feedback from these practice sessions should not be included in the final report.

8.6 Conducting a Test

Conducting the actual test requires organization, planning, and people to carry out roles. The material that follows is based on standard procedures used in industrial usability labs and by usability consultants [Rubin 1994, Orr 1996].

8.6.1 Format

Arrangement. A common room arrangement for user testing is shown in Figure 8–4. The (human) computer sits to one side or across from the test user. The facilitator sits beside the test user and is able to see facial expressions and converse easily. The observer is completely out of the line of sight of the user but can see the user and the prototype.

Videotaping. Videotaping adds several considerations. If there is only one camera, place it to record the prototype and the user's actions with the prototype. A good place to position the camera is behind the user, looking over the user's shoulder and trained on the prototype. A more sophisticated setup uses a second camera trained on the user's face and a video mixer combines the two views into a single screen showing a small inset of the user's facial reaction while the rest of the screen shows the user's actions.

Perhaps it does not need to be said, but the test user must be fully informed of any planned videotaping, and permission to conduct it must be included in the informed-consent agreement. Surreptitious videotaping is completely off limits.

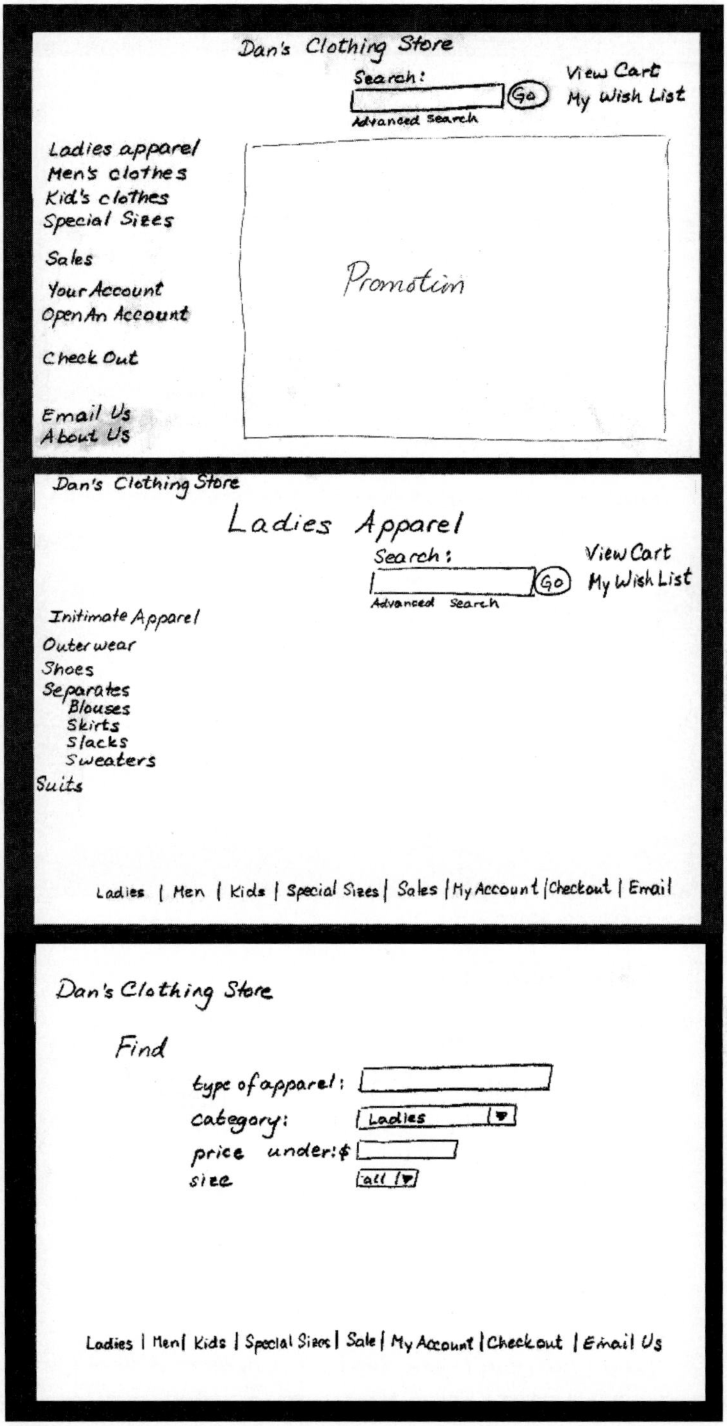

Figure 8–2 Prototypes for the home page, ladies' apparel page, and a search page.

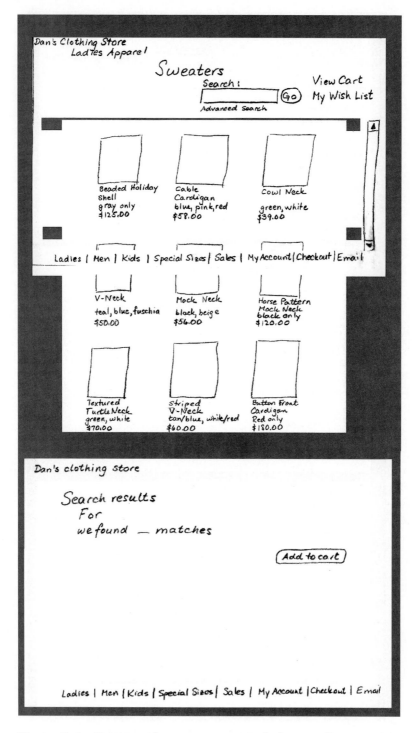

Figure 8–3   Prototype for sweater page, including scrolling inset, and partially prototyped page for search results.

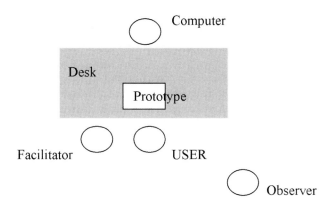

Figure 8–4   Seating arrangement.

8.6.2 Roles

There are four roles on a test team. They are *greeter, facilitator, computer,* and *observer.*

Greeter.   At the beginning of the test, the greeter welcomes the test user to the test facility and carries out all the necessary pretest activities, which include ice-breaking, explaining the purpose and format of the test, obtaining informed consent, and perhaps administering a pre-test questionnaire. To break the ice, the greeter can use some of the same social interactions that a good host would use to put a guest at ease. This includes greeting the test user by name, shaking hands, introducing the team, and offering the test user a seat and refreshments.

Then, reading from a written script, the greeter explains the purpose and the general format of the test. An important goal at this stage is to empower the user, to remove any sense that the user is being tested, and to try in any way possible to relieve the anxiety that many people feel in this situation. The greeter's own manner, tone of voice, and body language convey that this is an everyday business situation, one in which the test user is performing a valuable service. While it is helpful to say, "This website is being tested, not you," you should also develop other phrases to empower users. Here are some examples:

> "Any difficulties you experience are a sign of trouble in the design and not a reflection on your abilities. Any problem you have with the site will help us make it better."

> "We appreciate your taking your time to help us test. Your feedback will help us make this a better website."

> "There are no right or wrong responses."

The script explains how to interact with the prototype. It mentions that the interface is a paper prototype, and that the user will use his or her finger as the mouse and will touch the paper to simulate clicking. If the user needs to type in information on a fill-out form, the greeter supplies a felt-tip pen to the user and explains its use as a substitute.

It's best to read from a script because you could forget important points when speaking conversationally. It's also better than memorizing the script because this puts additional pressure on the greeter not to muff the speech. Yes, it is unnatural to read to a person, but you can begin by saying, "So that I don't forget anything, I'm going to read from a script," which users readily accept.

Computer Science Curriculum Study

Informed Consent and Privacy Statement

The study in which you are being asked to take part is an evaluation a website for a new textbook. A member of the team that is developing the text is conducting this study.

The general purpose of this study is to get feedback on the course topics and supporting materials during the early stages of development.

Please be informed that you must sign this informed consent before participating in the study. This informed consent document is intended to provide you with general information about the study and to assure you that, as a participant, your privacy will be maintained.

Please also be informed that:

Your participation in the study is fully voluntary. You have the right not to participate, and you will not be penalized in any way if you do not participate.

All information you provide in this study is confidential. Any report of the study results will be used only to evaluate the topics and materials in question.

Other than seeing a preview of the text's subject matter, there is no direct benefit to you. There are also no foreseen risks from participating in this study.

At the completion of the study, you will be given a thorough explanation of the research techniques, possible publication, and impact of the study, if you request it.

By signing this informed consent you certify that you are 18 years of age or older.

Figure 8–5   A sample Informed Consent document.

The greeter also obtains *informed consent* from every test user. An informed-consent form states the purpose of the test, explains the fact that it is being videotaped (if that is the case), and promises confidentiality. It contains a statement of benefit and risk, and the test user gives consent for the recording and the use of results. It also includes contact information for both the testing team and the testing team's supervisor. Figure 8–5 contains a sample informed-consent document.

In an industry setting, management might want test users to sign a nondisclosure form, which stipulates that the user will not discuss anything seen during the test.

To verify that the test user does indeed fit the desired user profile, the greeter could ask the user to fill out a pretest questionnaire. It establishes the user's background and experience, which will have to be taken into account in evaluating results.

Facilitator.   This is the person who actually conducts the test and is the only person who speaks to the user during testing. The facilitator presents the test scenarios to the user, one scenario at a time. Each scenario is written on a separate card. The facilitator reads the task to the user and then places the card in a convenient place for the user to refer to. The reason for this presentation technique is that some users prefer taking in information through their eyes; others prefer to listen. When a user finishes, the facilitator goes on to the next scenario.

Sometimes a test user will get "stuck." The facilitator must resist the natural urge to help the user and instead allow the user to struggle, because the point of the test is to see whether the user can complete the task unaided. Sometimes a user will ask for help. Rather than giving the answer, a facilitator can reflect back what the user is saying and help draw out his or her thoughts. Occasionally, a user will take more time than your team has allotted for the task. In this case, it is all right to move on to the next task, taking care not to imply that the user has performed badly.

Assist users only as a last resort. Sometimes you can let a test user know that you sympathize with the frustrating circumstances and can encourage him or her to stay with a task a little longer. If a user becomes so frustrated that it appears that he or she might just stop working and leave, provide small pieces of information.

A good facilitator draws out a user's thoughts. One way to do this is to ask users to provide a running commentary on what they are doing and why they are doing it. This is called *thinking aloud*. As mentioned in Chapter 3, thinking aloud has the advantage of providing insights into a user's preconceptions and reactions to the interface and provides a rich set of feedback for further improvements to the interface. A drawback to this technique occurs when a user encounters difficulties. When people encounter a problem, they tend to quit speaking so they can focus more thought on the task. When the user is puzzled, or stuck, it is important to say things like, "What are you thinking now?" or "You seem frustrated—what is causing that?" or "What did you expect to see?" It is important that these questions do not imply right or wrong answers or indicate a value judgment of the test user's actions.

An effective facilitator remains neutral at all times. When serving as a facilitator, it is useful to develop a set of neutral phrases to indicate the beginning of the next task. If a facilitator says, "Good job!" after a user successfully completes a task, but says nothing when a task is completed incorrectly, the user can correctly infer that something went wrong. For practice, try to find ten different ways to get the user to think aloud while working.

Thinking aloud provides valuable insights. It is important to know *where* the user had trouble; at the same time, it is very valuable to know *why*. It might be difficult to ask "why?" directly, but the facilitator needs to attempt to keep the user talking.

Key points in what the facilitator does:

- Gives test scenarios to the user, one at a time.
- Maintains a neutral demeanor.
- Lets the user struggle.
- Never explains the interface. If the interface requires explanation, it is deficient.
- Encourages user to "think aloud."

The facilitator is also responsible for keeping things moving. The test team will have decided on a maximum time to finish each task. The facilitator keeps track of the time and, if necessary, moves on to the next task.

Computer.   When using a paper prototype, the person playing the role of computer[4] has to move the parts of the prototype in response to user actions. The computer must know the program logic thoroughly, to be able to respond quickly and correctly. The goal is to sustain the illusion that what the user is interacting with is an electronic computer.

The user's actions will provide the input. Pointing with a finger will "move the mouse." Touching the appropriate place on the paper prototype simulates a "mouse click." In response,

---

[4]This relates to the original usage of the term: a computer, in the 1940s, was a person sitting at a desk calculator. This is why ACM stands for "Association for Computing Machinery," which has a strange sound now. In 1948 when ACM was founded, "Association for Computing" would have been misunderstood to be for people who operated desk calculators.

the computer rearranges the pieces of paper—putting in a pull-down menu, putting up a dialog box, or whatever the real computer would do in the situation.

Observer. The observer's job is primarily to take careful notes. Index cards work well for this purpose. The observer records only one observation per card, because the team will sort the cards in the evaluation phase. Depending on the interface, an observer may also time a user's completion of a task. Observers record any incident where the user encounters difficulty and make notes of the task and of relevant displays. In the way of preparation, it is helpful to write each test scenario at the top of several cards, so there is no need to record this information while the test is taking place.

The facilitator cannot take notes and run the session at the same time. Just running the test and keeping the user talking will require the facilitator's full attention.

The decisions made while setting usability specifications will have a big influence on what the observer records on the cards. The step of setting usability specifications occurs just before the design phase in the user-centered development methodology. Recall from Chapter 3 that setting usability specifications includes the selection of performance measures and preference measures. The observer will be responsible for recording the data for the performance measures while the test is taking place.

8.6.3 Team Demeanor during Test

It is critical that everyone on the team present a neutral demeanor to the test user. This has been touched upon already, but it is so important that it warrants further discussion.

It is fine to smile and generally put the user at ease at the onset. It is not fine to convey, in any way, approval or disapproval of either the interface or the user. Consider the possible situations:

The user makes a mistake, takes longer than expected, or gets completely lost, and members of the team frown, sigh, squirm, or convey disapproval by other body language and tone of voice. As a result the user feels even more pressure than is inherent in the situation to begin with. The added stress biases the results and invalidates the test.

The team treats the user in a neutral manner, but they let slip that the interface is their own design, or that the interface developer is watching, or that there is great pressure to get the product out the door. This tells the user that it is risky to criticize. Most users will avoid saying anything negative, for fear of hurting feelings or causing problems for the developer. This biases the results and invalidates the test.

Be aware of body language. Nervous motion, such as knee bouncing or absently tapping a pencil, can signal impatience with a user's progress in completing a task. Users will also pick up on any exchange of significant glances.

Neutral demeanor is not a natural response. It requires practice. But it is a skill that can be learned, and it will facilitate the gathering of useful information to improve the interface.

8.6.4 Debriefing the User

When the session is completed, the facilitator asks whether the user has any questions or suggestions for improvement. Depending on the product, it could be appropriate to ask for general impressions or to solicit more information about the tasks that caused problems.

Gathering of any preference measures occurs at this point, in the form of a posttest questionnaire. Questionnaires can be administered orally or on paper. Although it lacks the compelling quality of a verbally posed question, a paper questionnaire has the advantage of providing a written record of the user's responses.

Questions can be either *closed-ended* or *open-ended*. Closed-ended questions allow a user to choose one of several preselected responses in a manner similar to what is used on a multiple-choice exam. An open-ended question is analogous to a short answer to an essay question; a user is free to respond in any that that seems appropriate. Examples of open-ended questions that might be useful include the following:

- What did you like best about the site?
- What was the worst thing about the site?
- What improvements would make the site better?

Open-ended questions are particularly helpful in early rounds of usability testing, when the website design is still fluid. In many cases, responses from an open-ended question will be useful in shaping the next version of the prototype.

After the posttest questionnaire, the team then thanks the user and either the greeter or the facilitator escorts the user to the door, at which point perhaps the greeter takes over to make the transition to the next user. Sometimes there will be several users in succession. Three one-hour sessions could be scheduled for a half-day, for instance. The facilitator needs a break between users; maintaining focused attention for an hour is tiring.

8.7 Evaluating Results

Whether immediately after each user or at a later time, the team sorts the notes from the testing session and looks for patterns.

8.7.1 Sort the Note Cards

Label each card by user name or number, and then sort all the cards by category. Here are possible problem categories, for a hypothetical consumer e-commerce site, where, for a concrete example, the task was to find and buy a pair of men's cotton slacks, size 38, in gray [Spool 1998]:

- User could not find the men's pants section at all.
- User lost time exploring categories that were not helpful, such as looking for "pants" when the only available link was "men's clothing."
- Choice of size and choice of color were on separate pages, and user had to write down a vendor's catalog number.
- User made errors entering address information, error messages were not helpful, and the user gave up.
- User tried to type in a two-letter state abbreviation and was frustrated by having to use a pull-down menu instead.

8.7.2 Associate Cards with Prototype and Prioritize

Return to the note cards and classify each according to what feature of the interface it involves. Prioritize the problems according to their frequency and the amount of damage they do to the usability of the site. A simple severity rating scale of "low," "medium," and "catastrophic" can be useful for this purpose.

8.7.3 Review Usability Specifications

This is the time to revisit the performance and preference measures that were chosen as part of setting usability specifications. From the data collected by the observer, compute the numerical values for each performance measure. From the posttest questionnaires, determine the preference measures. Compare the results to the target values you specified for each measure. If you haven't met your target, this is an indication that another iteration of design, prototyping, and testing is in order.

8.8 Refining the Design

User-centered development is a highly iterative process. A round of carefully planned and well-executed usability testing will provide information to redesign the interface or website.

If the usability testing revealed no serious problems, congratulations! Your job is easy: Tell everybody what a great job they did, collect your accolades or your fee, and carry on. However, there will usually be problems, of greater or lesser severity.

If the difficulties that users encountered revealed problems that will require a redesign, then the project team should make changes in the prototype and test the new version.

Whether you are in-house or a consultant, you are in the position of needing to convince the developers or management that there is more work to do. Naturally, this is a challenge. The most powerful way to convince them that a redesign is necessary is to have them watch users struggle. A testing setup where developers can watch a test from behind a one-way mirror is ideal. That will prevent them from trying to help the user, or whispering to you that the user is stupid, or anything else that would compromise the testing.

You can often evoke the same effect by reviewing your videotapes from the test and picking out the critical sections. It does not have the immediacy of a live test, but you might persuade a developer to watch for a period of 5–10 minutes who would not be willing to spend an hour to watch an entire test.

8.9 Writing the Report

The final step is to put the test results and recommendations in writing. When organizing your report, think in terms of improvement ideas, not criticisms [Tognazzini 2001]. If all you do is list problems, then management still has nothing but problems. Instead, provide a suggested solution. Don't just state your finding:

> Difficulties due to poor labeling arose in relating a specific heading to a specific task.

Instead, give a solution:

> The button label "Upload logo" was confusing to users. The label "Add logo" made more sense to them.

Avoid stating general design rules:

> Use color carefully and always use something other than color to convey information.

Instead, be specific:

> The red text on a green background was difficult to read. Consider using red text on a white background and use green for a border.

Clearly state the recommended action. Be wary of passive voice:

> Feedback pages are necessary to display order completed and error status.

The following states the recommendation more clearly:

> Add feedback pages to indicate that the order is complete or that an error has occurred.

Draw on your normal writing skills, keeping in mind that the first rule of writing is to identify your reader clearly. What Jakob Nielsen says about people not liking to read Web pages [Nielsen 1997] is also true about usability reports. Busy clients and bosses have no time to wade through thick documents. The most effective format for a usability report is starkly different from the familiar form of a traditional term paper. At first, this format can seem unnatural, but it is well worth practicing.

Place an executive summary at the beginning of your report. Place general findings first. In one paragraph, point out the areas of strength; in another, list recommendations for improvement.

Keep it short. Clients do not want a lot of background about the product or the value of testing. They just want to know what is wrong enough to justify the cost of more development time. However, a short review of the user profile is worthwhile, just as a refresher on the website's audience, their needs, and their skill levels.

Continue to the specifics. If there are many recommendations, group and prioritize them. People become discouraged when confronted with large "to-do" lists. Some successful consultants suggest limiting yourself to the top three problems.

Make it understandable. Avoid the jargon of testing, which, like any other specialty, has its own vocabulary.

Be direct. Do not be shy about using phrases like "We recommend" or "We suggest." Make the suggestions specific and easy for a developer to implement, and avoid mentioning general design rules. For example, a specific suggestion would be: "When a user clicks on 'add to shopping cart', display the shopping cart with the part number and description of the selected item already filled in. Users didn't like having to remember the part number." A developer will be able to follow up on that suggestion. In contrast, the suggestion "Avoid overtaxing a user's short-term memory" gives the developer no useful information.

Pair recommendations with rationale. Avoid phrases like "the user found" or "the user said" except when providing evidence for a recommendation. Think of the user reactions as being the raw data that you will summarize and convert into suggestions.

Put the testing procedure in an appendix, not in the main body of the report. Put raw data, the testing instrument, and any accompanying material into an appendix. Most of the time, clients will not look at this information, but it is always good form to include it.

8.10 Summary

Congratulations. You are now familiar with the entire user-centered development methodology, which will help you create effective websites that provide convenience for your site's audience. This methodology is useful for any product that involves a user interface. This includes things ranging from automobile dashboard displays and microwaves to spreadsheet programs and video games.

The remaining chapters in the book cover color, typography, multimedia, how to make sites accessible to people with disabilities, how to globalize a site, and how to create a site that is personalized and inspires trust.

Review Questions and Exercises

1. How is program debugging similar to testing with a prototype?
2. How do the role and timing of user testing in user-centered development differ from more traditional software-engineering methodologies?
3. What is the difference between formative and summative evaluation?
4. In each of the following activities, identify what is being tested, and describe the test as formative evaluation or summative evaluation:
   a. A school board tests various Internet filters to choose one for the elementary school libraries.
   b. A project team creates a local prototype to decide if a single search box will work for the intended audience.
   c. An animation team tries several motion capture systems and decides to use hand animation instead.
   d. The project catches and fixes several severe usability problems before the site goes live.
   e. Before starting the process of creating a new version of the website, a project evaluates the current version of the website, looking for major usability problems.
5. What is the difference between user-based and expert-based evaluation?
6. What is a test scenario? Where should you look for information to build test scenarios?
7. What should a test scenario include?
8. When testing with a paper prototype, how much of the website do you need to prototype?
9. Why are family and friends not good test users? What is the one exception to this?
10. What are a greeter's responsibilities?
11. List four ways to reassure and empower test users.
12. Why should a greeter use a script?
13. What should be included in an informed consent document?
14. What are the facilitator's responsibilities?
15. What should a facilitator do if a test user gets "stuck"?
16. What is thinking aloud? Why is it valuable during a user-based test?
17. What is the role and goal of neutrality during a test?
18. What does the computer do during a user test with a paper prototype?
19. What responsibilities does an observer have?
20. What activities should the team carry out after the testing sessions?

Project Activities

21. If you are developing a website for a client, and you are ready to prototype a website, now is the optimal time to perform your initial round of user testing. Answering the following questions will help prepare you for the test.
22. What are the usability specifications you decided on?

23. How are you going to measure each usability specification?

24. What will your test scenarios be? List them and show the correspondence to your usability specifications.

25. What parts of your website will you need to prototype to support the test scenarios? Create the prototype.

26. How will you need to modify the sample informed-consent document shown in Figure 8–5 so that you can use it for your testing sessions?

27. Create a pretest questionnaire to determine if a person fits your user profile.

28. Carry out usability tests on your prototype.

29. Write up the results of your testing. Begin your report with an executive summary. The body of the report should be no longer than four pages. Put your test scenarios, the raw data, your testing procedure, and your informed consent and pretest questionnaire in an appendix.

References

[Bailey 1992] Robert W. Bailey, Robert W. Allan, and P. Raiello. Usability Testing vs. Heuristic Evaluation: A Head-to-Head Comparison. *Proceedings of the Human Factors Society 36th Annual Meeting, Computer Systems: Usability and Rapid Prototyping*. Vol. 1, 1992. 409–413.

[Donahue 1999] George Donahue, Susan Weinschenk, Julie Nowicki. *Usability is Good Business*. July 27, 1999. http://www.compuware.com/intelligence/articles/usability.htm

[Hackos 1998] JoAnn Hackos and Janice Redish. *User and Task Analysis for Interface Design*. New York: Wiley, 1998.

[Kantner 1997] Laurie Kantner and Stephanie Rosenbaum. Usability Studies of WWW Sites: Heuristic Evaluation vs. Laboratory Testing. *Proceedings of SIGDOC 97 Snowbird Utah*. (1997) 153–160.

[Nielsen 1997] Jakob Nielsen. "Be Succinct! Writing for the Web," *Alertbox*. March 15, 1997. http://www.useit.com/alertbox/9703b.html

[Orr 1996] David Orr, Principal, Orr & Associates Corporation. Personal communication. http://www.orrnet.com/

[Rettig 1994] Mark Rettig. "Prototyping for Tiny Fingers," *Communications of the Association for Computing Machinery* 37: 4. April 1994, 21–27.

[Rubin 1994] Jeffrey Rubin. *Handbook of Usability Testing*. Wiley, 1994.

[Scriven 1991] Michael Scriven. *Evaluation Thesaurus* (4th ed). Newbury Park: Sage Publications, 1991. 169.

[Schroeder 1998] Will Schroeder. "Scheduling Hard-to-Find Users," *Eye for Design* 5:1. January, 1998. 9–10.

[Simonsen 1997] Jesper Simonsen and Finn Kensing. Using Ethnography in Contextual Design. *Communications of the Association for Computing Machinery* 40:7. July 1997. 82–88.

[Spool 1998] Jared Spool, Tara Scanlon, Will Schroeder, Carolyn Snyder, and Terri DeAngelo. *Web Site Usability: A Designer's Guide*. Morgan Kaufman, 1998.

[Tognazzini 2001] Bruce Tognazzini. "How to Deliver a Report Without Getting Lynched," *AskTog*. June 2001. www.asktog.com/columns/047HowToWriteAReport.html

[User 2000] User Interface Engineering. *Eye for Design*. November 2000.

9

Color

9.1 Introduction

Color is one of the pleasurable aspects of eyesight and is an integral part of Web pages. Properly used, color makes a page both attractive and usable. It can provide cues that indicate a button's function or state. It can distinguish between navigational aids and content, unobtrusively guiding the user through a page. This chapter presents some color basics and design tips to enhance both the effectiveness and appeal of a website.

Goals of this Chapter

In this chapter, you can do the following:

- understand physical and perceptual aspects of color
- become aware of several color models and learn the advantages of each
- learn to apply four different color harmony schemes
- explore how color can make Web pages pleasing and easy to read.

9.2 The Physics of Color

Color is both a physical phenomenon and a perception. To understand how people react to color, it is important to know a little about both of these aspects.

As a physical phenomenon, visible light is a small portion of the electromagnetic spectrum [Foley 1990]. As shown in Figure 9–1, visible light has wavelengths that range from approximately 400 to 700 nanometers (nm). A nanometer is a billionth (10^{-9}) of a meter. Figure 9–2 shows the visible wavelengths. Different wavelengths correspond to different colors in a rainbow. Light with a wavelength greater than 610 nm is perceived as red; light with a wavelength between 450 and 480 nm looks blue [Murch 1987]. Light that contains an equal mixture of all wavelengths appears white. White does not correspond to any single wavelength. Black is the absence of light.

When light enters a human eye, it strikes the retina. Embedded in the retina are approximately six million cones, whose function is to sense color [Wyszecki 1982]. There are three types of cones. One type is sensitive to the longer wavelengths corresponding to the red portion of the visible spectrum; a second type reacts to the spectral midrange corresponding to the green portion; the last type responds to the blue end of the spectrum. Figure 9–3 displays a graph of these responses [Foley 1990].

Figure 3–1. The home page for www.funschool.com.

Courtesy of Kaboose, Inc.

Figure 3–3. Home page for Urban Decay at www.urbandecay.com.

Courtesy of Urban Decay Cosmetics.

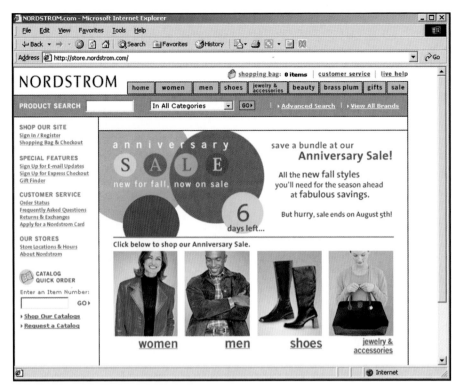

Figure 4–3. A hybrid organizational scheme www.nordstrom.com.
Courtesy of Nordstrom, Inc.

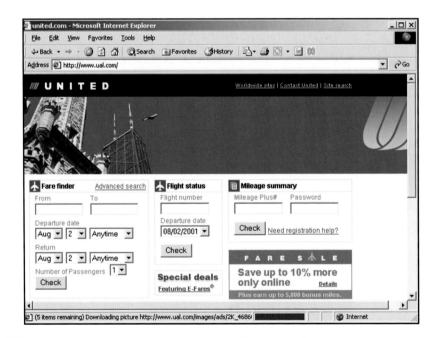

Figure 4–25. Exercise 15, part E. Home Page of www.ual.com.
© 2002 United Air Lines, Inc.

Figure 6–6. Screen shot of a portion of Amazon.com's Health and Beauty subsite,
`www.drugstore.com`.

Figure 6–7. The Books subsite of Amazon.com.

Figure 6–11. The appeal of graphical navigation bars, from `www.burpee.com`.
Courtesy of W. Atlee Burpee & Co.

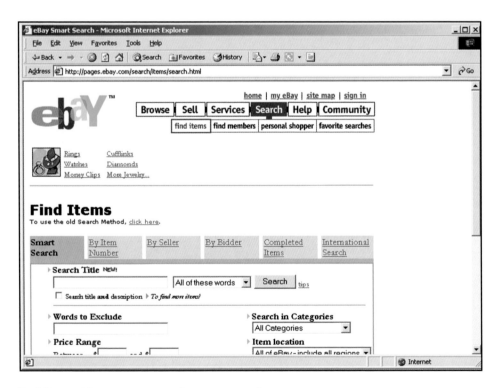

Figure 6–12. Building context with navigation bars.
These materials have been reproduced with the permission of eBay Inc.
© EBAY INC. ALL RIGHTS RESERVED.

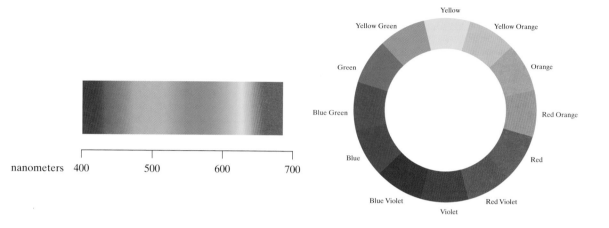

nanometers 400   500   600   700

Figure 9–2. The visible spectrum.

Figure 9–4. An artist's color wheel.

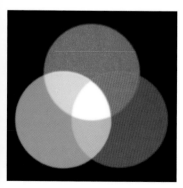

	Red	Green	Blue
Red	Yes	No	No
Yellow	Yes	Yes	No
Green	No	Yes	No
Cyan	No	Yes	Yes
Blue	No	No	Yes
Magentha	Yes	No	Yes
White	Yes	Yes	Yes
Black	No	No	No

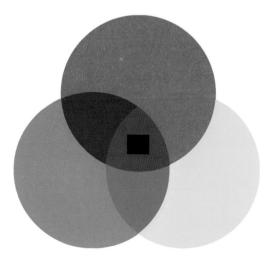

Figure 9–5. A demonstration of additive color, using the RGB color model.

Figure 9–6. Demonstration of the CMYK color system.

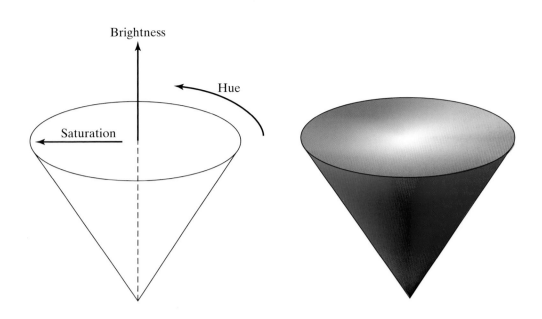

Figure 9–7. The HSB color model of hue, saturation, and brightness.

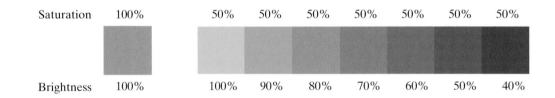

Saturation	100%		50%	50%	50%	50%	50%	50%	50%
Brightness	100%		100%	90%	80%	70%	60%	50%	40%

Figure 9–8. The effect of varying brightness.

Hue	30									
Brightness	85%									
Saturation	100%	90%	80%	70%	60%	50%	40%	30%	20%	10%

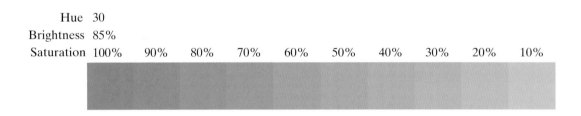

Figure 9–9. The effect of varying the saturation with brightness and hue fixed.

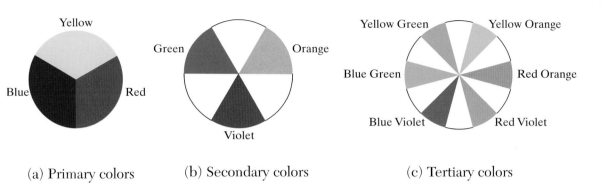

(a) Primary colors   (b) Secondary colors   (c) Tertiary colors

Figure 9–10. Three color wheels.

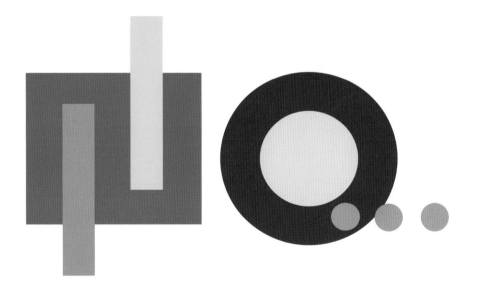

Figure 9–11. Two examples of a monochromatic (one hue) color harmony scheme.

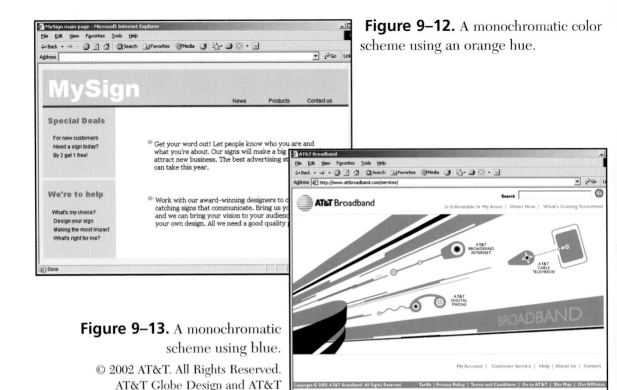

Figure 9–12. A monochromatic color scheme using an orange hue.

Figure 9–13. A monochromatic scheme using blue.

© 2002 AT&T. All Rights Reserved. AT&T Globe Design and AT&T Broadband are service marks of AT&T.

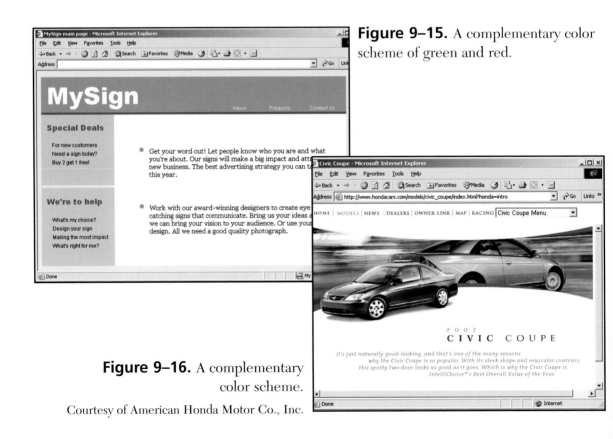

Figure 9–15. A complementary color scheme of green and red.

Figure 9–16. A complementary color scheme.

Courtesy of American Honda Motor Co., Inc.

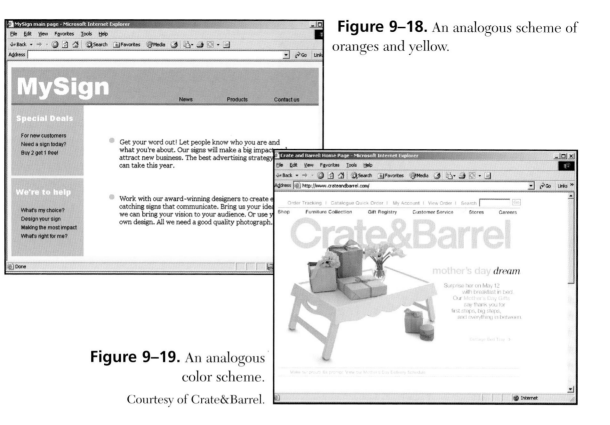

Figure 9–18. An analogous scheme of oranges and yellow.

Figure 9–19. An analogous color scheme.

Courtesy of Crate&Barrel.

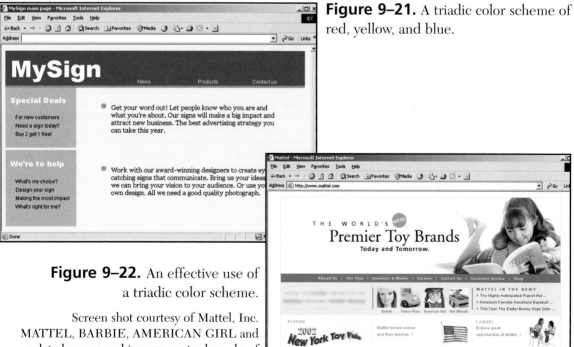

Figure 9–21. A triadic color scheme of red, yellow, and blue.

Figure 9–22. An effective use of a triadic color scheme.

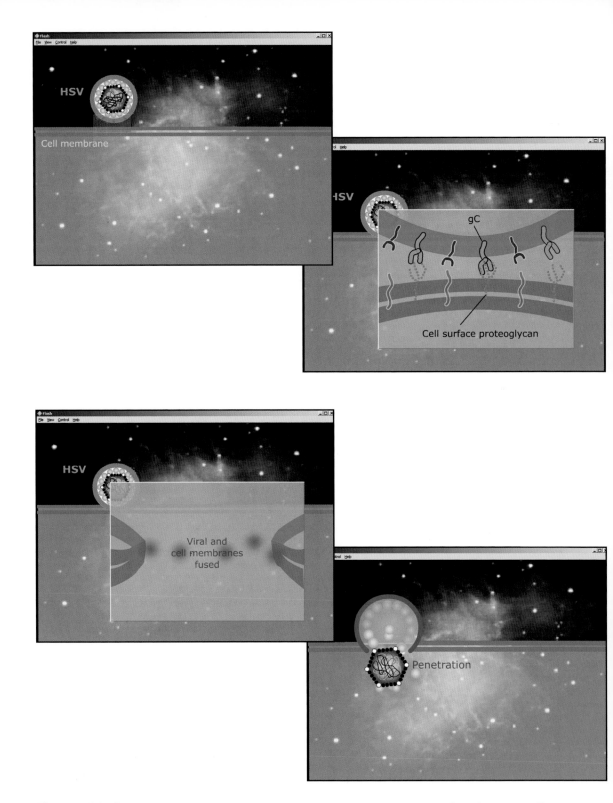

Figure 11–8. An animation depicting changes in time: A virus attacks a human cell.
Courtesy of Karin Christensen and Dr. Edward K. Wagner.

Figure 11–10. Depicting parking regulations.
Courtesy of Erik B. Steiner.

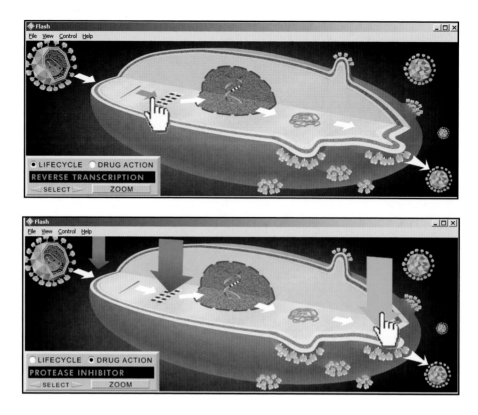

Figure 11–14. Animation depicting HIV infection and possible drug actions.
Courtesy of Roche.

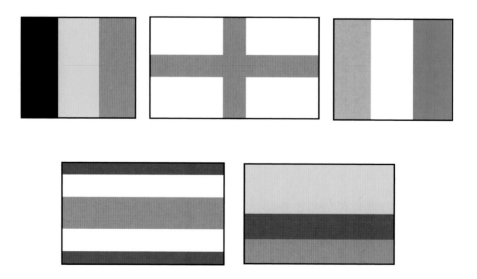

Figure 13–11. Flags from five countries. For exercise 11 in chapter 13.

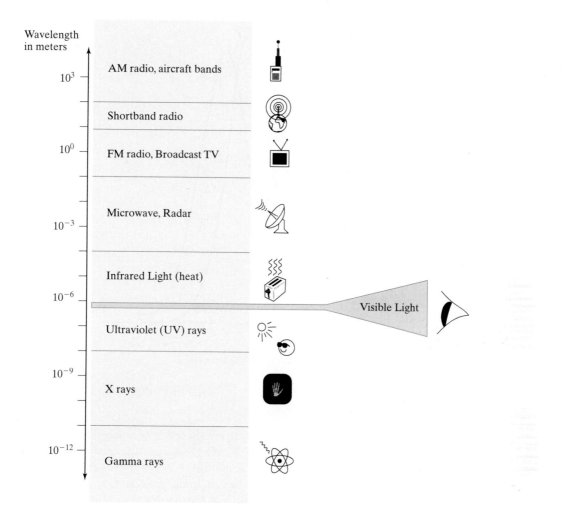

Figure 9–1 Human eyes perceive a small range of electromagnetic radiation.

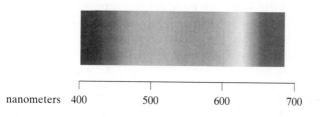

Figure 9–2 The visible spectrum.

There is quite a bit of overlap in the response curves. The peak sensitivities for the first and second types are actually in the yellow range. There is a big disparity in the height of the three curves. This is due to the fact that human eyes are most sensitive in the green range of the spectrum and are dramatically less sensitive in the blue range.

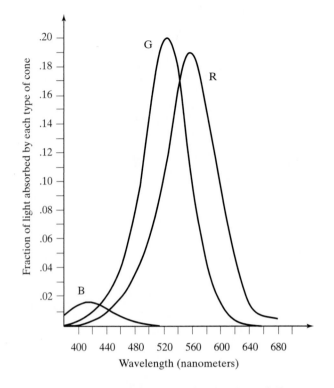

Figure 9–3   Response curves for the three different types of cones.[5]

Colors in the spectrum are quite unusual in that each one is composed of a single wavelength. In real life, such light is extremely rare. Most light is a mixture of wavelengths; when a mixture of wavelengths strikes a human retina, all three types of cones respond, according to the wavelengths present in the mix. How a human brain assimilates and categorizes the response falls into the area of color perception. The *tristimulus theory* of color mixing attempts to explain some aspects of how humans perceive mixtures of wavelengths as color.

The fact that there are three types of cones forms the physiological basis for the tristimulus theory of color mixing [Hall 1989]. It states that, if all three sets of cones sense equal amounts of light, then the brain will interpret this mixture as white light. As mentioned previously, natural white light is a mixture of all visible wavelengths, but a combination of three properly chosen wavelengths can produce the same perception. This is why a color television or computer monitor can display most of the colors found in nature by using mixtures of only red, green, and blue.

9.3 Color Models

A person with normal vision can distinguish between one and two million colors [Horton 1991], but it is nearly impossible to describe a particular color precisely without using a color model. A color model is a representation system for describing a color more precisely than would be possible with nouns and adjectives. There are over a dozen color models in current usage. This section examines several that are useful in Web development.

---

[5]Foley/Feiner/Hughes/Van Dam. *Computer Graphics.* Adapted from Figure 13–18 (page 577). © 1996, 1990 Addison–Wesley Publishing Company, Inc. Reprinted by permission of Pearson Education, Inc.

9.3.1 A Time-Tested Model: RYB

Artists, philosophers, and scientists have tried to understand the nature of color since antiquity. One aspect that intrigued them was the challenge of identifying *primary colors*, or colors that could be mixed to create all other colors. As early as 1613, Francis Aguilon suggested that, in addition to black and white, the colors red, yellow, and blue could be mixed to create all other colors [Hoffman 1999]. The RYB color model takes its name from these three colors.

Figure 9–4 shows a common method of display called a *color wheel*. The first person to order colors in a circular pattern was Sir Isaac Newton in 1702 [Gage 1999]. In 1766, Moses Harris created the first printed color wheel that used the RYB model [Linton 1991]. Today, artists still use this style of color wheel for creating coordinated color schemes [Weinman 1997].

9.3.2 Additive Color: RGB

The RGB model describes colors as a mixture of red, green, and blue primary colors. It is an example of an *additive* color model. In additive color models, mixing two colors results in a brighter color. Additive models are used to describe colors that emanate from glowing bodies such as lights, televisions, and computer monitors [Glassner 1995].

One way to explore the behavior of additive color is to use three projectors to beam red, green, and blue light onto a white wall in an otherwise darkened room. Arrange the projectors so that their beams overlap. The result resembles Figure 9–5. The area of overlap between red and green produces yellow; the addition of green and blue creates cyan; the colors red and blue add to magenta. Combining all three produces white. Where no light falls, there is black.

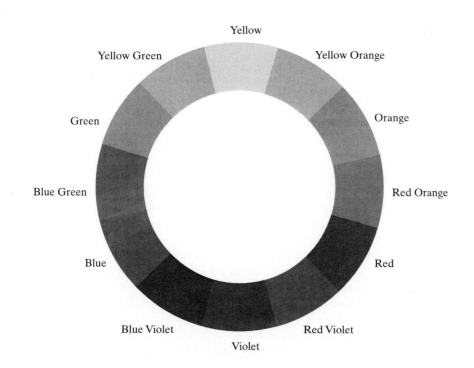

Figure 9–4 An artist's color wheel.

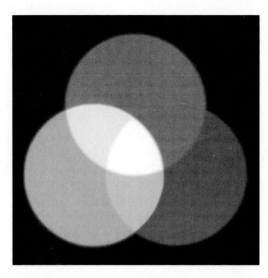

	Red	Green	Blue
Red	Yes	No	No
Yellow	Yes	Yes	No
Green	No	Yes	No
Cyan	No	Yes	Yes
Blue	No	No	Yes
Magentha	Yes	No	Yes
White	Yes	Yes	Yes
Black	No	No	No

Figure 9–5 A demonstration of additive color, using the RGB color model.

Another way to explore this color model is to view a color television or computer monitor at close range with a magnifying glass. The tiny glowing phosphor dots on the surface each have one of only three colors—red, green, or blue. Viewing from a normal distance, a human eye blends these tiny dots together and so performs the mixing necessary to create other colors.

There are several variations of the RGB system. In some applications, the values for R, G, and B range between zero and 255. In others, the values are expressed as a percent ranging from zero to one hundred.

What you see on a monitor depends significantly on the other light sources in a room. In a darkened room, colors will look more "alive" than in a room that is brightly lit. Subtle color effects that are clear in a darkened room can be invisible in a well-lit one [Durrett 1987].

9.3.3 Subtractive Color: CMYK

In real life, only a few objects emit light. Most of them reflect light instead. If a shirt appears blue in daylight, this is because its material has absorbed—or subtracted—all but the blue wavelengths from the incoming light, and only the blue is reflected.

To describe the colors of reflecting objects requires a different type of color system, called a *subtractive color system*. In a subtractive system, mixing two colors creates a darker one. This is the realm of paint and of printer's ink. For example, mixing red and green paint will produce a muddy brown.

CMY is one such subtractive system, taking its name from its three primary colors: cyan, magenta, and yellow. Cyan, magenta, and yellow are complements of red, green, and blue, respectively. Where cyan and yellow are printed on top of each other, the cyan subtracts red and the yellow subtracts blue, to leave green. Where cyan and magenta overlap, red and green are subtracted, leaving blue. Where magenta and yellow overlap, the result is red.

However, CMY is not practical for most color printing. In theory, where the three inks overlap, red, green, and blue are all subtracted, leaving black. However, this does not work

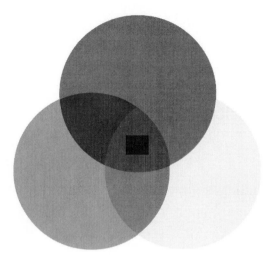

Figure 9–6 Demonstration of the CMYK
color system.

well in practice. The inks do not produce a rich, strong black, but make a dark gray instead.
In reality, a solid black needs to be printed with black ink. The letter K is used to represent
the color black, because B already means blue. This is the reason it's called the CMYK color
model. (See Figure 9–6.)

CMYK is the basis of a large portion of color-printing technology, ranging from the commercial presses for magazines to inexpensive inkjet printers. It uses four inks, so it is called
four-color printing. When printing a paper copy of an image, driver software converts the
image from RGB to CMYK before printing it. Inks vary, so the conversion is not a simple
numeric formula. Instead, the software uses a manufacturer-specific CMYK profile to complete the conversion [McDowell 2000].

9.3.4 The HSB System

The HSB system (for *hue, saturation*, and *brightness*) resembles traditional paint-based
systems for describing color [Hoffmann 2002]. *Hue* is the color name, such as red, blue, orange, or green, and is often presented in a circular arrangement reminiscent of a color
wheel. The numeric values for hue are given in degrees going around the circle. The value
zero represents the hue red, the value 120 represents green, and 240 represents blue.

Saturation refers to the purity of a color. Pure green, not mixed with any white, is fully
saturated. Pale green, on the other hand, includes a large amount of white mixed with the
green and thus has a low saturation. White has zero saturation, as do black and all shades of
gray. Numeric values for saturation are given as percentages and range from zero percent
for shades of gray to one hundred percent for fully saturated colors.

Brightness describes where the color falls on a scale running from white to black, with
white having the highest brightness. The numeric values for brightness range from zero
percent to one hundred percent. Figure 9–7 shows the relationship of these terms. As the
brightness decreases, there is a smaller range in saturation, and the hues become more
compressed in a tighter circle. This corresponds to the fact that humans are less able to
sense differences in hue and saturation in darker colors.

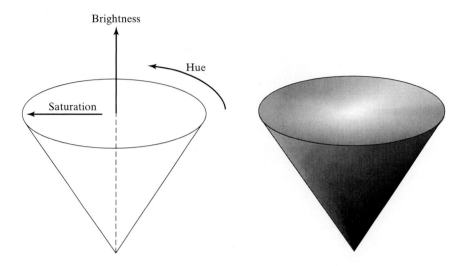

Figure 9–7 The HSB color model of hue, saturation, and brightness.

Figure 9–8 and Figure 9–9 demonstrate the difference between brightness and saturation. Figure 9–8 contains an isolated orange square with 100% brightness and 100% saturation. The other squares all have the same orange hue, and all are 50% saturated. Only the brightness level varies, from 100% down to 40%. The colors range from peach through dark brown.

Figure 9–9 shows the effect that saturation has on color. In the squares in this figure, the hue and brightness are held constant while the saturation varies. Notice the change: from a fully saturated, bold orange, through colors that appear increasingly washed out, to the extreme, a faded grayish color.

Saturation	100%		50%	50%	50%	50%	50%	50%	50%

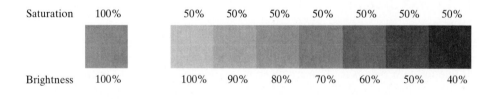

Brightness	100%		100%	90%	80%	70%	60%	50%	40%

Figure 9–8 The effect of varying brightness.

Hue 30									
Brightness 85%									
Saturation 100%	90%	80%	70%	60%	50%	40%	30%	20%	10%

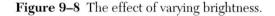

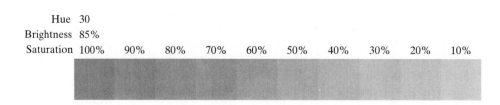

Figure 9–9 The effect of varying the saturation with brightness and hue fixed.

9.3.5 Comparing the Four Models

The RGB color system is hardware oriented. The phosphor dots on a color monitor glow in the colors red, green, and blue. Early software provided only simplistic tools to manipulate these dots, so the first interface developers used the color model of the display hardware to express the color they needed. Without a graphical tool such as a color picker, it takes years to develop the skill necessary to look at a color and to specify it in terms of its RGB components. This was an area of frustration for early interface designers. Similarly, CMYK is technology oriented, because it describes ink colors.

The goal in creating the HSB system and similar color systems was to develop a way of describing colors more easily [Smith 1978]. A problem with both the RGB and the CMYK systems is that people find it difficult to estimate numeric values for a desired color without the help of an interactive color-selection dialog. In either system, it takes much practice to name three numbers that describe such common colors as brown or slate blue. A client is more likely to talk in terms of a "light blue" or a "dark green" instead of CMYK or RGB values. Such verbal descriptors are more directly recast in HSB.

Each color system has a *gamut*, or a range of expressible colors. Not all colors can be expressed in all color systems. CMYK has a smaller gamut than RGB or HSB. In particular, CMYK cannot reproduce colors high in saturation and brightness. A bright red on a screen having the RGB values (255, 0, 0) or the approximately corresponding HSB values (0, 100, 10) will appear on a printed page as a much darker, duller red, because it lies outside the CMYK gamut.

Both the RYB and the HSB system use a circular arrangement as a method for ordering hues. Thus, they are useful for creating and analyzing color harmonies, which is the topic of the next section.

9.4 Color-Harmony Schemes

An effective color scheme can greatly enhance a website's appeal. The question of what combination of colors looks attractive is a complex amalgam of theory, personal preference, experience, and cultural influences. However, there are time-proven combinations of colors that tend to be pleasing. They arise from four color-harmony schemes: monochromatic, complementary, analogous, and triadic. These methods describe a systematic methodology for picking colors that work together effectively [Whelan 1994].

Color-harmony schemes depend on references to a color wheel, as shown earlier in Figure 9–4. To artists using traditional media (paint, water color, etc.) the primaries are red, yellow, and blue. The leftmost wheel in Figure 9–10 shows just these primaries.

Mixing equal amounts of any two primary colors yields a *secondary color.* On a color wheel, these colors are located halfway between the primary colors. The middle wheel in Figure 9–10 shows the three secondary colors, which are orange, violet and green. Mixing

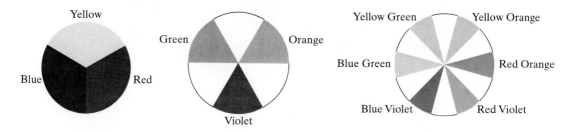

Figure 9–10 Three color wheels.

equal amounts of a primary and a secondary color yield a *tertiary color.* On a color wheel, these appear interleaved between the primary and secondary colors. The six tertiary colors are red–violet, blue–violet, blue–green, yellow–green, yellow–orange, and red–orange; they appear in the rightmost wheel in Figure 9–10.

Finally, these 12 colors can be described as *warm* or *cool.* On the color wheel, the warm colors include red-violet through yellow, with red-orange being considered the warmest. The cool colors range from yellow-green to violet, with blue being the coolest. In other words, the colors of the sun (yellow, orange, or red) are warm colors, and the colors of lake or ocean water (blue or green) are cool colors [Whelan 1994].

This background lays the groundwork for discussing the four color-harmony schemes.

9.4.1 Monochromatic

In a monochromatic scheme, all colors have hues that are exactly the same or that are within a few degrees of each other. Speaking in terms of the HSB color model, colors in this scheme will vary in saturation or brightness, but the hue is constant for all of them. For example, a monochromatic scheme based on blue could include a sky blue, a slate blue, several gray shades, midnight blue, black, and white.

Figure 9–11 shows two designs, one using variations of blue and the other using variations of orange. The background rectangle is a saturated medium blue. The upper vertical bar is brighter and less saturated. The lower vertical bar has the same saturation as the upper bar, but less brightness. In the design on the right, all colors are variations of a reddish orange. The outer ring has low brightness, but fairly high saturation.

A monochromatic scheme enhances the sense of cohesiveness of the overall layout of a Web page. Figure 9–12 and Figure 9–13 show two examples of Web pages with monochromatic color schemes. Even with a small range of hues, it is possible to create appealing pages. Note in Figure 9–13 how the blue in the corporate logo forms the basis of the color scheme. The hue of the corporate logo is 195; the blues in the rest of the design have hue 207.

9.4.2 Complementary

Instead of a single hue, a complementary color scheme uses a pair of *complementary* hues. Two colors are *complementary* if their hues appear opposite one another on a color wheel.

Figure 9–11 Two examples of a monochromatic (one-hue) color-harmony scheme.

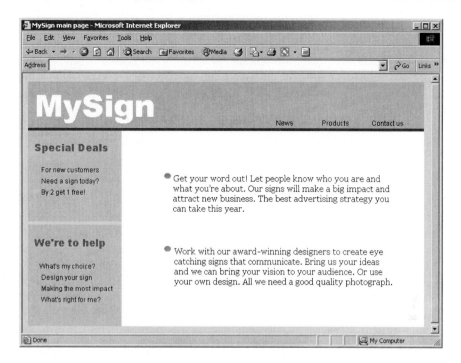

Figure 9–12 A monochromatic color scheme using an orange hue.

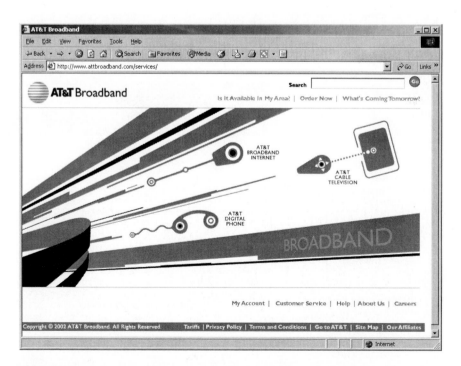

Figure 9–13 A monochromatic scheme using blue. Copyright © 2002 AT&T. All Rights Reserved. AT&T Globe Design and AT&T Broadband are service marks of AT&T.

Figure 9–14 shows some pairs of complementary hues. The colors in a complementary scheme can have any saturation or brightness, as long as they use one of the two complementary hues. When using this color scheme, pick one of the hues to be the dominant one. Use colors based on the dominant hue to fill in the large areas of a page. The other hue serves as an accent. Use it in small areas to add interest. In Figure 9–15, the dominant hue is green, and red is the accent. In the home page shown in Figure 9–16, the dominant hue is blue, seen on the car and in the lettering, and the accent hue is orange, seen on the car's running lights.

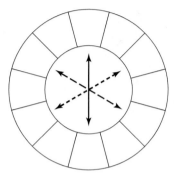

Figure 9–14   Three pairs of complementary colors.

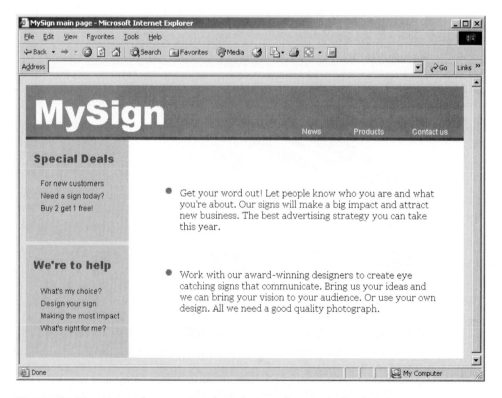

Figure 9–15   A complementary color scheme of green and red.

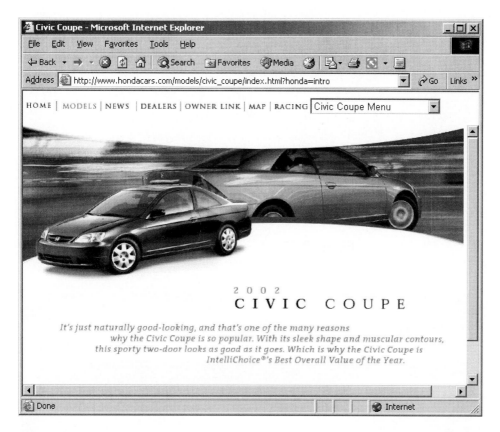

Figure 9–16   A complementary color scheme. Courtesy of American Honda Motor Co., Inc.

9.4.3 Analogous

Two or more colors whose hues lie close together on a color wheel can form an *analogous* color scheme. Analogous schemes echo the color schemes found in nature, such as in a field of grass, the fur of an animal, or the brilliance of a sunset. They often make a pleasing combination. Figure 9–17 shows an analogous color harmony scheme on a color wheel, and Figure 9–18 shows an analogous scheme in the context of a Web page. The Crate&Barrel home page, as seen in Figure 9–19, uses orange, yellow, and green.

As demonstrated in these examples, color combinations in an analogous scheme are more interesting if the colors do not all have the same brightness and saturation.

9.4.4 Triadic

Any three colors that are spaced approximately equally around a color wheel are called a *triad*, as in shown in Figure 9–20. A triadic color scheme uses colors whose hues form a triad. This color scheme offers a wide variety of color choice and can create excitement; however, it can become overpowering and interfere with the textual communication of the page. One way to avoid this is to choose colors that vary in brightness and saturation, as is demonstrated in Figure 9–21.

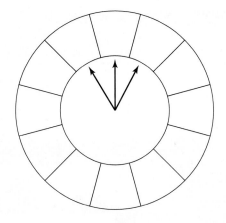

Figure 9–17   An example of an analogous color scheme.

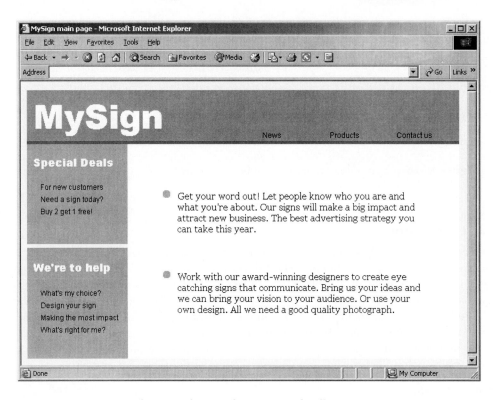

Figure 9–18   An analogous scheme of oranges and yellow.

Another way to avoid the problem is to restrict the number of text and background colors. In addition to black and white, use no more than seven colors [Silverstein 1987]. The Mattel home page shown in Figure 9–22 follows both of these guidelines. It uses a triadic color scheme of red, yellow, and blue, but it has only three shades of yellow (the background on the middle yellow band; the lettering on the blue stripe; the text "2002"), one shade of red

Figure 9–19   An analogous color scheme. Courtesy of Crate&Barrel.

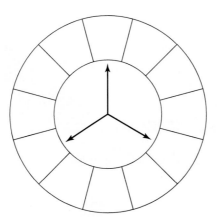

Figure 9–20   A triadic color scheme.

(the text in the middle of the yellow band), and two shades of blue (the remainder of the text on the yellow band; the blue stripe above it; and the words "New York Toy Fair").

Color-harmony schemes come in handy in many situations. Most of the time, a client will have some specifications about color usage. For example, the client might want the color of a logo to dominate the site. Many colleges prefer that the home page and administrative subsite

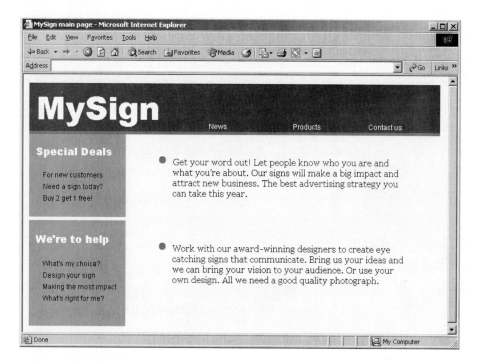

Figure 9–21 A triadic color scheme of red, yellow, and blue.

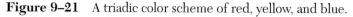

Figure 9–22 An effective use of a triadic color scheme. Screen shot courtesy of Mattel, Inc. MATTEL, BARBIE, AMERICAN GIRL, and related names and images are trademarks of and used with permission from Mattel, Inc. © 2001 Mattel, Inc. All Rights Reserved.

use the school colors. When you have been given some of the colors you must use, color-harmony schemes can help you pick other colors that will work well with them. These schemes are also useful even if you have total control of the site. Using these schemes will help elicit positive comments about your site's professionalism and polish.

9.5 Color in Text and Background

One of the most important issues in website design is assuring that text be legible. Studies [Murch 1984, Hill 2000] investigating the effect that color has on user performance and preference have shown that there are several color combinations that facilitate ease and speed of reading. Having a large contrast between the text and background colors is important. In tests involving short and long text passages, black text on a white background and black text on a light gray background rated high. In both cases, the background has a high level of brightness and a low saturation. The text was always low on the brightness scale. Dark text on a light background tested better than light text on a dark background. As a general guideline, use dark text on a white background or a background that has a high brightness and low saturation.

The same studies give strong indications of what color combinations were less effective. In particular, avoid text and background colors that differ only in blue. For example, people have great difficulty in reading bright yellow text on a white background. In terms of RGB values, these two colors are identical in their red and green components and differ only in blue, as demonstrated in Figure 9–23. On the other hand, a brown, which is a type of dark yellow, works well with white because it differs from white in its red and green components. This weakness in seeing differences in blue is closely linked to the fact that the human eye is less sensitive in the blue range of visible light.

It's important to maintain contrast between text and background, but the type of contrast is also important. When choosing text and background combinations, it's best to avoid bright, saturated colors. Combinations of bright colors such as red and green, red and blue, or magenta and green create a perception of vibration between the two colors and cause eye fatigue.

	Color	R	G	B	
Text	**Yellow**	**255**	**255**	**0**	
Background	**White**	**255**	**255**	**255**	
Difference		**No**	**No**	**Yes**	**Not a good combination**
Text	**Brown**	**64**	**64**	**0**	
Background	**White**	**255**	**255**	**255**	
		Yes	**Yes**	**Yes**	**Good combination**

Figure 9–23 Avoid text and background colors that differ only in blue.

9.6 Color as Organizer and Attention Getter

Color can help organize a Web page visually. When selected portions of text have the same color, those items are perceived as being related. This is an example of the Gestalt principle of similarity, discussed in Chapter 2. For example, color can distinguish between first and second-level navigation links. Figure 2–2 and Figure 5–4 reinforce the visual hierarchy of navigation bars by using color as well as position to group each set of links.

Color can organize a web page into distinct areas. In Figure 5–3, the navigation bar is set off from the content area partly by its position on the left side of the page and partly by the fact that its background is a different color. In Figure 5–8, the background color divides the page into four distinct areas. The topmost one contains navigation information, including current position within the information hierarchy, and a search box. The one directly below it contains the website's name. Below this are two columns, one devoted to permanent content and the other to news.

In addition to helping add structure to a page layout, color can focus a user's attention. For example, in Figure 5–4, it's possible to tell at a glance which top-level link has been selected: Its background color not only differs from that of the others, but also matches the color of the secondary menu.

Color, especially bright, saturated color, can also attract attention. In everyday life, a saturated red often appears on signs warning of danger. Highway traffic cones that temporarily redirect the flow of quickly moving cars have a bold orange color that is easily noticeable. Color functions in the same manner on Web pages. Bright, highly saturated colors compete for attention and should be used sparingly. Limit their use to small areas of the screen and do not place them side-by-side or one on top of the other. Figure 9–22 is a good example. Only the red in the logo and the blue in the narrow band are highly saturated. Together, they occupy less than five percent of the screen's real estate. Use bold colors on a page in the same way you would use spice to season food. Too much will spoil the dish.

9.7 Summary

It is rare that the color choices for Web pages are left entirely in the hands of a developer or designer. In most cases, the client will already have some colors in mind, ones based on a corporate logo, a school insignia, or personal preference. Color harmonies provide options for choosing colors that are compatible with the client's wishes. Applying guidelines for text and background color will foster readability. Finally, using color to organize text and focus attention will result in easier navigation. Properly used, color enhances both the usability and appeal of a site.

Review Questions

1. What is the range of wavelengths of visible light? What colors correspond to the shorter wavelengths?
2. What portion of the visible spectrum appears blue? What portion appears red?
3. What is the physiological basis for the tristimulus theory of color mixing? How does it relate to the manufacture of color monitors?
4. What is a primary color? A secondary color? A tertiary color?
5. Name four different color models and name each component in the model.
6. What are the advantages of the HSB color model?

7. What is a subtractive color model? How does it differ from additive color models?

8. Suppose you plan a user manual that will be available on the Web, but users have said that they will want to be able to print it out as well. What colors should you avoid? Why?

9. Describe four color-harmony schemes.

10. What color combinations work well for text and background? Which ones should you avoid?

11. Why should you avoid using more than seven colors for text and background?

Exercises

There is some software on the book's companion website that will help you with the following exercises. The two items are called "Color Conversion" and "Color Matching." See the instructions on the CD for locating and installing the programs.

12. Identify the harmony scheme for each of these sets of colors. To find the answer, it might help to convert the colors to a different color model or to refer to a color wheel. You can do this either by using the Color Conversion software or by accessing the color-selection dialog in a commercial paint package.

   a. HSB values:

0	75	80
0	75	52
120	100	60
120	37	80
120	16	90

   b. HSB values:

41	100	100
30	50	80
30	67	60
30	35	85
62	20	100

   c. HSB values:

23	90	100
23	50	100
23	38	100
23	93	38
23	20	0

   d. RGB values:

255	255	204
54	53	154
255	0	0
153	153	204
62	62	128

   e. RGB values:

64	177	255
0	154	255
99	193	255
0	0	0
255	255	255

   f. RGB values:

53	53	204
255	246	148
212	79	98
60	60	145
232	214	21

13. In the previous question, half of the color sets were posed in RGB values, the others in the HSB color model. For the purposes of creating and using a color harmony, which is easier to employ? Why?

14. Which of the following combinations for text and background should you avoid? In each case, give your reasons. To find the answer, it could help to convert the colors to a different color model or to refer to a color wheel. You can do this either by using the Color Conversion software or by accessing the color-selection dialog in a commercial paint package.

   a. Text: (60,100,0) HSB Background: (180,10,100) HSB

   b. Text: (0,0,100) HSB Background: (180,0,100) HSB

    c. Text: (0,0,0) HSB Background: (180,0,100) HSB

    d. Text: (0,100,100) HSB Background: (120,100,100) HSB

    e. Text: (300,70,100) HSB Background: (0,70,100) HSB

    f. Text: (60,70,100) HSB Background: (120,0,100) HSB

15. In this exercise, you will use the Color Matching software to explore color spaces. Start the software. On the opening screen, select a color and a color model. This will take you to a screen with two color patches and a set of sliders. Adjust the sliders until the two squares match in terms of color. You will know when this happens because the two squares will appear to be one long rectangle and the word "Match" appears. You will also see the number of adjustments you made during the matching process.

    a. Use the software to match 10 colors. For five of these colors, use a hardware-oriented color model; for the other five, choose an artist's model. Make a table to record information about your session. Use the following format:

    Color Name   Color Model   Number of Adjustments

    _____   _____   _____

    b. After matching 10 colors, which model did you find easier to work with?

    c. Relate your answer for part B to the table you recorded for part A.

16. Use the Color Matching software to test people's performance and preference for the RGB and HSB color models.

    a. Recruit 30 people to take the test. Each person will match 10 colors. Divide the people into two groups. The first group will use the RGB model for the first five matchings they complete, and the HSB model for the second five. The second group of people will use the HSB model first, followed by the RGB model.

    b. In a written pretest questionnaire, ask the test participants to list any computer graphics, Web, or graphics design classes they've taken. Also ask them if they're colorblind.

    c. Be sure to administer informed consent. Review Chapter 8 for a discussion on informed consent.

    d. Test each user individually. Ask each user to match 10 colors, one at a time. For each matching, tell the user which model to select.

    e. During a test session, record the color name, the color space, and the number of adjustments that the user made for each matching. At the end of the matching sessions, ask the user which was the better system for color matching.

    f. Analyze the data you collected, and answer the following questions:

      i. What colors were easier to match?

      ii. Which colors caused the most difficulty?

      iii. Were some colors easier to match in a particular color space? If so, which ones? Explain, in terms of the data.

      iv. Which color system did users prefer? Is there a relation between the number of adjustments they made and the model they preferred?

      v. Does previous experience have any effect on their preference? Justify your answer.

      vi. Does previous experience have any effect on their performance? Explain your answer in terms of the data you collected.

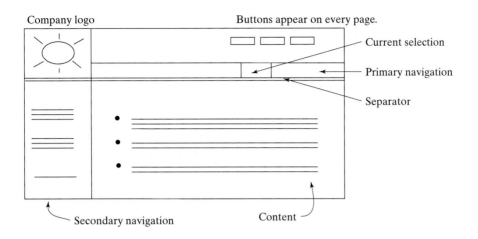

Figure 9–24 For question 17.

17. Suppose you are working for a client who likes the color yellow and wants it to be the dominant color on a website. Further, the client wants a white background for everything outside the navigation layout. The agreed-upon main page layout is given in Figure 9–24.

   Using a monochromatic color scheme, make suggestions for the elements of the page. Explain the underlying principle for each choice. Fill in the table below.

Element	Color	Reason
Background of primary navigation bar		
Background of current selection in primary navigation bar		
Background of secondary navigation bar		
Background of buttons at top of page		
Separator		
Background of content area	HSB: (0,0,100) White	Client specified
Text of primary navigation bar		
Text of selection in primary navigation bar		
Text of secondary navigation bar		
Text of content area		
Corporate logo	HSB (47, 100, 100) Yellow	Client specified
Bullet		

References

[Durrett 1987] H. John Durrett, editor. *Color and the Computer*. Boston: Academic Press, 1987. pp. 43–44.

[Foley 1990] James D. Foley, Andries van Dam, Steven K. Feiner, and John F. Hughes. *Computer Graphics: Principles and Practice.* 2nd ed. (in C). Reading, Massachusetts: Addison–Wesley, 1990–96. Chapter 123: Achromatic and Colored Light. pp. 563–604.

[Gage 1999] John Gage. *Color and Culture: Practice and Meaning from Antiquity to Abstraction.* University of California Press, 1999.

[Glassner 1995] Andrew Glassner. *Principles of Digital Image Synthesis.* Vol. 1. San Francisco: Morgan Kaufmann, 1995. Chapter 3: Displays. pp. 71–114.

[Gleitman 1998] Henry Gleitman. *Basic Psychology*, 4th ed. New York: Norton, 1998.

[Hall 1989] Roy Hall. *Illumination and Color in Computer Generated Imagery.* New York: Springer-Verlag, 1989. Chapter 3: Perceptual Response. pp 45–62.

[Hill 2000] Alyson Hill and Lauren Scharff. "Readability Of Websites With Various Foreground/Background Color Combinations, Font Types And Word Styles," *Optics Express* 6(4), February 2000. pp 81–91. Also available at `http://www.opticsexpress.org/abstract.cfm?URI=OPEX-6-4-81`

[Hoffman 1999] Kenneth Hoffman. *Understanding Color in a Digital Workflow.* Rochester, New York: Rochester Institute of Technology, 1999. Available at `http://www.rit.edu/~kfhnvc/StoC/colorcurricsample.pdf`

[Hoffmann 2002] Gernot Hoffmann. *Color Order Systems: RGB, HLS, HSB.* Available at `http://www.fho-emden.de/~hoffmann/hlscone03052001.pdf`, updated March 2002.

[Horton 1991] William Horton. *Illustrating Computer Documentation: The Art of Presenting Information Graphics on Paper and Online.* New York: John Wiley, 1991.

[Linton 1991] Harold Linton. *Color Consulting: A Survey of International Color Design.* New York: Van Nostrand Reinhold, 1991.

[McDowell 2000] David McDowell. Color Management: What's Needed for Printing and Publishing. *The Prepress Bulletin.* March/April 2000. 11–17.

[Murch 1984] Gerald Murch. "The Effective Use of Color: Perceptual Principles," *Tekniques* 8(1). pp. 4–9.

[Murch 1987] Gerald Murch. Color Displays and Color Science. In *Color and the Computer.* H. John Durrett. Boston: Academic Press, 1987. pp 1–26.

[Silverstein 1987] Louis Silverstein. Human Factors of Color Display Systems: Concepts, Methods and Research. In *Color and the Computer.* H. John Durrett. Boston: Academic Press, 1987. pp. 27–61.

[Smith 1976] Alvy Ray Smith. Color Gamut Transform Pairs. *Computer Graphics. (Proceedings of SIGGRAPH 78)* 12(3), August 1978. 12–19.

[Weinman 1997] Lynda Weinman, Bruce Heavin, and Ali Karp. *Coloring Web Graphics.* Indianapolis: New Riders, 1997.

[Whelan 1994] Bride M. Whelan. *Color Harmony 2: A Guide to Creative Color Combinations.* Gloucester, MA: Rockport Publishers, 1994.

[Wyszecki 1982] G. Wyszecki and W. Stiles. *Color Science: Concepts and Methods, Quantitative Data and Formulae.* New York: John Wiley, 1982.

10

Typography

10.1 Introduction

Typography has a long and proud history extending back to 1455, when Gutenberg invented printing from movable type. In five-and-a-half centuries, a subject area of such great usefulness as typography can build up quite a vocabulary. In the past ten years, designers have adapted this knowledge for Web use. As in the previous chapter, the presentation here discusses basic tools for making Web pages easy to read and provides a basis for good communication with graphic designers.

The basic, most essential elements found on a Web page are words—words in links, words in section headings, words in isolated sentences and in blocks of text. To communicate effectively with an audience, it's important that these words be easy to read. This chapter covers *typography*, which is the act of arranging text with attention to placement, size, and font choice.

Goals of this Chapter

After studying this chapter, you will have done the following:

- understood the basic terminology and concepts of working with type
- learned a dozen typefaces, their characteristics, and where and why they are useful
- become aware of how typography on the Web differs from typography in print
- become able—using guidelines provided at the end of the chapter—to design the typography for a Web page that is readable, effective, and attractive.

10.2 Concepts and Terminology

In the context of typography, *type* is any set of printed characters, including letters, numbers, or symbols. These characters can appear on paper or on a computer monitor [Holtzschue 1997]. A *font* is a set of all the printable (printer fonts) or displayable (screen fonts) text characters in a specific style and size. A *typeface* is the design for a set of fonts. A *typeface family,* or *font family,* consists of all the sizes and variations (bold, italic, small caps, etc.) of a typeface. Thus, Times New Roman is a typeface family, Times New Roman bold is a typeface, and 12-point Times New Roman bold is a font.

Here is some sample text set in the 16-point Times New Roman font provided with Microsoft Word:

abcdefghijklmnopqrstuvwxyz

ABCDEFGHIJKLMNOPQRSTUVWXYZ

`1234567890-~!@#$%^&*()_+

[]\;',./{}|:"<>?

Figure 10–1 shows a word and some more terminology.

Uppercase and *lowercase* designate large and small characters. The terms come from the days when the type for individual characters was held in boxes called cases, placed at the back of the compositor's worktable.

A *serif* is a decorative line, circle, or other flourish at the end of a stroke in a letter. The most basic distinguishing characteristic of type families is that between *serif* and *sans serif* forms. "Sans" is French for "without."

The *baseline* is an imaginary line on which most letters appear to rest. The *midline* is an imaginary line that runs along the tops of most lowercase letters. The vertical distance between the baseline and the midline is called the *x-height*; the lowercase letter x is a representative of the letters that extend to the midline. An *ascender* is the portion of some letters that extends above the midline; a *descender* is the portion of some letters that extends below the baseline.

Figure 10–2 shows the same word as before, but this time in a common sans-serif typeface, Arial.

The terms *body type* and *display type* describe two different contexts in which text can appear. Body type is what you are reading. It is a collection of text, ranging from a few lines to hundreds, in a relatively small size. Display type is used for things like chapter and section

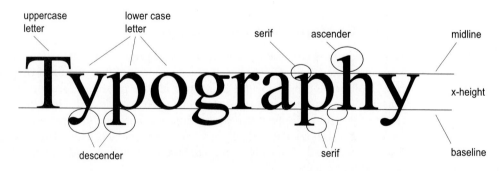

Figure 10–1 Uppercase and lowercase serifed characters in a serif font, Times Roman.

Typography

Figure 10–2   A sans-serif font, Arial.

headings in a book, and for page and section headings on a Web page. Display type is larger than body type, sometimes much larger.

A *point* is 1/72nd of an inch; points are used to measure vertical and sometimes horizontal sizes and distances. A *pica* is 1/6 of an inch; picas are used to measure horizontal sizes and distances. It is useful to know these conversions:

- There are 72 points in an inch.
- There are 6 picas in an inch.
- There are 12 points in a pica.

The size of type is given in points. We might say "12-point Times New Roman" or "18-point Arial." It is important to be clear on what is meant by point size. The point size of type is the vertical distance from the bottom of the lowest descender to the top of the highest ascender, measured in points—*plus a little bit*.

The size of the "little bit" varies from one typeface to another. Figure 10–3 displays two lines of type set in Times New Roman, showing the "little bit." The point size is also the distance between baselines, assuming no space is added between lines. Without the "little bit," the letters in successive lines would touch, hampering legibility.

Readability of text type is enhanced by adding even more space—beyond that provided in the design of the typeface—between lines. The added space is called *leading* (pronounced "ledding"); the term comes from the days of metal type, when adding space meant inserting a thin piece of a lead alloy between two lines of type. At the top of the next page are two paragraphs, both set in 10 point Times New Roman. The first has one point of leading; the second has three points of leading. The shorthand description of the latter is "10 on 13," or "10/13."

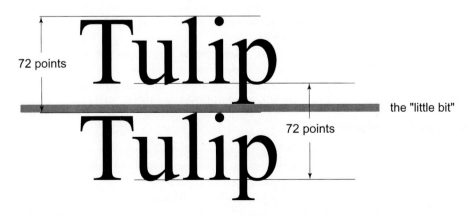

Figure 10–3   The size of a font is given in points.

Typography has a long and proud history extending back to 1455, when Gutenberg invented printing from movable type. A subject area of great usefulness can build up quite a vocabulary in five and a half centuries. In the past ten years, designers have adapted this knowledge for Web use. As with color in the previous chapter, the presentation here discusses basic tools for making Web pages easy to read and provides a basis for good communication with graphic designers.

Typography has a long and proud history extending back to 1455, when Gutenberg invented printing from movable type. A subject area of great usefulness can build up quite a vocabulary in five and a half centuries. In the past ten years, designers have adapted the knowledge for Web use. As with color in the previous chapter, the presentation here discusses basic tools for making Web pages easy to read and provides a basis for good communication with graphic designers.

An *em* is a linear measure, equal to the point size of the font. In any 12-point font, an em is 12 points, 1/6 of an inch. The em is a *relative* measure, whereas points and picas are *absolute*. If you specify a distance between words in points, that distance does not change if you change to a different font size. If you specify a distance in ems and change the font size, then that distance changes also. A related measure, the *en,* is half the width of an em.

The angles of the characters of a font family can be characterized as *normal* (also called roman) or *italic*. Normal means upright; italic means slanted, along with other more subtle changes. The terms go back many centuries, to a time before Italy was a country: Rome was the city, and Italia was the rest of the Italian peninsula. Much early font design was done in this region. Having a typeface called Times Roman is awkward in this context: "Times Roman italic" and "Times Roman roman" both make sense despite the strange appearance of the latter. This is why most of today's commercial software uses the equivalent term "normal" or "regular" in font-selection dialogs.

10.3 A Dozen Font Families

In thinking about text fonts, it can seem that there is a nearly infinite variety that is overwhelming. However, most professional graphic designers tend to find a small number of fonts that they like and understand and do most of their work using this small set. *The Designer's Guide to Text Type* [King 1980] shows " . . . fifty-one popular text typefaces . . . " Fifty-one type fonts are still quite a few, and it helps to classify them into categories based on common characteristics. This section presents a dozen font families, grouped into five categories: *serif, sans serif, monospaced, script,* and *miscellaneous and decorative*. Most of the typefaces shown are provided in Windows 2000.

10.3.1 Serif Typefaces

Printing from movable type began with serif typefaces, which were used exclusively for over two centuries. A majority of newspapers, magazines, and books use serif typefaces. Much of the body text on the Web appears in a serif typeface.

The most widely used font family for print is Times Roman, designed by Stanley Morison in 1932 for The Times of London [Craig 1990]. It was intended to be readable in small sizes on the low-quality newsprint used during a worldwide depression. Today, it's still a good first choice for print work.

Times Roman was a great success in meeting its intended goal of enhancing the legibility of printed materials. However, what succeeds in print might not work on a computer monitor. Monitors have far coarser resolution than does print. Their resolution ranges from 72 to 120 pixels per inch. Laser printers for home use have resolutions of 600 dots per inch, and ink jet printers go as high as 4800 by 1200. The fine detail available in print technology is not a possibility on a computer monitor.

Microsoft commissioned Matthew Carter to design a typeface along the lines of the familiar Times New Roman, but optimized for screen display [Will-Harris 1997]. The result is called Georgia. Here are sample lines in Times New Roman and Georgia, considerably enlarged to bring out the differences:

Times New Roman

Web Typography

Georgia

Web Typography

Several changes make for improved readability of Georgia on the screen. Compared with Times New Roman, in Georgia,

- The strokes that make up the letters are a little heavier.
- The letters are slightly larger, in each dimension.
- The x-height is slightly greater.
- There is less variation between the thin and thick strokes in the characters.

In Georgia, letters like o, e, and about half a dozen others have *vertical stress*, meaning that a line drawn through the thinnest parts of a letter is vertical. Here is the letter o in Times Roman and in Georgia, enlarged to bring out the difference:

On a typical monitor in 2002, one pixel is about one point, and curved portions of small letters come out jagged. (These areas are commonly called *jaggies*.) Here is a 12-point letter o, in Times New Roman on the left and Georgia on the right, greatly enlarged:

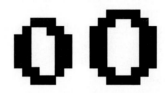

In the Times New Roman, there are two places where pixels touch only at their corners; this does not happen with Georgia. Also, the size of the letter is increased. The overall effect is that Georgia has a smoother appearance. Type families like Georgia, which were designed for better legibility in small sizes on computer screens, are called *screen friendly*.

Neither of these fonts is intended for use in the large sizes used to illustrate issues here. Georgia comes into its own in extended bodies of text on the screen. Figure 10–4 shows a small body of text in each typeface, both set at 10 points. The sample set in Georgia takes part of another line, reflecting its larger characters and its greater letter spacing.

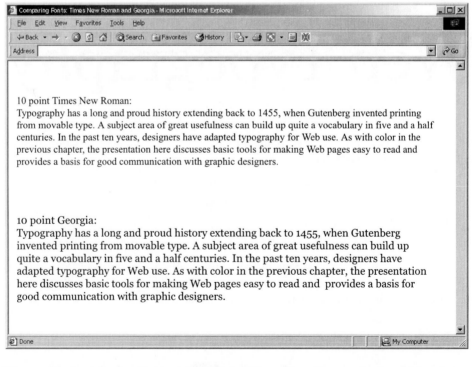

Figure 10–4   A body of text set in 10-point Times New Roman, top, and 10-point Georgia, bottom.

10.3.2 Sans-Serif Typefaces

When sans-serif typefaces emerged in the nineteenth century, they were called grotesque, because they seemed so unusual [Adobe 2000]. A typeface named Grotesque, in use today, recalls that heritage. The most widely used sans-serif typeface on the Web is Arial® — which, as it happens, is similar to Grotesque. Any reader of this book has seen type set in Arial thousands of times.

Besides Arial, we shall consider Verdana, Arial Black, Impact, Comic Sans MS and Trebuchet. Here they are together for easy comparison:

Arial

Web Typography

Verdana

Web Typography

Arial Black

Web Typography

Impact

Web Typography

Comic Sans

Web Typography

Trebuchet

Web Typography

Arial and **Verdana**. When compared to Arial, Verdana has two advantages for Web use. The letters are a little wider, and the standard letterspacing is slightly greater. These factors spread the type out by about 10%. Further, Verdana letters have fewer and more gradual curves, thus reducing jaggies. Compare the letters b, y, p, and a in these samples. The effect of these differences is to make Verdana somewhat easier to read in the small font sizes normally used for extended bodies of text.

Arial Black is a much heavier typeface than Arial. It is useful for attracting attention. Arial Black is noticeably different from Arial bold. Here are a few letters set twice, both at 36 points (half an inch), in Arial bold on the left and in Arial Black on the right:

Web Dev Web Dev

Compare the thickest and thinnest parts of the lower case 'b' in both fonts. The stroke is wider and gives Arial Black more contrast when compared to other fonts.

Impact.   Compared to Arial, Impact creates even more contrast than does Arial Black. Impact gains its effect by going to letters that are tall and narrow and by using a very large x-height. Here are two words in Arial and in Impact:

Web Dev Web Dev

Comic Sans MS is an informal style inspired by the lettering in comic books. It can be used to give a distinctive touch to a heading. Here are Arial and Comic Sans:

Web Dev Web Dev

Trebuchet has the easy screen readability of Verdana, but gives a more relaxed, informal appearance. In the following example, Arial is on the left and Trebuchet on the right:

Web Dev Web Dev

10.3.3 Monospaced Typefaces

In all of the previous typefaces, the characters had different widths. The letter "M" takes more horizontal space than the letter "i", and "W" is wider than "f". In typefaces that have *proportional spacing*, each character is allotted a width proportional to its natural geometry. For most purposes, proportional spacing is appropriate, because it enhances legibility.

There are times, however, when it's important for all the characters of a font to be the same width, because then it's easier to align text without the use of word-processing software. Such typefaces are called *monospaced*. One of the most prevalent uses of monospaced typeface is to display program code.

Courier is one of the most familiar typefaces, having been adapted from a widely used typewriter font. Here are a few words in Courier and in Times Roman:

```
cout << "Hello, World!";
```

cout << "Hello, World!";

This is C++ code, for which monospaced fonts are customary. Notice that, in Courier, the comma, the exclamation point, and the letter W all get the same horizontal space. In the proportionally spaced Times Roman, a character gets an amount proportional to its width. Notice the *typographic quotes* in Times Roman, compared with the *straight quotes* in Courier. The Times Roman version would cause a compiler error.

Here is a little more code, showing how indentation is clearly conveyed when all characters (including blank) are the same width:

```
// Hit(): return true if mouse is inside bug
// and update hit taken count
bool Bug::IsHit(const Position &MousePosition) {
  if (GetBmp(GetDirection()).IsInside(MousePosition)) {
    ++HitsTaken;
    return true;
  }
  else
    return false;
}
```

The indentation nicely conveys the nesting of the statements: each new level is indented two spaces to the right of the preceding. It is easy to see, for example, that the first and last lines are aligned, and that the fourth and seventh lines are indented by the same amount. In reading programs, this matters. Now look at it in Times New Roman:

```
// Hit(): return true if mouse is inside bug
// and update hit taken count
bool Bug::IsHit(const Position &MousePosition) {
  if (GetBmp(GetDirection()).IsInside(MousePosition)) {
   ++HitsTaken;
   return true;
  }
  else
   return false;
}
```

If you are a programmer, you probably have never seen a program set in Times Roman, because a monospaced font is much more suitable for your purposes. The user's comfort zone has to be considered.

Andale Mono is a screen-friendly monospaced font family from Microsoft. Here is the same C++ code in Andale Mono:

```
// Hit(): return true if mouse is inside bug
// and update hit taken count
bool Bug::IsHit(const Position &MousePosition) {
  if (GetBmp(GetDirection()).IsInside(MousePosition)) {
   ++HitsTaken;
   return true;
  }
  else
   return false;
}
```

Choosing which monospaced font to use is a matter of personal preference, but keep in mind that many users will not have access to the more exotic typefaces. Essentially all machines have Courier, so it is a safe choice.

10.3.4 Script Typefaces

Script typefaces are designed to look something like handwriting. Sometimes the intent is to give the informal appearance of a quick memo; at other times, it is to produce a formal invitation with the appearance of an engraving.

Nuptial Script suggests a wedding invitation. A website selling wedding accessories might use a little Nuptial Script to suggest the connection. Here is a sample:

A Perfect Wedding

This is 36-point type, which is fine for a heading. An extended body of text set in Nuptial Script at an ordinary body text size, such as 12 points, would be quite hard to read.

Without some custom installation work, today's browsers do not support script typefaces. If it is crucial to a client that a particular heading appear in a script typeface, there are two alternatives. The first is to convert the text into an image. For example, a GIF image with a transparent background can take the place of a text heading. The second is to use Scalable Vector Graphics (SVG), but this option also requires that the user download additional software.

10.3.5 Miscellaneous and Decorative Typefaces

This umbrella category covers a large number of typefaces that do not fit elsewhere. Here is a small sample—very small—of the large number available, with suggestions for how they might be used.

Webdings is a typeface developed by type designers at Microsoft and at Monotype, a major type supplier. The characters are graphic images, but in the form of characters. If a user's browser has the typeface, a single character can take the place of a graphic file that would require hundreds of bytes. The following are examples:

You will recognize the icons for controls on a tape or DVD player, some other familiar icons, and a few characters for making borders or patterns. There are many typefaces of this kind, which go under the generic name *wingdings*.

A site about New York City could use two characters in Webdings and two in Arial Black, to produce an iconic version of a familiar slogan:

Symbol is a typeface containing the letters of the Greek alphabet, a number of mathematical symbols, and a few other things. It can be used for simple mathematics, as in the next example.

The speed of propagation c equals the product of the frequency f and the wavelength λ:

$$f\lambda = c$$

Be aware that the setting of general mathematical expressions is far beyond the capability of XHTML. Look into MathML if this is your interest. See `http://www.w3.org/Math/`.

10.4 A Web Page Is Not a Printed Page

A print designer starts a project knowing that the result will be ink on paper. The size and quality of the paper are known. If a print designer specifies 36-point Arial, then the printed words will be 36 points high, or the printer doesn't get paid. A Web designer doesn't have this luxury.

Here are some of the things the Web type designer doesn't know [Williams 1992]:

- The resolution of the monitor, which depends on the type of monitor and perhaps on the video card. This affects the size of everything.

- The size of the browser window. It could be a window four inches wide and seven inches high, or it could be all of a 21-inch monitor. This could result in lines of 12-point text that are over a foot long—which is very difficult to read.

- The text size. Users can specify that the browser display text in a size that's different from what's specified on the Web page. Older people will often want to display text in a larger size. Those with younger eyes may direct that the text be smaller, to reduce scrolling.

- The settings and quality of the monitor, in terms of brightness, contrast, color balance, and a number of technical factors.

- The fonts available to a user. If Beesknees is just the right font for the heading on a funky page, feel free. Just be aware that what a user sees could be totally different.

The user is the boss: On most browsers, it is a simple matter to specify text and background colors, font, and font size. However, there is no way the reader of a book or magazine can check some boxes and override every decision a designer has made.

Do not despair. This section lays out a worst-case scenario. Sticking to familiar font families that most users do have will pay off.

10.5 Text in Graphics

Suppose you have found a font that is just right for the heading of a page; the client loves it, but it is one that most users are unlikely to have. Is the situation hopeless? Not at all. If the text is short, it's possible to use an image instead.

There are many ways to make a graphic containing text; Adobe Photoshop is one possibility among many. It's not necessary to have access to Photoshop. Another alternative is to format the text in a word-processing program and make a screen capture. Paste the screen grab into a paint program and crop it so that it contains only the desired text. Save the result as an image file. Figure 10–5 shows nonsense expression from the 1920s set in 30-point ITC Beeskness STD:

IT'S THE BEE'S KNEES

Figure 10–5 An image containing a decorative font.

The image file that contains this text is only 1800 bytes, which will not normally cause problems with download times. With appropriate software you can add shadows, make the type look embossed, and employ many other effects. Figure 10–6 displays a sample, using a drop shadow:

Figure 10–6   Adding effects to text. This is a drop shadow.

The accompanying increase in file size is usually acceptable, for small amounts of text. When using this approach, remember to add an ALT tag[6] that contains the text that's portrayed in the image file.

10.6   Guidelines: Body Type on the Web

You might be wondering how to apply all the new information in this chapter while you are still trying to make sense of the unfamiliar concepts and terminology. This section applies to body type (extended bodies of text in small sizes).[7] The following section deals with display type (small amounts in bigger sizes). Here are some suggestions that will help you get started. The way you specify your choices depends on the software involved. In working with Web pages, we use tags in XHTML or attributes in Cascading Style Sheets. There are numerous examples in the Appendix.

Use Georgia or Verdana.

There doesn't seem to be much difference in legibility between serif and sans-serif faces on the screen, in these very legible choices, but don't intermix them in body text [Boyarski 1998]. Trebuchet is also a screen-friendly sans-serif option.

Use 10-point or 12-point type.

For people under the age of 65, font sizes smaller than 10 points will slow a person's reading speed. People over the age of 65 prefer 12 or even 14-point fonts [Tullis 1995, Bernard 2001].

Avoid bold or italic text in body type.

Extended bodies of text in italic are quite difficult to read, and bold type competes with headings for attention. Use italic and bold only for emphasis, and with small amounts of text.

Use uppercase only for the first letter of sentences, of proper names, and so on.

All UPPER CASE, also called ALL CAPS, is much harder to read than the usual uppercase and lowercase. It's fine for labels, but not for regular text.

Use 2 points of leading between lines, unless you are using a font that automatically supplies that.

---

[6]For more information on HTML tags, see the appendix.
[7]See [Miyazaki 2000] for another set of guidelines. The recommendations are largely the same, but organized a little differently, and Miyazaki has some additional material.

Specify the leading in a Cascading Style Sheet (CSS) with the line-height attribute. To see whether leading is supplied, specify a line height the same as the font size; if this causes the lines to move closer together but they still do not touch, you already had leading.

Use left alignment.

Centered and right-aligned text is difficult to read: when the eye reaches the end of a line it has trouble finding the start of the next line. Both are OK for variety with a small amount of text, but not otherwise. Justified type can cause unacceptably large spaces between words if the browser window is narrow.

Use black text on a white background.

This isn't rigid. Dark blue or dark gray text on a warm white background is pleasant and easy to read. If you insist on using white text on a black background, increase the font size; white on black is harder to read.

Never use underlining for emphasis.

Users assume that underlined text is a link. Instead, use a bold or italic font.

10.7   Guidelines: Display Type on the Web

Display type is larger than text type because titles and headings should be bigger than body text. There is no firm boundary, but you should strive to make it twice as large as body type. In these sizes, legibility is not an issue. The rules are less restrictive, and your freedom to innovate is greater. Here are a few guidelines:

Big is beautiful.

This has limits: the text does have to fit in a browser window, but there is lots of room to maneuver. Do you want to put one word in inch-high (72-point) letters? Feel free, if the impact is worth the screen real estate it uses.

Use any typeface that is legible.

This comes with the proviso that either your user's machine should have the font or that you should substitute an image that contains the text in the font you want.

Use the line-height attribute for control of line spacing, to get the graphic effect you want.

That effect can be anything from making the letters touch to spreading them out a lot.

Use letter spacing and word spacing to get effects you want.

Example: you decide to set up a website for the second volume of Tolkien's *The Lord of the Rings*. "The Two Towers" isn't very many characters long, so, for impact, you decide to got to all caps and add extra space between letters and between words:

THE TWO TOWERS

This clearly has more snap and pizzazz than

THE TWO TOWERS

Don't use any form of animation of text.

Users hate it. They will scroll the ugliness off the screen or cover it with their hand. Some develop "animation blindness," in which they don't "see" the text: some action of the brain filters out anything animated.

Review Questions

1. Make a photocopy of Figure 10–7 and label the following. The font is Garamond, designed by Claude Garamond around 1540 and still in use.

   a. Uppercase

   b. Lowercase

   c. Ascender (2 instances)

   d. Descender (2 instances)

   e. Serif (two types)

   f. x-height

   g. Baseline

Biographical

Figure 10–7   For question 1.

2. The terms *point*, *pica* and em are all units of measure in typography. Explain the relationship between point and pica and how they differ from an em.

3. What is leading? What is its purpose? Explain "set solid" in terms of leading. Is "set solid" a good choice for body text on a Web page? Why or why not?

4. How is font size measured?

5. Suppose a website were offering the Caslon Open Face typeface for download. To show users what it looks like, the Web page display the text in Figure 10–8. What can

Figure 10–8   A sample of the Caslon Open Face typeface. For exercise 5.

you do to guarantee that users will be able to see the font's appearance, even if they haven't downloaded it? (William Caslon was an influential English type designer of the 18th century.)

6. What is the effect of a "screen-friendly" typeface? Name at least three characteristics that make a font screen-friendly.

7. Match the font family name with the text sample:

1.	Arial	a.	Sample Text
2.	Nuptial Script	b.	**Sample Text**
3.	Times Roman	c.	Σαμπλε Τεξτ
4.	Impact	d.	*Sample Text*
5.	Verdana	e.	Sample Text
6.	Courier	f.	Sample Text
7.	Symbol	g.	Sample Text
8.	Georgia	h.	**Sample Text**

8. You have chosen a font family and font size that give very good legibility, and your site is directed to people with normal vision. What is the smallest font size you would use?

9. You have chosen a font family and font size that give very good legibility for a website that caters to retired people. What is the smallest font size you would use?

10. What is the difference between letter spacing and word spacing?

Exercises

11. Create a Web page containing a paragraph of text that fills approximately six lines in a 12-point serif font. The text should be in normal uppercase and lowercase. Left-justify the text, and use black text on a white background. Now create additional Web pages that contain the same text but have the following variations:

    a. Original version (no changes)

    b. All caps; same colors for foreground and background; single spaced

    c. All italic; same colors for foreground and background, single spaced

    d. Same font and colors, but break up the text into lines with no more than eight words each, single spaced. Center each line.

    e. Video reverse: use white text on a black background. Single spaced.

    Ask 10 people to tell you which variation is the easiest to read and which is the worst. For testing purposes, set up a presentation that will allow users to look at each Web page as many times as they want. Perhaps you will want to have an initial page containing links to each of the different variations that you want the users to see. Also, to avoid any bias that would come from the order of seeing the variations, set up a method to present the pages in a different order for each viewer. Report on your findings.

12. The large type shown in Figure 10–9 is in a 72-point Arial font. Use a ruler to verify that the distance between the two horizontal lines is one inch on the printed page. Create a Web page that contains the same text in 72-point Arial. Display the result on a computer monitor. How much vertical space does the font take up on the screen? Use a ruler on the screen surface to check. Answer this question again after changing your monitor resolution to the largest and smallest available. What are your conclusions?

Figure 10–9   For exercise 12

13. Review the following Web pages:

    • Figure 4–8 (a page of Google search results)

    • Exercise 4d in Chapter 4 (a campus calendar of events)

    • Exercise 9d in Chapter 4 (MyNews.com)

    • Figure 5–9 (www.eddiebauer.com)

    • Figure 6–8 (www.useit.com)

For each, answer the following questions:

a. Which font category (serif, sans-serif, monospaced, script, decorative/miscellaneous) was used for the logo or main title?

b. Which font category was used for headings?

c. Which font category was used for body text?

d. How many font categories appear on the page?

14. You have decided that you will design a title so that it looks good in any screen resolution from 640 × 480 to 1024 × 768. You want the heading to be dramatic, which you have decided means as big as possible without it breaking into two lines on a small screen. The title is "Typography is Fun!" Create a Web page with several versions of the title, each using a different typeface. Use at least different three different typefaces. For each version, specify the typeface and size for the font. Note: there is no unique "correct" answer. Restrict yourself to the typefaces described in this chapter.

15. Search the Web for free or shareware fonts. Find three typefaces that could serve as body type and at least three typefaces that would work as display type, but not body type. Install these typefaces on your computer. For each typeface,

a. Print a sample paragraph of text using the new typeface. Give its name.

b. Identify it as being appropriate for body or display type.

c. Justify the answer you gave in part B.

References

[Adobe 2000] Adobe, Inc. *MyriadPro: A Versatile Sans Serif OpenType Family*. 2000. Available: `www.adobe.com/type/browser/pdfs/MyriadPro.pdf`

[Bauermeister 1988] Benjamin Bauermeister. *A Manual of Comparative Typography: The PANOSE System*. New York, Van Nostrand Reinhold.

[Bernard 2001] Michael Bernard, Corrina Liao, and Melissa Mills. "Determining the Best Online Font for Older Adults," *Usability News*. Wichita State University, Winter 2001. `http://psychology.wichita.edu/surl/usabilitynews/3W/fontSR.htm`.

[Craig 1990] James Craig. *Basic Typography: A Design Manual*. New York: Watson–Guptil Publications, 1990. p. 32.

[Craig 1992] James Craig, *Designing with Type*. New York: Watson–Guptil Publications, 1992.

[King 1980] Jean Callan King and Tony Esposito. *The Designer's Guide to Text Type: Leaded showings of fifty-one popular text typefaces in 6 point through 12 point plus 14 point*. New York: Van Nostrand, 1980.

[Miyazaki 2000] Jerry Greenfield Miyazaki. "Web Page Legibility Guidelines," `http://www.miyazaki-mic.ac.jp/faculty/JGREENFI/WebLegibility.html`.

[Will-Harris 1997] Daniel Will-Harris. Matthew Carter. "Typefaces Designed for the Screen," *Web Review*. November 7, 1997. Available at `http://www.webreview.com/1997/11_07/webauthors/11_07_97_10.shtml`

[Williams 1992] Robin Williams. *The PC is Not a Typewriter*. Berkeley: Peachpit Press.

11

Multimedia

11.1 Introduction

Since long before the advent of computers, the world has been filled with multimedia. Sights, sounds, tastes, textures, and aromas range in variety from splashes of color or a blur of motion to the feel of well-worn jeans or the smoothness of a door handle polished by thousands of hands. These sensations add richness and variety to everyday living. Similarly, electronic multimedia can offer a richer user experience for website visitors. Used appropriately, these sensations add enormous appeal. Multimedia can engage the senses to inform, persuade or entertain. Used poorly, multimedia can annoy or alienate an audience.

The term *multimedia* refers to a combination of two or more media [Weinschenk 1997]. There are many media available for the Web, including printed or spoken words, music and other audio, images, video, animations, and interactive animation. This chapter will examine three major types of multimedia: audio, video, and animation. These appeal to the sense of sight, the sense of hearing, or both. They are available to the majority of computer users, because most moderately priced computer systems now have graphics and sound capability. There have been recent developments in using the sense of touch as part of an interaction, but the required hardware is still considered a specialty item and is not widely available [Konrad 2001].

Goals of this Chapter

This chapter covers the various types of commonly available multimedia, shows some examples, and discusses design tips for effectively incorporating multimedia on a website. In this chapter, you will learn

- basic multimedia types and available file formats
- advantages and disadvantages of using multimedia
- technology considerations when using multimedia
- design guidelines for using multimedia on the Web
- new developments in multimedia delivery.

11.2 Audio

Audio can supplement the visual aspects of a Web page by adding speech, sound, or music. Spoken words can serve as an alternative to printed text for user populations that have poorly developed reading skill or limited eyesight. Music can help set a mood in an interactive game or an electronic greeting card. Some e-commerce sites invite users to download sample music clips to entice them into buying music CDs. Sound, when properly used, can grab a user's attention away from his or her current task. A commonly experienced example of this is the sound that announces the arrival of new e-mail.

There are a variety of audio file formats available for the Web, but they all fall into two basic categories: *streaming* and *nonstreaming* [Niederst 98]. In a nonstreaming format, the entire file is downloaded and saved on disk. In contrast, with the newer streaming formats, the entire file is not saved to disk. Both can allow a user to begin listening to the audio while the download is still in progress.

Figure 11–1 lists commonly used audio file formats [Bagwell 2000, Directorate 1999, Dunn 2000, Fraunhofer 2001, Midi 2001]. In addition to streaming capability, the newer MP3 and RealAudio formats also incorporate more effective file compression, so that sound can be stored more compactly and require less time to download. In fact, the new formats store speech in such small files that users owning a 56Kbps modem can initiate a download and begin listening almost immediately. Further, there are no pauses or gaps in the speech, because the bits arrive quickly enough that the media player does not have to wait. Current bandwidth also supports some types of recorded music, and Internet radio is becoming popular [MeasureCast 2002].

When considering the use of audio on a site, keep the following guidelines in mind:

- Be sure that the dialog contained in any audio file is also available as text on the site. Some people prefer to read the text instead of listening to it. Users might be working a computer without sound capabilities or be in a location (such as a library) where sound is inappropriate. Others are deaf and cannot make use of audio.

- When using audio to set a mood, keep the volume low. If the music loops continually, give users a way to turn off the repetition.

- When using sound to focus attention, keep the sounds short and quiet. In addition, any sound used for attention-getting purposes should happen only occasionally, or users will learn to ignore it. Give users the option to turn off the sound without affecting the rest of the website.

Extension	Format Name	Originator	Streaming?	Additional software?
.wav	Waveform	Microsoft	No	No
.au	Sun Audio	Sun Microsystems	No	No
.aiff	Audio Interchange	Apple	No	No
.mid	Musical Instrument Digital Interface	International MIDI Association	No	No
.mp3	MPEG Audio (Layer 3)	Fraunhofer IIS-A and the International Standards Organization	Yes	No
.ra	Real Audio	Real Networks	Yes	Yes. Available: www.real.com

Figure 11–1 Audio file formats.

11.3 Video

Video is an appealing medium, as is evidenced by the fact that, on average, people in the United States watch television four hours a day [Byrd 2001]. For this reason, it is tempting to use video on a website. Unfortunately, storing video in digital form requires a large amount of disk space, and downloads are extremely slow. Figure 11–2 gives a sampling of video clips, with their run times, file sizes, and download times at 56 Kbps. Recall the discussion of wait times from Chapter 2. Some studies show that people working with computers are willing to wait no longer than 10 seconds before moving on to another task. How many of the videos listed in Figure 11–2 will arrive in time?

To compensate, many developers reduce the resolution of the video picture, but this also has the effect of reducing image quality. When attempting to reduce the size of a video file, always ask some test users what they think before making a final commitment.

Web developers face a second problem when working with this medium. When people see video, they immediately compare it to broadcast television video, which is an extremely high standard for content presentation. Few Web developers have access to people who are as dynamic as actors or news anchors, and few possess the caliber of equipment needed to produce the polished look of broadcast television. Any video on a website will be competing against the best that television has to offer.

For most situations, it is best to avoid using video altogether. Consider other means of communication. For example if the video shows a "talking head" – a close-up shot of a speaker – consider using a static image of the speaker and storing the speech as an accompanying audio file [Nielsen 1999].

If it's absolutely necessary to use video, break it into segments. For each segment, create a still image indicative of the video's content and include a text summary; include the run time of the video clip and the size of the file. When creating the segments, keep in mind that it takes approximately three minutes to download a megabyte on a 56K modem.

When taping video, several simple things will reduce the resulting file size and increase image quality at the same time [Chamberlin 2002]. First, mount the camera on a stationary tripod. While frantically roving hand-held camera work in the style of the *Blair Witch Project* is

Description	Run time	Screen resolution	File size (MB)	Download time at 56 Kbps
Museum tour (high quality video) www.dungarvanmuseum.org/index.cgi?art_id=73 click "High"	7 min, 30 sec	320 × 180	24	1 hour, 12 min
Museum tour (medium quality video) www.dungarvanmuseum.org/index.cgi?art_id=73 click "Medium"	7 min, 30 sec	320 × 180	5.74	18 minutes
Museum tour (low quality video) www.dungarvanmuseum.org/index.cgi?art_id=73 click "Low"	7 min, 30 sec	320 × 180	3.07	10 minutes
Speech (high quality video) www.anglican.ca/gs2001/news/webcast/wwwelcome_dsl.rm	1 min, 19 sec	160 × 120	3.3	10 minutes
Speech (low quality video) www.anglican.ca/gs2001/news/webcast/wwwelcome_28k.rm	1 min, 19 sec	160 × 120	.2	1 minute
Helmet camera video from mountain bike trail www.mtbbritain.co.uk/images/kamikaze.wmv	1 min, 19 sec	170 × 145	9.5	30 minutes

Figure 11–2   File size and download time for selected video clips.

currently popular, it creates huge files when the video is digitized. The last clip listed in Figure 11–2 is a video taken with a camera mounted on the helmet of a cyclist who was traversing a mountain bike path. The run time is 1 minute, 19 seconds. Compare this to the video clips of people speaking. Which video clip has the larger file size? How much bigger is it?

A second technique for simultaneously reducing file size and increasing image quality is to avoid recording any unnecessary detail. Use a solid-color background. The presence of wood paneling or wallpaper does nothing for the content and adds kilobytes to the video. Encourage your speakers to wear solid-color clothing. Avoid tweeds, stripes and prints. As a guide, observe what television news anchors wear.

Third, if the video features a speaker, use an extreme close-up, as demonstrated in Figure 11–3. If you find that you need to reduce the file size or image resolution, a tight shot will retain more facial details and the result will be perceived as having higher image quality. Compare the still frames in Figure 11–4. Both have low resolution, but users will have a higher opinion of the one on the right.

Add any captioning to video after it is already in digital form. The result will be easier to read. In fact, if the aim of the caption is to enhance accessibility, consider not adding conventional captions to the video at all, but present the text on the accompanying Web page, or use one of the accessible multimedia formats, such as SMIL [World 2001a] or SAMI [Microsoft 2001]. See Chapter 13 for more details on making multimedia accessible to people with special needs.

Medium shot	Close-up shot	Extreme close-up – the best

Figure 11–3 Use tight camera work. Courtesy of Lori Smallwood.

Figure 11–4 Close-up shots retain more facial detail. (Magnified to show detail.) Courtesy of Lori Smallwood.

Figure 11–5 Text on a Web page is easier to read than captions on videos.

When compared to captions in a video, text on a Web page has the advantage of better clarity and greatly reduced bandwidth. See Figure 11–5 for a comparison of the clarity of text within a video and text presented on a Web page.

Commonly used formats for video include AVI, QuickTime, MPEG, and Real Video [Murray 1996, Apple 2000, MPEG 1998, RealNetworks 2000]. (See Figure 11–6 for a summary and comparison of these formats.) In reality, the AVI format is only a framework for using a video compressor/decompressor called a codec [Fischer 1999, McGowan 2001]. Commonly used codecs include Cinepak, Intel Indeo, and Microsoft Video 1. To play an AVI file, a video player needs to have a copy of the codec that created the file. If a player is missing the codec, it will display an error message, and the user will be forced to download the codec in order to see the video. Many modern media players will attempt to perform this download automatically before issuing the error message. Most current Web browsers come with bundled software that plays AVI videos. Although AVI was originally created by Microsoft, current media players on both Apple and Unix platforms are capable of playing them.

QuickTime is a video format developed by Apple for the Macintosh. Like the AVI format, it also has a codec-based framework. In addition to having sound and video tracks, QuickTime supports additional tracks for multiple languages and subtitling. It's possible to offer QuickTime as a streaming or nonstreaming format, depending on how the Web server is configured. Wintel and Unix players exist, so the format is cross-platform.

The MPEG standard is actually a group of formats for audio and video. The acronym came from Motion Picture Experts Group, the name of the international organization that developed them. From its inception, the goal of the group was to create an open standard, so that the format would be as platform independent as possible. Because the technical

Name	File extension	Originator	Additional codec?	Streaming?	Additional player?
Audio-Video Interlaced	.avi	Microsoft	Yes	No	No
QuickTime	.mov .qt	Apple	Yes	Configurable	No
MPEG Video (MPEG-4)	.mpg	Motion Picture Expert Group	No	No	No
Real Video	.ram .rm	RealNetworks	No	Yes – requires server software	Yes

Figure 11–6 Summary of video formats for the Web.

specifications for the format are available to the public, any developer who reads the specifications will have enough information to write a player for the format and distribute the player without having to pay a licensing fee. The MPEG standard completely specifies the compression/decompression method, so there is no need to download additional codecs. In general, MPEG compression can produce smaller files than the AVI or QuickTime formats. Originally, the MPEG video formats were not streaming formats, but recently a new consortium is trying to develop this capability [ISMA 2001].

In contrast, Real Video was designed to be a highly compressed, streaming format. The format is proprietary, and Real Video viewers currently do not come bundled with commonly available Web browsers. This approach forces a user to download a special player. The good news is that a free player exists; unfortunately, its size is substantial. At eight megabytes, it represents quite an investment in download time. Many users will not be willing to do this. In order to deliver the video as a stream, Web developers need to install additional server software that's available only from RealNetworks.

When considering video for a website, keep the following guidelines in mind:

- If possible, avoid video altogether. Most people connect to the Internet at a bandwidth that will not support video download at a satisfactory speed.

- If forced to use video, use recording techniques that will reduce the size of the video when it is digitized. These include using a stationary camera and a single-color background, avoiding patterned clothing for the speakers, and employing tight camera shots.

- When choosing the file format for the video, consider the user's willingness to download additional software.

11.4 Animation

Animation is synthetic apparent motion created through artificial means. This is in contrast to video, which is a recording of a motion that occurred in the real, physical world. In many cases, the synthetic nature of an animation allows the motion to be stored more compactly than video; such storage facilitates faster download times. For this reason, animations are often a viable alternative to video.

Animation offers a richer set of interactions than video. Video is essentially a linear medium, with user controls similar to those on a conventional VCR. The user is limited to positioning the playback head and starting or pausing the video. Animation goes beyond those options by offering hyperlinking and the possibility of creating custom interactions designed to support specific user tasks.

In addition to serving as an alternative to video, animations can be effective for attracting attention, demonstrating transitions, and explaining complex systems. Well-designed motion will attract and focus attention. The appearance of a drop-down menu draws attention to that menu. Highlighting is another example. The change in color focuses attention on the current selection. Figure 11–7 shows a tutorial in which animation plays a major role in focusing attention. The goal of the tutorial is to familiarize users with the interface of a software-development environment. As a user moves the mouse over each element, a pop-up appears that names the element and explains its purpose.

The motion in an animation attracts attention only if it occurs just once or in response to a user action. If the motion repeats endlessly, users will find it annoying and ignore it. For this reason, avoid using animations such as blinking text, marquees, crawling lines, or animated images continually flashing the word "New!"

Animation unfolds over time, so animations are a great way to depict transitions or changes that occur in time. The transitions in question might be a demonstration of a biological or

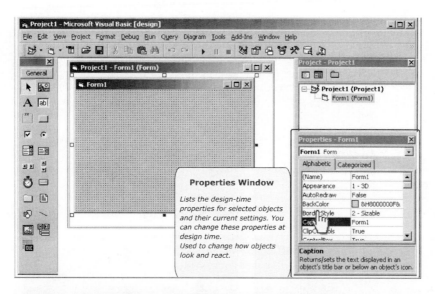

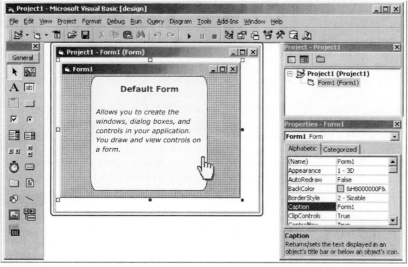

Figure 11–7   Using animation to attract attention. Courtesy of Jorge Toro.

manufacturing process. The transitions might be part of a "how to" manual that explains the operation of equipment or the rules of a game. Figure 11–8 shows a sequence of frames from an animation that illustrates how a virus attacks a human cell [Christensen 1999].

Animation can also help the user visualize complex structures or systems. The Visible Human Project [Ackerman 1995] has fostered the development of interactive visualization tools for exploring the anatomy of the human body [National 2001]. Other efforts have visualized algorithm behavior [Naps 1997], air pollution [NASA 2001], and microbiological processes [van Lieder 2002]. Some of these animations are in the form of interactive games [Web3D 2002]. Figure 11–9 demonstrates the operation of a laser printer. By clicking on the numbered circles, a user can see the paper trays, a view of the network connectors, and a method for reloading the ink cartridges.

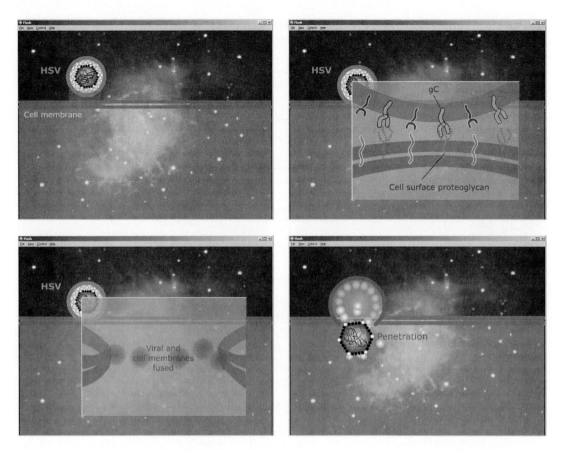

Figure 11–8 An animation depicting changes in time: A virus attacks a human cell. Courtesy of Karin Christensen and Dr. Edward K. Wagner.

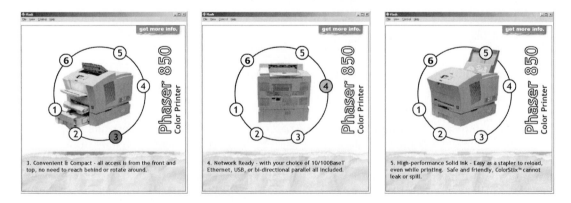

Figure 11–9 Animation demonstrating the operation of a Xerox Phaser® 850 network color printer. Courtesy of Xerox Corporation.

Animation can explain complex systems. Figure 11–10 shows how animation can effectively explain the intricacies of university parking regulations [Steiner 2001]. Once a user has chosen the type of parking permit and the desired building, the animation presents a map of the campus with a color code indicating the legal parking lots near that particular building. By clicking on the time line, a user can observe which lots are legal at different hours of the day.

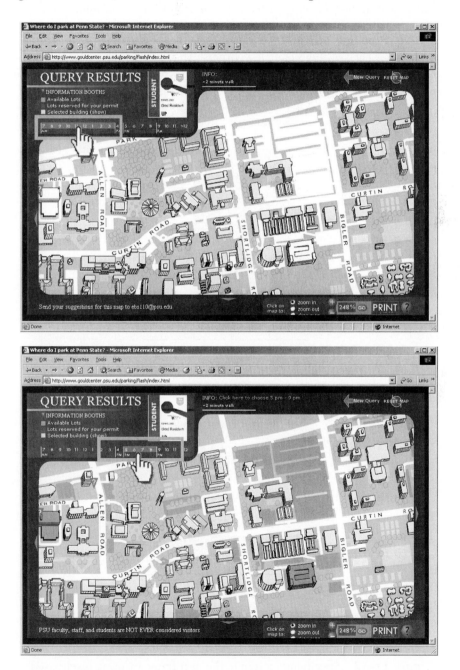

Figure 11–10   Depicting parking regulations. Courtesy of Erik B. Steiner.

There are three different approaches to delivering animation on the Web. One is to use one of the video formats mentioned in the previous section. Most animation packages have options to do this. A second is to use one of the vector-based formats; the third is to use a programming or scripting language, such as Java or JavaScript.

Vector-based formats differ from the older, pixel-based formats in that they list the shapes that appear in the animation instead of explicitly storing color information for every pixel. This strategy results in compact file sizes. (See Figure 11–11 for a comparison of the two approaches.) In this example, the vector-based approach will need to store only eight numbers – two for each of the rectangle's corners. The pixel-based approach will need to store 25 numbers, one for each pixel in the image. To record the motion of the rectangle in the next frame, the vector-based system needs only two numbers. In contrast, the pixel-based approach needs to indicate which pixels changed color. How many pixels changed color in Figure 11–12? How does this compare to the vector-based approach?

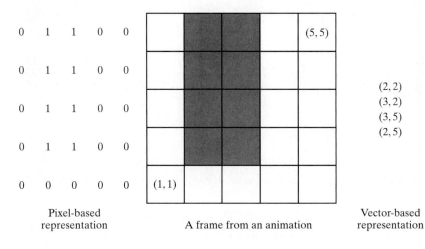

Figure 11–11   A comparison of pixel-based and vector-based formats.

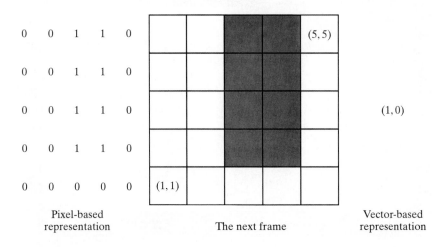

Figure 11–12   Specifying motion in the next frame by using pixel-based and vector-based formats.

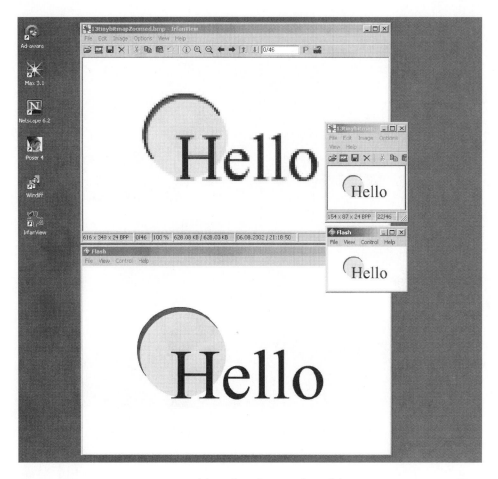

Figure 11–13   Comparing pixel-based and vector-based formats.

Another advantage of vector-based formats is the idea of reuse. Suppose a designer wanted a night sky with a field of stars. Once a single star shape is created, it takes very little space to include additional stars, because the star shape itself is stored only once. It's also possible to resize vector-based formats without losing image quality. Figure 11–13 compares images of vector-based and pixel-based graphics. It is a screenshot of a desktop and contains two little images and two big ones. Of the two little images, the upper one is pixel based, the lower one vector based. At this size, their image quality looks comparable. The two large images are zoomed versions of the small ones. The lower image, which is vector based, is clearer and sharper.

In addition to having a compact format that yields superior image quality, the commonly available vector formats allow for customized user interactions. For example, it's possible to include buttons that allow a user to control the animation. Figure 11–14 is a tutorial on the mechanism of HIV infection and the approaches to disabling the virus [Hoffman 2001]. The user can choose to see either the course of infection or the sites for drug action. If clicked, the large arrows display the name of the particular stage in the infection or the type of inhibiting drug action.

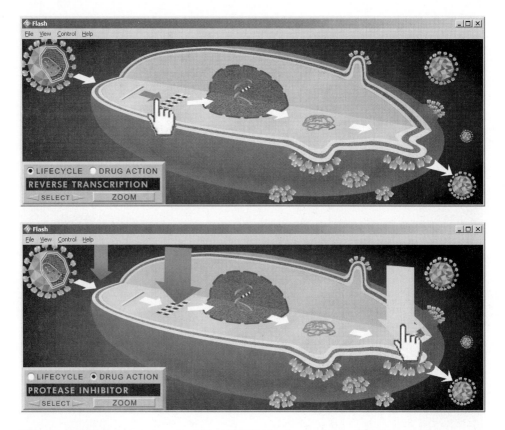

Figure 11–14　Animation depicting HIV infection and possible drug actions. Courtesy of Roche.

When creating an interactive animation of this type, be vigilant about making the controls visible and easy to understand. Unlike static Web pages, where there are some conventions about the appearance of a link or a button, there are no conventions about the appearance or behavior of controls in animations. It is very easy to create interactive animations that are difficult to understand and frustrating to use.

Avoid the temptation of using an animation to create an opening "splash page" on your website. The novelty of these animations is rapidly wearing off. Eye candy is fun for the person who makes it, but it delays users in completing the tasks they wish to perform.

One big disadvantage of all of the vector-based formats is that no conventional browser comes equipped to display them. In order to view these files, a user must be willing to download a player. At present, the most commonly used vector-graphics format is Shockwave Flash (swf), developed by Macromedia [Macromedia 2001, Macromedia 2002]. Macromedia supplies a freely downloadable player and contends that 98% of all Web browsers currently have access to its player. The Shockwave Flash format is proprietary; however, there is a new open standard called Scalable Vector Graphics (SVG), created by the World Wide Web Consortium (W3C) [World 2001b]. There are several free viewers for SVG, and the W3C website lists several free SVG authoring tools as well.

A third approach to delivering interactive animation is to use a programming language, such as Java or JavaScript. Java has been used quite successfully in creating simulations that a user can control and observe. Figure 11–15 is a simulation that allows a user to add successively

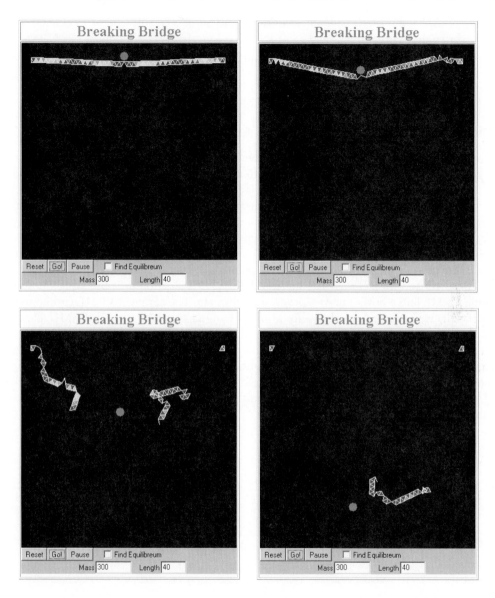

Figure 11–15 Java applet simulating structural failure. Courtesy of John McDonald.

more weight to a bridge until it breaks [McDonald 1998]. JavaScript provides such interactive elements as drop-down menus and rollover buttons without forcing the user to download special viewers to see them. This approach does offer the ultimate flexibility in developing customized user interactions, but it requires in-depth knowledge of programming. Further, users wanting to experience this type of animation will need to have JavaScript and Java enabled in their Web browsers.

In general, when considering animation for a website, keep the following in mind:

- When using animation to attract attention, limit the frequency of the motion's occurrence. If it is not activated by user control, it should occur rarely, or users will find it annoying and ignore it.

- Consider the user's willingness to download additional software or to change their browser security.

- When creating interactive controls in an animation, take extra care to make them visible and understandable.

- Be mindful of download time.

11.5 Future Developments: 3D Animation

A very specialized type of animation for the Web is three-dimensional (3D) animation. Figures 11–7 through 11–10 and Figure 11–15 are examples of conventional two-dimensional (2D) animation. True 3D animation provides more information and flexibility than the 2D version. It allows a user to choose any viewpoint and to examine items in a scene from any angle. As a comparison, refer to the 2D animation of the color printer in Figure 11–9. For this animation, a developer created images from a fixed set of viewpoints, and the user is limited to choosing from among those preselected positions. With 3D animation, users are free to look at a scene from any vantage point they choose.

There are several technologies that can deliver 3D animation over the Web. These include VRML and a host of newer, proprietary formats. The acronym VRML (pronounced VERmull) is short for Virtual Reality Markup Language [VRML 1997]. VRML allows a designer to create virtual worlds. People with a VRML viewer can download and walk through a world, each choosing an individual path. Room designers and real-estate agencies have used VRML to offer tours of rooms or entire buildings. A notable example is a model of the terminal building at the Munich Airport Center [Van Nedervelde 2000]. See Figure 11–16 for a screen shot of the starting position at an entrance to the terminal and some views of its interior spaces.

Figure 11–16 Tour of Munich Airport Center, in interactive 3D. Courtesy of Phillippe van Nedervelde E-spaces n.v.

You can tour the mezzanine, take the elevators up to the second floor to visit office suites, or use the escalator to go down to the food court. The arrows visible in the images are additional navigation aids. Pressing on the arrow near the elevator will automatically bring the elevator to your floor, open the doors, bring you into the elevator car, and travel to the desired level.

It's possible for two or more people to visit a virtual world simultaneously. An *avatar* is an icon or character that represents a real person who is touring the virtual world [Lycos 2002]. It's possible to meet and interact with another person who is also visiting the virtual world.

VRML is an open standard. Related to VRML is H-Anim, which is a standard for human animation. It facilitates the download and display of avatars. See Figure 11–17 for an example. When set up correctly, the body geometry of the avatar does not need to be downloaded more than once. After this initial download, a small amount of additional information can make the avatar walk, jump, sit, or otherwise change position. Because of this, downloaded avatars can react in real time even at current bandwidths.

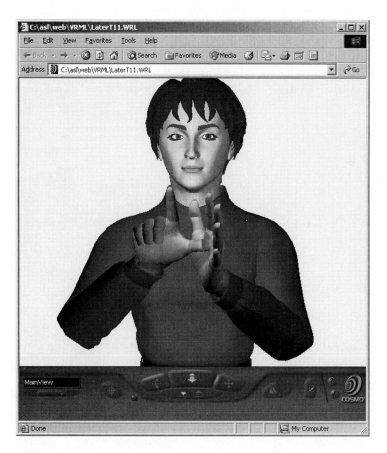

Figure 11–17   An avatar. Courtesy of the DePaul American Sign Language Project.

Figure 11–18   Level of Detail (LOD).

Interacting in three dimensions is an exciting concept, but there are some disadvantages that have kept it from being mainstream. The first is a long download time. To send enough information to describe an entire airport requires a long wait.

There are two approaches being developed to address the download problem. The first is called *level of detail* control or LOD for short [Gobbetti 1999]. When an object is located far in the distance, much of its detail is not visible to a viewer, and it is possible to use a coarser representation of the object that does not take as long to download. See Figure 11–18 for a demonstration. In each of the three images, the figure on the right has the lower level of detail, but downloads seven times faster than the one on the left. In a close up view, the imperfections are clearly visible, but from an intermediate or far view, the differences are barely noticeable.

The second approach is called *successive refinement* and does not actually reduce the amount of information that needs to be downloaded [Alliez 2001]. It is analogous to the technique used in interlaced GIF images. When downloading an interlaced GIF, a coarse approximation appears quickly, so users get an overall idea of what the image contains. As more information arrives, users see successively more detail. When downloading a 3D object via successive refinement, a coarse approximation arrives first. The user can start interacting with this coarse version while successively finer detail arrives to refine the object's appearance. In Figure 11–19, a crude approximation of a suit arrives first, followed by more geometric detail and color information. The user can begin interacting with the suit before all of the information arrives.

A second disadvantage to using 3D on the Web is the fact that VRML is only one of several competing formats [Macromedia 2001, Polevoi 2000, Pulse 2001]. Figure 120 gives a list of other 3D formats that are currently available. All of them require having either a plug-in or a Java-enabled browser. A further complication is the fact that 3D navigation is difficult for beginners and it requires an investment in time to learn how to use the controls to move about in space.

Web 3D holds exciting promise for the future, but currently it is available to only a small segment of Internet users. If you do provide it, always present the information in an alternative format (such as static images) to make it available to as wide an audience as possible.

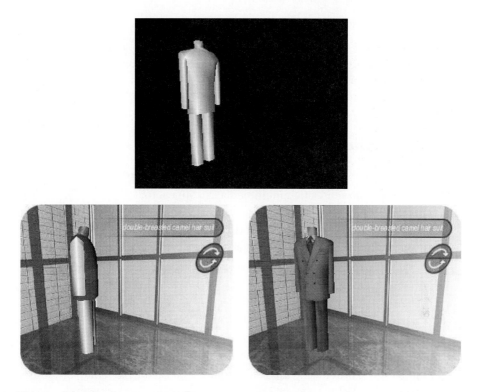

Figure 11–19   Successive refinement. Courtesy of Eyematic.

	Open standard?	Plug-in required?	Streaming?	LOD control?	Successive refinement?
VRML	Yes	Yes°	No	° °	No
Pulse 3D www.pulse3d.com	No	Yes	Configurable	Yes	No
Shout 3D www.shout3d.com	No	No–requires only Java-enabled browser	No	No	No
Shockwave www.macromedia.com	No	Yes	Yes	Yes	Yes

° Free browsers available at www.blaxxun.com and www.cai.com/cosmo
° ° LOD control is specified in standard, but browsers are not obliged to honor it.

Figure 11–20   Alternative 3D formats for the Web.

11.6   Conclusions

There is an exciting variety of media available for the Web, and it's a lot of fun to experiment with them. Nevertheless, however tempting it might be to add multimedia to a site, first ask the question, "Will including this media help support users in carrying out the tasks they want to perform?" If the answer is yes, by all means use it. As this chapter has shown, there are many ways to use multimedia effectively. Enjoy!

Review Questions

1. What types of media are available for the Web? Name at least six.
2. Which are the senses that multimedia can appeal to?
3. Audio signals such as the announcement "You have mail," can redirect a user's attentions away from a current task. In the context of computer use, name other situations where sound successfully attracts attention without overly annoying the user.
4. What is the difference between streaming and nonstreaming media? Name a streaming technology.
5. When creating a Web page, why is it important to include a text transcript of any speech that's offered as an audio file?
6. When shooting video for the Web, what can you do to help keep the file size as small as possible?
7. Suppose you are staffing the help desk for an e-commerce company. A user calls and says that his AVI player won't play an AVI file that is on your website. You test the file by downloading it to your computer. On your computer, it plays perfectly fine. Explain how this could happen.
8. Why should you try to avoid using video on the Web?

Exercises

9. Suppose you are considering the best way to present a round-table discussion of students discussing their reasons for choosing their majors. You know that your users are accessing the Web via 56Kbps modems. You are considering the following possibilities:

   i. Four images each having a resolution of 400×600 and a file size of 250 KB each, plus four audio clips that are 160 KB each. Each audio file is 20 seconds long.
   ii. Four video clips having a resolution of 160×120 and a file size of 375 KB.

   Answer the following questions:

   a. For each of these possibilities, what is the overall download time? (Your users are accessing the Web with a 56Kbps modem, so use the estimate of 3 minutes per megabyte.)
   b. What is the difference in download times? Give the answer in minutes. Which possibility has the faster download time?
   c. It's always important to consider download time when choosing a multimedia presentation. In this case, it's probably better to choose the possibility that has the slower download time. Why?

10. Suppose you are building a website that presents a tour of a submarine. You know that your users are accessing the Web over telephone modems. You have two possibilities for offering the video to your users:

    a. Four video clips having a resolution of 320 × 240 and a file size of 600 KB each.

    b. A single video clip having a resolution 320 × 240 and a file size of 2200 KB.

    What are the tradeoffs between these two possibilities?

11. If you have access to video-editing software, record a 320 × 240 video clip of a "talking head." Create three version of the video. By any means available to you, create a version that is 75% of the original file size. Create a second version that is 50% of the original file size, and create a third version that is 25% of the original file size. Invite eight different people to view the three versions, one at a time, and to rate each one after seeing it. Report on your results.

12. How do pixel-based and vector-based animation formats differ in how they represent images?

13. What are the advantages of using vector-based animation formats? Are there any disadvantages? If so, what are they?

14. What is the appeal of 3D animation as compared with 2D animation?

15. What is an avatar? What advantages does it offer that are lacking in conventional animation clips presented as AVI files?

16. How can level-of-detail (LOD) control be useful in reducing download times?

17. Although it is an exciting medium, 3D animation is still a curiosity on the Web. Why? List several reasons.

18. If you have not done so already, visit some website that offers tours of 3D virtual worlds. Record your experiences. Discuss the following:

    a. length of time to download and install the player

    b. the process of learning to navigate the world

    c. download times for the virtual worlds.

19. Download and install two or more 3D browsers. Try out their navigation controls, and compare the strengths and weaknesses of each.

References

[Ackerman 1995] M. Ackerman. "Accessing the Visible Human Project," *D-Lib Magazine*. October 1995. http://www.dlib.org/dlib/october95/10ackerman.html

[Alliez 2001] P. Alliez and M. Desbrun. "Progressive compression for lossless transmission of triangle meshes," *Proceedings of the 2001 conference on computer graphics.* Los Angeles, 2001. 195–202.

[Apple 2000] Apple Computer. *Inside QuickTime: QuickTime File Format.* http://developer.apple.com/techpubs/quicktime/qtdevdocs/PDF/QTFileFormat.pdf 2000.

[Bagwell 2000] C. Bagwell. *Audio File Format FAQ.* December 28, 2001. http://home.sprynet.com/~cbagwell/audio.html

[Byrd 2001] R. Byrd. *Pediatricians urge reduced TV exposure.* UC Davis School of Medicine, April 20, 2001. http://healthtip.ucdavis.edu/purtve.html

[Chamberlin 2002] C. Chamberlin, B. Ormand, and K. McNutt. *Shooting and Choosing Digital Video.* New Mexico State University College of Agriculture and Home Education. January 15, 2002. `http://www.cahe.nmsu.edu/streaming/shooting.html`

[Christensen 1999] K. Christensen. *The Replication of Herpes Simplex Virus.* `http://darwin.bio.uci.edu/~faculty/wagner/movieindex.html`

[Directorate 1999] Directorate of Information and Services. Chapter 26: How do I put sound and video in my Web pages? *WWW Information Pack.* University of Aberdeen, Scotland. May 1999. `http://www.abdn.ac.uk/diss/webpack/chap26.hti#26.3`

[Dunn 2000] J. Dunn. "How-to: Understanding digital audio formats," *Microsoft Uplink.* 2000. `http://www.microsoft.com/windowsce/uplink/tracks/digaudio.asp?style=5`

[Fischer 1999] B. Fischer and Udo Schroeder. "Video Formats and Compression Methods," *Tom's Hardware Audio Video Guide.* September 24, 1999. `http://www4.tomshardware.com/video/99q3/990924/`

[Fraunhofer 2001] Fraunhofer-Gesellschaft. *MPEG Audio Layer 3.* `http://www.iis.fhg.de/amm/techinf/layer3/`

[Gobbetti 1999] E. Gobbetti and E. Bouvier. Time-critical multiresolution scene rendering. *Proceedings of the conference of Visualization '99: Celebrating ten years.* San Francisco, 1999. 123–130.

[Hoffman 2001] F. Hoffman–La Roche, Ltd. The Lifecycle of HIV `http://www.roche-hiv.com/Roche_Template3.cfm?Pageid=56` Click on "Click here to see an animation of HIV."

[ISMA 2001] Internet Streaming Media Alliance. Welcome Page. `http://www.isma.tv/index.html`

[Konrad 2001] R. Konrad. "Researchers tout touchy-feely technology," *CNet News.com.* September 7, 2001. `http://news.com.com/2102-1017-272652.html`.

[Lycos 2002] Lycos, Inc. *Tech Glossary.* `http://webopedia.lycos.com/TERM/a/avatar.html`

[Macromedia 2001] Macromedia, Inc. Macromedia Director 8.5: Shockwave Studio with Intel Internet 3D graphics software. April 2001. `ftp://download.intel.com/ial/3dsoftware/3dshockwave.pdf`

[Macromedia 2002] Macromedia, Inc. Flash 5.0. `http://www.macromedia.com/software/flash/productinfo/product_overview/`

[McDonald 1998] J. McDonald. *Applets demonstrating 2-D physically based simulation.* `http://mcdonald.cs.depaul.edu/PhysicalModeling/maxwell/index.html`

[McGowan 2001] J. McGowan. *AVI Overview.* `http://www.jmcgowan.com/`

[MeasureCast 2002] MeasureCast. *Internet radio audience growth skyrockets in first full work week after holidays.* Press release, January 21, 2002. `http://www.measurecast.com/news/pr/2002/pr20020121.html`

[Microsoft 2001] Microsoft Corporation. *Understanding SAMI 1.0.* October 2001. `http://www.microsoft.com/enable/sami/`

[Midi 2001] Midi Manufacturers Association. *Sources of Midi Information.* `http://www.midi.org/about-midi/resource.htm`

[MPEG 1998] MPEG. *MPEG starting points and FAQs.* `http://www.mpeg.org/MPEG/mpeg`

[Murray 1996] J. D. Murray and W. vanRyper. *Encyclopedia of Graphics File Formats,* 2nd Ed. Sebastopol, California: O'Reilly, 1996.

[Naps 1997] T. Naps, J. Bergin, R. Jimenez-Peris, M. McNally, M. Patino-Martinez, V. Proulx, and J. Tarhio. "Using the WWW as the delivery mechanism for interactive, visualization-based instructional modules: Report of the ITiCSE '97 working group on visualization," *ACM SIGCUE Outlook.* 25(4) October 1997. 13–26.

[NASA 2001] NASA Goddard Space Flight Center. *Scientific Visualization Studio.* `http://svs.gsfc.nasa.gov/`

[National 2001] National Library of Medicine. *The Visible Human Project.* `http://www.nlm.nih.gov/research/visible/visible_human.html` (Over 425 papers have been written on this project.)

[Niederst 1998] J. Niederst. *Web Design in a Nutshell.* Sebastopol, CA: O'Reilly, 1998. 333–340.

[Nielsen 1999] J. Nielsen. *Designing Web Usability.* Indianapolis: New Riders, 1999.

[Polevoi 2000] R. Polevoi. *Interactive Web Graphics with Shout3D.* Alameda, CA: Sybex, 2000.

[Pulse 2001] Pulse Entertainment, Inc. *The Pulse Rich Media Platform.* February 2001. `http://www.pulse3d.com/developers/whitepaper.pdf`

[RealNetworks 2000] RealNetworks, Inc. *RTSP interoperability with RealSystem Server 8: RealSystem iQ white paper.* December 7, 2000. `http://docs.real.com/docs/rn/RealSystem_iQ_RTSP.pdf`

[Steiner 2001] E. Steiner. Where do I park at Penn State? `http://www.gouldcenter.psu.edu/parking/flash/index.html`

[van Liere 2002] R. van Liere, W. de Leeuw, J. Mulder, P. Verschure, A. Visser, E. Manders, and R. v Driel. *Virtual Reality in Biological Microscopic Imaging.* (ms submitted for publication.) `http://www.cwi.nl/~robertl/papers/2002/vr/paper.pdf`

[Van Nedervelde 2000] Philippe Van Nedervelde, E-spaces, n.v. *Virtual Munich Airport Center.* Description at `http://www.e-spaces.com/lbw/portfolio/projects/port_vmac.html` Virtual world at `http://www.mac-airport.de` Click on "Gast."

[VRML 1997] The VRML Consortium, Inc. *The Virtual Reality Modeling Language.* International Standard ISO/IEC 14772-1:1997 `http://www.vrml.org/technicalinfo/specifications/vrml97/index.htm`

[Web3D 2002] Web3D.org. Web3D Games. *The Web3D Repository.* `http://www.web3d.org/vrml/games.htm`

[Weinschenk 1997] S. Weinschenk, P. Jamar, and S. Yeo. *GUI Design Essentials.* New York: John Wiley and Sons, 1997.

[World 2001a] World Wide Web Consortium. Synchronized Multimedia Integration Language (SMIL 2.0). August 7, 2001. `http://www.w3.org/TR/smil20/`

[World 2001b] World Wide Web Consortium. Scalable Vector Graphics (SVG) 1.0 Specification, September 4, 2001. `http://www.w3.org/TR/SVG`

Accessibility

12.1 Introduction

> "The power of the Web is in its universality. Access by everyone regardless of disability is an essential aspect."
>
> —Tim Berners-Lee, W3C Director and inventor of the World Wide Web

Use of the Web has expanded into all areas of society, and it should be accessible to everybody. This includes people who have vision deficiencies, those with injuries or diseases that make it difficult or impossible to use their hands in ordinary ways, and the deaf and hard of hearing. This chapter explores some of the challenges that these people face and how to create websites that facilitate access for all.

Goals of this chapter

After studying this chapter, you will

- be aware of the major barriers to accessing the Web
- be familiar with assistive technologies for improving computer access
- know the guidelines and high-priority checkpoints from the W3C Web Accessibility Initiative
- be familiar with several ways to evaluate the accessibility of a website.

12.2 The Scope of the Challenge

Some people are born with disabilities; some become disabled later in life by accident or disease; others become temporarily disabled for any of a wide variety of reasons. Many of these physical challenges develop or become more severe with age.

Perhaps it does not seem that there are many people with disabilities, but a few statistics will indicate the range of issues and the number of people affected:

- In the United States, over 8 million people are blind or visually impaired [USHealth 1997].
- There were over 20 million deaf and hard-of-hearing people in the United States in 1994 [Holt 1994]. Of these, about a million cannot understand any speech at all.
- Over a quarter of a million Americans have spinal-cord injuries [NCSA 2002].
- About half a million Americans have cerebral palsy [NICHCY 2000].

- A third of a million Americans have multiple sclerosis [NMSS 2002].

- Physical impairments, minor and major, become more common with the passing years. More than half of the population in the United States over the age of 65 has some kind of impairment. This is a rapidly growing group. In the year 2000, there were 34.8 million people in this category, and current projections predict that this group will grow to 53.7 million by 2020 [Aging 2001].

The Web can be made *accessible* to most of these people. When visiting an accessible site, people with disabilities can achieve their goals in ways comparable to those of able-bodied people. Accessibility issues are wide ranging and many faceted. This chapter surveys assistive technologies and design guidelines for making websites accessible to as many users as possible.

12.3 Issues Involving Vision

The Web is so visually oriented that people who have visual impairments face significant challenges when using the Web. These impairments range in severity from total blindness to low vision to changes that are part of the natural process of aging. This category also includes color blindness and health conditions that are aggravated by visual stimuli.

12.3.1 Blindness

Information displayed on a conventional computer monitor is simply not available to people who are blind. At present, there are two alternative assistive technologies that address this issue: screen readers and refreshable Braille displays.

Screen readers include a speech-synthesizer component that reads aloud any text that appears on the screen [Alliance 2000]. This includes text in documents, in dialog boxes, and in error messages. Screen readers can also read menu selections and any text accompanying an icon. This makes it possible for people who are blind to work with Web pages.

Several vendors offer screen readers, including Freedom Scientific (`www.freedomscientific.com`), Dolphin (`www.dolphinuk.co.uk`), and GW Micro (`www.gwmicro.com`); the prices range from $300 to $1000. Several of them have downloadable trial versions that work for a limited period of time. Some operating systems now come bundled with screen readers, but they do not offer the same range of functionality.

So that a screen reader can cope with the text in a Web document, it's important to identify the natural language of the text and to mark any changes that occur, such as switching to Spanish or back to English. In HTML, this involves using the "lang" attribute. When this attribute appears in a document, it can serve as a signal to a speech reader to automatically switch to the new language. This makes the document more accessible to multilingual users [W3C 1999a].

To get a better understanding of the challenges involved in navigating a website with nothing but a screen reader, go to `www.webaim.org/simulations/screenreader-sim.htm`. The simulation presents the website of a mythical University of the Antarctic and asks a few simple questions, which require finding information on the site. However, the pages are not visible!

For people who are both deaf and blind, however, the audio output of a screen reader is not useful. A *refreshable Braille display* is a hardware device that reads and translates the text of a Web page into Braille [Mates 2000]. Braille is a tactile representation system whose basic unit is a *cell* having six dots, which can be raised in different patterns to represent letters, numbers, and punctuation. People who are blind read Braille with their fingertips. Because each cell takes up more space than a printed character, this representation requires

"It was a dark and stormy night."

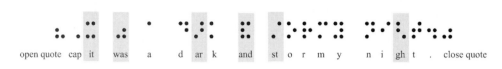

open quote cap it   was   a   d ar k   and   st o r m y   n i gh t   .   close quote

Figure 12–1 A sample of Grade II Braille. Shaded cells are contractions.

more space than the corresponding printed text. For this reason, Braille uses many contractions [Krebs 1974]. Some of these are present in Figure 12–1, which is a sample of grade II Braille, the form most commonly used [Holladay 2000].

Refreshable Braille displays can present text as Braille on a row of "soft" cells [Gallagher 2001]. (See Figure 12–2.) A soft cell has six or eight nylon pins. The device moves each pin up or down to display characters. If present, dots 7 and 8 can show the cursor position. Many Braille displays also include directional keys for navigating through a document. Several companies offer Braille displays, among them Freedom Scientific, Papenmeier (www.papenmeier.de/reha/rehae.htm), and ALVA (www.alva-bv.nl/braille/product.asp). This equipment is expensive. The low-end devices start at $4500 for a display containing 20 cells; others can cost over $14,000 for an 80-cell display.

Figure 12–2 A refreshable Braille Display. Courtesy of ALVA, Inc.

Both screen readers and Braille displays read text that appears on a Web page, but they are unable to interpret the graphic content of images. Images without ALT tags are useless, as are images used for navigation links. For this reason, it is important to provide a textual equivalent for all nontextual information, including JavaScript elements, Java applets, plug-ins, and multimedia objects [W3C 1999b].

Multimedia presentations require additional information, because the dialog alone does not always make sense without the visual portion of the presentation. *Descriptive audio* is a verbal explanation of important visual events, which are inserted into the natural pauses in dialog [Hoffner 2000]. For example, an audio portion of a video might contain the following dialog:

Susy:	Run.
John:	What?
Susy:	Go!
John:	Argh!

With descriptive audio, the drama of this exchange becomes clearer:

Descriptive Audio:	A large bear enters the campground. Susy sees the bear.
Susy:	Run.
John:	What?
Susy:	Go!
Descriptive Audio:	John turns and sees the bear.
John:	Argh!

It's possible to add descriptive audio into the current audio track of a video, but then there is no longer an option to turn it off. The television station WGBH in Boston pioneered a method of adding descriptive audio to the station's secondary audio program (SAP) channel. People with a stereo television can listen to the descriptive audio on closed-captioned programs by activating the SAP on their sets [Salsberg 1996].

There is similar technology available for the Web. A developer can add the descriptive audio either as an additional sound file synchronized to run with the video or as an additional track within the video itself [W3C 1999c]. In the future, a desirable development would be to add the descriptive audio as text instead of sound. There is a tradeoff in this approach. Natural audio is easier to understand than synthesized speech, but the text-based description would be accessible to people who are both blind and deaf.

For a person who is blind, it's important that the design of Web pages make sense in a linear ordering, without needing to refer to a visual organization as a whole. Multicolumn formats are very difficult to comprehend. When creating accessible pages, avoid using tables to position text for visual presentation purposes. Use style sheets instead. See the appendix for an introduction to style sheets. Reserve the use of tables for displaying tabular data [W3C 1999d].

Multiple columns *are* necessary when displaying tabular data [WebAIM 2001]. When a user is reading a data table visually, it could appear simple and easy to understand, but when the user is hearing it as a sequence of words, it could be far more difficult to comprehend. Consider the tabular data shown in Figure 12–3. Without the proper markup language, a speech reader would produce the following sequence of words:

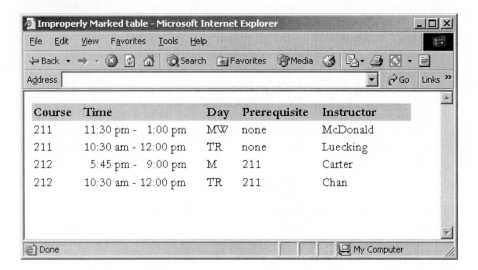

Figure 12–3   Tabular data, displayed as a table.

> Table 5 rows 5 columns Course Time Day Prerequisite Instructor 211
> 11:30 pm dash 1:00 pm MW none McDonald 211 10:30 am dash 12:00 pm
> TR none Luecking 212 5:45 pm dash 9:00 pm M 211 Carter 212 10:30
> am dash 12:00 pm TR 211 Chan.

When one is listening to the sequence of words, it becomes difficult to know whether the third occurrence of "211" is a course or a prerequisite. To make tabular data more accessible, do use TD tags to identify data cells and TH tags to identify headers. Use the "id" attribute in TH tags and the "headers" attribute in TD tags to aid in linearizing the data. Figure 12–4 shows an excerpt from the HTML that demonstrates this markup.

This additional markup makes it possible for speech readers to expose or read the contents of a table in a way that makes the significance of the data more accessible. In the following stream of words, the extra context given by the repetition of the column description makes it easier to distinguish the meaning of the number "211":

> Table 5 rows 5 columns Course 211 Time 11:30 pm dash 1:00 pm Day
> MW Prerequisite none Instructor McDonald Course 211 Time 10:30 am
> dash 12:00 pm Day TR Prerequisite none Instructor Luecking Course
> 212 Time 5:45 pm dash 9:00 pm Day M Prerequisite 211 Instructor
> Carter Course 212 Time 10:30 am dash 12:00 pm Day TR Prerequisite
> 211 Instructor Chan.

Users who are blind cannot use visual cues to orient themselves in a document. This is also an issue for people who can experience only a portion of a page at a time because they are using screen magnifiers. For these reasons, it is important to create meaningful, descriptive link text and to associate labels explicitly with their input elements.

When creating a form, specify a "label" attribute that describes the purpose of each form element. Place the label immediately before the element it describes. In Figure 12–5, the presence of label attributes allows a screen reader to announce the purpose of the text boxes [Thatcher 2001].

```
<table>
  <thead>
  <tr>
    <th id="c1"> Course </th>
    <th id="c2" Time </th>
    <th id="c3" Day </th>
    <th id="c4" Prerequisite </th>
    <th id="c5" Instructor </th>
  </tr>
  </thead>
  <tbody>
  <tr>
    <td headers="c1">211</td>
    <td headers="c2"> 11:30 pm -   1:00 pm</td>
    <td headers="c3">MW</td>
    <td headers="c4">none</td>
    <td headers="c5">McDonald</td>
  </tr>
  <tr>
    <td headers="c1">211</td>
    <td headers="c2">10:30 am - 12:00 pm</td>
    <td headers="c3">TR</td>
    <td headers="c4">none</td>
    <td headers="c5">Luecking</td>
  </tr>
  <tr>
    <td headers="c1">212</td>
    <td headers="c2">  5:45 pm -    9:00 pm</td>
    <td headers="c3">M</td>
    <td headers="c4">211</td>
    <td headers="c5">Carter</td>
  </tr>
  <tr>
    <td headers="c1">212</td>
    <td headers="c2">10:30 am - 12:00 pm</td>
    <td headers="c3">TR</td>
    <td headers="c4">211</td>
    <td headers="c5">Chan</td>
  </tr>
  </tbody>
<table>
```

Figure 12–4   A markup strategy to enhance linearization of tabular data.

Figure 12–3 is an example of a simple table. Many tables have a more complex structure, one involving divisions that go beyond rows and columns. Such tables contain densely packed information that can supply answers to a variety of complex questions. Figure 12–6 is an example. The leftmost column of the table contains data that are not all of the same type. Some of the entries are names of websites; others are dates. It is important to designate what *type* of information appears in each cell of the column. In HTML, the "axis" attribute in a TD or TH tag can supply this information. Figure 12–7 shows a fragment of HTML for the upper half of the table. The axis attribute helps categorize each data cell.

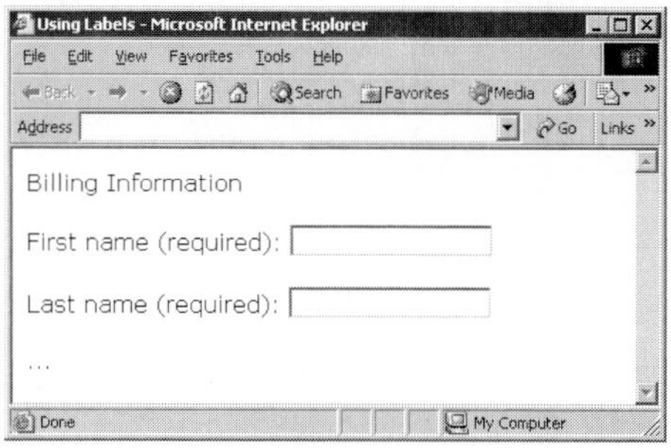

```
<form action="BilingInfo" method="post">
  <fieldset>
    <legend class="TitleLarge">Billing Information</legend> <p>
    <label for="firstname">First name (required): </label>
    <input id="firstname" type="text" tabindex="1"></p><p>
    <label for="lastname">Last name (required): </label>
    <input id="lastname" type="text" tabindex="2"> </p>
      ...
  </fieldset>
</form>
```

Figure 12–5   Label each element of a form.

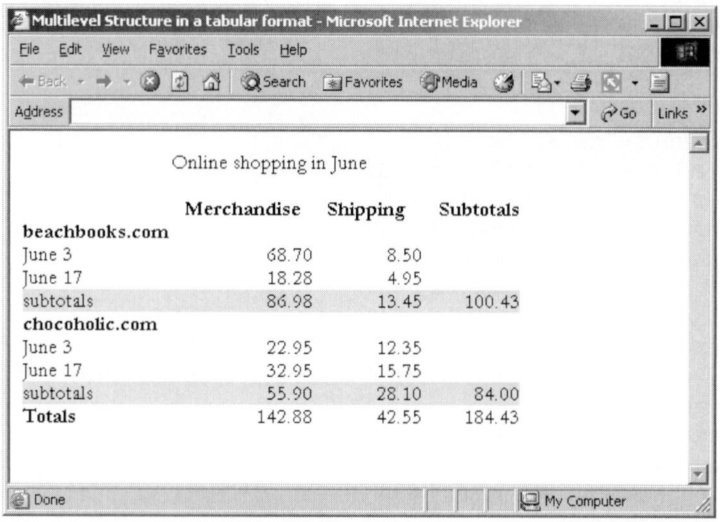

Figure 12–6   A complex table containing structure beyond simple rows and columns.

The table in Figure 12–6 contains numeric data having more context than what its row and column imply. For instance, the quantity "18.28" is not just the cost of the merchandise purchased on June 17. The table also indicates that this purchase was made at the website beachbooks.com. To glean the entire meaning of this numeric quantity, a user must be aware of this additional association. In HTML, using an expanded form of the headers attribute will capture this information. Lines 16–17 and 21–22 in Figure 12–7 demonstrate how the header attribute can refer to more than one heading and thus represent more than one association in a table.

This additional information makes it possible for future screen readers to make intelligent decisions about presenting the table as audio output. A "smart" screen reader could present the initial portion of Figure 12–6 in the following words:

Online shopping in June

Beachbooks.com June 3 Merchandise 68.70 Shipping 8.50

```
<table>
  <caption>Online shopping in June </caption>
  <tr>
    <th></th>
    <th id="h1Merchandise" axis="Cost" width="109">Merchandise </th>
    <th id="h2Shipping" axis="Cost" width="86">Shipping </th>
    <th> Subtotals     </th>
  </tr> <tr>
    <th id="h3WebSite" axis="WebSite"> beachbooks.com</th>
    <th> </th>
    <th> </th>
    <td> </td>
      </tr>
  <tr>
    <td id="h4June3date" axis="date" > June 3 </td>
    <td headers="h3WebSite h4June3date h1Merchandise" > 68.70 </td>
    <td headers="h3WebSite h4June3date h2Shipping" > 8.50 </td>
    <td> </td>
  </tr> <tr>
    <td id="h5June17Date" axis="date" > June 17  </td>
    <td headers="h3WebSite h5June17Date h1Merchandise" > 18.28 </td>
    <td headers="h3WebSite h5June17Date h2Shipping" > 4.95  </td>
    <td> </td>
  </tr> <tr>
    <td> subtotals  </td>
    <td headers="h3WebSite h1Merchandise"> 86.98 </td>
    <td headers="h3WebSite h2Shipping"> 13.45 </td>
    <td> 100.43 </td>
  </tr><tr>
  <th id="header10" axis="location" width="120">
    <div align="left">chocoholic.com</div> </th>
  <th width="109"> </th>
  <th width="86"> </th>
  <td width="77"> </td>
  </tr> ...
```

Figure 12–7   Demonstrating axis attribute and header attributes with multiple references.

Beachbooks.com June 17 Merchandise 18.28 Shipping 4.95

Subtotals Beachbooks.com Merchandise 86.98 Beachbooks.com Shipping 13.45 Subtotals 100.45

Another method for making a page more accessible is to give users an easy way to skip over navigational links that often appear at the top of each page, as is shown in Figure 12–8 [W3c 2000]. In HTML, include a link called "skip navigation" at the start of the navigation bar that points to the content portion of the page.

To know that a website is truly accessible to people who are blind, it's important to test it with users who *are* blind. There are several techniques you can employ to ascertain whether you're on the right track. Disable JavaScript and Java. Turn off image loading to see whether the pages still make sense without the images. Use a text-only browser, such as Lynx, to view the pages. Versions of Lynx for various operating systems are available at `lynx.browser.org`. If it's not possible to install Lynx, the site `www.deloric.com/web/lynxview.html` displays any page as it would appear in a Lynx browser. For an acid test, turn off the monitor. Now you are experiencing the page the way a blind person does.

12.3.2 Low Vision

For every person in the United States who is blind, there are seven more who have low vision [Trace 2002]. These people have some, but not all, of their sight. Internet browsers provide accommodation for these users by offering options to change the text size used to

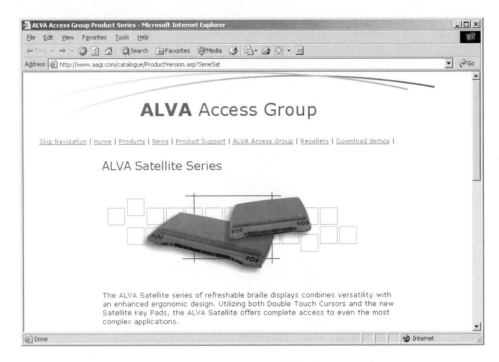

Figure 12–8   Example of a "Skip Navigation" link. Courtesy of ALVA, Inc.

display Web pages. Some browsers allow users to select from "normal," "larger," and "largest," but others let users select any font size they desire.

People with low vision can also benefit from *screen magnifiers* [King 1999]. A screen magnifier is software that enlarges a portion of the monitor display, making it easier to read. This improves the readability of small text, but, if the text is part of a graphic, the magnified version could be too smeary to be read easily. As Figure 12–9 demonstrates, only a fraction of a screen can be magnified at any one time; this limitation forces a user to scroll from side to side as well as up and down.

There are many screen magnifiers available, having a wide variety of special features. The sites `www.magnifiers.org` and `www.abilityhub.com` contain repositories of information on currently available products. Some of them even magnify multimedia, including videos and animation. Most can be downloaded for a free 30-day trial.

Each of these alternatives requires more knowledge than a novice user is likely to have. Remember to use combinations of text and background color that promote easy reading. Chapter 9 lays out some guidelines that address this issue. It is also important to avoid small font sizes. Chapter 10 gives some guidelines for selecting both typeface and font size. Again, using style sheets can help. See the Appendix for information on style sheets.

12.3.3 Color Blindness

True color blindness is defined as not perceiving any color at all and is extremely rare. Although cited figures vary, many sources estimate that 8% of the male population and 0.5% of the female population in the United States have some degree of *color deficiency* [Meyer 1988]. Although color deficiency is not always classified as a disability, sometimes Web developers

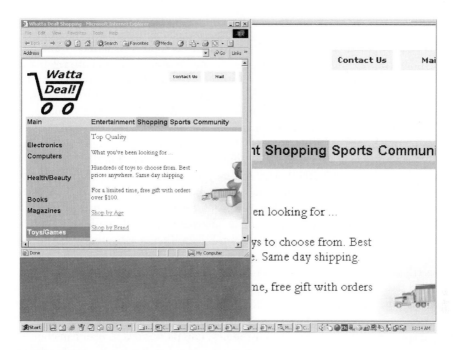

Figure 12–9   Results of a screen magnifier.

make poor design choices that can cause accessibility problems for people with this condition. The severity of the condition varies in type and degree. The most commonly occurring color deficiency is red/green confusion [Ishihara 1992]. Yellow/blue confusion also exists, but it is rare.

When creating Web pages, do not rely on hue alone to convey meaning. If you are using a color-coding scheme, be sure that the colors differ greatly in brightness. People who have red/green confusion would perceive a "fire engine red" and "bright green" as being two shades of brown. If you decide to use red and green to convey information, you can choose the fire engine red, but the color of the green should be quite dark, so that its brightness contrasts with that of the red. Even better, consider using other aspects such as position, size, alignment, or additional text to encode the same information [W3C 1999e].

Before testing with people having color deficiencies, there are two alternatives for assessing the accessibility of Web pages. The first is to view the pages on a black-and-white monitor or as a black-and-white printout. This is an extreme test, because most people with color deficiencies can perceive some colors. The second is to use a simulator, such as the one found at www.vischeck.com. At this site, a developer can type in the URL of a Web page and see how the page would look to people with varying types of color deficiencies.

12.3.4 Photosensitive Epilepsy

For some people, blinking text or flashing images are not just annoying, but actually dangerous. Flashing images can cause photoconvulsions, also known as photosensitive epileptic seizures. People with photosensitive epilepsy are sensitive to flashing in the range of from 4 to 59 times a second, with peak sensitivity at about 20 times a second [W3C 1999f]. Avoid using repetitive flashing in animations, and do not use flashing text as an attention attractor.

12.4 Issues Involving Mobility Impairments

This broad category encompasses conditions that affect a person's ability to use a conventional keyboard and mouse. These conditions can range from those that are relatively minor and do not have much effect on using the Internet to those that are so profound that they restrict most voluntary movements. Such impairments can be caused by diseases, such as arthritis, multiple sclerosis (MS), amyotropic lateral sclerosis (ALS—known as Lou Gehrig's disease), and muscular dystrophy. They can also be caused by stroke, by injury to the head or spinal cord, and by the loss of a limb [Trace 2002]. Repetitive strain injury caused by long periods of repeated movements is another condition that can result in mobility impairment [Pascarelli 1994]. The natural aging process can also be a factor.

Some people with mobility impairments are able to use a conventional keyboard and mouse, but with some difficulty. There are several technologies that can help. *Sticky Keys* (or latch key) is software that gives a person an alternative to holding multiple keys simultaneously [Apple 2002, AbilityHub 2002]. When Sticky Keys is activated, a user can press a key such as Shift or Control, then release it and then press the other key or keys. The sequence is treated as if all of the keys were pressed at the same time.

A second assistive technology alternative is *predictive typing,* which is software that guesses at the word that a user is typing [Garay 1997]. (See Figure 12–10, which is a demonstration of a predictive typing system [Madentec 2000].) After each keystroke, the software displays possible alternatives for the next complete word. A user can choose one of the alternatives by pressing the corresponding function key. Typing the sentence in the example through conventional means requires 53 keystrokes. With predictive typing, the user needed to press only 15 regular keys and 12 functions keys, a savings of nearly 50%. Further, most software of this kind will keep a history of a user's typing and, over time, "learn" to make more accurate predictions.

For some people, lack of fine motor control can make using a conventional keyboard difficult. To help, large keyboards offer keys that are four times the size of conventional ones. [Alliance 2000]. For others, typing is impossible. *Speech recognition* offers an alternative method of interacting with a computer [De Mori 1997].

Speech-recognition systems involve both hardware and software. A user speaks into a microphone connected to a computer. Software converts the incoming auditory signal into words. Users can not only simulate typing a document via speech recognition, but also navigate among documents.

There are several tradeoffs in speech-recognition systems. These are speaker dependence vs. independence, vocabulary size, and surrounding environment. Systems with limited vocabularies have higher rates of recognition accuracy. *Dictation systems* are capable of recognizing the largest vocabularies, but they are speaker dependent. Users must spend many hours in training the system to adapt its recognition to their individual voices. The noise in the surrounding environment has a big effect on recognition accuracy. For best results, the user needs to wear a headset microphone. Several companies currently offer dictation systems, including Scansoft's Dragon NaturallySpeaking and IBM's ViaVoice, and some newer operating systems have speech-recognition capability.

For people with profound mobility disabilities, speech recognition might not be a viable alternative. For them, devices such as mouth sticks, head wands, and eye-gaze trackers are sometimes useful. Together with an onscreen keyboard, these can emulate the functionality of a standard keyboard, although they are slower to operate [Alliance 2000]. It can be difficult and time consuming to switch from emulated keyboard to emulated mouse, so keyboard

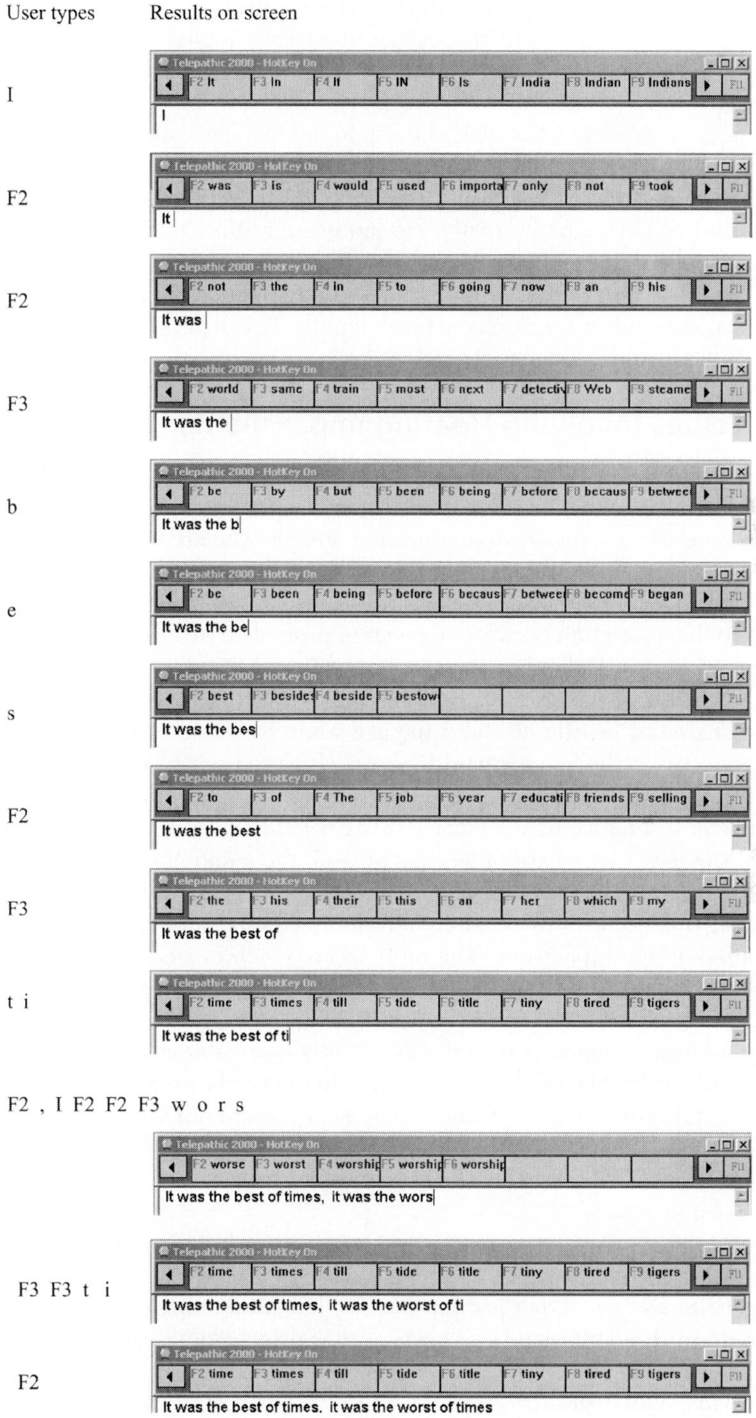

User types   Results on screen

I

F2

F2

F3

b

e

s

F2

F3

t i

F2 , I F2 F2 F3 w o r s

F3 F3 t i

F2

Figure 12–10   Predictive typing software saves keystrokes.

navigation of websites becomes crucial. For this group, requiring a mouse click to follow a link or activate a function will render that page or function less accessible [W3C 1999g].

Using some of these technologies can require extra physical effect and can be exhausting. Individuals using a head wand may become fatigued while making the necessary head movements to tab from link to link on a page. This can be especially tiring when skipping over a large number of links such as those found in a navigation bar [WebAIM 2002].

To help make a website more accessible to people with mobility impairments, make sure that the pages are navigable using only a keyboard. (Be aware that some JavaScript elements offer no keyboard alternatives to mouse activation.)

In many cases, it takes people with mobility impairments longer to fill out a form [W3C 1998]. Adjust any "time outs" the site might have to accommodate them. Avoid creating link text that is only a single character in length. This makes a very small target for people having issues with fine motor control.

12.5 Issues Involving Hearing Impairments

Hearing impairment refers to any type and severity of auditory disorder. *Deafness* refers to an inability to recognize conversational speech through hearing. Deaf people cannot use their hearing as a means of communication. People who are *hard of hearing* are still able to use their hearing for communication, but require an amplification device such as a hearing aid [Trace 2002].

Loss of hearing often occurs as a result of prolonged exposure to noisy environments. In the United States, 23% of people between 65 and 75 years of age have hearing impairments, and the portion rises to 40% in those over 75.

The degree of hearing loss and the age when the loss occurred has a large effect on a person's access to the hearing world. Those who lose their hearing later in life have already mastered a native language, such as English. However, people who are born deaf typically do not acquire a native first language [Schein 1974].

For people who are hard of hearing or deaf, the audio portion of multimedia should be *captioned* to make it accessible. Captions are a textual presentation of the sounds and spoken dialog that occur in video and other multimedia presentations. These usually appear at the bottom of the display area. The captions are synchronized with the spoken dialog. Captions also indicate who is speaking. Nondialogue audio, such as a door slam or a dog barking, also appears in the captions [National 2002].

Captions can be open or closed. *Open captions* are always visible. They differ from subtitles, which are text translations that appear in foreign films. Subtitles do not include sound effects or indicate who is speaking. *Closed captions* are not visible unless a user chooses to make them so. Recent versions of several media players (including Real Player, Windows Media Player, and Apple QuickTime) can display captioned multimedia. See Figure 12–11 for an example.

At present, captioning is labor intensive because a human must manually transcribe the audio. However, once stored, the captions can be indexed and searched, thus increasing accessibility for all groups, not just for those with hearing impairments.

There are three alternative formats available for adding captions to Web multimedia. These are the Synchronized Multimedia Integration Language (SMIL)—created by the World Wide Web Consortium (W3C)—Apple's QuickTime, and Microsoft's Synchronized Accessible Media Interchange (SAMI). SMIL (pronounced "smile") allows a Web designer to integrate video, audio, pictures, and captions so that the multimedia is accessible to all.

Figure 12–11 Captioned multimedia. Courtesy of Lori Smallwood.

Users can choose which media they prefer to experience. Both SMIL and SAMI are text-based formats that are similar to HTML. The QuickTime format offers similar flexibility via multiple tracks. Information in these additional tracks is normally hidden from user view. Multimedia developers can use the tracks to add captions and descriptive audio. Users can then choose the option of experiencing the additional tracks.

For people who lose their hearing later in life, captioning is an effective means of making audio more accessible. However, this is not a satisfactory solution for those whose primary means of communication is sign language.

Most hearing people in the United States mistakenly believe people who are born deaf use English as their first language. This is not the case. American Sign Language (ASL) is the language most widely used among the deaf in North America. It does have some vocabulary in common with English, but ASL is a completely different language, with its own unique grammar. It is not possible to translate English word-for-word into ASL. Thus, most deaf people who consider ASL their primary language are not as proficient with English as hearing people. In fact, the average reading level of adults in this group is between the third and fourth grade [Roffé 1998]; as a result, websites written in English can be less accessible to this group.

For this group of people, seeing the audio portion interpreted as ASL would provide better accessibility than closed captioning. In England, the BBC experimented with an alternative to captioning for television that added a small image of an interpreter [Family 2002]. In a similar vein, for multimedia presentations, one could add the option of viewing a second video of the interpreted dialog, but this would effectively double the bandwidth requirements.

An experimental approach involves using an avatar as an interpreter. As mentioned in Chapter 11, an *avatar* is an icon or character that represents a real person. Once the avatar is downloaded to a user's computer, the additional bandwidth required for sending the sign language itself is less bandwidth intensive [Visicast 2002, DePaul 2002].

12.6 The Web Accessibility Initiative

The Web Accessibility Initiative (WAI) is an outgrowth of the commitment of the World Wide Web Consortium (W3C) to promoting usability for people with disabilities. This group works with organizations around the world to develop technology, guidelines, and tools to promote Web accessibility [Paciello 2000].

Central to WAI philosophy is the goal of *universal access*. If content is correctly designed, organized, and formatted, the information on a website can be accessible to all users, including those with special needs or those working under special conditions such as noisy surroundings or a work environment requiring hands-free or heads-up operation. An important concept underlying this goal is the *user agent*. A user agent is any software that accesses and presents Web content. Examples of user agents include desktop graphical browsers, text browsers, multimedia players, mobile phones, PDAs, plug-ins, and such assistive software as screen readers, screen magnifiers, and voice-recognition software.

12.6.1 Guidelines

To promote universal access, the WAI has created a set of Web Content Accessibility Guidelines. These guidelines enable user agents to present information in the format that is most easily accessible to a particular user. Proponents point out that the guidelines are not meant to discourage designers from creating such content as multimedia, but are meant to make all content more available to all users.

Figure 12–12 lists the 14 guidelines. They address two general themes:

- Ensure graceful transformation.
- Make content understandable and navigable.

---

1. Provide equivalent alternatives to auditory and visual content.
2. Don't rely on color alone.
3. Use markup and style sheets, and do so properly.
4. Clarify natural-language usage.
5. Create tables that transform gracefully.
6. Ensure that pages featuring new technologies transform gracefully.
7. Ensure user control of time-sensitive content changes.
8. Ensure direct accessibility of embedded user interfaces.
9. Design for device independence.
10. Use interim solutions.
11. Use W3C technologies and guidelines.
12. Provide context and orientation information.
13. Provide clear navigation mechanisms.
14. Ensure that documents are clear and simple.

Figure 12–12 The guidelines of the Web Accessibility Initiative from [W3C 1999h].

Pages that can transform gracefully will remain accessible, no matter the special needs of the person using them. Documents should work for people who cannot see or cannot hear. For this reason, it's important to separate structure from presentation in Web pages. The structure of a document is what designates its organization. In HTML, <h1>, <p>, and <table> are all examples of structural elements. On the other hand, presentational elements specify how the document should appear visually and include such considerations as text color and background graphics. Structural elements convey more information about the context of content. Structural elements make it easier for user agents to communicate the document's content more clearly and to preserve the author's original intent.

Pages that transform gracefully do not rely on one single type of hardware. Pages should be accessible by a user with a small screen, one without a mouse, and one using only voice-based or text-based displays. It is important to provide text equivalents for all images, multimedia, applets, and JavaScript elements, because text is the content found in Web documents that is most nearly universally accessible.

Guidelines 1-12 address the theme of graceful transformation. Guidelines 13 and 14 address the second theme: developing content that is understandable and navigable. This encompasses not only writing text in a style that is clear and easy to understand, but also providing straightforward and easy-to-use navigation.

12.6.2 Checkpoints

Each of the fourteen guidelines has a number of *checkpoints,* which explain how the guideline applies to creating Web content. Each checkpoint is specific enough that someone reviewing a page can judge whether the checkpoint has been satisfied.

Each checkpoint also has a priority. *Priority 1 checkpoints* are basic requirements for accessibility. (See Figure 12–13 for a list of these checkpoints.) These *must* be satisfied; otherwise, the page's content will not be available to one or more groups of users. Adhering to *Priority 2 checkpoints* will remove significant barriers to content accessibility. Content developers *should* address Priority-2 checkpoints, because failure to do so will cause difficulties for some groups of users. To improve access to Web content further, a developer *may* address *Priority 3 checkpoints.*

A document that adheres to all Priority-1 checkpoints is at WAI Conformance Level A. A document satisfying all Priority-2 checkpoints is at WAI Conformance Level Double-A. Documents satisfying all three sets of checkpoints are at WAI Conformance Level Triple-A. The WAI has a strict format for any conformance notices posted on a page, subsite, or site. For details, consult the Web Content Accessibility Guidelines at `www.w3.org/TR/WCAG10/`.

12.6.3 Evaluating for Accessibility

The W3C outlines a two-phase approach to evaluating website accessibility that combines manual review (expert-based review), semiautomatic accessibility checks, and user testing. The two phases are a *preliminary review* and *comprehensive conformance evaluation.*

In a preliminary review, the goal is quick identification of the scope of the problems. W3C suggests manually checking a set of representative pages, in addition to using semiautomatic accessibility checkers. The manual checking should include all of the following:

1. An examination using a graphical browser, such as Netscape or Internet Explorer. Examine accessibility under the following browser settings:
   - Images and Java turned off.
   - Sound turned off.

1. Provide a text equivalent for every non-text element (e.g., via "alt", "longdesc", or in element content). *This includes*: images, graphical representations of text (including symbols), image map regions, animations (e.g., animated GIFs), applets and programmatic objects, ascii art, frames, scripts, images used as list bullets, spacers, graphical buttons, sounds (played with or without user interaction), stand-alone audio files, audio tracks of video, and video.
2. Ensure that all information conveyed with color is also available without color, for example from context or markup.
3. Clearly identify changes in the natural language of a document's text and any text equivalents (e.g., captions).
4. Organize documents so they may be read without style sheets. For example, when an HTML document is rendered without associated style sheets, it must still be possible to read the document.
5. Ensure that equivalents for dynamic content are updated when the dynamic content changes.
6. Until user agents allow users to control flickering, avoid causing the screen to flicker.
7. Use the clearest and simplest language appropriate for a site's content.
8. Provide redundant text links for each active region of a server-side image map.
9. Provide client-side image maps instead of server-side image maps except where the regions cannot be defined with an available geometric shape.
10. For data tables, identify row and column headers.
11. For data tables that have two or more logical levels of row or column headers, use markup to associate data cells and header cells.
12. Title each frame to facilitate frame identification and navigation.

Figure 12–13   Priority-1 checkpoints of the Web Accessibility Initiative [W3C 1999i].

- Font sizes larger than normal.
- Small screen size.
- Black-and-white display. A printout of the page on a black-and-white printer is an effective substitute.
- Without a mouse.

2. An examination of pages using a text browser (such as Lynx) or a voice browser (such as IBM's Home Page Reader).
3. Use of two semiautomatic accessibility checkers. Three tools mentioned by the W3C include Wave (`www.temple.edu/inst_disabilities/piat/wave`), Bobby (`bobby.watchfire.com`), and A-prompt (`aprompt.snow.utoronto.ca`).

Semiautomatic accessibility checkers get their name from the fact that no existing software can automatically carry out a complete evaluation. Wave and Bobby offer online services that will check individual pages for usability problems. Both Bobby and A-prompt offer downloadable software that will check multiple pages. In addition to listing problems that it can identify automatically, Bobby will offer suggestions about issues that should be reviewed manually. A-Prompt will not only identify potential accessibility problems but also provide structured help in editing the page to correct the problem.

In a comprehensive conformance evaluation, W3C recommends a combination of manual review, semiautomatic evaluation, and user testing. In addition to the semi-automatic accessibility checkers, it is important to use a syntax checker to verify that there is no illegal or improperly formed markup in the documents. There are quite a number of validation services, including W3C's own HTML validation service at `validator.w3.org` or `validator.w3.org/file-upload.html`. Another one is Dave Raggett's Tidy HTML [Raggett 2002], which also features an HTML editor.

No software tool or manual (expert-based) evaluation will catch all usability problems. Getting users to participate in the process is critical. Invite people with differing disabilities to carry out representative tasks on the site and give you feedback. Make a note of where they encounter problems.

With the knowledge gained from these three techniques, make any necessary changes to the site. W3C suggests that the site display an e-mail address for feedback regarding accessibility. In this way, users can point out any remaining problems.

12.7 The Human Side

> "T.J. Parker was a happy-go-lucky sort of 20-year-old guy who liked to horse around with friends after a hard day working as a roofer. He and his friends went fishing one May evening in 1991, catching mullet in a gill net and just fooling around as young guys are known to do.

> "When they impulsively decided to dive off the end of a pier to rinse off before going home at 10:30 p.m., it turned out to be what T.J. calls the biggest mistake of his life. The depth of the water was tragically misjudged: it was only two and a half feet deep.

> "He woke up a few days later in the hospital, with a respirator helping him breathe, and two vertebrae—the C1 and C2—fractured, leaving him paralyzed from the neck down. He was to spend the next 11 months in the intensive care unit and another three months in the rehab center."

This is the beginning of a Web story by Christine Rowley [Rowley 1997] that describes how assistive technology can help a person lead a productive and fulfilling life in the face of severe problems.

With help from the State of Florida Vocational Rehabilitation Program, T. J. learned to use a computer with speech recognition and a head mouse. The head mouse is a device that tracks a dot on the end of his nose. The computer operates light switches, the thermostat, and other household devices under voice control.

Using this equipment, T. J. can type 25 words a minute. He taught himself programming and Web design and has designed websites on a volunteer basis. He used the computer to play games with his daughter. He used voice recognition at first, but, as of 2002, he needed a ventilator for assistance in breathing most of the time.

The real story here is the indomitable human spirit: a man whose future changed forever in one brief moment, who picked himself up and put together a life. Designing Web pages to conform to accessibility guidelines not only makes them easy for able-bodied people to use, but also makes the information, resources, and communities on the Web available to people like T. J.

Review Questions

1. What are three major categories of physical impairment?
2. What technologies help make printed or displayed text accessible to blind people?

3. What technology makes video more accessible to people who are blind? Does it also make video accessible to those who are deaf and blind? Why or why not?

4. Why is it a bad idea to use tables for visually formatting a page?

5. What markup techniques can help make tabular data more accessible to people who are blind?

6. What is the purpose of a "skip navigation" link? Why is this beneficial to people who are blind? What other group would benefit from "skip navigation" links? Justify your answer.

7. When enhancing the accessibility of Web pages for people who are blind, why is it useful to review the pages in a text browser, such as Lynx?

8. What two colors do people who are colorblind most often confuse?

9. What guidelines can a Web developer follow to ensure that Web pages are accessible to people who are colorblind? As a preliminary check, what tools or techniques can help assess the accessibility for this group?

10. What are the drawbacks of Web-based advertisements that flash to get a person's attention?

11. Some people with mobility impairments can use a conventional keyboard and mouse, but only with difficulty. What technologies can help make it easier for people in this group to use a keyboard?

12. Many long-distance telephone companies offer automated directory services, where a caller can select among a set of options by speaking the number instead of pressing a key on the phone. This is a type of speech-recognition software that is speaker independent. Suppose a marketer proposes to simply repackage this software and offer it as a alterative to keyboard input for a computer. Analyze this proposal, and give your opinion.

13. Why is it important to ensure that Web pages are navigable without a mouse?

14. What is captioning? How does it differ from subtitles?

15. Is captioning an effective assistive strategy for everyone who is deaf? Justify your answer.

16. What is a user agent? Give some examples. What purpose does each serve in enhancing Web accessibility?

17. Explain the difference between Priority-1, Priority-2, and Priority-3 checkpoints in the Web Accessibility Initiative.

18. Name the three main categories of techniques that developers can use to evaluate Web accessibility.

Exercises

In the following six exercises, you will be carrying out some user testing that simulates the accessibility challenges faced by users who have special needs.

19. As preparation for the remaining five of these exercises, you will first gather some baseline information about the speed, accuracy, and satisfaction of four able-bodied users as they carry out some common tasks on an e-commerce site. Choose one of the major e-commerce sites that sells books. You will use this site for all user testing that you perform.

   a. Prepare an informed-consent document. See Chapter 8 for tips on preparing it.

b. Prepare a written introductory orientation script. In it, mention that you are gathering information on how an able-bodied person carries out several common activities on an e-commerce site. See Chapter 8 for a discussion of the important points to make in this script.

c. Prepare a short pretest questionnaire that assesses the following:
- Familiarity with Web browsing.
- Familiarity with buying merchandise online.
- Familiarity with the particular site you're testing.
- (optional) Any disabilities the user might have.

d. Use the following procedure to test the users:
- **i.** Configure the computer to have a Web browser open and displaying the home page of the site. Record the following measures:
  - Time to complete the task.
  - Number of mistyped characters.
  - Number of pages visited.
  - Number of positive comments.
  - Number of negative comments.
- **ii.** Here are the test scenarios:
  - Find the search box.
  - Use the site to find the author of *War and Peace.*
  - Find the cheapest edition of *War and Peace* that the site sells.
  - Place one copy of the cheapest edition into the shopping cart.

e. Write up the results. Give a summary of the responses to the pretest questionnaire. For each task, create a table showing the measures for each user.

f. Create a summary table that gives the average measures for each of the tasks.

Before completing any of exercises 20–24, complete exercise 19 to gather some baseline information about able-bodied users.

20. In this exercise, you will simulate a user experiencing low vision. Get a cheap pair of sunglasses and smear a little Vaseline® onto the lenses. Calibrate the blurriness by distributing the Vaseline until it's possible to read 36-point type but impossible to read 12-point type. Clean up the rims and frame so they're not too repulsive to wear.

Recruit four people to test. These cannot be the same people who participated in the baseline test. When testing, do obtain informed consent and administer the same pretest questionnaire that you developed for exercise 19. Before each test, configure a Web browser to use the largest font size available. Display the home page of the e-commerce site. Use the same scenarios and record the same measures that you did in exercise 19.

a. Write an orientation script that explains that the user will be wearing a set of specially prepared glasses to simulate low vision and will perform some common tasks on an e-commerce site.

b. Write up the results. Give a summary of responses on the pretest questionnaire. For each task, create a table showing the measures for the four users.

c. Create a summary table that gives the average measures for each of the tasks.

d. Compare the measures from this group to the measures you collected in exercise 19. What are the differences? What do you conclude?

21. This exercise is similar to exercise 20. This test also explores low vision, but, instead of using a browser with a large font, use a browser with the normal font size and a screen magnifier. Install a screen magnifier or use the one that comes with the operating system. Recruit four users who did not participate in the testing you performed in exercise 19.

    Carry out the test as outlined in exercise 20 and answer parts a–d from exercise 20.

22. This exercise is similar to exercise 20, but this test simulates total blindness. Install a screen reader. Verify that the screen reader will recognize and read the text on the test site's pages. During the test, you will turn off the computer monitor. To prevent users from seeing their hands, construct a cardboard box that's 24 inches long, 4 inches high, and 8 inches deep. During the test, you will place the box over the keyboard and mouse. Leave one of the long sides open so that users can reach inside to the keyboard and mouse.

    Recruit four people to test. These cannot be the same people who participated in the baseline study. When testing these users, do obtain an informed consent and ask them to fill out the same pretest questionnaire that you developed for exercise 19.

    a. Write an orientation script that explains that you will be testing a screen reader and that, to simulate blindness, the screen will be turned off and the keyboard covered.

    b. Write up the results. Give a summary of responses on the pretest questionnaire. For each task, create a table showing the measures for the four users.

    c. Create a summary table that compares the average measures for each of the tasks.

    d. Compare the measures from this group to the measures you collected in exercise 19. What are the differences? Why might it be necessary to reconsider "time out" periods when serving users who are blind?

23. In this exercise, you will explore the impact that limited mobility has on using the Web. The setup for the user tests will be the same as for exercise 19, but the user will not be allowed to use more than one finger. Before beginning the test, set up the browser to display the home page of the test site, and turn on Sticky Keys.

    Recruit four people to test. These cannot be the same people who participated in the baseline study. When testing these users, obtain an informed consent, and ask them to fill out the same pretest questionnaire that you developed for exercise 19.

    a. Write an orientation script that explains that you will be testing the effects that mobility limitations have on accessing the Web. Tell them that, to simulate a motor disability, they will be on able to use more than one finger and will not be able to use the mouse. Explain how to use Sticky Keys to simulate simultaneous key presses.

       Use the same test scenarios and record the same measures that you did in exercise 19. You might need to remind the user not to use more than one finger.

    b. Write up the results. Give a summary of responses on the pretest questionnaire. For each task, create a table showing the measures for the four users.

    c. Create a summary table that gives the average measures for each of the tasks.

    d. Compare the measures from this group to the measures you collected in exercise 19. Are they different?

24. In this exercise, you will assess the challenges that severely limited mobility has on navigating a website. The setup for the tests will be the same as for exercise 19, but, to simulate severe motor impairment, give the users a new unsharpened Number 2 pencil to put between their teeth for accessing the keyboard. Before beginning the test, set up the browser to display the home page of the test site, and turn on Sticky Keys.

   a. Write an orientation script that explains that you will be testing the effects that mobility limitations have on accessing the Web. Tell them that, to simulate a severe motor disability, they will be able to use only the pencil between their teeth to touch the keyboard and they will not be able to use the mouse. Explain how to use Sticky Keys to simulate simultaneous key presses.

      Use the same test scenarios and record the same measures that you did in exercise 19. You might need to remind the user to rely only on the pencil for navigating the site.

   b. Write up the results. Give a summary of responses on the pretest questionnaire. For each task, create a table showing the measures for the four users.

   c. Create a summary table that gives the average measures for each of the tasks.

   d. Compare the measures from this group to the measures you collected in exercise 19. Compute a "frustration measure," which is the ratio of negative comments to total comments for each task for both groups. How do they compare?

25. Test a website by using Bobby, Wave, A-prompt, or another automatic checking program that evaluates accessibility. Ideally, the site should be one of your own, no matter how simple, so that you can correct the accessibility faults that will be reported. In your report, include a printout of the feedback that the checking program generated. Categorize and summarize the types of accessibility issues detected and suggest steps you can take to rectify them.

26. Research any of the following topics, using the Web. Write a short paper (2–5 pages) explaining the basics to a reader assumed to be unfamiliar with the subject. Set up a demonstration.

   a. Predictive typing, also called word completion.

   b. Voice recognition.

   c. Screen narration in relation to page layout.

27. Contact the Office of Disabilities on your campus and interview one of the staff about the number of students they serve and about the types and severities of the disabilities. Ask about the frustrations that students with disabilities have when using computer technology. Give a presentation on your findings.

References

[AbilityHub 2002] AbilityHub, Inc. Sticky Keys. Available at
   www.abilityhub.com/keyboard/stickykey.htm

[Aging 2001] Administration on Aging, U. S. Department of Health and Human Services. *A Profile of Older Americans 2001.* Available at
   www.aoa.gov/aoa/STATS/profile/2001/12.html

[Alliance 2000] The Alliance for Technology Access. *Computer and Web Resources for People with Disabilities: A Guide to Exploring Today's Assistive Technology.* Alameda, CA: HunterHouse Books, 2000.

[Apple 2002] Apple Computer. Accessibility Features. Available at
www.apple.com/disability/easyaccess.html#sticky

[De Mori 1997] Renato De Mori. *Spoken Dialogues with Computers.* San Diego: Academic Press, 1997.

[DePaul 2002] DePaul University American Sign Language Project, 2002. Available at
asl.cs.depaul.edu.

[Family 2002] The Family Centre (Deaf Children). Television Listing. Accessed May 2, 2002 at www.fcdc.org.uk/tv_listings.htm

[Garay 1997] Nestor Garay-Vitoria and Julio González-Abascal. Intelligent word-prediction to enhance text input rate (a syntactic analysis-based word-prediction aid for people with severe motor and speech disability). International Conference on Intelligent User Interfaces Proceedings of the 2nd international conference on Intelligent user interfaces 1997. Orlando, Florida. pp. 241–244.

[Hoffner 2000] Randy Hoffner. "Video Description Is On the Way," Tvtechnology.com—October 31, 2000. Available at www.tvtechnology.com/features/
Tech-Corner/f-RH-video-description.shtml

[Holladay 2000] David Holladay and Jesse Kaysen. *American Braille Basics.* Duxbury Systems, 2000. Available at
www.duxburysystems.com/resources/about_amer_braille.asp

[Holt 1994] Judith Holt, Sue Hotto, Kevin Cole. *Demographic Aspects Of Hearing Impairment: Questions And Answers.* Gallaudet Research Institute, 1994. Available at
gri.gallaudet.edu/Demographics/factsheet.html

[Ishihara 1992] Shinobu Ishihara. *Ishihara's Tests for Colour-Blindness.* Tokyo: Kanehara, 1992.

[King 1999] Thomas W. King. *Assistive Technology: Essential Human Factors.* Boston: Allyn and Bacon, 1999. p. 19.

[Krebs 1974] Bernard M. Krebs. *Transcribers' Guide to English Braille.* New York: Jewish Guide for the Blind, 1974. p. 2.

[Madentec 2002] Madentec. *Telepathic 2000.* Available at
www.madentec.com/products/comaccess/telepathic/telepathic.html

[Mates 2000] Barbara T. Mates. *Adaptive Technology for the Internet: Making Electronic Resources Accessible to All.* Chicago: American Library Association, 2000. pp. 53–59.

[Meyer 1988] Gary W. Meyer and Donald P. Greenberg. "Color-Defective Vision and Computer Graphics Displays," *IEEE Computer Graphics and Applications.* September/October, 1988. Vol. 8, No. 5. 28–40.

[National 2002] National Association of the Deaf. Captioning and Accessibility Information. *Captioned Media Program.* Accessed April 29, 2002. Available at
www.cfv.org/caai/nadh12.pdf

[NCSA 2002] National Spinal Cord Injury Association. Spinal Cord Injury Statistics, 2002. Available at www.spinalcord.org/resource/Factsheets/factsheet2.html

[NICHCY 2000] National Information Center for Children and Youth with Disabilities. General Information about Cerebral Palsy. Fact Sheet Number 2 (FS2), May 2000. Available at www.nichcy.org/pubs/factshe/fs2txt.htm

[NMSS 2002] National Multiple Sclerosis Society. Frequently Asked Questions About MS. Available at www.nmss.org/faq.asp

[Paciello 2000] Michael G. Paciello. *WEB Accessibility for People with Handicaps.* Lawrence, KS: CMP Books, 2000.

[Pascarelli 1994] Emil Pascarelli and Deborah Quilter. *Repetitive Strain Injury: A Computer User's Guide.* New York: John Wiley, 1994.

[Raggett 2002] `http://tidy.sourceforge.net/`

[Roffé 1998] Sarina Roffé. "The 'Dumbing Down' of Language," *Hearing Health.* Vol. 14 No. 3. May/June 1998. Also available at `www.cuedspeech.org/vp-dumbing.html`

[Rowley 1997] `http://www.folksonline.com/folks/ts/roofer.htm`

[Salsberg 1996] Bob Salsberg. "New technology helps blind enjoy Hollywood's classics," *SouthcoastToday.com.* May 18, 1996. Available at `www.s-t.com/daily/05-96/05-18-96/1dvs.htm`

[Schein 1974] J. Schein and M. Delk. *The deaf population of the United States.* Silver Spring, MD: National Association of the Deaf, 1974.

[Thatcher 2001] James W. Thatcher. Accessible Forms. Course notes written for the *Information Technology Technical Assistance and Training Center.* Available at `jimthatcher.com/webcourse8.htm`

[Trace 2002] Trace Center. A Brief Introduction to Disabilities. Trace Center, College of Engineering, University of Wisconsin-Madison. April 5, 2002. Available at `trace.wisc.edu/docs/population/populat.htm#visual`

[USHealth 1997] Office of the Assistant Secretary for Planning and Evaluation, U.S. Department of Health and Human Services. *Trends In The Well-Being Of America's Children & Youth,* 1997. Available at `aspe.os.dhhs.gov/hsp/97trends/Pf1-1.htm` and `aspe.os.dhhs.gov/hsp/97trends/hc2-4.htm`

[Visicast 2002] The Visicast Project. Available at `www.visicast.co.uk/`

[W3C 1998] World Wide Web Consortium. Voice Browsers. *W3C NOTE,* 28th January, 1998. Available at `www.w3.org/TR/NOTE-voice`

[W3C 1999a] World Wide Web Consortium. Clarify Natural Language Usage. *Web Content Accessibility Guidelines 1.0.* Available at `www.w3.org/TR/WCAG10/#gl-abbreviated-and-foreign`

[W3C 1999b] World Wide Web Consortium. Provide equivalent alternatives to auditory and visual content. *Web Content Accessibility Guidelines 1.0.* Available at `www.w3.org/TR/WCAG10/#gl-provide-equivalents`

[W3C 1999c] World Wide Web Consortium. Accessibility Features of SMIL. *W3C NOTE 21.* September, 1999. Available at `www.w3.org/TR/SMIL%2Daccess/`

[W3C 1999d] World Wide Web Consortium. Create tables that transform gracefully. *Web Content Accessibility Guidelines 1.0.* Available at `www.w3.org/TR/WCAG10/#gl-table-markup`

[W3C 1999e] World Wide Web Consortium. Don't rely on color alone. *Web Content Accessibility Guidelines 1.0.* Available at `www.w3.org/TR/WCAG10/#gl-color`

[W3C 1999f] World Wide Web Consortium. Ensure user control of time-sensitive content changes. *Web Content Accessibility Guidelines 1.0.* Available at `www.w3.org/TR/WCAG10/#gl-movement`

[W3C 1999g] World Wide Web Consortium. Design for device-independence. *Web Content Accessibility Guidelines 1.0.* Available at `www.w3.org/TR/WCAG10/#gl-device-independence`

[W3C 1999h] World Wide Web Consortium. *Web Content Accessibility Guidelines 1.0.* Available at `www.w3.org/TR/WCAG10`

[W3C 1999i] World Wide Web Consortium. *Checklist of Checkpoints for Web Content Accessibility Guidelines 1.0.* Available at `www.w3.org/TR/WCAG10/full-checklist.html`

[W3C 2000] World Wide Web Consortium. Navigation. Core Techniques for Web Content Accessibility Guidelines 1.0. *W3C Note 6.* November, 2000. Available at www.w3.org/TR/WCAG10-CORE-TECHS/#navigation

[WebAIM 2000] WebAIM.org. How to Create Accessible Tables. Web Accessibility In Mind, 2000. Available at www.webaim.org/howto/tables

[WebAIM 2002] WebAIM.org. The User Perspective: Motor Impairments. Web Accessibility In Mind Accessibility Training Event, April 2002. Available at www.webaim.org/training2002/week1/motor.php

13

Globalization

13.1 Introduction

The demographics of Web users have changed dramatically over the past ten years. In 1996, over 87 percent of them were native speakers of English [Moon 1996]. Although current estimates vary, most experts agree that this percentage has fallen to less than 50 percent [Global 2001]. The U.S. government predicts that, by 2005, the number of non-English speakers using the Internet will outnumber English speakers by a factor of three to one [Goble 1999].

The term World Wide Web emphasizes the fact that the Internet is global. Many organizations and companies have realized that the best way to meet the needs of multilingual users is to create multilingual websites [He 2001]. These sites enjoy the advantage of reaching a wider audience and a bigger market.

At the present time, however, 70 percent of Web content is still in English [Bowan 2001]. However, reaching international audiences requires more than translating text. It involves presenting information in a way that is not inappropriate or offensive. The process of converting Web content to a different language and culture is called *globalization.*

Goals of this Chapter

This chapter examines the considerations and challenges involved in globalization. While reading it, you will learn

- the differences between internationalization and localization
- two approaches to text translation
- cultural considerations that extend beyond language
- screen layout guidelines to accommodate globalization
- tips for testing with international users.

13.2 Internationalization and Localization

Creating a website that appeals to a different culture requires extensive attention to content organization. The first step, called *internationalization,* identifies and isolates culturally specific items that appear on a site. This includes text, numbers, and dates, but also extends to images and colors [Belge 2001]. The second step, *localization,* adds cultural context to a previously internationalized site. This involves translating extant textual content, but can also require the creation of new content relevant only for particular locations. This might include local news, job postings, announcements of events and seminars, contact information, and directions to office or store locations [Huang 2001].

There is more to localization than translation and the addition of site-specific content. In addition to the language, the new site should reflect the values and customs of the target culture. The following two sections examine these issues.

13.3 Text Considerations

At present, there are two approaches to translating text for a website. The first is to use human translators exclusively; the second is to use semiautomatic translation with human oversight. Automatic translation, also known as machine translation, is not an option. For purposes of producing a website, machine translation is not capable of producing high-quality results without human intervention [Huang 2001].

When preparing for either method of translation, begin by re-editing the website text to conform to Standard English. Avoid jargon, colloquialisms including sports metaphors, slang, and marketing hype, because they are easy to mistranslate. It can be time consuming and embarrassing to correct such errors. A slogan of the Coors Brewery, "Turn it Loose" became "Suffer from diarrhea" in Spanish [Henning 2001]. For technical terminology, develop a controlled vocabulary of preferred terms and use them consistently.

It is important to express dates, times, units of measure, and names of locales in an unambiguous manner. Avoid using a purely numeric form for expressing a date without including additional context. In the United States, the characteristic interpretation of "03/10/2005" is March 10, 2005, but most of the rest of the world will interpret it as October 3, 2005. It's possible to use the numeric form for a date if the month, day, and year are clearly labeled. Another possibility is to use the name of the month instead of the numeric equivalent [Merrill 1992]. Figure 13–1 demonstrates six different methods for expressing dates unambiguously.

When listing a time, use a 24-hour clock instead of the "A.M." and "P.M." abbreviations. In addition, specify the time zone. This can either be Greenwich mean time (GMT) or an appropriate local zone.

When referring to money, always include the country as well as the numeric amount. Countries other than the United States also use the dollar symbol and name to indicate a monetary quantity [Belge 2001]. Adding the country name removes ambiguity. When specifying a size measurement, include the unit of measure. Most of the world, including England, has abandoned the English system of inches, feet, yards, and miles and would interpret an unlabelled measurement as being in the metric system. The same holds true for expressing quantities of weight.

When mentioning a city, always include the country name, and if the city is located in the United States, include the state. Although the most famous Boston is located in

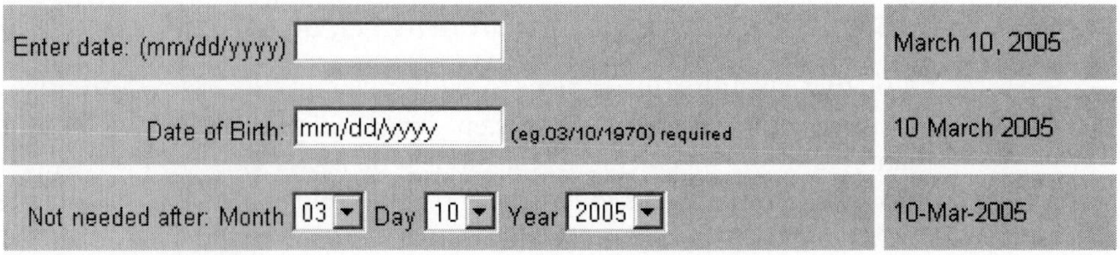

Enter date: (mm/dd/yyyy)		March 10, 2005
Date of Birth: mm/dd/yyyy (eg.03/10/1970) required		10 March 2005
Not needed after: Month 03 ▼ Day 10 ▼ Year 2005 ▼		10-Mar-2005

Figure 13–1 Express dates in an unambiguous manner.

Massachusetts, there are ten other cities named Boston located in the United States, one in Ireland, and one in England [Mapquest 2002, Ireland 2001, British 2001].

Translation goes beyond the vocabulary and grammar of a language. An effective translation also considers the communication of concept in the context of a culture. For example, the weekend occurs on different days of the week, depending on the locale. In Arabic countries, a day begins at sundown, not at midnight. The number 13 is not considered unlucky in Japanese culture, but the number 4 is [Smithsonian 2000].

Another consideration is the appropriate writing style for communicating information. Readers in the United States put a premium on efficiency. They prefer prose that is straightforward and specific. In contrast, Japanese admire prose that contains long flowing sentences with many relative clauses. To come directly to the point is rude [Spragins 1992]. A phrase such as "Buy now!" would be considered extremely distasteful.

For these reasons, it is important to find a translator who knows the target language and the target culture. Further, the translator should be familiar with the subject matter described in the text. It was clear that the translator who worked on the Cantonese version of the Sun *Open Windows Developer Guide* was not familiar with computers. The term "menu" became "list of food items" [Russo 1993].

Without knowing the target language or culture, it is difficult to judge the quality of a translation. One possible quality check is to have a second translator bring the translated text back into English and compare this with the original [Elnahrawy 2001].

The second approach to localizing text to a target culture is semiautomatic machine translation. Machine-translation efforts have been going on for nearly 50 years and have had moderate success [Hutchins 1995]. However, relying exclusively on machine translation for a website is ill advised. An alternative is semiautomatic translation. After a software package performs an initial translation, a human checks the result and makes changes as necessary [Huang 2001].

Regardless of the translation approach, the results will need to be displayed. The old seven-bit ASCII character set was designed to express English only and is inadequate for other languages. The ISO 8859-1 standard is a little bit better. It is an eight-bit standard capable of expressing such diacritical marks as acute accent (é in café), dieresis (ö in coöperate) and circumflex (ô in rôle) that occur in Western European Languages [Adams 1993]. A second eight-bit standard, ISO 8859-2, can express Slavic languages such as Czech, Polish, and Serbian. Other parts of the 8859 standard accommodate the Arabic, Cyrillic, Greek, and Hebrew alphabets.

Representing Japanese, Korean, traditional Chinese, or simplified Chinese poses even greater problems. There are between 20,000 and 50,000 distinct characters in each of these languages, so they are impossible to express as an eight-bit code. In 1991, the Unicode Consortium was formed to find a way to express all characters of all languages in one system [Unicode 2001]. The result was the ISO 10646 standard, more commonly known as Unicode.

Unicode is actually a suite of three encoding forms. The first, UTF-8, is an eight-bit (one-byte) form that includes the familiar ASCII character set. The second, UTF-16, is a two-byte form that can express a far larger number of characters. UTF-32 is a four-byte code capable of expressing all characters of all known languages.

Web browsers and other applications supporting Unicode can display characters from any language, as long as the relevant code page has been loaded into the software [Page 2000, Wood 2002]. Without the proper code page, the characters will not appear correctly. (See Figure 13–2.) The Web page contains the same passage in English, Arabic, and Chinese. The first screen capture shows a browser that is lacking the simplified Chinese and Arabic code pages.

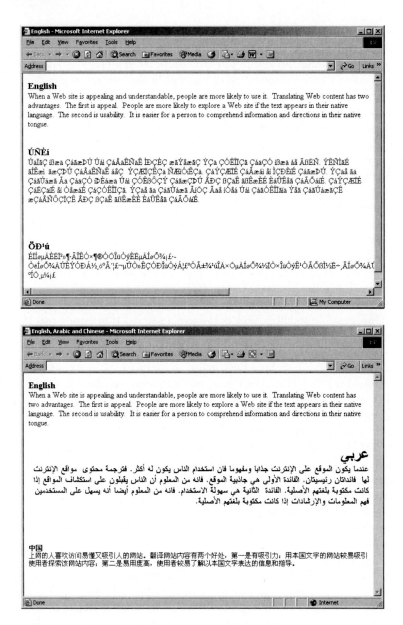

Figure 13–2 Even with Unicode-capable browsers, the proper code page needs to be loaded.

Clearly, translating text is a major consideration when localizing a website. However, another important aspect of localization is the use of color and imagery.

13.4 Color, Icons, and Images

Color associations vary widely between cultures, and the reaction to a color used out of context can be strongly negative. For example, in the United States and much of Europe, the color of a bridal dress is white. In China, a bride who wore white would shock the assembly

	Egypt	**China**	**Japan**	**India**	**France**
Red	Death	Happiness	Anger, Danger	Life, Creativity	Aristocracy
Blue	Virtue, Faith, Truth	Heavens, Clouds	Villainy		Freedom, Peace
Green	Fertility, Strength	Ming Dynasty, Heavens, Clouds	Future, Youth, Energy	Prosperity, Fertility	Criminality
Yellow	Happiness, Prosperity	Birth, Wealth, Power	Grace, Nobility	Success	Temporary
White	Joy	Death, Purity	Death	Death, Purity	Neutrality

Figure 13–3   Color Symbolism in Different Cultures [Russo 1993].

and cause pain for her parents, because white is the color worn to funerals and has a strong association with death. In China and parts of India, red is the preferred color for a bridal dress; in the United States, this would have a strong negative connotation.

Figure 13–3 and Figure 13–4 demonstrate the wide variety of cultural interpretations for color [Russo 1993, Horton 1994]. Note that there are differences of opinion among experts. This underlines the importance of consulting people who are natives in the target culture to get their reaction.

Icons are another nontextual aspect that is tricky to localize. In some cases, an icon describes a term that does not have a direct translation in the target language. For instance, many countries do not use the term "home page" to describe the main page of a website [Lacoursière 2001]. In France, it's called the welcome page (*page d'accueil*).[8] In Germany, it's often called the starting page (*Startseite*).[9] In Spanish, it's the beginning (*início*) or main (*principal*)[10] page. In these languages, an icon of a house does not convey the message, "Click here to go to the main page of this site."

Another type of problem arises from the fact that an object might have an entirely different appearance in another culture, and thus the U.S. icon makes no sense. For instance, the familiar shopping-cart icon is not universally successful in Europe, because many people there use a handheld basket or bag when grocery shopping [Woods 1999]. In fact, the British version of amazon.com uses a shopping basket, not a cart.

In the past, some websites have used flags from different countries to serve as links to the translated versions of their pages. However, this is not the best approach. In some countries, such as Switzerland, multiple languages are spoken. Another complication occurs when multiple countries use the same language, as is the case with Spanish, French,

---

[8]Accueil is used at Bank of Montreal www.bmo.com/francais, Amazon.com www.amazon.fr, Le Figaro www.lefigaro.com, FNAC www.fnac.com, Ebay www.ebay.fr, and the French edition of the BBC www.bbc.co.uk/french/.

[9]Starting page (Startseite) is used at www.ebay.de, Medicine World Wide www.m-ww.de, and World Time Clock www.weltzeituhr.com. However, many sites use "home," including BMW www.bmw.de, Amazon.com www.amazon.de, and der Spiegel www.spiegel.de. The German Parliament www.bundestag.de uses both terms.

[10]Beginning (início) is used at Monster www.monster.es, Microsoft www.bcentral.com.ar, Yahoo www.yahoo.es, and the Government of Aruba spanish.aruba.com. Main (principal) is used at Alta Vista eses.altavista.com and Yupi/MSN www.yupimsn.com.

	Arabia	China	Japan	India	Western Europe
Red	Strength	Festivity, enthusiasm	Anger, danger	Auspicious	Danger
Blue	Truth	Illusion	Villainy		Masculinity, authority
Green		Life	Youth, energy	Life, Nature	Safety, sourness
Yellow	Happiness	Honor, royalty, pornographic	Grace, nobility, childish		Cowardice, caution
White		Death, mourning, purity	Death, mourning	Purity (dress of widow)	Purity
Black		Sober mood	Evil	Mourning, Protest	Death
Orange		Warmth		Rebellion, fire	
Purple		Female			

Figure 13–4   Color Symbolism in Different Cultures [Horton 1994].

and English [Foreign 01]. A better approach is to display the name of the language as it is spelled in that language. Figure 13–5 demonstrates this idea.

Newer software allows Web servers to query the locale or preferred language of a user's Web browser. It is possible to write scripts, typically in JavaScript, to use such information as the basis for automatically sending pages in the proper language instead of forcing users to select language-specific links [Flanagan 1998].

When creating icons for localization, test them with users from the target culture to see whether the icons actually convey their intended meanings. When using an icon, always include supporting text that explains its meaning.

Figure 13–5   Giving a user a choice of languages.

Figure 13–6   Outside of the U.S., this gesture
rarely has a positive meaning.

Icons and images depicting people can pose great difficulties. Depicting any sort of hand
gesture has a high probability of causing offense. The "OK" sign shown in Figure 13–6 has
few positive connotations outside of American culture. The French interpret this as meaning "zero" or "worthless" [Axtell 1991]. In Turkey, it refers to an indelicate sphincter. In
Brazil, it is the equivalent of the middle-finger gesture in the United States [Betts 2000].

Horton [1991] suggests displaying a hand only in the context of performing work with an
object. When depicting people, he recommends using line drawings instead of photographs
and to use an abstract, unisex style, such as stick figures.

13.5 Formatting and Page-Layout Considerations

Text and imagery are both central elements in Web-page design. Creating layouts that are
flexible enough to accommodate localization is a challenging project. This section will examine a number of issues, ranging from the word level to the page level.

In the formatting of numbers, the commas and periods sometimes change function [del
Galdo 1990]. In France, it is customary to write the quantity 1,256.68 as 1.256,68. When
expressing weights or measures, convert to the units most familiar to the culture. In most
cases, this means using the metric system. In the case of measures, an inch is a larger unit
than a centimeter and a mile is longer than a kilometer, so the new number will take up
more space on the page. Compare the quantity 50 inches and its metric near-equivalent,
127 centimeters.

Consider expressing any money in units of the target culture. As with weights and measures, allocate extra space. (See Figure 13–7.) Use the appropriate currency symbol or the

	Formatted with currency symbol	ISO 4217 designation
United States	$100.00 USD	USD
European Community	114,914 €	EUR
Great Britain	£ 69.932	GBP
Japan	¥ 13.475,98	JPY
Canada	$159.784 CAD	CAD

Figure 13–7 Expressing currency.

three-letter ISO 4217 currency designation [ISO 2001]. If using the monetary units of the target culture is not possible, clearly label the amount as being in U.S. currency and add a link to one of the many currency calculators available on the Internet [Elnahrawy 2001]. To find them, use the term "currency calculator" with your favorite search engine.

When creating a form for international use, keep in mind that physical mailing addresses vary from country to country. When designing the shipping and billing sections of a form for locations outside the U.S., do not force people to select a state. Outside the United States, "ZIP codes" are referred to as postcodes or postal codes, and they sometimes are not numeric. The number of digits in a phone number also might differ [Gutzman 2001].

When designing text-alignment schemes, consider the reading direction of the target language [Ishida 2000]. Western European languages are read from left to right. Arabic and Hebrew are read from right to left. Chinese, Japanese, and Korean can support either a vertical (top to bottom) or horizontal (left to right) direction, but vertical organization is becoming rare [Chan 2002]. When aligning left-to-right languages such as English, use predominantly left alignment. When aligning right-to-left languages, use predominantly right alignment. See Figure 13–8 for a comparison of English and Hebrew.

The page design needs to accommodate the size of the translated text. Avoid using horizontal navigation bars, because they lack flexibility. English prose expands when it is translated to other European languages; often, the shorter the phrase, the greater is the expansion. For single words, Merrill [1992] suggests allocating two to three times the amount of space required in the original. For example, consider the translations of some commonly used words shown in Figure 13–9.

13.6 User Testing

Any website needs usability testing. A localized website will surely require this, even if its content is simply a translated version of the original [Nielsen 1990].

International usability testing entails even more considerations than conventional usability testing [Dray 2001]. First, identify people living in the target locale to help with recruiting users, scheduling tests, and finding translators. Second, localize the test. This includes modifying the test scenarios, the introduction, the informed-consent document, and any questionnaires. If at all possible, conduct the usability tests in the target language rather than in English. This will encourage people to discuss their reactions and offer suggestions more freely.

Finally, allow more time for testing. If you are not a native speaker of the target language, allot additional time between test sessions. Even if you are fluent, it will take more concentration to conduct a test and you will need more time to recover between sessions. If

Figure 13–8   Use predominantly right alignment for languages that are read from right to left.

	Spanish	**French**	**German**
News	Noticias	Actualités	Nachrichten
Exit	Salir	Quitter	Verlassen
Sign In	1. Login	Identifiez-vous	Melden Sie sich
	2. Validación de Clave		
	3. Identifícate		
Print	Imprimir	Imprimer	Drucken
Buy	Compra	Achetez	Einkaufen
Next	Siguiente	Suivant	Forward
File	Archivo	Fichier	Datei

Figure 13–9   Short words in English tend to expand when translated into other European languages.

you are working with an interpreter, allow for longer test sessions, because it will take additional time to translate anything that you or the test user will say.

13.7 Conclusions

Creating a website for a culture other than your own is a challenging activity. To maximize your chances for success, do apply the same user-centered development methodology that you would use for any site. The guidelines and tips from this chapter will help you avoid some known pitfalls as you localize your site. Globalization is not an exact process, but if you remember the principle "Know Thy User" and employ usability testing with people who fit your user profile, the result is more likely to be a useful site that is appealing to your new audience.

Review Questions

1. What is internationalization? What is localization? Why would it be important to consider both during the globalization process?

2. Why is it important to edit the English text on a website before translating it to a new language? What types of phrases or terminology should you eliminate?

3. What are the different interpretations of the date 05/06/2005? Give three alternative formats for this date that would remove the ambiguity.

4. A website runs a contest; in the rules, it says that all email entries must be received by October 15, 2004 at 5 P.M. Is this a precise date and time? If not, explain how to correct the problem.

5. Why are the following ambiguous? For each name, give two possible locations.
   a. Rome
   b. Athens
   c. Paris
   d. Notre Dame

6. What is Unicode? What purpose does it serve?

7. Locate a website that's in Japanese. Find and install the Unicode code pages to make your Web browser display the characters correctly. Print a copy of the page, and document the steps you took to install the code pages.

8. Compare Figure 13–3 and Figure 13–4. Where do they differ? Do they have any areas of agreement?

Exercises

9. Survey ten people. Ask them what each of the following colors means to them:

   a. Red

   b. Black

   c. White

   d. Green

   e. Yellow

   f. Purple

   List their responses for each color. Analyze the responses. Is there consensus? Where are there differences? Compare your results with Figure 13–3 and Figure 13–4. List areas of similarity and difference.

10. Analyze the icon in Figure 13–10, which is often used as a link for e-mail:

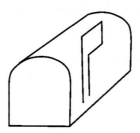

Figure 13–10   An icon used to represent e-mail.

   Describe the nationality and location of users who own one of these. Are there users in that country who don't own one? What portion of the users do they represent? Can you think of an icon that would be recognizable to a wider audience? If the flag is up, does that mean "You've got mail," or "I've got mail I want you to pick up"?

11. Suppose a website displayed the following flags, shown in Figure 13–11:

   a. Which flag(s) should Spanish speakers choose? Why?

   b. What flag(s) should French speakers choose? Why?

   c. What flag(s) should English speakers choose? Why?

   d. What is the drawback of this approach?

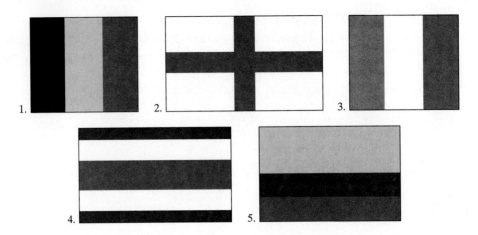

Figure 13–11   Flags from five countries. For Exercise 11.

12. A U.S. company named Victory Autos has a website featuring the company logo, shown in Figure 13–12. Why might this company want to reconsider this design before setting up an Australian website?

13. Why is it important to allow a little extra space when localizing measurements?

14. Suppose you need to accommodate measurements in inches and centimeters on your new website. Both units need to be accurate to two decimal places. The maximum length you need to represent is 50.05 inches.

    a. How many characters do you need to represent the maximum value in inches?

    b. How many characters do you need to represent the maximum value in centimeters?

15. You are visiting the French version of a favorite shopping site when you see a music CD that you know your cousin wants. The price is listed as 1.000 EUR. Given that the Euro currency is roughly equivalent to a dollar, is this a good deal? Explain.

Figure 13–12   A corporate logo for a fictitious U.S. company. For Exercise 12.

16. Suppose you had the following navigation bar on your U.S. site, shown in Figure 13–13:

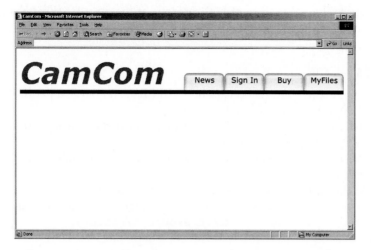

Figure 13–13   A U.S. website with a horizontal navigation bar. For Exercise 16.

What problems will you encounter if you decide to create a French version of this page? Demonstrate the problem, and suggest a solution.

17. Many U.S. websites have buttons similar to these, shown in Figure 13–14:

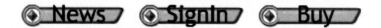

Figure 13–14   Buttons. For exercise 17.

What problems might these cause if the site is translated?

18. Find two students who are taking a second year of a foreign language. Bring them into a computer lab and bring up one of your favorite U.S. websites. Ask one of them to critique the site for five minutes *in the foreign language they're studying*. Suggest that the critique include positives, negatives, and suggestions for improvement. Ask the other student to translate for you. Alternatively, ask a non-U.S. student to critique a U.S. site.

a. How many positive comments did they give

b. How many negative comments did they offer?

c. How many suggestions for improvement did they give you?

d. What does this outcome suggest about conducting usability tests in a language other than the user's native tongue?

19. Experiment with changing the locale or preferred language on your favorite Web browser. First, point your browser at either `www.google.com` or `www.msn.com`. Once you have changed the preferred language to something other than English, point the browser at the site again. Answer the following questions.

a. What browser did you use? Give the name and version number.

b. What steps were necessary to change the preferred language?

   c. Print out screen captures of the English and foreign-language version.

   d. Compare the appearance of both versions of the website. What changed? What remained the same?

References

[Adams 1993] G. Adams. "Internationalization and Character Set Standards," *Standard View,* Vol. 1., No. 1. September 1993. 31–39.

[Axtell 1991] R. Axtell. *Gestures: The Do's and Taboos of Body Language Around the World.* New York: John Wiley and Sons, 1991.

[Belge 1995] M. Belge. "The Next Step in Software Internationalization," *Interactions.* January, 1995. 21–25.

[Betts 2000] M. Betts, C. Sliwa, and J. Disabatino. "Global Web Sites Prove Challenging," *Computer World,* August 21, 2000. [Online]. [No pagination]. Available at `http://www.computerworld.com/itresources/rcstory/ 0,4167,STO48799_KEY52,00.html` Accessed September 10, 2001.

[Bowan 2001] T.S. Bowan. "English Could Snowball on Net," *Technology Research News,* November 21, 2001. [Online]. [No pagination]. Available at `http://www.trnmag.com/Stories/2001/112101/ English_could_snowball_on_Net_112101.html` Accessed February 11, 2001.

[British 2001] The British Library. *About Us: Locations.* [Online]. [No pagination]. Available at `http://www.bl.uk/about/locations/yorkshire.html` Accessed February 11, 2001.

[Chan 2002] S. Chan. Personal communication. February 12, 2002.

[del Galdo 1990] E. del Galdo. Internationalization and Translation: Some Guidelines for the Design of Human-Computer Interfaces. In *Designing Human–Computer Interfaces for International Use.* J. Nielsen, Ed. Amsterdam: Elsevier, 1990. 1–10.

[Dray 1996] S. Dray. "Designing for the Rest of the World: A Consultant's Observations," *Interactions,* Vol. 3 No. 2. March 1996. 15–18.

[Elnahrawy 2001] E. Elnahrawy. Users from Other Cultures than the U.S. April, 2001. [Online]. [No pagination]. Available at `http://www.otal.umd.edu/UUPractice/culture/` Accessed February 6, 2002.

[Flanagan 1998] D. Flanagan. *JavaScript: The Definitive Guide.* Sebastopol, California: O'Reilly, 1998.

[Foreign 2001] Foreign Exchange Translations, Inc. Secrets of Successful Web Site Globalization. [Online]. [No pagination]. Available at `http://www.fxtrans.com/resources/web_globalization.html` Accessed September 9, 2001.

[Goble 1999] P. Goble. World: Analysis From Washington—The Other Y2K Problem. June 8, 1999. [Online]. [No Pagination]. Available at `http://www.rferl.org/nca/features/1999/06/F.RU.990607122007.html` Accessed February 4, 2001.

[Gutzman 2001] A. Gutzman. The Internet Arsenal: Chapter 10—Globalization and Multicurrency Capacity (Part 1). Internet.com, March 26, 2001. [Online]. [No pagination]. Available at `http://ecommerce.internet.com/news/insights/ectech/ article/0,3371,10378_724311,00.html` Accessed February 2, 2002.

[He 2001] S. He. Interplay of Language and Culture in Global E-commerce: A Comparison of Five Companies' Multilingual Websites. Proceedings of SIGDOC'01. October 21–24, 2001, Santa Fe, New Mexico, USA. 83–88.

[Henning 2001] K. Henning. Localization. Bridging the usability gap. [Online]. [No pagination]. Available at `http://www.vertebrae.net/insight/thoughtpaper_3.asp` Accessed February 9, 2002.

[Horton 1991] W. Horton. *Illustrating Computer Documentation.* New York: John Wiley and Sons, 1991.

[Horton 1994] W. Horton. *The Icon Book.* New York: John Wiley and Sons, 1994.

[Huang 2001] S. Huang and S. Tilley. Issues of Content and Structure for a Multilingual Web Site. Proceedings of SIGDOC'01. October 21–24, 2001, Santa Fe, New Mexico, USA. 103–110.

[Hutchins 1995] W. J. Hutchins. Reflections on the History and Present State of Machine Translations. Proceedings of MT Summit V. Luxembourg, July 10–13, 1995. 89–96.

[Ishida 2000] R. Ishida. Challenges in Designing International User Information. Xerox Global Design. January 30, 2001. [Online]. [No pagination]. Available at `http://www.xerox-emea.com/globaldesign/paper/NonLatin/iuc18h04.pdf` Accessed February 10, 2002.

[ISO 2001] International Standards Organization. Codes for the representation of currencies and funds. ISO 4217:2001 [Online]. [No pagination]. Available at `www.iso.ch` Accessed February 13, 2002.

[Ireland 2001] Local Ireland, Inc. Boston. [Online]. [No pagination]. Available at `http://clare.local.ie/boston/` Accessed February 2, 2001.

[Lacoursière 2001] G. Lacoursière. Re: International Internet Icons. Newsgroup communication. April 02, 2001. [Online]. [No pagination]. Available at `http://lists.w3.org/Archives/Public/www-international/2001AprJun/0005.html` Accessed September 10, 2001.

[Mapquest 2002]. Mapquest.com. Available at `www.mapquest.com` Enter "Boston" in the textbox labeled "City" and click "Map it." Accessed February 2, 2002.

[Merrill 1992] C. Merrill and M. Shanoski. Internationalizing Online Information. Proceedings of SIGDOC'92. Ottawa, Ontario, Canada, 1992. 19–25.

[Moon 1996] K. Moon. Who's Surfing the Web? A Look at GVU's Fifth User Survey. IS/OOP Group's Online. [Online]. [No pagination]. Available at `http://www.online-magazine.com/survey.htm` Accessed September 10, 2001.

[Nielsen 1990] J. Nielsen. Usability Testing of International Interfaces. In *Designing Human–Computer Interfaces for International Use.* J. Nielsen, Ed. Amsterdam: Elsevier, 1990. 39–44.

[Page 2000] B. Page. "Building the Tower of Babel: The Web Goes Global," TechWeb News, November 6, 2000. [Online]. [No pagination]. Available at `http://content.techweb.com/wire/story/TWB20001106S0003` Accessed February 9, 2002.

[Russo 1993] P. Russo and S. Boor. How Fluent is Your Interface? Designing for International Users. Proceedings of the INTERCHI'93 Conference on Human Factors in Computing Systems. Amsterdam, The Netherlands, 1993. 342–347.

[Smithsonian 2000] Smithsonian Institution. Dinner for Five: Japanese Serving Dishes for Elegant Meals. October, 2000. [Online]. [No pagination]. Available at `http://www.asia.si.edu/press/prdinner.htm` Accessed February 5, 2002.

[Spragins 1992] E. Spragins. Developing Hypertext Documents for an International Audience. Proceedings of SIGDOC'92. Ottawa, Ontario, Canada, 1992. 27–34.

[Unicode 2001] Unicode Consortium. The Unicode® Standard: A Technical Introduction. August 10, 2001. [Online]. [No pagination]. Available at `http://www.unicode.org/unicode/standard/principles.html` Accessed February 8, 2002.

[Woods 1999] J. Woods. Translation or Humiliation? DigiTrends Magazine. November 22, 1999. [Online]. [No pagination]. Available at `http://www.digitrends.net/marketing/13638_6357.html` Accessed February 14, 2002.

[Wood 2002] A. Wood. Creating Multilingual Web Pages: Unicode Support in HTML, HTML Editors and Web Browsers. January 16, 2002. [Online]. [No pagination]. Available at `http://www.hclrss.demon.co.uk/unicode/htmlunicode.html` Accessed February 8, 2002.

14

Personalization and Trust

14.1 Introduction

Organizing content to help users locate information and creating navigation to help them locate it quickly are both important aspects of user-centered Web development. The goal of these activities is to serve groups of people within a user profile. *Personalization* takes this a step further. It encompasses techniques to structure content organization and enhance navigation to meet the specific needs of each individual user. This has also been called mass customization and one-to-one marketing [Rossi 2001].

To provide this service, a website needs to gather information on individuals, an approach that has caused many users to become concerned about their privacy when using the Internet. This chapter examines the privacy issue and explores ways that websites can instill trust in their users.

Goals of this Chapter

In this chapter, you will do the following:

- learn about different types of personalization on the Web
- become aware of privacy issues
- understand what inspires trust and how it can be applied to websites.

14.2 Benefits of Personalization

Personalization is a strategy for gaining a competitive advantage. Surveys have consistently reported that users want convenience when they visit a website [Georgia 1998, Rosenfeld 1998, Consumer 2001]. They want to be able to find what they want and find it quickly. If the website has a method of customizing a page for the current user by identifying the most relevant information and placing it closer to the top of the page, the site will become even easier to use.

In many instances, this approach can result in value-added service for a user. For example, if a website knows a user's ZIP code, then, when the user searches for, say, a restaurant offering Thai cuisine, the site not only can display a list of Thai restaurants, but also can sort them by driving distance. With a ZIP code, when a user looks up a new movie title, Yahoo delivers not only information about who's starring in the movie, but also a list of show times at local theatres [Manber 2000]. Both of these

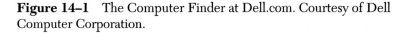

Figure 14–1   The Computer Finder at Dell.com. Courtesy of Dell
Computer Corporation.

scenarios are examples of a type of personalization that requires active involvement on the
part of the user. The site requests an item of information that the user supplies.

The solicited information is not always personal in nature. The "Computer Finder" on
Dell.com is an example. (See Figure 14–1.) By selecting answers to a small number of simple
questions, users can quickly winnow 96 possibilities into a manageable number of choices
[Dean 2000]. Another site that uses personalization to speed task completion is Amazon.com.
Its "1-Click" feature offers the convenience of automatically supplying the shipping and
billing information for repeat purchases. Users who have previously stored this information
with Amazon.com need only click on the "1-Click" icon to purchase merchandise.

Other personalization strategies are less intrusive and do not require users to fill out a form
or answer questions. For example, a website can track a user's *click stream,* which lists the
pages that a user browsed while visiting a site. This technique can help produce more relevant
searches. Software can record the search terms that a user typed and track the pages the user
chose to view. If another person requests a similar search, the software can use the information from previous users to rearrange the order in which the search results are displayed.

Regardless of whether the information required active user participation, a website server will use *cookies* to store some indication of a user's personalization preferences. A cookie is an HTTP header containing a string that a browser stores on a user's hard disk as a
small text file. The cookie can help identify a particular computer and store preferences for
a user. For example, a server could store an identification number in a cookie. On subsequent visits to the site, the server can access the cookie to find the number and use it to re-
trieve customer information from the server's databases [Bonner 1997].

The manner in which the personalized pages are displayed will vary from site to site. Amazon.com presents book recommendations that are based on past purchases. These appear as lists of links accompanied by small amount of text. (See Figure 6–7.) The site my.netscape.com gives people the opportunity to customize the actual content of the page, in addition to specifying the page's appearance. Users can choose content from many sources, including news, travel, sports, shopping, weather, and even a horoscope. Figure 14–2 shows a default version of my.netscape.com, and Figure 14–3 shows a personalized one.

The times at which sites solicit the information also differ. Some sites ask users to register before making content and personalization services available. Others permit users to browse or search site content freely and require user-supplied information only when the user wants to engage in a transaction. Supplying information typically involves choosing options from a menu, answering yes/no questions, or supplying a small amount of text, such as a street address and credit-card information. However, there is a promising new approach on the horizon called *conversational interfaces* [Lucente 2000]. In a conversational interface, a software "expert" engages the user in a dialog that is conducted in natural language; see Figure 14–4 for a sample interaction. At present, these experts are effective only in restricted domains, where the conversations are structured and are limited in variety. However, in these areas, they are highly effective. At the ShopAcer.com subsite for notebook PCs, 30 percent of shoppers who experienced the conversational interface went on to make a purchase. Of the site visitors who did not use the interface, only two percent made a purchase.

Personalization has the potential to benefit users who visit a website, and it also has benefits for the company that owns the websites [Fowler 2000]. Properly carried out, personalization can increase the percentage of people who buy merchandise while visiting the site. It can also be used to leverage further sales. Knowing more about users allows marketing departments to focus the types of advertisements they deliver more tightly. They can send additional e-mail to people who have browsed or made previous purchases on their site. In fact, the data about a user's purchasing habits, coupled with an e-mail or street address, have become a valuable commodity in their own right. Companies sell this information to others seeking new audiences for their goods and services; often, this practice generates spam, to the user's dismay.

14.3 Privacy Concerns

At present, there is no umbrella "right to privacy" for U.S. citizens seeking to block a company from selling or otherwise disseminating information about their buying habits [Bresnahan 2000]. The laws restricting this type of information flow are very limited. Laws do prevent the *government* from disseminating certain types of personal information, and state licensing laws place restrictions on people in some professions. Not only is there no broad right to privacy in the U.S., but the courts have upheld the contention that the redistribution of this type of data is protected as free speech under the First Amendment.

The best protection that users currently have is the law of contract [Volokh 2000]. If a company promises not to distribute information that a user supplies and then does so, the user can sue. Recently, in fact, a bankrupt e-commerce toy company was blocked from selling its customer database containing information about customer buying habits, mailing addresses, and the names of family members. The company's privacy policy had stated that the information would not be distributed to anyone, and the courts ruled that selling the information would constitute a breach of contract.

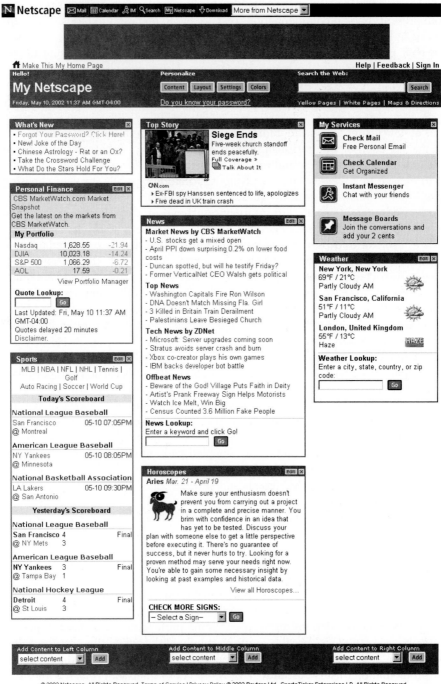

Figure 14–2 Home page of my.netscape.com, without personalization.
Netscape website © 2002 Netscape Communications Corporation. Screenshot
used with permission.

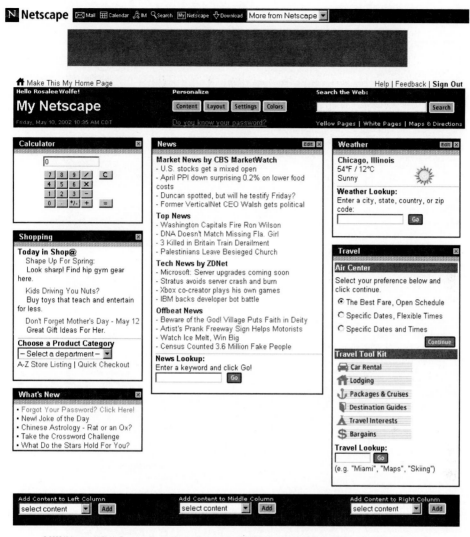

Figure 14–3   Home page of my.netscape.com, with personalization. Netscape website © 2002 Netscape Communications Corporation. Screenshot used with permission.

Even if users are not aware of the lack of privacy laws, they are very aware of the ramifications. Users of all kinds receive unsolicited messages in their e-mail queues daily. As a result, they are extremely reluctant to furnish personal information when they visit a website. Users report that, when they didn't want to supply requested information, they would leave the site or supply false information and refrain from buying merchandise.

This, then, is perhaps one of the causes contributing to the fact that, in general, people do not trust websites. In a recent survey of 1500 Web users, people were asked to rate several types of organizations in terms of their credibility [Princeton 2002]. These included small business, newspapers, financial companies such as banks, charities, the federal government

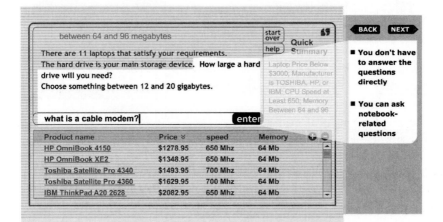

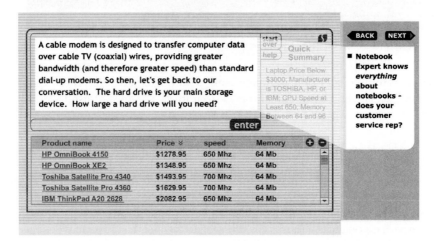

Figure 14–4   A conversational interface. Courtesy of Soliloquy.com.

in Washington, health-care companies, and large corporations. Websites selling goods or services came in last. Less than a third of Web users said they trusted this type of site most of the time or almost always.

The same survey found that credibility, or trust in a website, was an overwhelming reason for choosing a site. Credibility ranked second in importance only to ease of navigation and finding what users wanted. Over 95 percent rated navigation and "findability" as either "very important" or "somewhat important." A whopping 94 percent also said that being able to trust the information on a site is "very important" or "somewhat important." This is a clear indication that the issue of trust should be addressed during the creation of a website.

14.4 Factors Affecting Trust

Trust is "firm reliance on the integrity, ability, or character of a person or thing" [Dictionary 2002]. To gain a better understanding of the factors affecting a user's sense of trust in a website, this section steps back and examines what factors affect trust in everyday life. An intriguing tool for studying trust uses a game called "social dilemma" [Olson 2000]. In this game, people choose to act either in the spirit of cooperation, thus showing trust, or in their own self-interest. Many factors affect trust, including the following:

- Context
- Perceived similarity
- Standing or station in an organization
- Behavior
- Certification
- References.

Context has to do with the potential for loss. When the stakes are low or when there is little potential for costly loss, people tend to be more trusting. When the potential for loss goes up, the tendency to trust goes down. For example, divulging a credit-card number to someone with criminal intentions can result in a loss of both time and money and in a damaged credit rating. In the context of a website, people have high expectations when divulging their credit-card information.

People tend to trust others when they judge them to be similar to themselves [Cassell 2000]. When meeting for the first time, people engage in social interactions, including small talk and the disclosure of details about themselves. An awareness of shared vocabulary and shared experiences tends to foster trust, so self-disclosure is important. For example, Staples lost customers when the company added a ZIP-code request page that appeared any time that a user clicked on a link to a product [Schwartz 2000]. The reason Staples needed the information was to tell customers whether the item was in stock at a local store; if not, they would have to wait while Staples shipped it. The intent was to offer a better service to customers, but people thought the company was collecting marketing information. To rectify the situation, Staples disclosed the reason for needing the zip code by adding the following:

> **To view real-time inventory availability, please enter the ZIP code where products will be shipped.**

By disclosing this information, Staples reduced the abandonment rate by 75 percent.

People also consider a person's standing in a community and past behavior. They tend to assume that a person would not have risen to a recognized station without some degree of trustworthiness. Similarly, people whose actions are consistent with their words will inspire trust. When people do not have the time to observe a person's behavior for an extended period, they often rely instead on certifications and references [Shneiderman 2000]. A college degree is a form of certification, as is a license to practice medicine. There are several organizations offering certification for websites, including WebTrust (`www.webtrust.net`), TrustE (`www.truste.com`), VeriSign (`www.verisign.com`), and Better Business Bureau Online (`www.bbbonline.org`). These certifications range from assurances of privacy for personal information to a broad guarantee of business practices associated with supporting the website.

Referrals are a form of transferring trust. A new person, new information, or a new website that is recommended by trusted people will also tend to be trusted. For example, Amazon.com features book reviews written by private individuals who have decided to share their thoughts about the book. There is also an option for people to "review the review" by indicating whether they found the review helpful. Both the review and its rating appear with the book listing.

14.5 Fostering Trust in Websites

Establishing credibility for a website relies on the same principles that people use in day-to-day living for determining trustworthiness. Self-disclosure is an example [Princeton 2002]. Users want a statement of all fees they will be charged for the goods or services they plan to purchase. This includes shipping and handling costs, applicable taxes, and any other transaction fees.

Users will also want to know how a site will handle credit-card and other personal information. A *security statement* addresses this issue by listing the precautions that a website takes to protect sensitive information. It should mention the type of encryption technology the site uses to transmit information. Some sites, such as Gap.com, also explain how to check a browser window for indications confirming that the page being displayed is on a secure server. Some sites, including Amazon.com, also mention how their pages will display credit-card information. Figure 14–5 shows some examples of how to display credit-card information in a form that is recognizable to the owner but cannot be utilized by others for unauthorized purchases. It's vital that people be able to find this information easily. Many e-commerce sites now display a link to this information at the bottom of each page.

Some companies combine their security statement with a *privacy statement.* A privacy statement lists the types of information gathered by the site and the manner in which it is obtained. It also explains its policy for disseminating the acquired information. The site

Credit Card: 3787 ****** ***** **American Express**

Credit Card: AmEx ****-25003

Figure 14–5   Secure display of credit-card information.

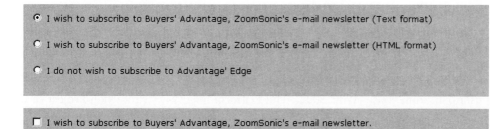

Figure 14–6 Giving a user a choice.

might give people a choice in this matter. An *opt-in* policy states that the information will not be shared without a user's explicit consent. An *opt-out* policy states that the information *will* be shared unless a user expressly forbids it. Whether a company gives users a choice of opting in or opting out can be deduced from the checkbox that often appears at the end of a form, as in Figure 14–6. Which of the two pages represent an opt-out policy?

Almost as important to users as privacy and security statements is confirmation of expected delivery date and information about the company's policies for returned items [Princeton 2002]. A clearly labeled link to a page outlining shipping and return policies is a good first step. It's also a good idea to include information about the expected delivery times on the form where a user chooses shipping options. (See Figure 14–7.) The third place to include information about the delivery date is in the confirmation page or e-mail that is generated after a person has committed to the purchase. In addition, users like to be able to check on the status of an order. Amazon.com puts the link to this information under the heading "Where's my stuff?" Most users also want a link to contact information, including e-mail address, street address, and telephone number, so they could reach someone in the company in case they encounter a problem.

Interestingly, most users do not consider certification as important as these other issues. One possible explanation is that, during the early days of the Internet, there was a proliferation of seals of approval, certificates, and awards. At the time, it was easy to obtain such seals and awards; that ease likely lowered their value. New Web users, however, attach more importance to these than do experienced users [Princeton 2002].

> ⦿ Standard Shipping $4.95 (3-7 business days)
>
> ○ Priority Shipping $15.00 plus additional $20.00 for orders over $200.00 (2 business days)
>   We are unable to offer priority shipping for orders containing furniture.
>
> ○ One Day Shipping $25.00 plus an additional $40.00 for orders over $200.00 (1 business day)
>   We are unable to offer next day shipping for orders containing furniture.

Figure 14–7 Supply information about expected delivery times on the order form.

14.6 New Developments in Controlling Privacy

Although the methods mentioned in the last sections will help ease user concerns, the fact remains that most current browsers and websites do not adhere to any standard method for preserving a user's privacy. In an effort to rectify this situation, the World Wide Web Consortium (W3C) has recently created a set of recommendations for an infrastructure to protect user data from abuse [W3C 2002]. The Platform for Privacy Protection Project (P3P) now provides a standard way for a website to communicate its practices for collecting, using, and distributing personal information.

From a user perspective, P3P offers a simple-to-use, automated way to exercise more control over how sites utilize personal information. It outlines a mechanism that can make privacy policies easy to find and presented in a standard form that makes them easier to understand. A browser that is P3P enabled allows a user to set personal privacy preferences; see Figure 14–8.

As part of the P3P implementation process, developers answer a standardized set of multiple-choice questions addressing a website's privacy policy. A site that is P3P enabled can furnish this information when it sends a Web page to a user. A browser that is P3P enabled can "read" this information and compare it to the user's privacy preferences. If the site wants to record information that the user is not willing to divulge, a dialog appears to explain the nature of the requested information. A user then has the option of supplying or not supplying the information.

Several major sites have already adopted P3P, including Msn.com, Yahoo.com, and About.com. Now that the specifications are finalized [W3C 2002a], expectations are that more sites will adopt it soon. The first browser to feature P3P was Microsoft's Internet Explorer 6.

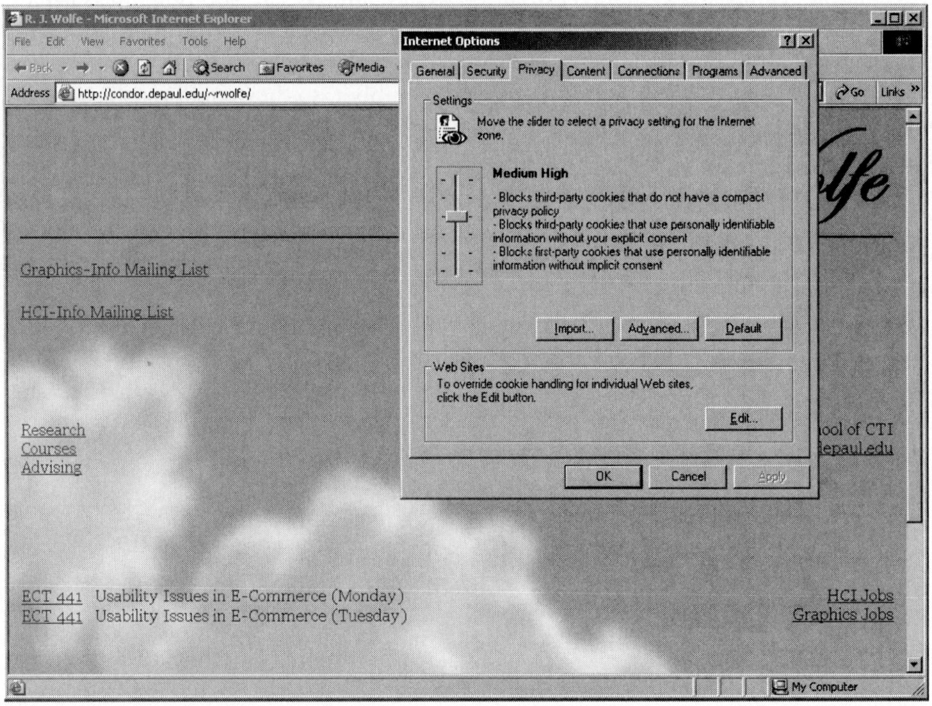

Figure 14–8   Privacy preferences in a P3P-enabled browser.

Its P3P implementation focused on a part of the P3P standard that addresses cookie acceptance. It can also display a report of a website's P3P policy.

An application that implements the entire P3P policy is AT&T's Privacy Bird, which installs into Internet Explorer. It appears as a bird icon in the browser's title bar [ATT 2002]. The bird chirps and changes color to tell the user whether a website's P3P policy matches the user's privacy preferences. If there is a mismatch, the bird caws and turns red. Users can get detailed information about any mismatches, plus a full or summary report of a site's P3P policy, by clicking on the bird.

14.7 Conclusion

Personalization has the potential for offering more convenience to users, but it also raises concerns about privacy, because people are aware of the fact that many sites collect and disseminate personal information. The new P3P standard holds the promise of giving users more control over personal information. Adherence to this standard, coupled with attention to making full disclosure about such issues as credit-card security, delivery dates, and contact information for problem resolution, will help instill trust. These measures will encourage people who come to browse to stay and buy.

Review Questions

1. How does personalization differ from conventional user and task analysis?

2. Discuss the advantages of personalization from the viewpoint of users. Give three Web examples of personalization not mentioned in the text.

3. List the advantages of personalization from the viewpoint of a company. Do these advantages benefit users as well? Explain.

4. The site my.netscape.com allows users to customize the page content according to personal taste. Find two other sites that also offer this service to users. Are there any commonalities in the services they offer?

5. What laws protect a U.S. citizen's right to privacy? Would this have any bearing on people's perception of personalization?

6. Here are several items of information:

   - ZIP code
   - Credit-card number
   - Phone number

   a. Which will users be most willing to divulge?
   b. Which will users be least willing to divulge?

   Explain your answers in terms of one or more factors that affect trust.

7. From a user's privacy perspective, which is the more desirable information policy, opt-in or opt-out? Justify your answer.

Exercises

8. What visual indications in a browser window inform users that they're viewing a page from a secure server? In terms of browser real estate, what percentage of the display changes? When writing a security statement for a website, why would you want to mention these indications explicitly?

9. Print a copy of the home page of a favorite e-commerce site, and analyze it for content that would inspire trust.

10. Using a P3P-enabled Web browser, choose a high level of privacy, and then visit a website that has previously offered you personalized services. Describe what happens. Give an explanation.

11. Install Privacy Bird and visit

   - www.w3.org
   - www.lycos.com
   - www.msn.com

   a. Are the sites P3P enabled? How can you tell?
   b. Compare and contrast the privacy policy of the three sites. What are the commonalities? What are the differences?

References

[ATT 2002] AT&T. *Privacy Bird.* April, 2002. Available at privacybird.com

[Bonner 1997] P. Bonner. "Adding Cookies to Your Site," *Builder.com.* November 18, 1997. Available at builder.cnet.com/webbuilding/pages/Programming/Cookies

[Bresnahan 2000] J. Bresnahan. "Personalization, Privacy, and the First Amendment: A Look at the Law and Policy Behind Electronic Database," *Virginia Journal of Law and Technology,* Vol 5. No. 3. Fall, 2000. Available at http://www.vjolt.net/vol5/issue3/v5i3a08-Bresnahan.html

[Cassell 2000] J. Cassell. and T. Bickmore. "External Manifestations of Trustworthiness in the Interface," *Communications of the ACM,* Vol. 43, No. 12. December, 2000. 50–56.

[Cranor 2002] L. F. Cranor. and R. Wenning. Why P3P is a Good Privacy Tool for Consumers and Companies. *GigaLaw.com.* April, 2002. Available at www.gigalaw.com/articles/2002-all/cranor-2002-04-all.html

[Dean 2000] R. Dean. Top Personalized Sites. *Builder.com.* June 6, 2000. Available at http://builder.cnet.com/webbuilding/pages/Business/Personal/ss07.html

[Dictionary 2002] Dictionary.com—Search word: trust.

[Fowler 2000] D. Fowler. "The Personal Touch," *Networker,* Vol. 4, No. 12. December, 2000. 25–29.

[Georgia 1998] Georgia Institute of Technology. GVU WWW 10th User Survey. October, 1998. Available at www.gvu.gatech.edu/user_surveys/

[Lucente 2000] M. Lucente. "Conversational Interfaces for E-Commerce Applications," *Communications of the ACM,* Vol. 43, No. 9. September, 2000. 59–61.

[Manber 2000] U. Manber. A. Patel. and J. Robison. "Experience with Personalization on Yahoo!" *Communications of the ACM,* Vol. 43, No. 8. August, 2000. 35–39.

[Princeton 2002] Princeton Survey Research Associates. *A Matter of Trust: What Users Want From their Web sites. Results of a National Survey of Internet Users of Consumer WebWatch.* Consumers Union, 2002. Available at www.consumerwebwatch.com/news/1_TOC.htm

[Olson 2000] J. Olson. and G. Olson. "i2i Trust in E-Commerce," *Communications of the ACM,* Vol. 43, No. 12. December, 2000. 41–44.

[Rosenfeld 1998] L. Rosenfeld. and P. Morville. *Information Architecture for the World Wide Web.* Sebastopol, CA: O'Reillly, 1998.

[Rossi 2001] G. Rossi. D. Schwabe. and Guimarães. Designing Personalized Web Applications. *Proceedings of WWW10.* Hong Kong, May 2001. 275–284.

[Schwartz 2000] M. Schwartz. "Sharper Staples," *ComputerWorld.* June 12, 2000. Available at `www.computerworld.com/softwaretopics/software/appdev/story/0,10801,45787,00.html`

[Shneiderman 2000] B. Shneiderman. "Designing Trust into Online Experiences," *Communications of the ACM,* Vol. 43, No. 12. December, 2000. 57–59.

[Volokh 2000] E. Volokh. "Personalization and Privacy," *Communications of the ACM,* Vol. 43, No. 8. August, 2000. 84–88.

[W3C 2002] World Wide Web Consortium. *The Platform for Privacy Preferences Project.* April, 2002. Available at `www.w3.org/P3P/`

[W3C 2002a] World Wide Web Consortium. *The Platform for Privacy Preferences 1.0 Specification.* April, 2002. Available at `www.w3.org/TR/P3P/Index`

Appendix: Introduction to XHTML and Cascading Style Sheets

Goals of this Appendix

After reading this appendix and completing the exercises, you will be able to do the following:

- author Web pages
- set up links between pages
- write HTML in a form that is acceptable to the increasingly important XML (eXtensible Markup Language), but which can be displayed in current browsers. This is called XHTML
- use styles to control format and layout of pages.

If you already know some HTML, but have not worked with style sheets or XHTML, reading this appendix will benefit you. The standards body for Web work, the World Wide Web Consortium (W3C), has said there will be no further HTML standards; all future standards will be for XHTML. In addition, the W3C recommends the use of style sheets.

All of the examples in this appendix are available on the book's companion website. See the Preface for details.

The Internet and the World Wide Web: Definitions and a Brief History

Informally, "The Internet" and "The Web" are used almost interchangeably, and little harm is done. As we delve into ways to prepare information for viewing via a Web browser, however, it is appropriate to get the terms straight.

A *network of computers* is a collection of computers, from two to millions, that "talk to" each other over copper wires, through transoceanic fiber optics, via satellite communications, and in a growing list of other ways.

Computers, at their heart, deal only in bits and bytes. To send messages containing a wide variety of types of data, from telephone numbers to baby pictures to live video, there have to be *protocols* about message formats and many other things. For an everyday example, suppose I tell you that the following six digits contain a date: 050241. Does that mean May 2, 1941, or February 5, 1941? The first form is used in the United States, where the month is given first; the second is used in Europe, where the day is given first. There is no way to decide between the two, unless you and I agree on the format of dates. Such an agreement would be a *protocol* for sending dates from one computer to another.

There are two protocols involved in the Internet. One is the Transaction Control Protocol, TCP, which " . . . allows one computer to send the other a continuous stream of information by breaking it into packets and reassembling it at the other end, resending any packets that get lost" [Berners-Lee 2000]. A packet is a small collection of data. The way packets are sent across the Internet is governed by the other key protocol, the Internet Protocol, or IP. "TCP uses IP to send the packets, and the two together are referred to as TCP/IP" [Berners-Lee 2000].

This means that the Internet (note capital letter) is a large network of computers, all of which use TCP/IP to control sending and receiving of data. In other words, it is a combination of hardware (the computers and communications gear) and software (programs for breaking apart messages at the sending end and putting them back together at the receiving end, both programs obeying the TCP/IP protocols).

The term "the Web" is short for "the World Wide Web." The World Wide Web is the set of all information that is accessible by using computers and networking. Each unit of information on the Web has its own URL, or *Uniform Resource Locator*. A URL "identifies anything" with the familiar combination http:// followed by characters that identify the "anything," whether that be `http://www.ibm.com`, which is the main address for the IBM site containing over a million pages, or `http://ccnyddm.com/599SyllabusUrdu.htm`. Nobody really knows how many pages are accessible on the Web via this addressing scheme, but it is well over several billion.

The HTTP in a Web address stands for HyperText Transfer Protocol, which is "a computer protocol for transferring information across the Net in such a way as to meet the demands of a global hypertext system" [Berners-Lee 2000].

Hypertext, in turn, is a term that Berners-Lee defines as "nonsequential writing." The term was invented by Ted Nelson in the 1960s, who used it to mean text that contains links to other things—other text, other pictures, other documents, and so on [Nelson 1965]. The idea behind hypertext was introduced by Vannevar Bush at the close of World War II [Bush 1945]. Bush spoke of a ". . . a sort of mechanized private file and library." Remove the "private," and emphasize that "file" means "filing system," and you have a capsule definition of the World Wide Web. It consists of a large amount of information and a way of accessing it.

The Web is founded on three concepts of Berners-Lee. The first was the URL, HTTP was the second, and the third was HTML, the main subject of this appendix. HTML stands for HyperText Markup Language, a "language for representing the contents of a page of hypertext; the language that most Web pages are currently written in" [Berners-Lee 2000]. Thus, the Internet is a large interconnection of hardware and software; the Web is all the information accessible by using the URL/HTTP/HTML trio.

A browser allows us to read information on the Web. Currently, the most common browsers are software packages that run on personal computers. The most widely used are Microsoft's Internet Explorer (IE) and Netscape Communications' Netscape (NN); Opera has a loyal band of devotees. Browsers can be hand-held wireless (mobile) devices, or a device that makes an ordinary TV set work like a browser. One can be software that reads a Web page aloud for a blind person; another can be a kiosk in a store or airport. The generic term for all of these is *user agent*. This term is not common yet, and we'll use "browser."

Current browsers owe much to a number of pioneers. Doug Englebart invented the mouse in the mid-1960s and contributed to the ideas of windows and the application of hypertext [Englebart 1962]. Alan Kay led a group at Xerox PARC (Palo Alto Research Center) that introduced the Graphical User Interface (GUI) that was implemented in the Apple Lisa and Mac and was later picked up by Microsoft as Windows [Brate 2002].

The precursor to today's browsers was a program called Enquire, written by Berners-Lee in 1980. Other early browsers included Erwise (Helsinki University of Technology), ViolaWWW

(Pei Wei), Arena (Dave Raggett), and Lynx (University of Kansas). The first point-and-click browser was developed at the National Center for Supercomputing Applications (NCSA) at the University of Illinois at Urbana-Champaign by Marc Andreessen and Eric Bina. The result was Mosaic, which was first made available over the Web in February, 1993. Versions for the PC and Mac became available in 1994. It is from these that the rocket called *The Web* blasted off.

In April 1994, Andreessen and several others formed what became Netscape, and their product was named Netscape Navigator. (NCSA held rights to the name Mosaic.) Microsoft took a while to realize how important all this was, but not forever. Their Internet Explorer currently holds the majority of the browser market.

Berners-Lee created the World Wide Web, working over a period of years earlier, but it was the appearance of Mosaic that triggered the major explosion of Web usage. This text is being written in 2002. The infiltration of the Web into homes, offices, governmental agencies, and all the rest has taken place in a mere eight years.

Authoring Your First Web page

Figure A–1 is a first example of a Web page. The text in the top half of the figure produces the Web page you see in the lower half of the figure.

```
<html>
<head>
<title>The Basic Structure</title>
</head>
<body>
   <p>This is the basic  structure of HTML. The whole thing must be
enclosed between the opening and closing html tags, there must be
a head section which must contain a title,and there must be a
body. The
body is where the content of the page is specified. If you put
nothing in the body, the page will be blank.</p>
   <p> The major parts (html, head, title, and body) must appear
in this order, but the spacing
is up to you. The first three lines as shown here could be
all on one line, for example, and the page would be the same.<p>
</body>
</html>
```

Figure A–1   Netscape window produced from first XHTML example.

You can try this out for yourself by using a text editor, such as Windows NotePad, or SimpleText on the Mac. Activate the editor, and type in the text in Figure A–1. Save the file with the extension **htm**.[1] To see the page you created, double-click on the file name to activate your Web browser. You can also see your page by using the File menu in your browser. Note that there is no correspondence between the line breaks in the file and the line breaks in the browser window.

Anything enclosed in angle brackets, such as **\<html>**, **\<body>**, **\<h1>**, or **\<p>** is called a *tag*. Each tag has a *tag name*, which appears immediately after the opening angle bracket. Almost all tags occur in pairs called *opening tag* and *closing tag*. Each of **\<html>**, **\<body>**, **\<h1>**, and **\<p>** is an opening tag. The closing tag looks similar to an opening tag, except that a forward slash precedes the tag name. Each of **\</html>**, **\</body>**, **\</h1>**, and **\</p>** is a closing tag. An *element* consists of an opening tag, the corresponding ending tag, and all the text between them.

Visible Web-page content appears between the body element. Each paragraph is enclosed between the paragraph tags **\<p>** and **\</p>**. In Figure A–1, the head element contains one element, the title, which appears in the title bar of the browser window.

A First XHTML Example

Figure A–2 contains a sample document that conforms to XHTML, or *eXtensible HyperText Markup Language*. XHTML is the newest generation of HTML and is compatible with newer technologies, such as handheld devices.

The first four lines in Figure A–2 tell a browser that the document is written in XHTML. Each XHTML document you write will start with these same four lines.

Figure A–2 contains three headings and three paragraphs. The headings appear larger than the body text. There are six possible heading tags, **\<h1>** through **\<h6>**; the **\<h1>** heading is the largest. In the middle of the second paragraph, a line break tag, **\
**, forces a line break before the second sentence.

To lend emphasis, you can enclose words between the **\<em>** and **\</em>** tags. Most browsers will display the enclosed text in italics. Words enclosed between the **\<strong>** and **\</strong>** tags will appear in boldface.

Figure A–2 also demonstrates some of the rules you need to keep in mind in order to write correct XHTML:

1. All tag names must be in lower case. Thus **\<body>** is legal, but **\<BODY>** is not.

2. Every opening tag must have a matching closing tag. For example, if you use a **\<p>** tag, at some point you need to include a **\</p>** tag.

3. A few tags, such as **\
** in the previous example, do not enclose text and are called *empty tags*. These tags do not need a separate closing tag, but you must include a slash **/** at the end of the tag.

4. Tags must be properly nested. For example,

    \<p>\<em> my text \</em> \</p>

    is correct XHTML, but**\<p>\<em> my text \</p> \</em>**

    is not.

---

[1]To save a file with an htm extension in Windows Notepad, use the File > Save as command. When the "Save as" dialog box appears, select "All Files" in the "Save as type" menu. Be sure that your file name ends in **.htm**.

```
<?xml version="1.0" encoding="iso-8859-1"?>
<!DOCTYPE html PUBLIC "-//W3C//DTD XHTML 1.0 Strict//EN"
    "http://www.w3.org/TR/xhtml1/DTD/xhtml1-strict.dtd">
<html xmlns="http://www.w3.org/1999/xhtml" xml:lang="en"
lang="en">
<head>
<title>A page with Two Levels of Headings</title>
</head>
<body>
  <h1>Levels of Headings </h1>
  <h2>Introduction</h2>
  <p>A Web page can have from one to six <em>levels of
headings,</em> where a heading is like a chapter heading or a
section heading in a book.</p>
  <p>This simple page does not make any provisions for the style
 (formats) of headings. <br /> For things like the size of the
type in the headings there are default values that are used if we
specify nothing different.</p>
  <h2>Things To Come--Shortly</h2>
  <p>The separate specification of style, which controls
the <strong>appearance</strong> of our content,
from the <strong>content itself</strong>, is not difficult.
We introduce this central subject in the next example.</p>
</body>
</html>
```

Figure A–2   A Web page with two *levels of headings*.

You can check the correctness of your XHTML by going to `http://validator.w3.org/file-upload.html` and following the directions for validating a file. You will receive a detailed report indicating any errors you have made.

Exercises: Basics

1. Produce a page with an **<h1>** heading, "My First XHTML Experiment," and a few lines of body text of your choosing.

2. Create a Web page with several paragraphs and all six levels of headings. Open it in Opera, Netscape Navigator, and Microsoft Internet Explorer. What differences do you see?

3. Make a page with an **\<h1\>** heading, at least two **\<h2\>** headings, and some body text. Experiment with **\<em\>** and **\<strong\>** to see what italic and boldface look like in your browser. Try using both of these within headings.

A First Look at Styles

The first two examples did not include any provisions for specifying the *appearance* of Web-page content. Using styles will give you this control. When used properly, an advantage of using styles is the ability to update the look and feel of an entire website by simply changing a single file!

Figure A–3 shows a first example using styles. The style information is contained in the **\<head\>** section of the XHTML document and is enclosed by the opening tag **\<style type="text/css"\>** and the closing tag **\</style\>**.

```
<style type="text/css">
  body {
    font-family: Georgia;
    background-color: white;
  }
  h1 {
    font-family: Verdana;
    font-size: 18pt;
    font-weight: bold;
    text-align: center;
  }
  h2 {
    font-family: Verdana;
    font-size: 12pt;
    font-weight: bold;
  }
</style
```

Styles

Introduction

We can use styles in the heading of a document to control the size, color, and font of type; the centering of text; the color of the background, and many other things.

The Styles in This Example

We specify that the h1 heading be shown in a font named Verdana, which is easily readable on a computer screen, in a size of 18 points, which is 1/4 of an inch. The heading will be centered (horizontally) in the browser window.

See text for discussion of other style matters.

Figure A–3   A page in Netscape Navigator, based on styles in the XHTML.

A little terminology will save time. Consider this part of the style section:

```
body
    font-family: Georgia;
    background-color: white;
}
```

The whole thing is called a *rule*. **body** is a *selector*. **font-family:Georgia** is a *declaration*. In that declaration, the **font-family** is a *property*. The word **Georgia** is a *value*. Declarations must be separated by semicolons, which means that a semicolon after the last one is not required. The **body** rule applies to all text between **<body>** tags. This one specifies Georgia as the font family and white as the background color.

The **h1** rule specifies 18-point Verdana boldface font with centered alignment. The **h2** rule specifies 12-point Verdana boldface. No alignment is specified, so the text will be left aligned, which is the default. Compare the appearance of the headings in Figure A–2 and Figure A–3 to see the effects of these rules.

A Second Look at Styles

Figure A–4 is our first example that takes advantage of *inheritance*. Inheritance is closely related to the elements of a Web page. Recall that an element consists of an opening tag, its matching closing tag, and the text between them. In any Web document, the largest element is the *html element*. It has two *child* elements, which are the *head* and *body elements*. The body element in Figure A–2 contains six children, namely, three paragraphs and three headings. Turning this around, each paragraph element has the body element as a parent.

In terms of Web authoring, inheritance helps reduces the size of the style section in your Web pages. If you do not specify a value for an *inheritable property* in a rule, then the rule inherits a value from its parent element. In Figure A–4, the inheritable properties include color, font-family, font-size, font-weight, and text-align. The properties background-color and margin-left are not inheritable.

Figure A–4 takes advantage of inheritance in several ways, among them by setting the text size for the headings and by specifying the position and color of the h2 headings.

In the **h1** rule, the declaration **font-size:2em** specifies a font size twice as large as the parent's font size. The term *em* is a relative measure referring to the font size. The parent of **h1** is the body element, so this declaration has the effect of making the text in the **h1** headings twice as large as the body text. If a user chooses to view the page with larger type, the **h1** headings will still remain twice as big as the body text.

The positioning of the **h2** headings also takes advantage of inheritance. The declaration **margin-left:-1.5em** is a directive to "indent in the opposite direction by 1.5 em." This negative indentation is often referred to as an *outdent*. You can see the effect in Figure A–4's Web page. The **h2** headings stand out from the body text.

The last example of example of inheritance involves the color of the **h2** headings. Because a value is not specifically declared in the **h2** rule, the **h2** headings will get their color from the parent, the body element.

The **body** rule specifies the text color **#000066**, which is in *hexadecimal* notation. The first two digits specify red, the next two specify green, and the last two specify blue. The possible values range from **00** to **ff** in hex, which correspond to 0 to 255 in decimal. Hexadecimal numbers use a base-16 representation, with 16 digits: **0**, **1**, **2**, **3**, **4**, **5**, **6**, **7**, **8**, **9**, **a**, **b**, **c**, **d**, **e**, and **f**.

```
<style type="text/css">
  body {
    font-family: Georgia, "Times New Roman", serif;
    color: #000066;
    background-color: #eff;
    margin-left: 10%;
    margin-right: 10%;
  }
  h1 {
    font-family: Verdana, Arial, sans-serif;
    font-size: 2em;
    font-weight: bold;
    color: maroon;
    text-align: center;
  }
  h2 {
    font-family: Verdana, Arial, sans-serif;
    font-size: 1.1em;
    font-weight: bold;
    margin-left: -1.5em;
  }
</style>
```

Figure A–4   A page with more extensive use of styles.

The "digit" **a** has the decimal equivalent 10; the digit **f** has the decimal equivalent 15. The place-value of adjacent digits goes up by 16, not 10, so 66 in hex = $6 \times 16 + 6 = 102$ in decimal. We are thus asking for no red or green, and a low-to-medium amount of blue.

The **background-color: #eff** specifies the background color of the page in a convenient condensed notation: in a property value, a three-digit hexadecimal number means to use each digit twice, so this is the same as writing **#eeffff**. The font color could have been written **#006**, of course, but we wanted to show both ways.

The body rule specifies its left and right margins as percentages. The margins will be 10% of the browser window width and will change if the user resizes the window. The margins can also be specified in absolute units, such as inches or centimeters, but relative values keep proportions better, which is often what we want.

The body rule specifies three alternatives in the font-family declaration. In addition to Georgia, the declaration lists Times New Roman and a generic name, serif. This means that that browser should use Georgia if it has that font, Times New Roman if not, and if it has neither of these use whatever serif font it does have. Times New Roman appears in quotes because it has spaces in its name.

Putting Styles in a Style Sheet

Let's suppose we're satisfied with the look of the previous page and want to make those style decisions apply to all documents in the site. To do this, create a file that contains all of the rules that you previously specified between the two style tags, and store it with a file-name that ends in **".css"**. Suppose we call it **Style1.css**. A file such as this is called a *style sheet*.

Now, instead of writing out all of the style rules in new XHTML files, you can add the following to the head element:

```
<link rel="stylesheet" type="text/css" href="Style1.css"/>
```

The entire head section is now a lot shorter:

```
<head>
<title>Styles with a Style Sheet</title>
<link rel="stylesheet" type="text/css" href="Style1.css"/>
</head>
```

As long as this new file is in the same directory as **Style1.css**, the new Web page will follow the same style rules as the page you saw in Figure A–4.

The benefit of using a style sheet is that the same style sheet can be referenced from many pages. That could be hundreds or thousands of pages. If it is decided that, say, the background is just a little too dark, there is an easy solution: change the background color declaration in the external style sheet, and the background is lighter in all the pages of your site.

If the same property is specified in more than one place, it is the latest one in the list of links that governs. If **Style1.css** is right for the major design matters, but the Engineering Department wants a different look to their pages, the head section might be

```
<link rel="stylesheet" type="text/css" href="Style1.css"/>
<link rel="stylesheet" type="text/css" href="Engineering.css"/>
```

If **Engineering.css** wants its **h1** heads to be green instead of dark red, then green they are.

Internal styles override the declarations in an external style sheet. Suppose that for a particular page **Style1.css** is right for everything except the **h2** color and outdent:

```
<link rel="stylesheet" type="text/css" href="Style1.css"/>
<style type="text/css">
  h2 {
```

```
        color: black;
        margin-left: 0;
    }
  </style>
```

The **color: black**, since it appears after the link to the external style sheet, overrides the inherited body text color. The **margin-left: 0** puts the margin back to whatever the default is.

Finally, we can override some specifications by putting style information within the body. Staying with the same example, suppose that we want almost all **h2** to be normal (not italic), but that we want a particular one to be in italic. We can write:

```
  <h2><em>Special Note to Systems Administrators</em></h2>
```

The basic idea thus is that the browser looks first for a link to a style sheets; then looks at style information in the head section, if any, overriding anything in the style sheet that is re-defined here; finally, it obeys style information in the body. If any attribute is specified more than once in all this, it is the last one that controls.

Exercises: Styles

Enter the necessary code to make a complete XHTML document, and then check it in a browser.

1. Modify one of the earlier examples, one without any styles, to experiment with text and background combinations. Create a **<style>** ... **</style>** section, and within it write rules to examine some of the good and bad color combinations mentioned in Chapter 9. Experiment with different ways of expressing a color. For example, try writing fuchsia as a color name (which XHTML knows), **#f0f**, **#ff00ff**, and in two ways we didn't discuss, **rgb(255, 0, 255)** and **rgb(100%, 0%, 100%)**.

2. In an earlier example without styles, enter a style section and a rule to make the body font size 1.0em. This should not produce any change: you have said to use the same size as the default. Now try 0.7em, 1.5em, 2em, and 3em.

3. Write a short XHTML code containing an **h1** head, an **h2** head, and some body text. In a style rule, specify the body font-size as 1em, the **h1** font-size as 2.0em, and the **h2** font-size as 1.5em. Check the result. Now change only the body text size, to 2em. What happened to the headings? Explain why it happened.

4. Make an **h1** head six times as big as the body text. Use the font-family Impact if the user's browser has it; if not, then Arial Black; if not, then Arial; if none of these, sans-serif. Right-align the headings. Write the necessary rule.

5. A graphic designer has given you some specifications. Convert them into XHTML style rules.

   a. **h1**: 4 times body text size, centered, Arial Black, fallback to Arial, then sans-serif.
   b. **h2**: 2 times body text size; Comics Sans MS, fallback to Arial, then sans-serif; left aligned (which is usually the default).
   c. **h3**: 1.5 times body text size, Arial falling back to sans-serif; italic. (Write font-style: italic;)
   d. **h4**: Same size as body text; Arial falling back to sans-serif, bold. (Write font-weight: bold;)
   e. **body**: default size, Georgia, falling back to Times New Roman and then to serif.

6. Remove all style information from the code you produced for the previous exercises, place it in a style sheet, and place a link to that style sheet in your head section. The new page should be identical in appearance. (Remember that, in the external style sheet, you do not write the **<style>** and **</style>** tags.)

Hypertext Links

What makes the World Wide Web interesting is the ability to get around from one place to another with ease. A *link*, or *hyperlink* as it is more formally called, takes us to another location. That might be another page on the same site, or it might be an international site halfway around the world. This ability to "jump around" gives the Web much of its distinctive flavor.

Figure A–5 shows two linked pages. You already know how to author everything on these pages except for the hyperlinks. The following text creates the hyperlink on the first page:

```
<p><a href="FirstLinkChild.html">Click anywhere in the
    underlined part of this line</a> to go to the second page.</p>
```

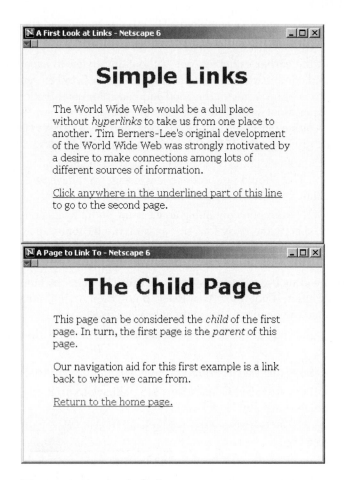

Figure A–5   Two linked pages.

The new tag **<a>** is called the *anchor tag*. Within the opening **<a>** tag, the **href** *attribute* specifies the address, or URL, of where the link will take us. Always enclose the address in double quotes. After the opening tag comes the text that will appear to the user as a link, and finally comes the closing **</a>**.

The link in this example has a *relative address*, which means that the destination is on the same machine as the current page. To refer to a document stored on another computer, you need to write out an *absolute address*, which begins with **http://** For the second page, the source code that creates the link is:

```
<p><a href="Links1.html">Return to the home page.</a></p>
```

The **href** entry in the anchor tag is an example of a tag *attribute*. An attribute supplies additional information to a tag. You have already seen attributes in other tags, including the **type** attribute in the style tag and the **rel**, **type**, and **href** attributes in the link tag. Attributes have two components: a name and a value, separated by an equals sign. Always place the value in double quotes.

Unordered Lists

Figure A–6 shows a Web page that describes the trial gardens at the University of Minnesota Extension Service. It includes four links in an unordered list, which looks like a bulleted list in printing.

The XHTML for an unordered list begins with the unordered list tag **<ul>**, contains one or more *list items*, and ends with a closing **</ul>** tag. Each list item begins with a list item **<li>** and ends with a **</li>** tag.

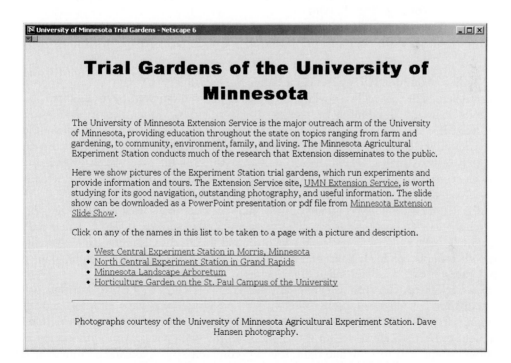

Figure A–6 A home page with links to four child pages, plus links to the University of Minnesota Extension Service website.

The XHTML for this page has links to two external style sheets: **Style1.css** and **GardenStyle.css**. Here they are, side by side for easy reference:

```
Style1.css                          GardenStyle.css

body {                              body {
    font-family: Georgia,               margin-top: 2%;
        "Times New Roman", serif;       color: #003;
    color: #000066;                     background-color: #eee;
    background-color: #eff;             text-align: center;
    margin-left: 10%;              }
    margin-right: 10%;             h1 {
}                                       font-family: "Arial
                                            Black",
h1 {                                                Arial,
                                                    sans-serif;
    font-family: Verdana, Arial,        background-color: #eee;
            sans-serif;            }
    font-size: 2em;                ul {
    font-weight: bold;                  text-align: left;
    color: maroon;                 }
    text-align: center;            p.left {
}                                       text-align: left;
h2 {                               }
    font-family: Verdana, Arial,   p.caption {
            sans-serif;                 margin: 0% 15%;
    font-size: 1.1em;              }
    font-weight: bold;
    margin-left: -1.5em;
}
```

The link to **GardenStyle.css** comes after the link to **Style1.css**, so any properties that are named in both will be governed by what appears in **GardenStyle.css**.

In its body rule, **GardenStyle.css** specifies text and background colors, so these values override what is in **Style1.css**. **GardenStyle.css** does not change the left and right margins, but it does specify a 2% top margin and centered alignment for the text. Because the body is the parent of everything within it, everything on the page will be centered, unless we override that in some rule. This is the reason that the unordered list rule, **ul**, specifies left alignment, to override the centering of the body rule.

All paragraphs would be centered, for the same reason, but we want some paragraphs to be left aligned. To provide this capability, we have a *class selector*, **p.left**. The **p** means paragraph; **left** is a class name of our own invention. In this case, paragraph elements starting with a simple **<p>** tag will be centered, but specifying a class attribute in a paragraph tag **<p class="left">** will left-align the paragraph.

Similarly, the **p.caption** will affect any paragraph elements with a class attribute value of **"caption"**. Unless we specify otherwise, all paragraphs will have 10% left and right margins, from **Style1.css**, and a 2% top margin, as specified in the body rule in **GardenStyle.css**. However, for the captions on the child pages, we want zero top and bottom margins and 15% left and right. It is very common to want top and bottom to be the same, and left and right to be the same, so we are permitted the shorthard **margin: 0% 15%**, which has the same effect as **margin: 0% 15% 0% 15%**. In a rule like this, where all margins are set with a margin property, the order of the margin values is: top, right, bottom, left. A useful mnemonic is *TRouBLe*.

The head section of the XHTML for Figure A–7 is identical to that for the page in Figure A–6. Here is its body section:

```
<body>
<h1>West Central Experiment Station</h1>
<p> <img src="WestCentralExpSta.jpg"
          alt="West Central Experiment Station"/>
</p>
<p class="caption">The West Central Experiment Station in
Morris, Minnesota, attracts hundreds of visitors on its
popular Hort Night, usually held in late July.</p>

<p><a href="UMExtensionGardens.html">Home Page</a>
  <a href="NorthCentalPage.html">Next</a></p>
</body>
```

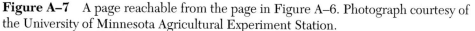

Figure A–7 A page reachable from the page in Figure A–6. Photograph courtesy of the University of Minnesota Agricultural Experiment Station.

The image tag **<img>** displays the picture specified by the URL in its **src** attribute. It also has an **alt** attribute with the value **"West Central Experiment Station"**. This is called *ALT text*. When a user holds the pointer over the picture more than a second or so, this text will appear. If the picture has not yet downloaded or is not available at all, the ALT text will appear in the space reserved for the picture. Finally, and most important, a screen narration program will read this text aloud, so that a blind user can tell what the picture is about. It is good practice to include ALT text with all images.

In Figure A–6, we want the two links to be on one line—but we want a little space between them. Adding the text ** **; tells the browser, "Put a space here, but do not consider breaking the line here." The result is a one-character space between the two links. The term for this special type of space is "nonbreaking space." Additional occurrences of ** **; will place additional spaces in the displayed document. Note that the closing semicolon is required.

The nonbreaking space is an example of a *character entity*. There are many others, such as **&quote**; for a quotation mark and **&copy**; for the copyright symbol, ©. They are readily accessible through the Web—for example, at `http://www.w3.org/TR/REC-html40/sgml/entities.html`.

Exercises: Links

1. Add a third page to the first links example; make it reachable via the second page. The new third page should have a link back to the first page.

2. Set up a hierarchical organization structure with a home page that has links to three pages, each of which has links to two additional pages. Each third-level page should have a link back to its parent. All subsidiary pages should link to the home page.

3. With the same pages as in Exercise 2, set up global navigation, where every page has a link to every other page.

4. Set up a "Favorite Links" page, something that you might have in your personal website. Provide links to your instructor's home page, to the website for this book, and perhaps to the home page, for your school, your favorite baseball or soccer team, and half a dozen others.

5. Set up a page that links to four other pages. Use graphics for the links.

Ordered Lists

A common requirement is a numbered list. We could type in the numbers, but a better approach is to take advantage of the ordered-list tag, **<ol>**. Figure A–8 shows the XHTML and the resulting page for a numbered list of the topics remaining to be covered in this appendix. The list items are enclosed in the tags for an *ordered* (numbered) list, **<ol>** . . . **</ol>**. Each item in the list is enclosed in the *list item tag*, **<li>** . . . **</li>**.

Definition Lists

A *definition list* specifies a list of terms together with their definitions. An example appears in the browser window in Figure A–9. A definition list begins with the **<dl>** tag. This tells the browser to expect a *definition term* **<dt>** followed by a *definition* **<dd>**. There can be many pairs of **<dt>** and **<dd>** tags. Figure A–9 also shows the XHTML used to build the definition list.

Nested Lists

Lists—ordered or unordered—can be used to produce a hierarchical outline. An ordered list can contain another ordered list, to any reasonable depth. Figure A–10 is taken from a section of the Encyclopedia Britannica, where the author, Donald G. Rea, outlines the encyclopedia's treatment of the solar system.

```
<body>
  <h1>Remaining Topics in this Appendix, </h1>
  <p>Note that the numbers are <em> not </em>
     part of the document. The browser adds
     them while formatting the list.</p>

  <ol>
    <li>More on lists.</li>
    <li>The box model.</li>
    <li>Tables for displaying thumbnails.</li>
    <li>Forms.</li>
  <ol>
</body>
```

```
N First List Example - Netscape 6                    _ |□| x|
```

Remaining Topics in this Appendix

Note that the numbers are *not* part of the document. The browser adds them while formatting the list.

1. More on lists.
2. The box model.
3. Tables.
4. Forms.

Figure A–8   An ordered list. The numbers do not appear in the XHTML.

When a list is placed inside another list, it causes a new level of indentation. The default numbering scheme uses Arabic numerals for all levels of ordered list. This means that there is no distinction in the numbering at different levels, which may be acceptable sometimes but is not customary.

To take control of the numbering style, we insert three class selectors for the ordered list into the style section, and then use class selectors in the list tags. Here's enough of the XHTML to give you the idea:

```
<style type="text/css">
  ol.decimal
    list-style-type:decimal;
  }
  ol.lowalpha {
    list-style-type:lower-alpha;
  }
  ol.lowroman {
    list-style-type:lower-roman;
}
</style>
...
```

```
<body>
...
<h2>Ordered Version 2: First Custom Numbering: 1. a. i.</h2>
  <ol class="decimal">
    <li>The Sun</li>
    <li>The major planets and their satellites</li>
    <li>Other constituents of the solar system</li>
```

(Continued on page 281.)

```
<dl>
  <dt>in</dt>
    <dd>inch</dd>
  <dt>cm</dt>
    <dd>centimeter; 1 inch = 2.54 cm</dd>
  <dt>mm</dt>
    <dd>millimeter; 1 inch = 25.4 mm</dd>
  <dt>pt</dt>
    <dd>point: 1/72 of an inch</dd>
  <dt>pc</dt>
    <dd>pica: 1 pica = 12 points = 1/6 of an inch</dd>
  <dt>em</dt>
    <dd>the font size of the current (parent) font</dd>
  <dt>ex</dt>
    <dd>the x-height of the current (parent) font</dd>
  <dt>px</dt>
    <dd>1 pixel on the current display device</dd>
</dl>
```

Figure A–9 A definition list showing CSS measures of length.

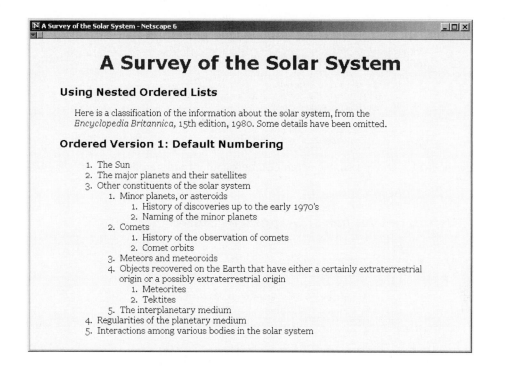

Figure A–10   An outline of the Encyclopedia Britannica coverage of the Solar System.

```
<ol class="lowalpha">
    <li>Minor planets, or asteroids
        <ol class="lowroman">
            <li>History of discoveries up to the early
                1970's</li>
            <li>Naming of the minor planets</li>
        </ol>
    </li>
<li>Comets
    <ol class="lowroman">
        <li>History of the observation of comets</li>
    <li>Comet orbits</li> ...
```

The values **decimal**, **lower-alpha** and **lower-roman** used for the **list-style-type** property are from the possibilities in the CSS standard. Other choices that would make sense with an ordered list include **upper-alpha** and **upper-roman**. Figure A–11 shows enough of the resulting window that you can see how it works.

There are environments where the ability to control numbering is much more than a pleasing nicety. In the legal system, different jurisdictions specify such things, and if your brief doesn't follow the specifications laid down by your court, the clerk of the court will simply reject it, unread.

The same kind of control is available for unordered lists, but in this case the style specifies the form of bullets or other decoration, not numbering schemes. Figure A–12 shows the same Solar System information as an unordered list, using small graphics files in place of the default bullet styles.

Ordered Version 2: First Custom Numbering: 1. a. i.

1. The Sun
2. The major planets and their satellites
3. Other constituents of the solar system
   a. Minor planets, or asteroids
      i. History of discoveries up to the early 1970's
      ii. Naming of the minor planets
   b. Comets
      i. History of the observation of comets
      ii. Comet orbits

Figure A–11 One possible custom numbering of an ordered list.

Unordered Version 3: Graphics as Bullets

- The Sun
- The major planets and their satellites
- Other constituents of the solar system
  - Minor planets, or asteroids
    - History of discoveries up to the early 1970's
    - Naming of the minor planets
  - Comets
    - History of the observation of comets
    - Comet orbits

Figure A–12 Graphics as bullets.

Listed next are the style rules that created Figure A–12. The **ul** rule is for the first level of an unordered list, the **ul ul** rule is for the second level of unordered list, and the **ul ul ul** rule is for the third:

```
ul {
   list-style-image: url(blueball.gif);
}
ul ul {
   list-style-image: url(orangeball.gif);
}
ul ul ul
   list-style-image: url(blackball.gif);
}
```

Instead of using the attribute **list-style**, these rules use the attribute **list-style-image**, followed by the URL for a small graphics file. As long as these files are in the same directory as the document, you will see the nicer, spiffier graphics bullets in the browser window.

Exercises: Lists

1. Pick any organization you know where there are organizational components (departments, clubs, city government, etc.) Create an unnumbered list of the components.

2. For each component in the previous exercise, show the leader (department chair, club president, etc.) as a one-element sublist.

3. Invent a list of toys suitable for small children. Find a suitable graphic for the bullet of each. For example, if one category is Stuffed Animals, find a picture of a stuffed bear or other representative image. Resize the graphic to about 1 cm square, making sure that it is recognizable in the small size.

4. XHTML offers standard bullets named disc, circle, and square. Make up a small list that uses all of them. Prepare XHTML code using all six permutations of the order of use of the bullets. Try all versions in at least three browsers. Write a summary of the differences.

5. Using any source material you please, produce a page having an unordered bulleted (disc) list nested within an ordered list.

6. You work for a law firm. Briefs for one court require the following style of outline numbering:

    1. The Jones Case
      a. Introduction
      b. Issues of law
        I. Delayed discovery
          a. New York
          b. New Jersey
            i. Types of cases where applicable
            ii. Statutory time limit
        II. Rules of evidence

      c. Issues of fact
        I. The Jones Company position
        II. Errors in the Jones Company position
          a. Dates are wrong
            i. Thanksgiving is always on Thursday
            ii. Starting date of contract has wrong year

In XHTML terms, the ordering is: Arabic numbers, upper alpha, upper roman, lower alpha, lower roman. Set up a style sheet that provides this numbering scheme.

7. The same law firm, but a different court. The ordering is upper alpha, lower alpha, upper roman, lower roman, and Arabic numbers. Make up a style sheet. The goal, of course, is to be able to change the outline number of an entire document—which could contain hundreds of pages—by changing only the reference to a style sheet.

The Box Model

A key concept in CSS is the *box model*. The box model offers great control over the appearance of a Web page, ranging from choice of backgrounds behind individual elements to the placement of elements on the page. The box model can be applied to a single element, such as a heading, or to any collection of parts of a page. The latter is done by including the section of XHTML within a **<div>**...**</div>** pair. Figure A–13 shows the terms and their relationships. The dotted lines in Figure A–13 are conceptual and do not appear on a Web page.

    Margins always have the same color as the containing element, and the **margins** property controls the spacing of the margin.

Figure A–13 The parts and relationships of the box model.

The property **border-style** controls the border's appearance. It can have any of the following values: **none** (the default), **dashed**, **dotted**, **double**, **inset**, **outset**, **ridge**, **groove**, or **solid**. The property **border-width** dictates the thickness of the border.

Padding refers to the space between the border and the content of the box, the latter often being some kind of text. The **padding** property controls the size of the padding and takes the same types of values as the **margins** property.

The padding will always have the same background color as the content.

Figure A–14 shows a sample page that has a box around the heading and part of the body has a yellow background.

Here are excerpts from the XHTML:

```
<style type="text/css">
  body {
    font-family: Georgia, "Times New Roman", serif;
    background-color: #eee;
  }
  h1 {
    font-family: Verdana, Arial, sans-serif;
    font-size: 1.8em;
    text-align: center;
    margin: 1em 4em 0em 4em;
    border-style: solid;
    background-color: #aff;
    border-width: 0.25em;
    border-color: #d00;
    padding: 0.5em;
  }
  .html {
    font-family: "Courier New", monospace;
    font-weight: bold;
```

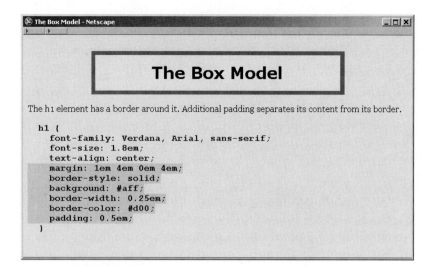

Figure A–14   An illustration using the box model; box specifications over a yellow background.

```
      white-space: pre;
      margin-top: -1.5em;
    }
    .new-material {
      background-color: yellow;
    }
</style>
...
<body>
  <h1>The Box Model: 3</h1>
  <p>The h1 element has a border around it. Additional
     padding separates its content from its border. </p>
<p class="html">
  h1 {
      font-family: Verdana, Arial, sans-serif;
      font-size: 1.8em;
      text-align: center;
<span class="new-material">        margin: 1em 4em 0em 4em;
      border-style: solid;
      background: #aff;
      border-width: 0.25em;
      border-color: #d00;
      padding: 0.5em;</span>
    }
</p>
</body>
```

Note that the style section features a new property called **white-space**. A value of **pre** for this property is a directive to a browser to preserve white space. Normally, a browser does not pay attention to multiple spaces or line breaks. The declaration **white-space: pre** tells the browser to reproduce white space—spaces, paragraph breaks, and tabs if any—exactly as they are in the document.

In addition to demonstrating the box model, Figure A–14 presents a new formatting technique, involving the **<span>** tag, and a new type of class selector. In past examples, class selectors always applied to a particular tag, as in the rules named **p.left** and **p.caption** in the Minnesota Trial Gardens example. Here, there are two class selectors, **.html** and **.new-material**, that begin with a period. This means that they can be applied to *any* tag simply by including one of the attributes **class="html"** or **class="new-material"**. For example, the paragraph opening with the tag **<p class="html">** invokes the **.html** rule.

A paragraph is an example of a *block-level element*. In a Web page, block-level elements always start on a new line. Any content that follows a block-level element also starts on a new line. Other examples of block-level elements are headings and lists. Block-level elements may contain other block-level elements, and they may contain inline elements. Inline elements follow each other like the words in this sentence, beginning a new line only when they have run out of space on the previous one. Familiar inline elements are **<em>** and **<a>**. Inline elements may contain only other inline elements, not block elements [Briggs 2002].

Until now, we have been able to specify a style only on a block-level element. In terms of a page's appearance, this meant that the style could not change except at the start of a new paragraph, a new heading, or a new list. Sometimes, we want to change the appearance of a few words *within* a paragraph. To accomplish this, use the **<span>** tags around the words to create an inline element, and apply the style to this new element by specifying a class attribute. For example, the tags **<span class="new-material">** and **</span>** create a different background for a few selected lines in the document.

Exercises: The Box Model

Copy the DDMmusic.htm and DDMMusic.css files from the book's companion website. The first several exercises ask you to modify the DDMMusic.css style sheet to change the appearance of the page.

1. Make the page background a very pale blue, without changing any other colors.

2. The list items are a little "cramped" in their surrounding boxes. Make the distance between the top border and first line greater; ditto for the bottom line and the bottom border.

3. The gray border around the **h2** heads is too close to the background color of those boxes. Make the border a darker gray, but not black.

4. There should be more space between the unordered list box and the following **h2** heading, so that each heading will be more closely associated with its items. There are two ways to do this; choose the way that does not increase the distance between the end of the body text and the first **h2** heading.

5. Dan has decided to change his name to Dimetriatropolis. Change both the title and the top-level heading accordingly. The resulting line wrap that occurs in the heading is not pleasing. Make changes to alleviate the problem. Both are graphic style decisions; figure out what they are and make the appropriate changes to the style sheet.

6. Change the **h2** heads to be centered over the **ul** boxes.

7. In as many browsers as you have, experiment with changing the text size from smallest to largest. Does the browser expand the padding around the **h1** text, even though it is given in points, a supposedly absolute measure? If you can't tell much difference,

try changing something else in the style sheet, such as font size, to points. Do your experiments suggest a good general policy? (Just for fun, write down your guess as to the answer before you test.)

8. In Dan's Music, remove the background-color declaration from the **ul** rule. Explain why part of the box has a yellow background while another part is the same as the body background. Does this violate the principle that background-color is not inherited? (*Hint*: The initial value for background-color is transparent.)

Tables

From a visual perspective, tables display data that is organized as a grid. Tables contain a series of *rows*, and each row consists of a series of *cells* that contain information. To make a table, begin with the **<table>** tag and end with **</table>**. A table contains a mandatory **tbody** element and optional **caption**, **thead**, and **tfoot** elements. The following lines demonstrate the structure for creating a table with two rows and two columns (the line numbers are for reference only and are not part of the XHTML):

```
1    <table summary="brief description of table contents">
2    <caption> Label or name for this table </caption>
3    <thead>
4      <tr>
5        <th id="label1"> Column 1 contents </td>
6        <th id="label2"> Column 2 contents </td>
7      </tr>
8    </thead>
9    <tfoot> <tr>
10        <td header="label1"> footnote for Column 1 </td>
11        <td header="label2"> footnote for Column 2 </td>
12   </tr></tfoot>
13   <tbody> <tr>
14        <td header="label1"> 1st cell, 1st row </td>
15        <td header="label2"> 2nd cell, 1st row </td>
16   </tr><tr>
17        <td header="label1"> 1st cell, 2nd row </td>
18     <td header="label2"> 2nd cell, 2nd row </td>
19   </tr> </tbody>
20   </table>
```

The **summary** attribute of the table tag gives an overview of the table's purpose. This information in a summary attribute can help blind users. Although sighted users can easily glance through a table to get a sense of its content, blind users cannot. However, a screen reader can read the summary text aloud, giving blind users the same sense of the table's contents.

The **caption** element, shown in line 2, can serve as a title for the table. It also provides additional identification information for a screen reader to convey to a blind user. If you want to include a caption for the benefit of blind users, but feel that it is unnecessary for sighted users, include a CSS caption style rule that includes the declaration **display:none**.

Lines 13–19 demonstrate the structure of the table body **<tbody>** element, which contains a series of row **<tr>** elements. Each row element is enclosed by an opening **<tr>** and closing **</tr>** tag. Within each row is a series of cells, each of which begins with a **<td>** tag and conclude with **</td>**. The **header** attribute in each cell can help screen readers to match the appropriate heading, or label, with cell contents. The headings themselves are located in the table head **<thead>** element.

Lines 3–7 demonstrate the **thead** element, which lists the column labels for the table. It contains a series of **<th>** elements. Each **<th>** element specifies an individual label for one of the columns in the table. Each **<th>** tag contains one attribute, the **id** attribute. The value of this attribute helps screen readers to match column headings with cells. Note how the value specified in a header attribute of each **<td>** element matches with the **id** value in one **<th>** elements. This enables a screen reader to give a label to each content item as it is spoken aloud.

Lines 8–12 show an example of a **<tfoot>** element. It lists footnotes, if any, that pertain to a column of data. Placing the **<tfoot>** element before the **<tbody>** helps screen readers to present the table contents more effectively to blind users.

Figure A–15 incorporates many of these features and is an example of a table whose cells all have the same size. However, there could arise circumstances under which you want a cell to occupy more than one column. To extend a single cell across multiple columns, use the **colspan** attribute in the **<td>** tag. For example, for a cell that occupies 3 columns, the opening tag would be **<td colspan="3">**. Similarly, the **rowspan** attribute can be used to extend a cell over multiple rows.

Figure A–15 An example of a table. All photographs used by permission of The University of Minnesota.

Exercises: Tables

The first four exercises make changes to the document
`ColorTableWithFullAccess8.html`, available on the book's companion website.

1. Make the following changes, one at a time to see the effects, to the Web page:

   a. The borders could seem too heavy to some graphic designers. Make them thinner; experiment with border color and style.

   b. The table might seem too crowded. Put more spacing between the cells.

   c. Make the table into a wall display, of the largest size you can conveniently print. Remove all text except the heading.

2. The cell borders are not all the same color. See if you can make them all the same color, still keeping either inset or outset.

3. Make the table into six columns, headed Color, Hex, Short Hex, Color, Hex, Short Hex. For any color that has a three-digit hex form, include the short form. Leave the Short Hex cell empty for any color that does not have a short form.

4. Look up the other eight of the 16 colors every browser is supposed to know and extend the table of color. One of many possible sources:
   `http://www.webreference.com/html/reference/color/named.html`.

5. If you are in school, get the information on about ten student clubs. Make a table giving club name, president or chair if known, meeting time if known, and any affiliation with a national organization.

6. Create a table showing the semifinalists in the current World Cup. For each team, list the team captain or captains, the goalkeeper, the team's position in the finals (1–4), and the names of each player who scored a goal, together with the number of goals each player scored.

Additional Navigation Techniques

Figure A–15 is a home page with *thumbnails* (small images) of eleven flowers that grow well in Minnesota. Each of these thumbnails acts as a link. Clicking on any of them will take a user to a page with a larger picture of the same flower.

Here is the XHTML for the first thumbnail link:

```
<a href="BegoniaPage.html">
<img src="BegoniasThumb.jpg" alt="Begonias" />
</a>
```

Observe that, instead of text between anchor tags, there is an image specified by the img tag. Note the use of ALT text to facilitate accessibility for users who are blind.

Figure A–16 shows an example of one of the website's subsidiary pages. At the bottom of each subsidiary page is a global navigation bar that permits the user to go to any other page in the site.

The following excerpt, which consists of a series of anchor tags, enclosed between opening and closing **<div>** tags, shows the XHTML that creates the global navigation:

```
<div class="globalNav">
<a href="MinnesotaFlowers.html">HOME</a> |
```

Figure A–16   One of the child pages of the home page of Figure A–15. Photograph used by permission of The University of Minnesota.

```
<a href="BegoniaPage.html">BEGONIAS</a> |
<a href="ColeusPage.html">COLEUS</a> |  
<a href="ColeusDucksFootPage.html">COLEUS DUCK'S FOOT</a> |
<a href="FlowerPouchesPage.html">FLOWER POUCHES</a> |
<a href="HeliotropePage.html">HELIOTROPE</a> |
<a href="ImpatiensPage.html">IMPATIENS</a> |
<a href="MossRosePage.html">MOSS ROSE</a> |
<a href="PansiesPage.html">PANSIES</a> |
<a href="PrimaryComboPage.html">PRIMARY COLOR COMBO</a> |
<a href="SenecioPage.html">SENECIO CINERARIA</a> |
<a href="ZinniasPage.html">ZINNIAS</a>
</div>
```

Using **div** tags allows a Web developer to treat any element or set of elements in a Web page as a single block element. The result can be formatted by using the box-model principles. In this case, a font-size and line-height were chosen after experimentation to see how things looked in both Internet Explorer and Netscape Navigator. The resulting size specifications are incorporated in a style using the class selector **div.class**, as shown here:

```
div.globalNav {
   font-family: Verdana, Arial, sans-serif;
   font-size: 75%;
   line-height: 150%;
}
```

In this example, both properties are specified as a percentage of the corresponding size in the parent element.

Conformance to Standards

In addition to the 11 flower thumbnails, Figure A–15 has small images at the bottom of the page. These attest to the fact that the page has passed several validation tests. The first attests to conformity to the XHTML standard. As mentioned previously, the World Wide Web consortium offers a free service for validating XHTML at `http://validator.w3.org/`. The second small image indicates that the page uses correct CSS. More information and a free validation service is available at `http://jigsaw.w3.org/css-validator/`.

The third image refers to Bobby, which is one of the tools you can use to make your site more accessible for people with disabilities. Bobby is available at `http://bobby.watchfire.com/bobby/html/en/index.jsp`. See Chapter 12 for more information on making sites more accessible.

Forms

Until now, you have not seen any provisions for interactivity. In XHTML, the *form element* provides interactivity by offering several ways to solicit information from a user. After filling out a form, a user can click on a special "submit" button that sends the user's information to a designated location for further processing. Typically the location is a Web server.

The following shows the format for the opening and closing form tags:

```
<form action="http://my.server/mycgi/myscript.cgi"method="post">
...
</form>
```

The **action** attribute specifies the URL of the application that will receive and process the user information. The value for the **method** attribute will be dictated by the application. The two legal possibilities are **"get"** and **"post"**. To know which one to choose, you will need to consult the people or organization supplying the application.

Server-side functionality is outside the scope of this book. However, if you have access to Internet Explorer and Outlook Express, you can simulate server-side functionality by using a slightly different set of attributes in the opening form tag:

```
<form action="mailto:myemail@myemaildomain"
      method="post"
      enctype="text/plain">
```

When one is using Internet Explorer and Outlook Express, the action **mailto:** will send the user information to the specified e-mail address. In order for the mailto action to work, the method must be **"post"**. The mailto action also requires an additional attribute, **enctype**, to specify the encryption type, which must be **"text/plain"**.

Caveat: The mailto action is recommended for debugging purposes only. Not everyone uses Internet Explorer as a browser. Furthermore, this technique transmits user information as unencrypted text, making it entirely unsuitable for handling sensitive information.

Although a form is a block element, you cannot include a form iniside another form. You can, however, include other block elements, such as paragraphs, headings, and lists.

Figure A–17 is a form that demonstrates a new block element, the *fieldset element*, which places a rectangle around its contents. A *legend element* adds a label to the rectangle. Here is the XHTML:

```
<fieldset>
    <legend> Music Survey </legend>
...
</fieldset>
```

Figure A–17 contains several interactive elements. First is a set of *radio buttons*. These provide a set of mutually exclusive choices. A user can select at most one radio button. Here is XHTML for this form's radio buttons:

```
<input type="radio" name="Year" value="1" checked ="checked" />
        Frosh <br/>
<input type="radio" name="Year" value="2"/> Sophomore <br/>
<input type="radio" name="Year" value="3"/> Junior <br/>
<input type="radio" name="Year" value="4"/> Senior <br/>
<input type="radio" name="Year" value="5"/> Grad <br/>
```

Figure A–17   A sample form.

In these input tags, the **type** attribute has the value **"radio"**. To preselect a particular radio button, include the attribute **checked** with the value **"checked"**.

The **name** attribute gives a name to the data being collected by the radio buttons. This is analogous to a variable name. The **value** attribute specifies the data that will be sent to the server if a user selects that radio button. For example, if a user selects the radio button preceeding the word "Junior," then the **"Year"** name will have the value **"3"** when the information is sent to the server.

All of the input elements discussed here have the **name** and **value** attributes. In all cases, the name attribute is required.

In Figure A–17, a *drop down menu* appears after the radio buttons. Drop down menus offer a set of preselected choices that take up less space than a set of radio buttons. To create a drop down menu, use the *select element*. Inside the select element, you will specify each menu choice via an *option element*:

```
<select name="Housing">
  <option value="1" > on-campus housing </option>
  <option value="2" selected="selected" >
                an apartment off campus</option>
  <option value="3"> other </option>
</select>
```

The text enclosed between the opening and closing option tags will appear as a menu choice. The optional **selected** attribute will preselect an item from the drop-down list.

In the sample form, a set of *checkboxes* appear, beneath the drop-down menu. Checkboxes allow a user to click in the box to indicate yes (checked) or no (unchecked). The optional **checked** attribute indicates that the box is initially checked. The following is the XHTML that produced the checkboxes in Figure A–17:

```
<input type="checkbox" name="jazz" /> Jazz <br/>
<input type="checkbox" name="Rock" checked="checked"/>
            Classic Rock <br />
<input type="checkbox" name="top40"/> Top 40 <br />
```

Sometimes, you will need to provide users with an opportunity to give free-form responses. You can do this with the *textbox* and *textarea* elements. Textbox elements allow a person to type in text, as long as the text is relatively short. In Figure A–19, the textbox for "Favorite Station" was created with the following XHTML:

```
<input type="text" name="Fave" size="10" maxlength="20" />
```

The **value** attribute is optional for textboxes. If omitted, the element will be blank. The **size** attribute specifies the textbox length in characters, and **maxlength** sets the total number of characters that a user can type in the textbox.

A textarea element offers a user the opportunity to type a response that's unlimited in length. It is enclosed in opening and closing **<textarea>** tags, as seen here:

```
<textarea name="comments" rows="4" cols="40" >
... </textarea>
```

Any text between the two tags will appear as text in the element on screen. If there is no intervening text, the element will be blank. The **rows** attribute specifies the number of text lines that are visible to the user at any one time. The **cols** attribute specifies the line length in characters.

The final interactive element in Figure A–17 is the *submit button*. Pressing the submit button on a form sends the user information to the destination specified in the action attribute of the form tag. Each form must have a submit button. Here is the XHTML that produced the submit button in Figure A–17:

```
<input type="submit" name = "submit" value="Send it in!"/>
```

The quoted string specified in the value attribute appears as text on the submit button. If it is omitted, the button has the label "Submit."

As mentioned previously, you will need to establish some server-side functionality in order to send and process the information supplied by users. If you are so inclined, you could explore installing server software yourself, or you can investiage the possibility of finding a Web host that will support server-side functionality. If your form does not require sophisticated data processing and you do not expect a high volume of traffic, it is possible to find sites that will provide server-side access for free. As of 2003, there are quite a few sites that will provide limited services for free or for a very nominal charge. Use your favorite search engine to find them.

For the purposes of debugging, however, you might decide to use the mailto alternative. With this approach, when a user clicks the "submit" button, an e-mail message will be sent to the recipient specified in the format's action attribute. Figure A–18 contains a side-by-side comparison of a filled-in form and the resulting e-mail.

Figure A–18 A filled out form and the e-mail with the user information.

In the body of the e-mail message, the information pertaining to a particular interactive element will occupy one line of the message. Each line will have the form

name = value

where **name** is the name of the interactive element and **value** is what was specified in the value attribute. For textbox and textarea elements, the value will be the characters that the user typed.

Conclusion

This ends our introduction to Web authoring using XHTML and CSS. You can now create commonly occurring elements of a Web page and can format them in a completely modern style that will serve you well now and in the future.

Learning more about XHTML and CSS

The World Wide Web Consortium site (`http://www.w3.org/`) contains a number of superb tutorials. `http://www.w3schools.com/default.asp` is the home page for W3Schools Online Web Tutorials. There are links to dozens of topics, with hundreds of examples. This is an amazing resource and is entirely free.

Dave Ragget, an early contributor to the Web, maintains two excellent tutorials. The first one, entitled, "Getting Started with HTML," is located at `http://www.w3.org/MarkUp/Guide/`. The second, "A Touch of Style," covers CSS and is available at `http://www.w3.org/MarkUp/Guide/Style`.

The site `http://www.w3.org/` is also the source for the formal specifications for XHTML and supplies information about Web accessibility. Enjoy!

References

[Berners-Lee 1999] Tim Berners-Lee, with Mark Fischetti. *Weaving the Web*. New York: HarperBusiness, 1999.

[Briggs 2002] Owen Briggs, Steven Champeon, Eric Costello, and Matt Peterson. *Cascading Style Sheets: Separating Content from Presentation*. Birmingham, UK: glasshaus Ltd., 2002.

[Brate 2002] Adam Brate. *Technomanifestos: Visions from the Information Revolutionaries*. New York: Texere, 2002. Chapter 7, "The Message in the Medium," describes Alan Kay's many contributions.

[Bush 1945] Vannevar Bush. "As We May Think," *The Atlantic Monthly*, July 1945.

[Englebart 1962] `http://www.histech.rwth-aachen.de/www/quellen/engelbart/ahi62index.html` (Pioneering paper with connection to hypertext, cited by Berners-Lee; no mouse story here.) Also try: `http://www.superkids.com/aweb/pages/features/mouse/mouse.html` See [Brate 2002] for a superb description of Englebart's pioneering contributions.

[Lie and Bos 1999] Håkon Wium Lie and Bert Bos. *Cascading Style Sheets: Designing for the Web*. Addison Wesley Longman, 1999.

[Nelson 1965] Theodor Nelson. A File Structure for the Complex, the Changing, and the Indeterminate. *Proceedings* of the 20th National Conference of the ACM.

Index